D1452052

History and Morality

History and Morality

DONALD BLOXHAM

OXFORD
UNIVERSITY PRESS

OXFORD

UNIVERSITY PRESS

Great Clarendon Street, Oxford, OX2 6DP,
United Kingdom

Oxford University Press is a department of the University of Oxford.
It furthers the University's objective of excellence in research, scholarship,
and education by publishing worldwide. Oxford is a registered trade mark of
Oxford University Press in the UK and in certain other countries

First Edition published in 2020

Impression: 1

Published in the United States of America by Oxford University Press
198 Madison Avenue, New York, NY 10016, United States of America

British Library Cataloguing in Publication Data

Data available

Library of Congress Control Number: 2019957828

ISBN 978-0-19-885871-3

Printed and bound in Great Britain by
Clays Ltd, Elcograf S.p.A.

To everyone who ever taught me history, and everyone who has ever discussed history with me.

Preface

I have worked on this book on and off since before the birth of my elder daughter, Yasmin, who will be 10 years old by the time of publication. She and her sister, Zahra, and their mother, Cordelia, all deserve my apologies as well as my profound thanks. The same applies to our wider families. I am grateful to the following scholars for their encouragement and for reading parts of the ever-changing manuscript: Adam Fox, Stephan Malinowski, Martin Shuster, Lucy Grig, Steve Rigby, Douglas Cairns, Thomas Ahnert, Tony Kushner, Cordelia Beattie, Tom Lawson, Jonathan Leader Maynard, Jürgen Matthäus, Michelle Moyd, Lissa Skitolsky, Matthias Thaler, Claire Duncanson, Jonathan Hearn, Gordon Pentland, Geoff Eley, A. Dirk Moses, Natasha Wheatley, Roberta Pergher, Mark Roseman, Tom Webster, David Patterson, Enda Delaney, Paul Boghossian, Patrick Joyce, Graham Stevens, Rick Sowerby, David Motadel, and Mark Levene. At Oxford University Press I thank Christopher Wheeler, who set the ball rolling, Robert Faber, Christina Wipf Perry, Stephanie Ireland, and Cathryn Steele. Not for the first time I owe a major debt of gratitude to the Leverhulme Trust. Significant sections of the book were written, and others revised, during a period of leave from my regular university duties facilitated by receipt of a Leverhulme Major Research Fellowship (MRF-2016-164). I hope the work constitutes a respectable part-repayment of the Trust's faith in me.

Contents

Introduction   1

Part 1. Contemplating Historical Actors in Context   16
         Introduction   16
         Misuses of Contextualization   18
         Cause and Context in Historical Explanation   30
         Different Sorts of Context   39
         On Ideology   52
         Political Morality and Special Roles   60
         The Importance of Hindsight   76

Part 2. Writing History: Problems of Neutrality   87
         Introduction   87
         History versus Social Science   88
         Evaluative and Evocative Language   91
         Rhetoric and Truthfulness   94
         Combining Perspectives   102
         Legitimacy Contests in the Past   113

Part 3. Justifying Judgement on Things Past   127
         Introduction   127
         History I: By Faith Alone   134
         History II: God Is With Us   175
         History III: To the Present   208
         Moving Beyond 'Their Own Terms'   225
         Tolerance, Respect, Relativism   234
         Past and Present in Conversation   249

Part 4. History, Identity, and the Present   251
         Introduction   251
         Influential Misunderstandings   252
         Relating to the Past   261
         Pride and Shame about the Past   271
         Material Legacies   282
         Closing Thoughts   288

Bibliography   291
Index   309

Introduction

The First World War: what caused it? The matter has fascinated every generation since the war and sparked controversy well beyond academia, but why?

The enduring urgency of the question relates to the character of the war itself, including the death toll and the nature of the killing: all of the imagery conjured up by names like Verdun, the Somme, and Passchendaele. Then there is the matter of the vast material and moral resources poured into the fray, plus its international, social, and psychological legacies. Some of the legacies of the conflict were also legacies of the post-war settlement; that is not a contradiction, since the settlement negotiations were themselves influenced by the extremity and cost of the war. Article 231 of the 1919 Treaty of Versailles, the first clause of the treaty's section on reparations, stipulated that 'The Allied and Associated Governments affirm and Germany accepts the responsibility of Germany and her allies for causing all the loss and damage to which the Allied and Associated Governments and their nationals have been subjected as a consequence of the war imposed upon them by the aggression of Germany and her allies.' Whatever the narrow legalistic meaning that the article's drafters may have intended, unsurprisingly the article became widely known as the 'war-guilt clause'. The *Kriegsschuldfrage*, the war-guilt question, then became a mobilizing issue in the interwar German politics of treaty revision and right-wing opposition to the Weimar Republic. In turn, the fateful legacy of German resentment fuelled historical interest in the question of whether Germans were right to feel aggrieved at having the blame for the war laid at their door and prompted inquiries as to whether the belligerence of Nazi Germany in the 1930s was continuous with the policies of Imperial Germany.

The political stakes are high indeed. As well as the issue of financial reparation, matters of national honour, political emotion, sovereignty, and territorial revision were thrown into the brew, guaranteeing that any explanation of the war's causes would upset some party. Some of the candidate ingredients for explaining the war date back to the wartime propaganda battle itself, and some are the stock of common memory. An archduke's assassination; the Habsburg Empire's nationalities problem; German hubris; German paranoia; the nature of the alliance system; the collective mentality of Europe's political and diplomatic elites: one may pick and mix. As with most historiographical debates, this one goes round and round, with revisionism sparking counter-revisionism and that, neo-revisionism. The quality of the arguments is inconsistent, but the present discussion is more concerned with what all explanations of the First World War share. They have in common a sense that what they are trying to account for was undesirable, traumatic, catastrophic. One can, of course, have natural catastrophes, but the matters in question were distinctly human phenomena resulting from human decisions. Some of the 'causes' or 'origins' of the war, to use the terms deployed in sundry book titles, inevitably indicate 'responsibility', in the language of Article 231. Given the negative associations of the war, conclusions as to responsibility will be conclusions as to 'blame' and 'guilt', whether or not their authors choose to deploy such terms. All that varies between accounts is who or what is to be blamed.

The evaluative association is reflected in the etymology of 'cause'. The ancient Greek αἴτιον, which became *causa* in Latin, meant 'fault', 'blame', or 'accusation' as well as 'cause'.[1] In the explanation of wars and so much else, just as in detective novels, whodunnit is at once a question about cause and guilt.[2] Likewise, when we talk of revolution we are apt to gesture at the weight and justness of revolutionary grievances, the governing regime's willingness to address grievances, or the proportionality of grievances to the violence of revolutionary action.[3] The characterizations are infused with evaluative appraisal.

Since historians today, as ever before, like to think of themselves as critical thinkers, it is of some interest that 'criticism' derives from the Greek verb κρίνω, which means to distinguish and discriminate and also to decide and judge.[4] Yet professional consensus today is against the argument of this book that it is legitimate, often unavoidable, and frequently important for the historian to make value judgements about things past.[5] In the contemporary profession 'critical thought' tends to be conceived as thought that would be polluted by any evaluative element. The philosopher Michael Oakeshott mocked the idea of treating the past as 'a field in which we exercise our moral and political opinions, like

---

[1] R. G. Collingwood, *An Essay on Metaphysics* (Oxford: Clarendon Press, 1969), 291.

[2] Heta Pyrhönen, *Mayhem and Murder: Narrative and Moral Issues in the Detective Story* (Toronto: University of Toronto Press, 1999), 4.

[3] I draw on Geoffrey Partington, 'Relativism, Objectivity and Moral Judgment', *British Journal of Educational Studies* 27/2 (1979), 125–39, here 131. For the endurance of such matters of judgement and rhetoric, see Christopher Pelling, 'Commentary', in John Marincola, Lloyd Llewellyn-Jones, and Calum Alasdair Maciver (eds), *Greek Notions of the Past in the Archaic and Classical Eras: History without Historians* (Edinburgh: Edinburgh University Press, 2012), 347–65, here 359–60.

[4] James Gordon Finlayson, 'Political, Moral, and Critical Theory', in Brian Leiter and Michael Rosen (eds), *The Oxford Handbook of Continental Philosophy* (Oxford: Oxford University Press, 2007), 626–70, here 632.

[5] This is not to say there have not been countervailing voices. There have, but they do not seem to have had much impact. For some important contributions, see Isaiah Berlin, *Historical Inevitability* (New York: Oxford University Press, 1954); Pardon E. Tillinghast, *The Specious Past* (Reading, MA: Addison-Wesley, 1972), 151–69; Gordon Wright, 'History as a Moral Science', *American Historical Review* 81/1 (1975), 1–11; Partington, 'Relativism'; Adrian Oldfield, 'Moral Judgments in History', *History and Theory* 20/3 (1981), 260–77; Richard T. Vann, 'Historians and Moral Evaluations', *History and Theory* 43/4 (2004), 3–30; James Cracraft, 'Implicit Morality' *History and Theory* 43/4 (2004), 31–42; Robert J. Richards, 'The Narrative Structure of Moral Judgments in History: Evolution and Nazi Biology', *University of Chicago Record*, 12 April 2005, 2–6; Jonathan Gorman, 'Ethics and the Writing of Historiography', in Aviezer Tucker (ed.), *A Companion to the Philosophy of History and Historiography* (Chichester: Wiley-Blackwell, 2011), 253–61.

whippets in a meadow on a Sunday afternoon'.[6] In somewhat higher diction the great historian Marc Bloch scorned the urge to play 'the role of Minos or Osiris' behind a desk.[7] H. S. Commager enjoined 'refrain from the folly and vanity of moral righteousness about the past',[8] while in more measured tones Richard Evans recently claimed that 'in history, the element of moral judgment, insofar as it is exercised at all, is in the end extraneous to the research rather than being embedded in the theory or methodology of it'.[9]

Formidable arguments accompany the pronouncements. Evaluation is pointless: even if it can be done in principle, why do it? Perhaps for the empty satisfaction of telling the deafened dead of the age of absolutism that they could have deconstructed the divine right of kings if only they had put their minds to it? Alternatively, evaluation is a category error, equivalent for Bloch to a chemist's separating 'the bad gases, like chlorine, from the good ones like oxygen'.[10] It is subjective at best; at worst, it is prejudice in disguise—the historian Herbert Butterfield had this in mind when writing of the 'whig' historian that 'the real burden of his indignation may fall on things which are anathema only to the whigs'.[11] Besides, the past is a foreign country with different ways and values, thus Butterfield again: 'historical explaining does not condemn; neither does it excuse; it does not even touch the realm in which words like these have meaning or relevance; it is compounded of observations made upon the events of the concrete world; *it is neither more nor less than the process of seeing things in their context*'.[12]

The final objection may be most resonant for historians because 'context' is one of the trump cards of the discipline of History. (The upper-case initial is used throughout to denote the discipline of History, while 'history' refers to the past.) The card is played to distinguish History from the generalizing, model-building or lesson-learning aspirations of philosophers, political scientists, and politicians. Characteristically, a philosopher will engage with some seventeenth-century document asking what it means to us, now. The historian will be concerned more with what it meant to 'them', back then. Her contextual questions might concern the circumstances of its writing, the motives of its author, or its influence on seventeenth-century readers. Oddly, given the centrality of 'context' to the discipline, few historians have tried to conceptualize it.[13] A contribution to that end is

[6] Michael Oakeshott, *Rationalism in Politics and Other Essays* (London: Methuen, 1962), 165.
[7] Marc Bloch, *The Historian's Craft* (New York: Vintage Books, 1953), 139.
[8] H. S. Commager, *The Search for a Usable Past* (New York: Knopf, 1967), 316.
[9] Richard J. Evans, *In Defense of History* (New York: Norton, 1999), 45.
[10] Bloch, *The Historian's Craft*, 139, 142.
[11] Herbert Butterfield, *The Whig Interpretation of History* (New York: Norton, 1965), 109.
[12] Butterfield, *The Whig Interpretation*, 117 (emphasis added).
[13] For relatively rare historians' forays, see E. P. Thompson, 'Anthropology and the Discipline of Historical Context', *Midland History* 1 (1972), 41–55; Giovanni Levi, 'I pericoli del Geertzismo', *Quaderni storici*, NS 20/58 (April 1985), 269–77; Peter Burke, 'Context in Context', *Common Knowledge* 8/1 (2002), 152–77. Intellectual History has produced more explicit work on the context than other fields, with a debt to Quentin Skinner's work: for relevant recent references and also a

made below by the investigation of different, sometimes competing, sorts of contextualization, but there is no ducking the point that some contexts are just very different across time, as across place. The intellectual historian Constantin Fasolt writes of the orthodoxy that acknowledging the contextual difference between past and present, a difference that is more than purely temporal and can denote great cultural and psychological diversity, 'is so elementary, so necessary for the very possibility of thinking about the past at all, that it may be considered the founding principle of history' in anything like its contemporary form. The other side of the coin of this contextual difference is 'anachronism', the erroneous projection of present values onto the past.[14]

History and Morality tries to meet all of the foregoing objections, arguing that if value judgements are illegitimate by the standards of the historical profession's 'common sense', the problem is with the common sense rather than the judgements. As such, there is no point trying to justify this project by today's historiographical standards. Rather one needs to revise those standards, which includes punching significant holes in common-sense thinking about evaluation, historical or not, in society at large. Sceptical readers are begged to bear with the book as it unfolds. At the least, it may get them to reflect more about how historians and other human beings think and judge, irrespective of what they say about how they think and judge.

Reflection might be stimulated by an example of the tangle historians can get into when forced to confront the question of value judgements head-on. Consider an open letter from fifty-eight Oxford University scholars, written in December 2017 in response to an article in *The Times* newspaper, 'Don't Feel Guilty about Our Colonial History', by another Oxford scholar, the ethicist and theologian Nigel Biggar.[15] The letter also mentioned 'the agenda pursued in [Biggar's] recently announced project entitled "Ethics and Empire"'. While defending Biggar's right to expound opinions that he finds persuasive, the scholars felt that his widely publicized views

> risk being misconstrued as representative of Oxford scholarship [*sic*]. For many of us, and more importantly for our students, they also reinforce a pervasive

discussion of the limitations of some analyses of context, see Daniel Wickberg, 'Conclusion: The Idea of Historical Context and the Intellectual Historian', in Raymond Haberski Jr and Andrew Hartman (eds), *American Labyrinth: Intellectual History for Complicated Times* (Ithaca, NY: Cornell University Press, 2018), 305–21, with references especially at n. 1 on p. 318. For an influential essay by a non-historian, see Jacques Derrida, *Limited Inc* (Evanston, IL: Northwestern University Press, 1988), 1–24.

[14]   Constantin Fasolt, *The Limits of History* (Chicago: University of Chicago Press, 2004), 4 and 6 for elaboration.

[15]   Nigel Biggar, 'Don't Feel Guilty about Our Colonial History', *The Times* (29 November 2017); The Oxford scholars' letter, 'Ethics and Empire: An Open Letter from Oxford Scholars', 19 December 2017, is available online at https://theconversation.com/ethics-and-empire-an-open-letter-from-oxford-scholars-89333.

sense that contemporary inequalities in access to and experience at our university are underpinned by a complacent, even celebratory, attitude towards its imperial past. We therefore feel obliged to express our firm rejection of them.

Such an opening invites the reading that these scholars are anti-imperialists, i.e. moral critics of empire, and the overall performative effect of the letter substantiates that reading. The letter was certainly interpreted thus by another historian of empire, Bernard Porter, and by the *Daily Mail* newspaper, which in an alarmist article accused the fifty-eight scholars of being 'hell-bent on rewriting history' and dwelt on the red herring of their supposed attack on freedom of speech.[16] The letter's impression of principled opposition to the empire was furthered by the signatories' endorsement of the seminal anti-imperial tract 'Aimé Césaire's morally powerful *Discours sur le colonialisme*'. The remainder of the letter, though, invited confusion as to the grounds for its opposition to Biggar's views and project. Sometimes it implied that a moral approach of any sort to the topic was conceptually misguided: 'The "Ethics and Empire" project asks the wrong questions, using the wrong terms, and for the wrong purposes.' Sometimes it implied that it was legitimate to deploy moral arguments but that Biggar had not done that very well: 'far from offering greater nuance and complexity, Biggar's approach is too polemical and simplistic to be taken seriously'. Accordingly, the letter dismissed

> such arguments as that the British empire's abolition of the slave trade stands simply as a positive entry in a balance-book against (for example) the Amritsar massacre or the Tasmanian genocide. Abolition does not somehow erase the British empire's own practice of slavery and the benefits it continued to reap from the slave trade long after it ended—such as railway investments in the UK or cotton imports from the US South.

What the letter did not do was hint at the nature of a moral inquiry that would have been nuanced and non-simplistic. Its conclusion did little to resolve the ambiguity:

> We welcome continued, open, critical engagement in the ongoing reassessment of the histories of empire and their legacies both in Britain and elsewhere in the world. We have never believed it is sufficient to dismiss imperialism as simply 'wicked'. Nor do we believe it can or should be rehabilitated because some of it was 'good'.

---

[16] https://bernardjporter.com/2018/01/04/oxford-and-the-ethics-of-empire/ and Guy Adams, 'Revealed: How Oxford University is "home to loud mouthed, Tory-loathing, anti-Israel academics who believe only they should have freedom of expression"<thin>', *Daily Mail*, 23 December 2017.

Whilst already having disavowed the use of terms like 'good' or 'wicked', at this point the letter might nonetheless be read as implying that empire could be considered wicked as long as it was not only considered wicked, or that it was indeed good if only in certain parts, but it is unclear, and the problematizing speechmarks only further muddy the waters.

Little was clarified by a follow-up newspaper article by the letter's principal author.[17] This article posited:

> We need a fuller public understanding of what Britain's empire was, and how its aftereffects have influenced Britain's multi-ethnic, multi-confessional society, its inequalities and injustices as well as its commonalities and opportunities.
>
> That debate should be equitable, rational and based on all the available evidence. It should not be about apportioning blame, instilling guilt or recovering pride.…It's important in understanding our collective present that we know what forces shaped it. But historical understanding is about recapturing the sense of things done by, and done to, other people at other times. It's not about us, and how we feel about it is entirely irrelevant.

It is not evident how the pronouncement that contemporary feelings are irrelevant can be reconciled with the letter's concern for the perceptions of Oxford students, or the obvious 'feelings' of the authors of the letter. And since by the article's account the legacy of empire has affected the present it is unclear why present 'feelings' (or at least reflective judgements) should be irrelevant whether they are of Oxford students or not. The overall tenor of the article is notably less anti-imperial than that of the letter, but its apparent aspiration to a state transcending value judgement is thwarted by its reference to 'injustices'.

Confusion was heaped upon confusion in Porter's intervention.[18] A self-proclaimed anti-imperialist in the political sphere, Porter claimed that he was 'a scholar and a professional historian before' being 'a political activist'—though he also wrote that his History informed his politics. In keeping with this unidirectional relationship between his two personae, he talked of the importance of the historian's contemplating imperialism in 'an objective and value-free' fashion. Then he went on to contradict his assertion about the importance of value-free History by applauding the 'Ethics and Empire' project's potential for introducing a nuance, which in this connection must have meant a moral nuance, that 'can only benefit…our historical understanding'. Indeed he identified instances in which a value-laden approach was positively useful: 'It may be worthwhile in some cases to

---

[17] James McDougall, 'The History of the Empire Isn't about Pride—or Guilt', *The Guardian*, 3 January 2018.

[18] All quotes in this paragraph from that intervention: https://bernardjporter.com/2018/01/04/oxford-and-the-ethics-of-empire/.

remind students about the crimes perpetrated under the aegis of the British Empire, but only in order to counteract excessive reactionary pride in the latter; and, in the same way, to remind the more rabid anti-imperialists of some of Empire's more positive or neutral sides.' It is difficult to know how to interpret this. Perhaps Porter felt that his evaluative corrections, negative and positive, would have the overall effect of neutralizing the moral issue. Yet casting himself as arbiter of what constituted 'excessive' pride and 'rabid' anti-imperialism implied that he was the arbiter of reasonable pride and reasonable anti-imperialism, and a concept of what was reasonable by way of praise and criticism could only have emerged from his own evaluative assessments of imperialism. At issue seems to be a matter of moral 'balance' rather than anything beyond the realms of moral thought.

If balancing acts were one of the things the fifty-eight Oxford scholars disapproved of, on other matters they were firmly in agreement with Porter. The camps concurred in their enthusiasm for 'nuance' and their appreciation of 'complexity'—and who would dissent from that? They further agreed that terms like 'good and evil' were 'useless to historians'. And they were roughly equal in their lack of precision about the place of evaluation in their, respectively, 'objective' and 'critical' historical work. With little effort one could imagine Porter and the fifty-eight swapping their existing positions on the desirability of *an* inquiry into 'ethics and empire', depending perhaps on the evaluative conclusions the inquiry seemed likely to reach.

The subject matter of the debate—empire and its legacies—is of great importance but the confusing way in which the subject matter was discussed is anything but unusual. The only surprising thing about the argument was that neither side explicitly mentioned anachronism, which tends to be one of the first responses on Britain's shores to any criticism of empire, as when one historian pre-emptively dismissed criticism of 'the conduct of the British empire in the 18th century': 'We know that today we would do it all differently,' he wrote, 'but that is not the point.'[19] In an earlier essay on a related matter Porter did reassert that 'The past *is* a foreign country', but that was less a way of suggesting that imperialists had different moral standards than to justify his claim that he and his government had 'an alibi—the best one of all. We weren't even born.' The German Chancellor Helmut Kohl had expressed the same sentiment in 1983 when he invoked the 'Gnade der späten Geburt', the good fortune of having been born recently enough not to have been complicit with Nazism. For Porter this was argument enough that contemporary Britons ought not feel guilt and ought not be blamed for empire. He did not address whether, if guilt and blame were inappropriate terms, the alternative concept of shame might still have salience. After all, today there is

---

[19] Max Hastings, 'High-Handed Moral Condemnation', *Daily Telegraph*, 19 February 2006.

manifestly a great deal of pride in Britain about the empire, irrespective of the late birth of so many of the proud, and if pride is possible, shame is too.[20]

The empire case exemplifies the consequences of the moral element's having been repressed in the historical discipline. The question of evaluation was never systematically worked through by the profession after a ban was placed on the sort of judgement common in classical and medieval historianship and the Enlightenment Histories of Voltaire and Condorcet. The issue cannot be relied upon to stay repressed. Its periodic resurgence is unpredictable and apt to manifest itself in unargued assertion or inconsistency even among highly intelligent and accomplished scholars such as those pitted against each other above.[21] Time and again, arguments against evaluation are embedded in tacit evaluations, and concluding 'both sides are to blame' is equated with obviating concepts like blame. Some of the same scholars who oppose evaluation—scholars including the philosopher-historian R. G. Collingwood—also suggest that a historical education encourages tolerance of other ways of being and doing, as if tolerance, like intolerance, could exist outside a sphere in which the evaluative faculties were operative.[22] In other words, there is little consensus on what is involved in jettisoning evaluation. Does scholarly 'neutrality' involve the complete absence of moral judgement, as Butterfield implies, or the sort of moral contextualism whereby it is acceptable to make judgements as long as they are in accordance with the standards prevalent in the historical actor's time? Such moral contextualism might then form the basis for the separate doctrine of moral relativism.

The term 'historicization' can have the implication of either relativization or 'mere' contextualism. Leopold von Ranke (1795–1886) was one of the greatest influences upon the German 'critical historical school' whose work become synonymous with the historical philosophy called historicism, or *Historismus*. When

---

[20] https://bernardjporter.com/2016/02/04/imperial-blame/. For a discussion on pride and shame, see Part 4 of this book.

[21] This is not to ignore a great deal of intelligent and sensitive discussion about historian's standpoints, the need for critical self-reflection, and so forth. Recent historiography and associated cultural and literary theory has been rich in addressing exclusions, silences, and the problems of representation. But discussion about moral judgement pertaining to the substance of the past has not played a large role in these discussions—indeed, moral judgement may loom large in the minds of historiographical theorists as precisely the sort of thing that a self-aware historian should avoid, its being conceived as a-contextual or even imperialist.

[22] Compare R. G. Collingwood's stance on judgement in his *The Idea of History* (rev. edn, Oxford: Oxford University Press, 2005), 402–6 and elsewhere with his belief in its ability to promote tolerance: Lionel Rubinoff, *Collingwood and the Reform of Metaphysics: A Study in the Philosophy of Mind* (Toronto: University of Toronto Press, 1970), 229; William M. Johnston, *The Formative Years of R. G. Collingwood* (Leiden: Martinus Nijhoff, 1968), 60; Alan Donagan, *The Later Philosophy of R. G. Collingwood* (Oxford: Clarendon Press, 1962), 246; and the review of Collingwood by Hayden White in *History and Theory* 4/2 (1965), 244–52. Richard J. Evans both opposes value judgements and espouses History's tolerance-building capacities in his 'What Is History?', in Harriet Swain (ed.), *Big Questions in History* (London: Jonathan Cape, 2005), 1–12, here 5 and 7. Alongside his pronouncements against judgements, Butterfield also hinted at the argument to tolerance in his discussion of the historian and the attitude about diversity: *The Whig Interpretation*, 95–6.

he wrote to the effect that the historian ought to do justice to all forms of moral life, since all peoples and epochs were 'immediate unto god',[23] he was halfway towards moral relativism.

The major claims of this book, most of which have yet to be substantiated, are as follows. They appear roughly in the order that they are supported as the book unfolds; the list is not a series of premises that follow logically from one another:

1. In many historical explanations, as in the First World War case, attributions of responsibility cannot be divorced from evaluative concepts of praise or blame.

2. Once historians establish the content of value systems in the past, they are establishing criteria for assessing actions in relation to those values. This contextualism is what historians pride themselves in providing when taking historical actors 'on their own terms', and it is consistent with a species of moral inquiry.

3. The language historians necessarily use to describe is often evocative, reflecting or prompting evaluative reactions. This is not problematic in itself since many of the things historians describe are not neutral. 'Neutralizing' non-neutral phenomena by one's descriptions is not neutral either.

4. Value judgements and hints as to judgements abound in works of History. Some of these judgements reflect the 'terms' of historical actors, others are external to those terms. Attempting to remove all external judgements would change History much more than would a consistent application of judgement.

5. In the past, as now, power was wielded positively and negatively, but never neutrally. The contestation of standards and power in the past and the capacity of the powerful to affect the lives of others for better or worse means that the way historians depict past acts ought not always be determined by the way in which the authors of those acts regarded them.

6. The world we live in, with its distribution of advantages and disadvantages, is a product of past acts, and so value judgements about the past may have political ramifications in the present. Nonetheless, such value judgements are intrinsically no more political than any other sorts of moral judgements.

7. In a world where History matters as an anchor of identity, historians with relevant expertise need to embrace their roles as contributors to identity debates, normative elements and all.

With a mind to the political ramifications of scholarship, while many historians are reticent about addressing the question of value judgement even when it

---

[23] Leopold von Ranke, *Aus Werke und Nachlass*, ii, ed. Theodor Schieder and Helmut Berding (Munich: Oldenbourg 1971), 59–63; Leopold von Ranke, *Aus Werke und Nachlass*, iv, ed. V. Dotterweich and W. P. Fuchs (Munich: Oldenbourg 1975), 295.

looms large, then others are surreptitious, meaning they engage in evaluation camouflaged as neutrality. It is unclear whether the German historian Friedrich Meinecke (1862–1954) was endorsing surreptitious or merely implicit evaluation when he wrote that

> Although the historian may, in form, abstain from value judgments of his own, they are there between the lines, and act as such upon the reader. The effect, then...is often more profound and moving than if the evaluation were to appear directly in the guise of moralizing, and therefore it is even to be recommended as an artifice. The historian's implicit value judgment arouses the reader's own evaluating activity more strongly than one which is explicit.[24]

Whatever Meinecke had in mind, if surreptitiousness needs to be challenged (though not necessarily implicitness[25]) then so does reticence, because the surreptitiousness thrives on the reticence.

A more conscious and consistent approach to the issue of value judgement will moderate the judgement in some areas of historical inquiry while amplifying it in some others; yet other areas will remain much as they are. Bloch illustrates a tendency to assume that judgements must come in the form of judicial verdicts and stem from a historian's god-complex.[26] This tendency can be attributed to a knee-jerk association of all moral thought with a hard-and-fast *moralism* that has no regard for differing circumstances or ways of life: Commager's 'moral righteousness', perhaps.[27] Thus conceived, evaluation seems like something other people do, and do, as Evans suggests, extraneously to their real business.

Evans is correct that historians are generally not trained in evaluative reasoning, but what is the thrust of this observation? If it is part of an argument against evaluation, as it is for him,[28] then that is also an argument against historians doing the very many sorts of History in which evocative (or neutralizing) descriptions and critical allocations of responsibility are unavoidable. If, however, the observation prompts historians to acquaint themselves better with the tenets of evaluative reasoning to complement their expertise in detail and contextualization, then that would seem to be a good thing.

---

[24] Cited in Robert Connor, *Thucydides* (Princeton: Princeton University Press, 1987), 7–8.

[25] Implicitness may be more conducive to the aesthetics that should rarely be consigned to the margins of the historian's artisanal practice. For important reflections on this, see Cracraft, 'Implicit Morality'. On the tendency to find moral and/or aesthetic fault in literary works that are too blunt in their moral didactics, C. A. J. Coady, 'The Moral Reality in Realism', *Journal of Applied Philosophy* 22/2 (2005), 121–36, here 131–2.

[26] A version of this is Arthur Marwick's concept of the superstar 'auteur' historian.

[27] For the morality–moralism distinction, see C. A. J. Coady, *Messy Morality: The Challenge of Politics* (Oxford: Oxford University Press, 2010); Stanley Cavell, *The Claim of Reason* (New York: Oxford University Press, 1999), 287<thin>ff.

[28] Richard J. Evans, 'History, Memory and the Law: The Historian as Expert Witness', *History and Theory* 41 (2002), 326–45, here 330.

Part 1 tackles the historian's signature practice of contextualization head-on, interrogating the concept of 'context' and examining different sorts of contextualization. It takes issue with Butterfield's severance of contextualization from evaluation. It shows how influential historians who have purported merely to be contextualizing, not evaluating, have failed to maintain this distinction, and failed in ways that confuse the issues at stake. This failure is not surprising since, as is further argued, contextualization often just is oriented to concerns in which empirical and moral elements go hand in hand. The commonplace and vital injunction to understand past actors in the contexts of their time or particular situation is, amongst other things, an injunction to understand the governing values of 'times' and situations and the choices made by past actors in relationship to those values. Whatever one's intentions, one often cannot avoid creating moral impressions through the process of relating actors' motivations and deeds to prevailing values and interests, since that process involves showing when the actors fell short of, or deliberately transgressed, those standards, as well as when they met the standards. Such moral impressions are not at all alien to a discipline in which causation is generally treated in humanistic fashion rather than by the lights of scientific determinism. Insofar as neutrality remains a scholarly aspiration in dealing with foreign countries past, it must pertain to the treatment of the values that governed at particular points in the past, not to the treatment of the way in which historical actors within those countries acted in relation to those values. As subsequent sections of the book show, however, even that standard of neutrality cannot be sustained.

If Part 1 concerns the way the historian conceptualizes the relationship of past actors to the value systems governing them, Part 2 concerns the historian's product—a work of History—as it conveys that relationship and more besides. As soon as one takes moral contextualization seriously, one has already fractured any consensus about what is involved in scholarly neutrality, and Part 2 goes further. It distinguishes a desirable aspiration to truthfulness from the problematic aspiration to neutrality. It shows that it is often impossible to create a quarantine area wherein the moral characterization of an historical act is 'historicized' to a standard in the past.

Part 2 expands on the point that value judgements on the historian's part can be implied by nothing more than choice of noun, adjective, or adverb. The matters to which words like 'theft', 'ruthless', and 'charitably' pertain are not value-neutral in anyone's mind, past or present, and in the way they 'speak' to contemporary audiences such terms can exceed the boundaries of the contexts within which past actors are otherwise discussed. Such terms of approbation and disapprobation are particular to humanistic disciplines. They are likely to evoke some sentiment in the reader, much as 'genocide' does, which explains why certain states fight tooth and nail to deny that they have ever committed it. Whether or not historians are prepared to take responsibility for the implications of their verbiage, readers are apt to make the inference. Contrary to the idea that conscious evaluation must issue in some grand verdict, or what Evans calls 'denunciation' and 'expressions of moral outrage',[29] it can just manifest itself through the validation or contestation of turns of phrase or particular evocative descriptions. Arguments about the justification of those judgements can only occur when historians recognize that as part of their business they may already be implicitly evaluating, and thus that evaluation is not a category error. One must acknowledge the presence of evaluation in order to control it.

At the other end of the scale from word choices, a work of History gives an overall impression and this can be a moral impression whether or not the historian sought to provide one. The moral impression given by a book or an article can be straightforwardly a function of the explicit argument as, say, when a historian of empire sets out to marshal evidence in support of the case that the project was driven by good intentions rather than greed. Or it can be a function of accumulated descriptions of historical occurrences and contexts, facts, rhetoric, and all. Theorists of narrative remind us that overall impressions can be more significant than particular word choices and the historian has as much responsibility for one as the other. Again, it is no good the historian washing her hands of responsibility by suggesting that readers can just make up their minds on the moral aspect, or any other aspect, of the story, since, consciously or not, she will have provided so many of the prompts that shape readers' thoughts.[30] The moral impression will rarely just be a reflection of the views of the major actors under consideration—those whose 'terms' the reader is enjoined to understand. As the historian explains the outlooks of those actors, she has to go behind those outlooks, contextualizing them in ways that might not have been familiar to the actors, and introducing a 'voice' that is external to the historical scenario under examination. As the historian explains the significance or consequences of what the actors did, she may have to harness latter-day perspectives (including her own), or the perspectives of contemporary onlookers or those affected by the acts in question. There is no reason that these sets of perspectives need cohere with the outlook of the principal actors. The overall moral impression of the work is shaped by how the historian elucidates and combines different contexts, perspectives, and experiences. There is no professional rulebook for creating such compositions, far less for rendering them morally neutral.

Part 3 moves from describing features of works of History to underwriting a range of judgements that are currently outlawed not just by advocates of neutralism and moral contextualism, but, finally, by certain moral relativists. This part of the book legitimates some of the apparently presentist value judgements that many historians already make and establishes criteria according to which other judgements can be formed or criticized. It is the longest section of the work

---

[29] Evans, *Defence*, 44–5.   [30] Evans, 'What Is History?', 5.

because it has to dig so deep through layers of occidental thought to trace the growth and flaws of an influential, though never uncontested, cluster of moral theories. The point of the opening three historical sections is to use historical investigation to undermine some of the prevailing standards of the disciple of History, showing that far from being self-evident for a properly scholarly undertaking, those standards emerge from particular, contestable standpoints in theology, strands of philosophy, and even theories of nationalism and *raison d'état*. Three concluding sections summarize the major issues at stake and address them from a more purely philosophical perspective.

The central problem animating Part 3 is that whatever the time and place, the world has been shaped for good and ill more by what people have done than their motives or justifications for doing it. One of its contentions is that just as an act has moral significance that is not always determined by the 'faith', good or bad, of its author, an actor's good faith is itself relative to a value that may be evaluated. In terms of evaluating acts, *though not necessarily actors*, 'good faith' can be irrelevant. There is a gulf between remonstrating with historical actors for failing to subscribe to concepts that were unavailable to them or failing to transcend values and structures that conditioned them—which is what some opponents of moral evaluation legitimately fear—and drawing out normative problems with the relevant structures and values in light of their worldly consequences for others who did not share the same outlook. At the simplest level there is no contradiction between being morally contextualist about the outlook of a seventeenth-century commodities trader who made a fortune on the products of slavery while criticizing slavery on more 'external' moral grounds. Reflecting morally on the crusades given their impact on peoples the crusaders encountered is not the same as condemning any and all crusaders that had a particular world-view.

Pushing the evaluative question 'back' or 'up' from the level of historical actors to the level of their value structures in different cultures past is, however, to step onto treacherous terrain, so some clarifications are in order. Cultures, in the sense of ways of life, cannot meaningfully be evaluated. They are immensely complex, multifaceted, and never entirely coherent. They are marked by internal diversity, and their members are capable of arguing, even fighting, about values. So we do not even need *cultural relativism* except as a useful shorthand marker of the incoherence as well as the colossal presumption of judging ways of life as such. Part 3 distinguishes between cultural relativism and moral relativism. It is moral relativism that this book interrogates, in order to show that it does not constitute an operative guide to the matters in hand. Unlike general ways of life, specific practices can be evaluated, and indeed are and have been evaluated, all the time, including by those sharing the same culture.

A further crucial point about relativism is often overlooked. Contextualisms and relativisms of all sorts—epistemic, aesthetic, and, for present purposes, moral relativism—presuppose some basic human commonality as the parameter against which particular differences are considered. Halibuts are notably absent from most discussions of 'difference' under the rubric of diversity or relativism, because relativism is an anthropocentric conception, no matter that the tacit underlying definition of shared humanity is unprovided. Part of the reason for the definitional deficit may be fear of a bias in any definition, which surely explains the absence of philosophical foundation for the Universal Declaration of Human Rights with its 'we hold these truths to be self-evident'-type assertion of human equality. But without a parameter of some shared quality, whether asserted, implied, or just taken for granted, the whole structure of relativism would fall down because we would have no means of establishing what it was that we needed to be relativist about. While we might be interested, say, in different social reasons for the infliction of pain, or different cultural forms and ways of experiencing pain, the pain itself lies within the ambit of the 'context' of a shared humanity. However various the concepts of justice across different societies past and present, the concept of injustice, and indignation at it, has transcultural reach. As elaborated at the end of Part 3, the sort of evaluation this book is concerned with gets its specifically historical colouring from inference about actual instances of happiness, suffering, justice, and injustice in foreign countries past. It does not issue forth from some ideal social theory designed in the present and then wielded in automatic criticism of all other societies, with no regard for how the inhabitants of those societies viewed their situation.

If Part 3 is more angled towards the principles of evaluating the behaviour of 'others', then Part 4 moves the focus more onto 'us' in the here and now. Part 4 gives the book explicit political relevance. It addresses the way in which moral evaluation feeds into the relationship between History and identity. It suggests that a major anxiety about making value judgements in one's History is not that judgements will hinder understanding of the past but that they have the potential to disturb the order of the present. In particular it addresses a common and especially important mode of engagement with History, a mode hereafter named Identity History.

Identity History in the upper case is founded on the idea that the past lives on in the present. It is not—or not necessarily—identical to the wide range of historical scholarship that simply examines the History of particular groups with, say, a desire to recognize their historical experience and write them back into the historical record. Identity History is prejudicial; its historians tend to be self-servingly selective about what moral aspects of the past they connect with, or how they make that connection. In particular, Identity History is characterized by inconsistency in the way its practitioners relate to historical actors. When the ways of the ancestors are embarrassing by the standards of the present, the Identity historian pleads that the past is a foreign country and criticism would be anachronistic. But the positive—or arguably positive—achievements and patrimony of the ancestors are embraced as if these forebears were close relatives rather than distant foreigners. Historical Identity debates about the British Empire often comprise a case in point of this process of alternating association and distancing.

Identity History should be taken seriously. The topics most likely to feature in it—wars, revolutions, suffering, triumphs, dynasties, national stories—tell us something about general interest in the past, and it is irrelevant if the nature of that interest contravenes the strictures of academic historians, many fewer of whom would have jobs without it. One aspiration of this book is that all relevant History becomes self-reflective *i*dentity History rather than upper-case Identity History.

To the extent that memories of the past bolster practices in the present, changes in the former will affect the latter. By extension evaluative interrogation is vital because, while parts of the same community and other communities beyond will surely remember different things, they will also remember some of the same things differently. When those memory clashes concern claims over rights and wrongs it is already too late for exhortations to neutrality or relativism, and 'tolerance' may just be a way of favouring the historical victor or aggressor.

Thinking harder about historical evaluation would improve the quality of many of the historians' judgements that are all around us anyway. It would also help reading audiences to distinguish an underlying moral stance of one sort from a competing and perhaps irreconcilable sort, to spot where judgementalism and moralism substitute for judgement and moral reasoning,[31] and to detect the influence of Identity narcissism as against critical reflection on identity.

---

[31] I hold judgementalism to stand in relation to judgement much as moralism does to morality.

PART 1

CONTEMPLATING HISTORICAL ACTORS IN CONTEXT

Introduction

The historian William H. Sewell Jr, who is also one of the most important contemporary theorists of History as an undertaking, encapsulated the centrality of 'context' to the practice of historians. 'Both history as transformation and history as context are recognized in the practice and training of professional historians. We would regard as incompetent any historian not capable of arguing in both modes.' He suggests, however, that accounting for context is generally regarded as more fundamental than the explanation of change:

> A historical work that makes no effort (or only the most passing effort) to expli-cate or explain a historical transformation but portrays effectively the context of some past lifeworld can be hailed as a masterpiece. Think of [Lewis] Namier's *The Structure of Politics at the Accession of George III* (1929), Emmanuel Le Roy Ladurie's *Carnival in Romans* (1979)...or Robert Darnton's essay on 'The Great Cat Massacre' (1983)...By contrast, a history that recounted a series of changes over time but failed to indicate the distance of the lifeworld being described from the present would be dismissed out of hand as 'anachronistic'—the histor-ian's equivalent of the anthropologist's 'ethnocentric' and perhaps the most damning term in the historian's lexicon of judgment.[1]

As against ethnocentrism, the historian's default mode today does include a 'presumption of qualitative difference' (in the phrase of another theorist) between worlds past and present.[2] One cultural historian writes of having 'been trained to

---

[1] William G. Sewell, *Logics of History: Social History and Social Transformation* (Chicago: University of Chicago Press, 2005), 183.
[2] Eero Loone, '"They Were Not Quite Like Us": The Presumption of Qualitative Difference in Historical Writing', in Henry Kozicki (ed.), *Developments in Modern Historiography* (Basingstoke: Palgrave, 1998), 164–81, here 169.

mark the exceptionality of an era, region, or cultural group'.[3] The historical discipline's 'cultural turn' in the later twentieth century merely reinforced this long-standing tendency, as did the promptings of sundry thinkers in the 'structuralist' and 'post-structuralist' traditions. The common point of contrast of these strands of thought, as of nineteenth-century German historicism and the romantic historianship with which it was affiliated, is a universalist tradition associated with elements of the Enlightenment. Where some thinkers in the universalist vein might seek the shared kernel of humankind or promote a particular way of life as an ideal to which all should aspire, historians now and for a long time have concerned themselves with illuminating different ways of life on their own terms and considering historical actors within the contexts of those ways of life.

This part of the book takes seriously the idea of doing justice to different ways and circumstances of life. One of the greatest obligations historians bear is not to caricature or traduce the historical objects of their investigations, and this obligation is honoured by care in depicting what one infers about the beliefs, motives, intentions, and situations of historical actors. The same obligation ought to be honoured for any actor under scrutiny, whether from a millennium ago or last year, whether Gulag guard or inmate. The following discussion paves the way for greater clarity and consistency in contextual understanding by bringing into focus what the practice of contextualization implies and examining the logics of different sorts of contextualization. It is a guide to what it means to deliver on the commitment to take historical actors on their own terms, and it highlights the unavoidable evaluative implications of the process. It has implications for revising how certain historians have evaluated and how others might yet evaluate, but it is the general fact of evaluation rather than the direction of any particular evaluation that is central.

Wary that discussion of conceptual matters can become too abstract, not to say abstruse, the first section anchors the others in concrete by examining some influential works of History that raise issues of general relevance. That section contemplates failed attempts in two famous books to neutralize a discussion by invoking a governing context by reference to which things are simply explained rather than justified, legitimated, condemned, excused, praised, etcetera. Then it examines a third work which uses a governing context not to neutralize but to provide arguably excessive mitigation for its chosen objects of inquiry. The point is to investigate ways in which 'ordinary' practices of contextualization can be normatively problematic.

The second section tries to demystify 'context', showing that it means nothing other than 'cause' and, generally in humanistic explanations, cause in the weaker

---

[3] Sharon Block, cited in Dror Wahrman, 'Change and the Corporeal in Seventeenth- and Eighteenth-Century Gender History: Or, Can Cultural History Be Rigorous?', *Gender & History* 20/3 (2008), 584–602, here 598–9.

sense of 'influence' as opposed to the stronger sense of 'determination'. In the absence of determinism, human choice comes into play, and where there is choice there is responsibility, which in morally salient matters cannot be considered without attributions of praise or blame.

The third section addresses the different evaluative implications of the two most popular sorts of contextualization: contextualization in societies with different values to the present, and contextualization in unusual situations. The discussion of those matters is interwoven with an account of the interaction of values and interests as motive forces for historical actors.

The fourth section addresses actors who consciously bring about or forestall change and establishes the limits of academically popular contextualizations that focus on *culture*. It brings the focus to bear on matters of more narrowly-defined and consciously-imbibed *ideology* and the inherently *political* nature of so much that is involved in social transformation or social reproduction. Again, as the type of contextualization changes, so do the evaluative connotations.

The fifth section addresses the range of special considerations associated with certain leadership and functionary roles and highlights common mistakes in evaluative thinking about the occupants of these roles. The sixth section builds on all the previous ones in addressing a matter that seems antithetical to any serious agenda of historical contextualization: the application of hindsight. It argues that certain forms of hindsight, evaluative implications and all, are legitimate even when 'taking people on their own terms'.

Misuses of Contextualization

The brilliant historian Carlo Ginzburg (b. 1939) famously contrasted the judicial process with the historian's investigation. The contrast is especially stark in the ways evidence is used—in court evidence is played against evidence to reach a final one-way-or-another verdict, while the historian seeks more holistically to understand the relationship between pieces of evidence and historical actors who can only be 'known' via the evidence. Marc Bloch's opinion on historical judgement was formed in reaction to a French historiography of the French Revolution that seemed but an extension of the major political divide in French politics in its determination to indict or exculpate.[4] The French Revolution provided the example par excellence of a controversial, event-centred History with high-profile individual players who might indeed be subjected to the verdict of posterity. Such was the sort of History Bloch sought to put in a different perspective. Surely it also shaped Bloch's philosophy that his History concerned a distant past, whereas

---

[4] Carlo Ginzburg, *The Judge and the Historian* (London: Verso, 2002), 13–15; Joep Leerssen and Ann Rigney, *Historians and Social Values* (Amsterdam: Amsterdam University Press, 2000), 72.

the present was turbulent in the most urgent manner—so turbulent that this courageous and wise man was murdered by the Gestapo in 1944.

Let us examine some of Bloch's thematic History, his classic *Feudal Society* (1939–40), to see how consistently he lived up to his famous demand: 'Robespierrists, anti-Robespierrists, just do us a favour: for Heaven's sake, tell us simply who Robespierre was.'[5] Bloch's admonition that 'the historian's sole duty is to understand', not 'pass judgment', suffixed a discussion of knightly adherence to the chivalric code of conduct that had emerged by the eleventh century:

> [A] It is hardly surprising that the realities of knightly life, with its frequent trickery and deeds of violence, should have been far from conforming always to these aspirations. [B] One might also be inclined to observe that, from the point of view either of a 'socially' inspired ethic or of a more purely Christian code, such a list of moral precepts seems a little short. [C] But this would be to pass judgment[6]

In sentence C, Bloch retreats from sentences A and B, which he sees as forming the grounds for a disapproval that would be illegitimate. Yet A and B are different: B concerns applying a code other than that which he thinks existed; whereas A concerns failure to meet the standards set by an extant code of his knights, and potentially provides the grounds for the very judgement from which Bloch ultimately resiles, despite his having already implied a judgement. Indeed Bloch's historical analysis sometimes fuses 'understanding' and 'judgement'. Immediately after the above-cited passage, he described the 'disturbing attenuation' of knightly values as they were translated from ecclesiastical theorists to lay popularizers: 'disturbing' is evocative. Now were this but a small performative contradiction over a few sentences it would be churlish to raise the matter, but in Bloch's own testament, 'war, murder, the abuse of power—these have cast their shadow over almost every page of our analysis'. So we have an invitation to dig deeper. Let us consider his account, especially of the 'first feudal age' which lasted from approximately the collapse of the Carolingian Empire in the early tenth century to the middle of the eleventh century, assuming for the sake of this discussion that all of his factual assertions are warranted.[7]

Feudal Society deals with the consolidation of a social system. For Bloch, the Church's endorsement of the social role of the warrior class provided knights with 'a religious justification of a social supremacy which had long been a recognized fact'. It strengthened the collective identity of the knights and, while notionally binding them to a set of moral precepts which they frequently ignored,

---

consolidated the sense that their earthly dominion over other men was part of the ordained scheme of things. Hence the romance of *Lancelot*: 'above the people must sit the knight. And just as one controls a horse and he who sits above leads it where he will, so the knight must lead the people at his will.' This philosophy, Bloch concludes, 'epitomizes the attitude of a dominant class: an attitude eminently favourable to the development of a nobility in the strictest sense of the term'.[8] Abuse and exploitation may have been characteristic of the new system which could not establish peaceful order for a long time, but there were, according to Bloch, good contextual reasons why 'violence became the distinguishing mark of an epoch and a social system'. New power structures emerged from the dislocation caused by the collapse of empire and then a series of invasions that had 'brought murder and pillage to every part of the land'. Yet 'violence was also deep-rooted in the social structure and in the mentality of the age'. This was so partly because of the temptations of plunder and brigandage when trade was insecure, and partly because of the absence of central, enforceable systems of justice, and the inherence of violence in such law as there was.

> Finally, violence was an element in manners. Medieval men had little control over their immediate impulses; they were emotionally insensitive to the spectacle of pain, and they had small regard for human life, which they saw only as a transitory state before Eternity; moreover they were very prone to make it a point of honour to display their physical strength in an almost animal way.[9]

This final and most generalized contextualization claims the broadest relevance, sitting as it does atop the discussion of more specific sociological conditions. In that final summation there is no distinction between, say, approximately symmetrical everyday violence and the violence of a heavily armed, retinued warrior class whose actions did not just affect their peer protagonists but the entire society over which they presided. There is, in other words, no distinction between degrees and deployments of social power. Yet such distinctions must be salient since in the same pages we read of how peacemaker lords were lauded above all else, with prospects for peace improving a little in the 'second feudal age' given the aggregation of larger political units and larger, more urbanized populations. So let us move to considering the actions of various lords.

Bloch's discussion of noble life earlier in the book provides insight into why the much-desired 'peace' might have been so hard to come by and it does so precisely by reference to the social class that had most say in the matter. For the nobility, fighting 'was sometimes a legal obligation and frequently a pleasure', and of course might be required as a 'matter of honour'. It was also a source of wealth. (Other

---

[8] Bloch, *Feudal Society*, 318–19, 349–51.   [9] Bloch, *Feudal Society*, 411.

scholarship has illustrated how later depictions of chivalric knighthood obscured the greed and crudely violent realities of much knightly behaviour, as judged by some of their contemporaries. Indeed, the aestheticization of violence was a central part of the self-justification of this class, much as it had been in classical epics.[10]) A 'share of the plunder' was 'the principal profit which the knight who fought on his own account in little local wars expected from his efforts'. And so 'by a series of transitions almost unnoticed by the rather simple minds of the time, forms of violent action which were sometimes legitimate—requisitions indispensable to armies without commissariat, reprisals exacted against the enemy or his subjects—degenerated into pure brigandage, brutal and mean'. Prepared for danger, and lauded for his courage, 'the knight found in war yet another attraction: it offered a remedy for boredom'. It was an expression of an 'appetite for diversions'. A 'roving disposition was especially widespread among the French. The fact was that their own country did not offer them, as did half-Moslem Spain, or, to a less[er] degree, Germany with its Slav frontiers, an arena for conquests or swift forays'. It 'has often been observed that Normandy was of all the provinces richest in bold adventurers', which was 'above all the effect of the state of relative peace which, in that remarkably centralized principality, the dukes established at an early date; so that those who craved the opportunity for fighting had to seek it abroad'. The 'bloodletting thus practised abroad by the most turbulent groups in the West saved its civilization from being extinguished by guerrilla warfare. The chroniclers were well aware that at the start of a crusade the people at home in the old countries always breathed more freely, because now they could once more enjoy a little peace'.[11]

It seems that 'peace' at home might come from the absence of some nobles as well as the presence of noble peacemakers, while the sojourns of the former coincided with a marked reduction of peace in their places of visitation. Indeed, it transpires that many nobles had their own reasons for not wanting peace at all. These distinctions of Bloch's are lost in his own later summary of the reasons for disorder. One popular piece of wisdom is that if all are responsible, then none is, which is evasive and incorrect, but still a product of moral discourse. Broad generalizations about mentalité, such as violence's presence in 'manners', seek to get outside moral discourse by recourse to the fundamental acculturation within which morality functions. But in the context at issue, not only is the argument to mentalité qualified by the author's own assessments of specific interests elsewhere, it also boils down to the circular claim that violence was the product of a violent age.

This sort of circularity is far from uncommon when 'historicization' is taken to mean the subsumption of individual or interest group agendas within what the

---

[10] For references, see Andrew Holt, 'Between Warrior and Priest', in Jennifer D. Thibodeaux (ed.), *Negotiating Clerical Identities* (Basingstoke: Palgrave, 2010), 185–203, here 187 and nn. 7 and 8 thereto.

[11] Bloch, *Feudal Society*, 294–7.

sociologist Émile Durkheim—a significant influence on the Annales school of historical thought within which Bloch worked—called *représentations collectives*. In that particular concept of contextualization, individuals and institutions are seen as 'embodying and applying collective beliefs and sentiments of "society" as a whole'. In this vein, Bernard Hamilton's *The Medieval Inquisition* (1981) claimed that the views of the persecuting clergy were 'shaped by the society in which they lived, which regarded the persecution of heretics as normal', as if the clergy, and indeed secular authorities, had not themselves been responsible for initiating and intensifying so much of the persecution that became 'normal'.[12]

If the reader is seeking any guide as to how an agenda of historical evaluation would look in practice, then Bloch gives us much before taking away at the last moment. Despite his well-known ban on judgement he provides so much of the grist for it, and even in refusing to remain with the logic of his analysis, he cannot retreat to a non-judgemental position. Instead he just blames an epoch rather than elements of a class. So: simply remove the ban on judgement, because it just tells us what Bloch thinks we should do, rather than exemplifying what he does, then qualify the misleading summation. In the case of *Feudal Society*, that is all that is needed.

The impulse to attempt a value-free explanation remains especially strong in controversial areas, as writers undertake a self-assigned task to add a sober or disinterested perspective to a divided field of inquiry. Ronald Robinson and John Gallagher's classic account of late Victorian Britain's role in the 'scramble for Africa' from the late 1870s, *Africa and the Victorians: The Official Mind of Imperialism* (1961), is such a work. The book's foreword states:

> The ethics of empire have always fascinated the moralist, just as the causes of their rise and fall have perplexed the historian... 'Imperialism' has become one of the most evocative myths of our time and it colours what Americans and Europeans, Africans and Asiatics think of each others' intentions. Today the motives imputed to national expansion have a world-wide significance. They console those peoples still clinging to memories of imperial glory. They inspire those countries even now extending their influence. They embitter those who, having inherited the achievements of others, may yet plunge into an imperialism of their own...
>
> This study is an enquiry into the motives behind Victorian expansion. Obliquely, it is therefore a commentary upon the historical truth of modern theories of imperialism, using the classic model of the African partition.

---

[12] For the quotes, and the contextualization and criticism of Hamilton, see R. I. Moore, *The Formation of a Persecuting Society* (2nd edn, Oxford: Blackwell, 2007), 3–4, 100–1. The relevant work of Émile Durkheim is 'Représentations individuelles et représentations collectives', *Revue de metaphysique et de morale* 6 (1898), 273–302.

The book is avowedly concerned with explanation alone: 'the morality of the conquest is not here our concern'.[13] To that end, it seeks to get behind the myths and the moralizing (and the Marxist explanations) and explore the real motives of some of the key agents of colonialism. The experience of empire, its impact upon and meaning for indigenous peoples, colonizers, or merchant, is largely absent. Britain's politicians and bureaucrats are to be taken on their own terms, the terms of what they intended and why they intended it. This is a legitimate thing for the historian to attempt as long as one thing is borne in mind.

As part of any competent technical inquiry, those 'own terms' of the inevitably select historical actors need to be interrogated just as rigorously as any other aspect of causation. Historians are not in the habit of taking historical actors at their word in other areas of causation but are constantly reading evidence 'against the grain', or in light of 'hidden agendas', underlying trends, self-justification, perceived interests, and so on. This is called source criticism. We know that historians have long speculated on the causes of the First World War, but whatever the ongoing disagreements in the scholarship, no debate hinges around believing everything that all of the relevant actors said at the time about why they got to the point of fighting. If the historians did stop at the self-justification of their historical subjects, their books would be nothing but litanies of mutually contradictory assertion. Historians would then indeed be guilty of taking the politicians at their own word rather than taking them on their own terms. Explaining events with reference to human volition entails giving motive reasons a meaning-in-context. Insofar as part of that meaning is morally salient, the historian's ascription of motive binds her to a judgement about how things were, morally speaking, at all relevant points in the tale. Thereafter come assessments of moral consistency, the relationship between values and interests, good and bad faith avowals, and so forth. With all this in mind some source criticism is called for. The source text is *Africa and the Victorians*, and the critical task is to assess how successfully the authors live up to their claim simply to avoid evaluation.

Robinson and Gallagher realize that telling it how it was necessitates identification of morally salient historical facts. We are duly notified at the outset of the introduction that the Victorians 'regarded themselves as the leaders of civilization, as pioneers of industry and progress'. In the same vein over the next two pages we learn that in 'the Utilitarian science of political economy, the earlier Victorians beheld the rules for improvement everywhere. They were not the first, nor were they to be the last people, to project their own image as the universal ideal.' 'Few doubted that *gesta Dei per Anglos*, however they might disagree about His choice of method.' The 'authentic mid-Victorian outlook on the world...was

---

[13] Ronald Robinson and John Gallagher with Alice Denny, *Africa and the Victorians: The Official Mind of Imperialism* (London: Macmillan, 1961), p. xi (from the preface)—note that the foreword has no page number.

suffused with a vivid sense of superiority and self-righteousness, if with every good intention'.[14] So far so good—the British way was held to be good for the rest of the world. This is clearly not an argument about discarding moral categories; it is an argument that the morally salient element is the motive sincerity of the relevant actors. Robinson or Gallagher are appealing to 'good intentions' relative to given standards, in much the same way as Lawrence James's *Empires in the Sun: The Struggle for the Mastery of Africa* (2016). 'Good intentions', like 'sincerity', have an affirming resonance.

As it happens, none of these general 'spirit of the times-like' assertions are tied to specific sources. As the book progresses, other generalizations are made but they are also importantly qualified. For the late Victorians, as for their predecessors, 'expansion in all its modes seemed not only natural and necessary but inevitable; it was pre-ordained and irreproachably right. It was the spontaneous expression of an inherently dynamic society.' This expansion was 'not essentially a matter of empire but of private commerce and influence...empire tended to be thought of as an auxiliary, in much the same way as the liberal state at Home. The main engine of expansion was enterprise.' And though by the end of the 1860s, 'this optimistic idealism was cooling, as disappointments piled up and the millennium of peace, brotherhood and free trade receded...[nevertheless] experience had only overlaid the earlier dreams, it had not erased them'. Then we read that 'however liberal in principle, Victorian statesmen in practice never minimized the role of government in all this'.[15] One important illustration of tension between principle and practice is to be found in British rule in India, when in 'the so-called era of laissez faire the country was being turned into a satellite of the industrial economy chiefly by state enterprise'. Crucially, we learn that 'such inconsistency rarely worried the pragmatic British'.[16] Within the space of ten pages of introduction, we have moved from Britain as the universalizer of its own deeply held beliefs to Britain the pragmatist, prepared to compromise its principles on the minimal role of the State on the basis of the 'Radical' Sir Charles Dilke's recognition that 'were we to leave Australia or the Cape, we should continue to be the chief customers of those countries: were we to leave India or Ceylon...falling into anarchy, they would cease at once to export their [primary] goods to us and to consume our manufactures'.[17]

The concepts pragmatism and practicality need interrogation, especially in relation to 'principle'. How do they relate to the purported belief of the officials that they were doing the right thing in principle? If pragmatism exists in a separate sphere to principle, which in turn derives from morality in some relationship to

---

[14] Robinson and Gallagher, *Africa and the Victorians*, 1–3.
[15] Robinson and Gallagher, *Africa and the Victorians*, 4–5.
[16] Robinson and Gallagher, *Africa and the Victorians*, 10.
[17] Robinson and Gallagher, *Africa and the Victorians*, 10.

culture, it scarcely makes sense for us to treat the Victorians as men of their times since they could choose whether to inhabit the universe of principle or that of pragmatism and were thus significantly free from the contextual influence of their culturally bequeathed beliefs. If, conversely, pragmatism exists within the constraints of a specific set of cultural or ideological precepts, we can assume that the movement from 'principle' to 'pragmatism' is not that at all, but instead a change in emphasis or parameter of rationality to another, within the confines of an overall framework of belief. The only inconsistency here is over which doctrine is best fitted to the pursuit of the higher, imbibed justification: the principle that purports to be universal, or the pragmatism that is really just a name for the retreat from quasi-universalistic principle to the pursuit of some other more fundamental imperative.

Presumably the more fundamental framework concerns the material prowess of the British state in an international system of competitive states. Suffice it to say that *Africa and the Victorians* adduces ample evidence of the awareness of British statesmen of some sort of 'bottom line' of imperial policy. This evidence is not the authors' unsourced distillation of the spirit of the times, but specific citations. In 1840 Lord Clarendon looked 'to what may be most for the honour and advantage of England, and to what offers the fairest prospects of extending her commercial relations and the sphere of her influence and power'. In 1863, Benjamin Disraeli said that 'there may be grave questions as to the best mode of obtaining wealth...but there can be no question...that the best mode of preserving wealth is power'. In the interim, according to the authors, 'the Palmerstonians insisted that the expanding economy needed the protection of power and that it was also one of the weapons of power'. Robinson and Gallagher then conclude that 'power remained an end in itself', and that 'trade and hegemony were manipulated deliberately as reciprocating elements...power must break open the world to free trade', and where it met with obstacles power was 'extended in its subtler forms—prestige, cajolery, threat, the dangled loan reinforced occasionally with blockade, bombardment or expedition'.[18] The logic of all of these pronouncements is that the view that *what was good for Britain was good for the world* in the eyes of the British has been reduced to the pursuit of *what was good for Britain simpliciter*.

In much the same deflationary vein we read that 'India by the mid-century no longer seemed likely to offer loyal partners on whom authority might safely be devolved', so the Victorians 'accepted the fact, and comforted their liberal consciences with the duty of an indefinite but benevolent trusteeship which pushed beyond the mental horizon teasing questions about nationalities struggling to be free'. Such dilemmas had apparently been present earlier in the century, in episodes in which Britain was 'generally ready to confront despotism and Holy

---

[18] Robinson and Gallagher, *Africa and the Victorians*, 4–5.

Alliances, and to give aid and comfort to rebels in South America, Greece, Belgium or Hungary'.[19]

Closer inspection of the Greek case rather qualifies Robinson and Gallagher's account of that instance and casts light on matter relevant to expansion into Africa. Official British support for the Greek rebels, culminating in support for independence from Ottoman rule, took years to develop out of a policy of neutrality in which the British foreign policy establishment hoped for a return to the status quo ante. It is unclear whether public philhellenism was a factor in the change of policy, or whether it merely provided additional justification for a shift that would have taken place anyway owing to other factors. Certainly British fears about commercial shipping were involved and a concern that were Russia to intervene alone it would adversely affect British strategic interests. Tellingly, after the Greek 'war of independence', British policy reverted for decades to sustaining the integrity of as much of the Ottoman Empire as possible as a counterweight to Russian influence in Europe and over the land routes to India.

The centrality of India and the Ottoman decline helps explain Britain's venture in Africa, as Robinson and Gallagher explain. Securing the alternative Suez canal route to India was key to understanding Britain's assumption of authority in Egypt and thereafter the acquisition of large parts of Africa can be explained by 'mission creep', under the pressures of general European competition for Africa as well as the land-hunger of white settlers in the south of the continent. There was no great economic justification, so the rationale was strategic and 'defensive', conceived to protect the large amount that Britain had in the world. Expansion into huge tracts of Africa was, nevertheless, the result. Under the pressure of other modern or fast-modernizing European states with their own expansionist agendas, and in a world that had rejected many of the liberal tenets of the mid-Victorian era, the late Victorians were in the mindset of retrenchment. This new turn of mind did not, however, stop them using older rationales. Of traders and philanthropists, Robinson and Gallagher conclude at the book's close that 'ministers usually listened to their pleas only when it suited their purpose...although their slogans were frequently used by government in its public justifications'. Such things as 'promises of African progress' were one of the '*ex post facto* justifications of advances'.[20] By this point this is good, discerning scholarship about the relationship between motives and justifications, but that is not how it began.

Robinson and Gallagher's claim that 'the morality of the conquest is not here our concern' equates to a refusal to assess the accuracy of their own claims about the purported impulses of their historical subjects in the light of the evidence that they (the authors) have themselves have brought forward. By their inviting us into the official mind of imperialism at the outset and telling us that it 'was

---

[19] Robinson and Gallagher, *Africa and the Victorians*, 4.
[20] Robinson and Gallagher, *Africa and the Victorians*, 463, 472.

suffused with a vivid sense of superiority and self-righteousness, if with every good intention', we are being told how it was in the moral world of the administrators of empire. On closer examination, by the authors' own account, it seems that that was never simply how it was, and at particular times some distance from how it was. Far from obviating or postponing the moral debate by their opening, scene-setting pronouncements, Robinson and Gallagher pre-empt it. Having professed to take the British actors on their own terms in order to get on to the real task of neutral explanation, the authors inadvertently provide a moral defence by their partial establishment of those 'terms' and the officials' good intentions relative to the terms.

Bloch, Robinson, and Gallagher each use contextualization to do some normative work. Bloch's concern to treat certain actors neutrally ended up producing a tacit evaluation of something else, namely the mentalité of the earlier Middle Ages. Robinson and Gallagher contextualize in a way that heads towards justification for their chosen actors. These three scholars are chosen not to cast any aspersions, but because their techniques are common. Many historians do what they do to some degree and in some fashion, with a greater or lesser self-consciousness and subtlety. Even when they do not use the term 'contextualization', historians' choices of master 'contexts' against which all else has to be discussed frame the moral issue in a particular pre-emptive way.

An example in which a form of contextualization is used not to justify, but certainly to mitigate, comes from the work of one of the world's best-known historians. In the historical case in question, one of mass murder and expulsion during the Second World War, it is impossible to hide from the moral purport of the actions under explanation, and there is no suggestion that the author, Timothy Snyder, seeks to hide from it. Nonetheless in the attribution of responsibility, meaning here blame, contextualization plays a sometimes ambiguous, sometimes problematic role.

Snyder's article 'The Causes of Ukrainian-Polish Ethnic Cleansing in 1943' (2003) is a finely researched exposition that is essential reading not just on that conflict but for any general student of ethnic cleansing or the Second World War. It is thoroughly persuasive in its argument that Ukrainian nationalism alone cannot explain why the contest over disputed Volhynian territory was resolved in the most violent manner by the killing and expulsion-flight of the ethnically Polish population. Nor, says Snyder, may we blame the mainstream Ukrainian nationalist leaders, who were either enfeebled, killed, or imprisoned before the 'ethnic cleansing'. Thus far, the normative overtones are starting to become clear, even if they are in the negative vein of telling us what not to blame. At the point of telling us what and who is to blame, Snyder places a relatively great emphasis on the overarching responsibility of Nazi Germany and the USSR, as opposed to the agendas of non-Nazi right-wing nationalists, specifically Ukrainian ones. The distinction between totalitarians and nationalists from various states in eastern

Europe was also marked in Snyder's subsequent works, notably the blockbuster *Bloodlands: Eastern Europe between Hitler and Stalin* (2010).[21]

Again, this is no crude apologetic for the chief Ukrainian actors: labelling them as ethnic cleansers, as Snyder does, cannot but combine evaluation with description—a combination that receives more systematic attention in Part 2 below. Nonetheless it is clear from Snyder's introduction and conclusion that 'triple occupation' provided 'the overarching institutional framework', indeed the framework, institutional or no, within which 'local particularities' like Ukrainian nationalist agendas must be examined.[22] By the triple occupation Snyder means the occupation of Volhynia by the USSR from 1939 to 1941, then by Germany from 1941 to 1944, and then again by the USSR from 1944, during which time institutional stability and established political elites were obliterated, and vast violence was committed by both totalitarian powers. Undoubtedly significant though such occupations were in polarizing Volhynian society, this framing does not include the Polish control of most of the relevant Volhynian territory in the interwar period—control that Ukrainian nationalists viewed as occupation too, and which was important in firming up some of the nationalist agendas that achieved the most extreme expression in 1943. Indeed, midway through the essay Snyder observes that one 'constant from the pre-war period was an ideology of ethnic homogeneity', and that the Organization of Ukrainian Nationalists (OUN) 'was founded, in 1929 [10 years before Soviet occupation], as an organization committed to removing all occupiers from Ukrainian soil'. Further, Snyder writes that both fractions of the OUN, i.e. the more radical OUN-B and the OUN-M, 'understood that Poland would not voluntarily relinquish Volhynia'. 'As proponents of an independent Ukraine including these territories, Ukrainians knew they had little to gain from wartime discussions with Poles. Both the OUN-B and the OUN-M believed that the situation would resolve itself if populations were moved in both directions.'[23] Now we might view this recognition of exclusionary endogenous nationalism's importance from well before the beginning of the war-time violence as Snyder explicitly qualifying his own insistence on the framing priority given to the German and Soviet occupations. Instead, what we have is an interpretative tension that is not reconciled in the conclusion. Oscillation between different causal factors and their importance replaces integration. One of the article's subsections is entitled 'ideology and circumstance', and the overall normative thrust of his essay is to foreground 'circumstance' in the explanation of

---

[21] Timothy Snyder, *Bloodlands: Eastern Europe between Hitler and Stalin* (London: The Bodley Head, 2010). On the issues in question, see Omer Bartov's excessively hostile review of *Bloodlands* in *Slavic Review* 70/2 (2011), 424–8 and Richard Steigmann-Gall's review of Snyder's *Black Earth* in *Humanity*, 7 Feb. 2016, at http://humanityjournal.org/blog/the-holocaust-between-scholar-and-public-intellectual/

[22] Timothy Snyder, 'The Causes of Ukrainian–Polish Ethnic Cleansing 1943', *Past & Present* 179/1 (2003), 197–234, here 200, 232.

[23] Snyder, 'The Causes of Ukrainian–Polish Ethnic Cleansing 1943', 212.

the actions of Ukrainian nationalists, by which he means circumstance from 1939 and especially 1941 as created by the ideological projects of Nazi Germany and the USSR. For 'circumstance', read 'mitigating context' as regards the relevant Ukrainian forces. It should be clear by now that the existence of a normative thrust itself is not a problem; the issue is whether the author is clear about what he is doing and whether the particular normative conclusion is appropriate in light of what we know.

One indication of excessive lenience towards the Ukrainian actors and Ukrainian political traditions involved in ethnic cleansing comes from the idioms of explanation Snyder employs when addressing specific agents of ethnic cleansing. Of the subgroup of extremist Ukrainian nationalists that did emerge (the OUN-B faction) out of a bloody conflict with other Ukrainian nationalists, his evaluation is that they were 'immature and angry'.[24] Carefully chosen words: in legalese, we might associate 'anger' with the crime of passion, which pleads mitigation in light of hot, not cold, blood. We might associate 'immaturity' with the age of minority, lack of full responsibility. Then we have a discussion of the c.12,000 Ukrainians who served in the German-run auxiliary police from later 1941 and provided vital manpower in that capacity for the murder of 150,000 Volhynian Jews. Snyder explains their employment as 'one of the few ways that young Ukrainians could draw a local salary and avoid deportation to Germany for forced labour'.[25] That is all; the murder of Volhynia's Jews is thereby detached from Ukrainian ethno-nationalism.

Those 12,000 men subsequently broke away from German ranks and provided the vanguard of the UPA, the paramilitary force of the OUN-B—a proactive move. But in explaining their subsequent killing actions against Poles Snyder puts them back into the reactive mode and finds an appropriate passive voice for the description. 'They had been taught how to kill. Former policemen brought not only their SS training and their weapons, but the irreplaceable experience of co-ordinated murder of designated populations. The OUN-B appealed directly to this experience, and to the widely held idea that the Ukrainians were next.' Accordingly, the 'people who became UPA soldiers knew about Jewish death, as they had brought it about as German policemen. The lessons were applied to Poles.' When they killed Jews, the reader infers, they did so purely as 'German policemen', and thereafter, once made into killers by an external agency, they could be instrumentalized for other tasks. German acts and agendas retain causal primacy. In the conclusion we learn that the 'final solution of the Jewish question', the Holocaust in Volhynia, 'was not only an effect but a cause', meaning a cause of the ethnic cleansing of Poles.[26] Again, when discussing OUN-B's 'voluntary'

[24] Snyder, 'The Causes of Ukrainian–Polish Ethnic Cleansing 1943', 208.
[25] Snyder, 'The Causes of Ukrainian–Polish Ethnic Cleansing 1943', 210–11.
[26] Snyder, 'The Causes of Ukrainian–Polish Ethnic Cleansing 1943', 210–12, 232–3.

resettlement scheme (for intermigration of Poles and Ukrainians across new Polish–Ukrainian borders), as proposed to the Polish Home Army in December 1941, Snyder writes 'that it could be [proposed] at all suggests the importance of the German precedent' of ethnic cleansing in Poland.[27] One would be forgiven for thinking that OUN had no choice but to endorse a precedent once it appeared, or that their own actions would have been unimaginable without that particular totalitarian precedent, as opposed, to, say, the precedent set by other ethnona-tionalists in the First and Second World War eras. The rhetorical device is par-ticularly jarring given that we know the OUN sought ethnic homogeneity from well before the war, but that fact of Snyder's own disclosure cannot be accommo-dated within the primary 'contextualizing' structure of the piece.

Cause and Context in Historical Explanation

Snyder's use of the occupations of 1939 onwards as a master context, rather than, say, the OUN quest for ethnic homogeneity, was an authorial choice, but the very idea of a master context is problematic. It is actually a special manifestation of a wider problem, which is the tendency of historians to give an interpretative prior-ity in their explanation to 'context' in the singular or plural. Context tends to be seen as more fundamental than 'cause', but there is, in fact, no conceptual distinc-tion between a cause and a context.

'Context' and 'cause' both have influence over an eventualization, and what has influence over an eventualization is a cause. 'Context' and 'cause' are just different names that we give pragmatically to elements of an argument as a result of the particular scope of our inquiry. Were one interested in the proximate origins of the First World War, the assassination of Archduke Franz Ferdinand might loom large as a cause, with the modernization of Russia, French Germanophobia, and German fears of encirclement part of the context, whereas an enquiry into both longer- and shorter-term origins would count both sets of things as causes.

By extension of the argument that there is no distinction in principle between a context and a cause, we need to resist any implication that a context is a particu-larly important sort of cause. In contrast to the implications of serried History essay and examination questions, in the explanation of any given outcome it does not make sense to assign one cause, or sort thereof, greater importance than another.[28] It makes no sense to claim of the First World War that, say, the alliance system, or German aggressive-defensiveness, or Austrian bellicosity towards Serbia, or the Franco-Russian alliance, were 'more important' causes than the

---

[27] Snyder, 'The Causes of Ukrainian–Polish Ethnic Cleansing 1943', 212–13.
[28] S. H. Rigby, 'Historical Causation: Is One Thing More Important Than Another?', *History* 80 (1995), 227–42.

assassination of Franz Ferdinand *if* one accepts that the assassination was causally relevant. In Snyder's Volhynian case it ought not be a question of portraying the triple occupation as being more important than the nationalist ideology of the OUN and the acts of Ukrainian agents. If all causes are needed for a certain outcome, then they may not be given in hierarchy of significance. (This sentence is not as startling as it may sound, especially to social scientists looking for shared causes in roughly similar classes of outcome; it does, however, emphasize the need for precision in defining exactly what outcome one is concerned with explaining.) What we sometimes call catalysts are also causes: a catalyst changes a situation by its introduction as a new element, and in plain speaking must be a cause of the modified situation. Now one might say that the situation had already to be unstable for the catalyst to have its effect (as in the Franz Ferdinand–First World War scenario), but it is eminently possible for unstable situations to continue indefinitely, or to stabilize by the introduction of yet other factors.

To say that no cause/context is more important than another is not to say that all are morally relevant. One does not blame a bullet for a lethal shooting even though its hardness is causally integral to the death. But amongst the causes that are morally relevant, the historian may not assume one to be solely relevant or most relevant. In the Volhynian case it ought not be a matter of totalitarian states *or* Ukrainian agents in the moral calculus any more than in the causal explanation; it is a matter of totalitarians *and* Ukrainian agents. Nor ought moral responsibility be treated as a finite quantity to be removed from one cause or actor in the measure it is attributed to another, as with Snyder's arguably excessive mitigation of Ukrainian elements.

The present section explores more systematically the relationship between causation and moral responsibility in a discipline—History—with a significant humanistic element. 'Humanistic' is used here only in the loose sense of inquiry that is concerned with human experience and agency, and by extension with matters of choice and conscious volition. In such an inquiry, one needs to be careful in establishing exactly what one means by the rather protean term 'causation'.

Let us first attend to what in the philosophy of social science is known as the relevant 'explanatory background'. Not blaming bullets for their hardness—a hardness that is causally relevant to explaining deaths by shooting—is not the same as subscribing to the argument underlying the popular expression 'guns don't kill people; people kill people'. The questions of arms manufacturers, availability of guns, and the culture around gun-usage would easily fit within the ambit of a humanistic inquiry in the aforementioned sense. The humanistic character of much historical explanation becomes clear when we consider the elements of explanation that historians have conventionally been most interested in. In perpetuating the tale of William Tell, the storyteller more often than not takes for granted, rather than providing, knowledge of how his synapses must have worked, how his arm muscles must have contracted, and of projectile dynamics, even though all of these elements would be required for a sufficient explanation of his best-known deed, and all might be more interesting to the natural scientist. The humanist is more interested in Tell's aim, in the senses both of his marksmanship and purpose in undertaking the shot. In either case the outcome—whether or not the aim is achieved—can only be assessed in accordance with a concept of success/failure that has no counterpart in the way that the chemist regards chemicals. Even when projectile dynamics and automatic bodily reactions play a greater—though still implicit—role in the humanistic account, as when the story is recounted of Harold II's (improbably) receiving an arrow in the eye at the Battle of Hastings in 1066, the interest is generated by the existential significance for Harold, and the broader sociopolitical significance for England.

Behind purposes like Tell's stand reasons, which are of much interest in humanistic explanations. By 'reasons' it is not necessarily intended to denote products of rational calculation, merely motive source. A sexual drive or a fantasy is a 'reason' of sorts, while the 'memory' that might also feed into purpose need not be accurate or relevant by anyone else's count than the actor's own. Now it should be stressed that humans are by no means the only entities capable of acting on reasons. The capacity to weigh courses of action ultimately rests on weights of attachment to different outcomes, and 'justification' in that sense is common to neurologically complex organisms in general. Abstract evaluative reasoning, and thus justification in the sense that we associate it with normative debate, is, however, plausibly unique on this planet to humans or at least the higher primates.

Thinking about justification in general, the eighteenth-century philosopher Immanuel Kant noted that it is only through our own self-conception as agents possessing some decision-making capacity and potential causal efficacy that we can make sense of our existence.[29] The evaluations on which human relationships are founded, from sentiments of love to those of hatred, can only exist on the assumption that praise, blame, admiration, and resentment mean something in a way they would not if we understood ourselves and others to be determined in all our actions by tradition, natural endowment, or divine purpose.

Even the theorists most associated with some species of determinism retain space for conscious individual contributions to the causal chain, much as when Otto von Bismarck claimed to the effect that one could not make events happen, one could only secure their fruits—as if acts of 'securing' did not comprise a species of event.[30] While Karl Marx predicted that the proletariat would be driven to

---

[29] Following Kant, and drawing directly on him, was Hans Vaihinger's *Die Philosophie des Als Ob* [The Philosophy of 'As If'] (1911; Lepizig: Feliz Meiner, 1922). One acted *as if* one's perceptions of things actually corresponded to how those things were because it would be hard to know how one could consistently act to the contrary. One acted *as if* one were a discerning, causally-effective moral agent because it made no sense to act otherwise. Separately, note a general influence on this section: S. I. Benn and R. S. Peters, *Social Principles and the Democratic State* (London: Allen and Unwin, 1966), ch. 9.

[30] Georgi Plekhanov, *The Role of the Individual in History* (London: Camelot Press, 1950), 27.

action by its immiseration, it would nevertheless have to recognize for itself what its predicament was, where its real interests lay, and how to rectify the situation. That applied theorist Lenin emphasized this element of Marx's thought in *What Is To Be Done?* when he rejected the economic determinism that he called 'economism' and emphasized the role of the political sphere:

> Class political consciousness can be brought to the workers *only from without*, that is, only outside of the economic struggle, outside of the sphere of relations between workers and employers. The only sphere from which alone it is possible to obtain this knowledge is the sphere of relationships between *all* the various classes and strata and the state and the government—the sphere of the interrelations between *all* the various classes.[31]

Lenin also recommended the Marxist Georgi Plekhanov's *The Role of the Individual in History* (1898). Some of Plekhanov's arguments resemble those of the Christian father Augustine as he rebutted the somewhat Stoic Cicero, who in turn had criticized other Stoics for their alleged fatalism.[32] Analogous considerations could be raised in objection to stereotypical portrayals of 'fatalistic orientals'. Both Augustine and Plekhanov sought to reconcile the existence of individual volition and its attendant responsibility with forms of determinism—historical materialism in Plekhanov's case, God's foreknowledge of all that comes to pass in Augustine's. Some of their arguments are fused with additional elements in the following exemplification.

In Augustine's and Plekhanov's cases the determinism at issue is teleological determinism, which needs to be distinguished from mechanical causal determinism of the sort that will be addressed separately in a moment. Consider someone who believes revolution inevitable as certain conditions come into existence, or that Christ is destined to return after a set of arrangements fall into place. The teleological determinist who believes that inevitability is incompatible with free will could say this person should just sit and wait, because whatever her attitude to the coming event, it is inevitable. The philosophy of reverse causation sheds light on why this is not so. Imagine a promise to do something in future—a similar notion to a prophecy of what will happen. At the moment it is uttered, the promise or prophecy is neither true nor false in virtue of its content. The illusion that a promise can be true (or false) prior to its fulfilment (or non-fulfilment) through future action 'derives from the idea that the present truth must compel the future action. The efficacy is in the reverse direction, however: a proposition

[31] V. I. Lenin, *Selected Works*, 2 vols (Moscow: Foreign Languages Publishing House, 1947), i. 201.

[32] Augustine, *City of God*, ed. David Knowles (Harmondsworth: Penguin, 1972), 190–5; cf. Plekhanov, *The Role of the Individual*, 10–22. Marcus Tullius Cicero, *Cato: or, An Essay on Old-Age* (London: J. Dodsley, 1773), 261: 'there is no precept of morality which they [the Stoics] inculcate more frequently nor in stronger terms, than an unlimited submission to the dispensations of providence'.

about what I am going to do is true in virtue of my later action.'[33] The prophecy will only be made true by its fulfilment, and insofar as the prophesied event is foreseen to occur under specific circumstances, then the bringing about (or prevention) of those propitious circumstances imposes a burden of responsibility on the converted (or their opponents) for the making-true (or proving-false) of a promise. Now the teleological determinist might counter that in virtue of the events' inevitability, inevitable too is the balance of the action for and against their advent, such that when they do transpire, they transpire at precisely the conjunction they are destined to all along. In other words, the historical actors' actions are all accounted for in the teleology of revolution or the Second Coming and those actions merely create the illusion of individual choice. But the return argument would be that, prior to the predicted events' coming to pass, participants in the historical process would, like everyone else, have imperfect knowledge of conditions, and ignorance of their precise 'assigned' role and how it was to play out. Accordingly, they would have to act *as if* their actions made a difference,[34] even if, as it might turn out, this difference were only to their chances of being remembered as a worthy member of the faithful. For the Christian or the revolutionary, the will would be freest precisely in the moment of acting to bring about that which was supposedly ordained, because the ordained would not only be the most ardently desired; its bringing about would constitute the making-true of the yet-unfulfilled promise.

History provides some empirical substantiation here. The self-perception of freedom that must accompany an act of will extends to self-conscious martyrs from all faiths, as also to those fundamentalist Christians, the Calvinists, who were so determined to prove by their deeds their place among an elect whose membership had been decided prior to any action they initiated.[35] The German Marxist Klara Zetkin's obituary for her murdered friend Rosa Luxemburg (1871–1919) reads: the 'great task and the overpowering ambition of this astonishing woman was to prepare the way for the socialist revolution, to clear the path for socialism. To experience the revolution, to fight its battles—that was the highest happiness for her.'[36] Whether or not our actor was participating in the creation of an *illusion of efficacy* by her actions, she was not creating an *illusion of intent*, and her motive and actions were hers in a very personal sense. Motive is desire. Intent is the effort to realize desire and with the ownership of such purposive effort, even if the effort is thwarted, comes an ownership of responsibility which is inseparable from human dignity as well as being a condition of concepts like praise and blame.

---

[33] Michael Dummett, 'Truth and the Past—Lecture 3: The Metaphysics of Time', *Journal of Philosophy* 100/1 (2003), 38–53, here 48.

[34] Here again the significance of Kant's and Vaihinger's *als ob*; see n. 29.

[35] For relevant considerations in one important contemporary politico-religious context, see Saba Mahmood, *Politics of Piety: The Islamic Revival and the Feminist Subject* (Princeton: Princeton University Press, 2005).

[36] Rosa Luxemburg, *Prison Letters to Sophie Liebknecht* (London: Independent Labour Party, 1972), 1.

To this point, the argument draws heavily on psychology—it concerns what Leo Tolstoy called 'consciousness' rather than 'reason', and as such Tolstoy called it a delusion. The individual's consciousness endorses the assumption of free will in herself, whereas reasoning about other people's affairs, especially with the perspective of distance, will tend to endorse the denial of free will, Tolstoy felt, as he came down on the side of the 'rational' conclusion. 'If the will of every man were free, that is, if each man could act as he pleased, all history would be a series of disconnected accidents.' Conversely, 'if a certain mode of government was established or certain migrations of peoples took place in consequence of such and such geographic, ethnographic, or economic conditions, then the free will of those individuals who appear to have established that mode of government or occasioned the migrations can no longer be regarded as the cause'. Here we move from teleological determinism associated with destinies to a claim more in keeping with the mechanistic causal determinism associated with the natural sciences.

How might one respond to Tolstoy? There is an increasing scientization that goes with expanding/exteriorizing the focus of historical inquiry to the level of planetary environment, or for that matter interiorizing it to the level of genes and biology. A sufficient level of aggregation, as with certain forms of quantitative History, or a sufficient degree of generalization, as with the comparative History of civilizations, makes the significance of wills and acts appear to fade into nothingness. But the perspective effects can be reversed by asking slightly different questions. Let us grant it true that the individual thinks she has control over some at least of her destiny, even the theorist who at the same time as he alerts his readers to the way their outlooks are shaped by pregiven contexts hopes to show how innovative and thus relatively unconditioned a thinker he is. At the same time, from her situated, local perspective, that individual is also likely to experience structures that confront her as permanent and immovable, which we might conceive as an argument against the belief in freedom. Let us also grant it true that a long-enough view will diminish the causal significance of individual action. At the same time, that long view, which we might call a historical view, will suggest that socio-economic structures at least, and even topographical and environmental structures, are anything but permanent or immutable, and that human action, individual and aggregate, is one of the causal factors of mutation. Ultimately, the further one gets from the study of the choices of people, the greater the appearance of mechanistic determinism, but this is because the historian who asks 'what is the significance of demographic change in history?' is just asking a different question to she who asks 'how have particular humans oriented themselves to demographic facts?'[37]

---

[37] An analogous response might be made to Timothy Mitchell, whose *Rule of Experts: Egypt, Techno-Politics, Modernity* (Berkeley and Los Angeles: University of California Press, 2002), 34, notes that 'Individuals may at times secure control of certain elements, and they may even claim to

Once his stark oppositions are rejected, Tolstoy's own acute point about 'disconnected accidents' might be turned on him. He is correct that with nothing but unconditioned will in the equation, it would be a matter of windowless human monads bumping into each other like atoms in the air, and with as little concern for consequences. The result would be just as arbitrary from the perspective of observers and participants as a world in which determinism operated at every level.[38] In neither world would there be mere relatively stable trends, or structures of middling durability. In neither, in other words, would there be the sorts of things that humans have fought to change, perpetuate, redirect. Such structures and trends of course shape the possibilities of action, but like a coral reef in perpetual metamorphosis they also constitute the objects of present-transforming action. The relationship may merely reflect the way that the existing architecture of a house influences the construction of an extension that will change that house, and the building techniques are influenced by the nature of the building materials. Bloch's colleague Lucien Febvre mentioned 'institutions, divorced from those who made them, and who, while upholding them, alter them constantly'.[39] This is roughly the lesson of sociologist Anthony Giddens's influential work on structuration: that structure and agency interact in a rather indeterminate fashion.[40] Theoretically speaking, it is not clear how much more precise one can be than invoking interaction: one can produce greater precision by empirical study of a given case, but what the case-study approach gains in specificity it loses in generalizability.

Now apply this sort of thinking to the concept of context, beginning with the etymology of 'context': the word stems from 'weaving together'. In the historian's weaving process, new evidentiary material does not simply get plonked on top of the tapestry, it should be woven in to alter the colour or texture of the fabric. Context is thus contingent on interpretation of new evidence, just as interpretation of new evidence is contingent on context, and new pieces of evidence add to context as well as being subsumed within it.[41] What is true of newly discovered

---

represent those elements in the social world. But no individual masters them, or submits the world to their intentions'.

[38] See also David M. Levin, 'On Lévi-Strauss and Existentialism', *American Scholar* 38/1 (1968–69), 69–82, here 74; and Bruce Wilshere, 'Pragmatism, Neopragmatism, and Phenomenology: The Richard Rorty Phenomenon', *Human Studies* 20/1 (1997), 95–108, here 105, on the unmediated opposition between 'sheer contingency' and 'blind mechanical necessity'.

[39] Febvre quote from Adrian Jones, 'Word and Deed: Why a Post-Poststructural History Is Needed, and How It Might Look', *Historical Journal* 43/2 (2000), 517–41, here 521.

[40] Anthony Giddens, *The Constitution of Society: Outline of the Theory of Structuration* (Cambridge: Polity Press, 1984).

[41] At this point we also encounter a problem that is not inherent to historical inquiry in principle but can be characteristic of its practice, namely the disproportionate influence accruing to the first historians of a subject, who get to establish 'the context' first and, as is the way with academic egos, frequently have a large investment in defending that interpretation. Subsequent historians then find that the burden of proof rests disproportionately heavily on them to correct the presumptive picture.

evidence is true of historical actors themselves, whether, individuals, organizations, or movements. And if actors can shape circumstances by their deeds and rationalizations, how can their actions then be entirely explained as a function of environment? The problem is easily presented by the case of inventions. Not only did they bring something new into the world, they can change that world more broadly. Given the impact on 'their times' of the printing press or the Maxim gun, it makes little sense to say that they can only be understood in the context of the time in which they were invented.[42]

Purposes are another of the things that compromise arguments about determinism by social or cultural context. Purposes are not the preserve of communities, societies, cultures, civilizations, structures, or circumstances. They are the preserve of individuals, and self-conscious collectives like teams, armies, and possibly status groups. Purposes are one of the elements that have no analogy in mechanistic accounts of causation. They derive from the interpretation of (prior) experience and from (future-oriented) will/aspiration. In anticipation of criticism about some notion of a fully autonomous actor unshaped by any context, the seventeenth-century philosopher Spinoza noted that desire, appetite, and fantasy are themselves indicators of limitation; the being that had the feeling of total fulfilment (for Spinoza this was God) would not have these, nor therefore the need of will to fulfil them. When non-divine 'purpose' is invoked here, it means the 'projection' described by a famous existentialist philosopher: 'No factual state whatever it may be (the political and economic structure of society, the psychological "state", etc.) is capable by itself of motivating any act whatsoever. For an act is a projection of the for-itself toward what is not, and what is can in no way determine by itself what is not.' Much the same goes for 'imagination'. Imagination is one of the things distinguishing causation in human affairs from causation as understood by natural scientists. Imagination projects from what is not to what is, and that vision of the future provides the motive force for action, with action complete when attempt has been made to realize vision.[43] Purposes/imagination are not sufficient to explain willed human actions (far less the outcomes of those actions), but they are necessary in any explanation of such actions.

The word 'determination' has tellingly different valences in different contexts of speech. Determined' in the sense of determinism is held to be antithetical to free will yet 'determined' in the sense of being hell-bent on achieving something is

---

New schools of historiography have to work hard to have their new sorts of evidence and new categories of inference validated as genuine contributions.

[42]   For relevant reflections, see Derrida, *Limited Inc*, 1–24, and Giovanni Levi, especially on the idea of 'immobile' contextualization in work produced under the influence of Geertzian anthropology: Levi, 'I pericoli del Geertzismo', 273.

[43]   The 'imagination' point comes from John Dewey; the quote is from Jean-Paul Sartre, *Being and Nothingness* (London: Methuen, 1957), 435.

held to reveal the very will incarnate. For an outcome to be determined in the mechanistic way in which a natural scientist would use the word does not mean that it is inevitable *simpliciter*, though that is how it is often construed in historical accounting, where the word 'determinism' can be used in a way that blends teleological and more mechanistic meanings. In natural science, for outcome X to be determined means that X is the inevitable result of the introduction of causal agent/mechanism Y under initial conditions Z.[44] In other words, given Y and Z, outcome X is predictable. But none of this means that outcome X is 'just determined' as such, i.e. absent Y and/or Z. In the event that change in interhuman affairs happened in ways substantively similar to this pattern, it is not given in advance that equivalents of Y and Z are already in place. Removing or forestalling one or both of them is the way to frustrate that particular 'determination'. Acting on an account of some past event in order that it 'doesn't happen again' is one commonplace recognition of this point.

Even the fact that one had a sword to one's neck does not provide a causal explanation, in the sense of a mechanistically deterministic explanation, of why one killed someone else on the swordsman's instruction, because one still had a choice, however dire. Appealing to the fact of the threat is to appeal for mitigation, not justification, and certainly not determination. At issue is a loose sense of cause, encapsulated by the concept of influence, or something that inclines, rather than determination, or something that necessitates.[45] In instances like these the causal explanation cannot be divorced from normative considerations.

Ordinary language captures the connection between reasons and the humanistic sense of cause, or it did until recently, if we consider the slightly archaic terminology by which one said 'she had cause' to act as she did, in the sense of her having had good or just reasons to act thus. Debates over the moral *character* of events, as well as their *causation*, can also devolve on that joint meaning. The atomic bombing of Nagasaki is an example. It appears to be a different sort of case to the war-guilt question about 1914 because there is no debate over who dropped the bomb. But the difference is reduced if we said that an agent 'had cause' to act in the sense of claiming that that agent had 'good reasons' to act. In the present case, 'good' may mean prudentially sensible, morally pressing, or both. When one asks who or what caused the Second World War, then, given that a complete causal explanation would be literally endless, much of the explanatory emphasis falls on whether salient parties 'had cause' in the sense of good reasons. Over the bombing of Nagasaki, the basic moral question is whether it was blameworthy, but this is also a

[44] One can see how the cause/context distinction might arise by analogy to the distinction between the causal mechanism and the initial conditions, but in both cases the distinction is pure heuristic convenience: in the scientific experiment both Y and Z are needed to produce X, so both are causes.

[45] Gottfried Wilhelm Leibniz, *Discourse on Metaphysics* (orig. *Discours de métaphysique*, 1686), §30, repr. in Gottfried Wilhelm Leibniz, *Discourse on Metaphysics and The Monadology*, trans. George R. Montgomery (Mineola, NY: Dover, 2005), 1–46, here 34–6.

question of whether it was justified, which can encompass either or both of what it was in response to and what it was supposed to achieve. The question could be whether it was a (morally) reasonable response to existing circumstances, or a reasonable measure with a view to achieving a morally desirable goal.

By whose standards the bombing might be evaluated is not relevant here. The point is that as soon as standards exist, which they always already do in affairs between humans, then actors can attain them or fall short of them because standards can only influence behaviour, not determine it.

Different Sorts of Context

Contexts are manifold, so 'contextualization' can mean very different things. (Remember that 'context' and 'cause' are not distinct things, and thus that 'contextualization' cannot be separated from 'explanation'.) This section addresses different sorts of contextualization and their differing consequences. The principle distinction is between what we might dub 'cultural' and 'functional' contextualizations. As the discussion progresses it encompasses debates about the motive force of values as against interests in order to show that satisfactory explanations of motivation must be open to the intrinsically evaluative concepts of good and bad faith.

Cultural contextualizations concern people who we consider to be 'just different to us' in their values and thinking; cultural arguments in this vein are 'people of their times' arguments. Functional arguments in their purest form concern people who we effectively treat as being 'like us' but in unusual situations; they assume a rationality and value system that adapts to different situations in ways that 'we would too'. Bloch's arguments were of the cultural sort, concerning as they did the mentalities of a far-removed time, whereas Snyder's explanation of the deeds of his Ukrainian nationalists was a more functional argument, given its emphasis on the extreme political conditions of the years 1939–43/4 and the appeal to a familiar idiom of youth and anger when explaining the radicalism of the OUN-B leaders.

Each sort of contextualization has different implications for evaluation, though this is rarely observed in a discipline that has not worked out how to handle normative elements. Cultural explanations may well tend to be more relativistic about context, or at least distancing in their character: 'that's just their way of doing things'. Functional explanations have a more assimilative character, whereby one passes tacit or explicit judgement: 'I'm sure I would have behaved in much the same way under those circumstances'; 'the circumstances were bad but they didn't justify *that*'. An imagined scenario helps to illustrate. The setting is a present-day class about the experience of the USSR during the 'Great Terror' or 'Ezhovschina', the Stalinist purges of the later 1930s. A student new to the topic criticizes a local administrator of whom he has read denouncing a colleague to the Soviet authorities. The History teacher then corrects the student along the following lines: 'you have to understand this wasn't a state like ours. The secret police were numerous and ruthless. There were no safeguards of liberty. In order to survive, one had to bend with the wind. We may not condone what the bureaucrat did, but it's easy to make judgements when you're not faced with those circumstances.' Now the teacher's assessment of the Soviet system's arbitrariness and terror is reasonable, but clearly explanation and warnings against knee-jerk judgement do not get away from judgement *tout court*. This sort of thinking does not encourage the student to jettison contemporary value systems, but rather to apply them in a particular, contrastive way, to reflect the extreme situational pressures of living under Stalinism. The implicit argument is that if that person had lived under a democratic regime more like 'ours', he would have behaved differently, just as 'we' would likely behave as he did under totalitarian circumstances. As regards the historical individual it is a moral argument in mitigation of negative judgement, not an argument against judgement. As regards the regime that constitutes the functional context the argument is straightforwardly, negatively evaluative.

Cultural and functional contextualizations can combine but systematic thought about cross-hatching has been hampered by the academic division of labour and by changing fashions within the discipline of History that reflect wider intellectual movements. Since intellectual fashions tend to compete with one another there is frequently a quest for explanatory primacy as well as a difference in focus.

In much political science and economics, trends including rational actor theory downplay cultural differences before the inquiry begins. Social psychological concepts like cognitive dissonance also claim significant transcultural purchase. If one took one's cue from philosopher Friedrich Nietzsche's reflecting on the will, or Sigmund Freud's theory of drives, one would be more likely to contend that local norms provide merely the idiom of camouflage in which individuals dress their basically self-interested behaviour. Much the same goes, *mutatis mutandis*, for some Marxist accounts of the relationship between class interest and dominant morality: interests are a function of 'objective', basic economic factors while morality exists in the universe of 'subjective', superstructural cultural factors, and unmasking the interests that determine the 'morality' is one of the major purposes of ideology-criticism. Marxist and Freudian approaches actually have some relationship to the 'rational actor' theory, with its emphasis on the instrumental pursuit of interests, even if Marxist and Freudian ideas of what constitute interest differ greatly.

Conversely, some influential historiographical trends that developed in symbiotic relations with different generations of anthropology have foregrounded cultural contextualizations. The nineteenth-century 'historicist' tradition associated with Ranke was founded upon the idea of national-cultural particularity, as in its own way was the British 'whig' tradition. The 'cultural turn' taken by the discipline from the 1980s speaks for itself and provides the best illustration of what one might term the 'neo-historicist' attitude. Neo-historicism shares with nineteenth-century historicism and romanticism more generally the emphasis on cultural difference but lacks the metaphysical basis in philosophical idealism and puts more emphasis on differences over time within the 'same' culture. The concept of culture that was deployed in History's cultural turn was opposed to the concept of ideology in its Marxist iteration, and is also to be contrasted with the more sociologically-influenced quantitative social History that had dominated in the USA especially from the 1960s to the 1980s and focused on questions related to socio-economic 'modernization'. In approaches foregrounding culture, acts of 'interest' could become mere epiphenomena when set against the more profound study of systems of meaning and value. In this vein the anthropologist Marshal Sahlins claimed that cultural 'unity' 'defines all functionality'.[46] Given its recent prominence in History, such thinking is subject to particular scrutiny over the next few pages. The coming critique shows what the recourse to certain conceptions of culture can obscure, especially when it comes to providing motive-based explanations for any particular action. Then the ramifications of that critique for moral evaluation are specified.

Clifford Geertz, the anthropologist most influential in History's 'cultural turn', provided useful pointers to combining different types of contextualization, while sometimes muddying the same waters. His helpful intervention came from criticizing the 'stratigraphic' approach to the study of relationships between 'biological, psychological, social, and cultural factors in human life. In the stratigraphic conception, the human is a composite of "levels", each superimposed on those beneath it and underpinning those above it.' Stratigraphic analysis involves taking one layer at a time and then peeling it off, in a way that happily reinforces the integrity of each of the relevant academic disciplines. A non-stratigraphic approach would consider the interplay of these different levels, showing how for instance cultural norms could channel or repress biological urges, or the different way cultural norms might be channelled in certain social situations.[47] There are similarities with the way Marxists can move beyond the idea of the base determining the superstructure, instead showing interaction and interpenetration.

Now to Geertz's less helpful offering. 'Culture is not a power,' he wrote, 'something to which social events, behaviours, institutions, or processes can be causally attributed; it is a context, something within which they can be

---

[46] Cited in Victor Li, 'Marshall Sahlins and the Apotheosis of Culture', *New Centennial Review* 1/3 (2001), 201–87, here 219. See also Talal Asad (referring to Edmund Leach's *Political Systems of Highland Burma*) on 'the theory which gives logical priority to the system of authentic meaning supposedly shared by an ideologically-defined community and independent of the political activity and economic conditions of its members', cited in the same article, 224.

[47] Clifford Geertz, *The Interpretation of Cultures* (New York: Basic Books, 1973), 37–8.

intelligibly...described.'[48] This is another false dichotomy of cause and context. Either culture has influence on outcomes like social events and so on, or it does not. If it does, then it is part of the causal explanation. If it does not, then it merits no mention in explanation. This particular Geertzian characterization of culture implies that culture has an especially deep explanatory function, within which more proximate, explanatorily discrete (and, to some, less interesting, even less important) causes play off each other. The cultural historian Alon Confino makes an analogous argument, but with contrasting terms. He downplays the significance of what he calls context in order to promote his own theory of the causal centrality of cultural developments. In 'reconstructing the context one describes the circumstances within which something happened, not necessarily why it happened'. In Confino's work 'context' is equated with 'circumstances' and both are opposed to cause which is equate with culture.[49] One way or another, we are back to a stratigraphic explanation, with, for instance, cultural and functional explanations firmly separated, and whatever happens to be one's favoured explanatory factor (in Geertz's and Confino's case 'culture') put in the box seat, whether it is called a cause or a context. It is no good, though, if (say) a historian criticizes clinical or social psychologists for disrespecting context if what he really means is that they are ignoring the contexts that he thinks are especially interesting or important. Psychologists are deeply concerned with particular sorts of context.

The word culture itself is vague enough to connote many matters, from linguistic and symbolic systems to law codes, manners, and folk-law, and a great deal besides. The term is yet further contested when we consider 'subcultures', 'countercultures', 'organizational cultures', and so forth. Any number of identity cleavages may run through any given society, and it is not uncommon these days to describe those cleavages in the idiom of culture. Urban, rural, regional, ethnic, gendered, and age-, occupation-, caste-, 'order'-, or class-based cultures constitute a non-exhaustive list. Since some subcultures can cut across other cultural divisions, they may also cut across time and place, collapsing to some extent the 'anthropological gap' between past and present or between different pasts or presents. The idea of military culture for instance, may bind together even opposed soldiers in a certain identity and value system, and may in some of its facets endure across generations. Taking culture in the broadest sense of a way of life, one certainly ought avoid what Geertz dubbed equally 'absurd positions—radical, culture-is-all historicism, or primitive, the-brain-is-a-blackboard empiricism—which no one of any seriousness holds'. He also wrote that

> The issue is not whether human beings are biological organisms with intrinsic characteristics. Men can't fly and pigeons can't talk. Nor is it whether they show

[48] Geertz, *The Interpretation of Cultures*, 14.

[49] Alon Confino, *Foundational Pasts: The Holocaust as Historical Understanding* (Cambridge: Cambridge University Press, 2012), 83–96, here 87.

commonalities in mental functioning wherever we find them. Papuans envy, Aborigines dream. The issue is, what are we to make of these undisputed facts as we go about explicating rituals, analyzing ecosystems, interpreting fossil sequences, or comparing languages.[50]

As it happens, some scholars who are considered to be serious have indeed subscribed to 'culture-is-all historicism'.[51] But cultural difference and similarity have to be argued for, not presumed by some theory of underlying similarity or difference. Simply being interested in difference ought not deny the possibility of similarity, or vice versa, and establishing difference or similarity in one area or at one point does not disprove similarity or difference in others, as an example from the literature of subaltern studies shows.

The historian Partha Chatterjee and the postcolonial theorist Dipesh Chakrabarty argued that Indian peasants reacted differently than English workers had to the encroachment of new market norms. They explained this difference with reference to fundamental, paradigmatic differences in the world-view of peasants in colonial India. Whereas British workers reacted according to some internalized utilitarian calculus about material interests, the choices of their Indian counterparts evinced the influence of communitarianism, religion, and an honour code. Now in some sense this supposed contrast is not one between British worker interests and Indian worker values, because, so the explanation goes, the British conception of 'interests' was itself related to something like the insinuation of bourgeois values/culture. So the argument could also be read as concerning different reactions in different cultures. Irrespective, Vivek Chibber has shown that Chatterjee's and Chakrabarty's conclusions as to the difference of British and Indian reactions are not supported by their own evidence, and moreover that a quite different interpretation was supported by that evidence. Chibber shows marked similarities across the cases in resistance to capitalism's expansion and its drive to control labour markets.[52] Put in the terms of this section, the assumption of 'cultural' difference determined Chatterjee's conclusions because it supposedly determined how Indian peasants would react to the situation in hand. The assumption was that, given cultural dissimilarity between Indians and English, there could be no functional similarity in human response. Chibber's conclusions, however, suggest one of two alternatives. Differently accultured people might act in broadly the same way in response to broadly the same pressures because there just are some obviously, widely identifiable 'interests' related to well-being and pride out there that a great diversity of people can recognize. Or

---

[50] Clifford Geertz, 'Anti Anti-Relativism', *American Anthropologist*, NS 86/2 (1984), 263–78, here 268.

[51] For the basic issues at stake and a range of examples, see Ian Hacking, *The Social Construction of What?* (Cambridge, MA: Harvard University Press, 1999). For some specific examples of historians' claims, see Wahrman, 'Change and the Corporeal'.

[52] Vivek Chibber, *Postcolonial Theory and the Specter of Capital* (London: Verso, 2013), chs 7–8.

there is some similarity in the situation and concern of certain sorts of workers, wherever they might be, that shapes the character of their responses to certain novelties—here the concept of 'peasant culture' might be deployed in a way that crosscuts 'Indian' and 'English' culture. The difference between these two positions may be slight and in any case one need not choose just now. But Chibber persuasively identifies problems in a certain hermetic tradition of thought about culture that so sharply divides one 'people' from another—and, as he points out, that tradition of thought ends up producing the same impression of radical cultural 'difference' that underpinned the 'orientalism' against which the likes of the theorist Edward Said set his face.

What superficially appears to be a cultural argument can sometimes be a functional argument. With moral evaluation in mind, consider the historical case of the Western social scientist's encounter with Inuits who walled-up aged relatives and left them to die, which seems the epitome of a culturally different practice. With further inquiry, though, what first looked like murder ended up looking like respectfully assisted suicide for incapable parents who felt themselves a burden on families living hard, subsistence lives.[53] This realization might persuade the observer that she would behave as the Inuits do were she in that economic-environmental situation. The role of cultural difference is now moot.

What goes for people in the face of roughly similar pressures can go for states and other polities. The relationship between war and social change is well established across different cultures. In the nineteenth and twentieth centuries, polities as different as the Romanov Empire, the Ottoman Empire, China, and Japan initiated revolutions from above in the form of modernizing reform projects that had many similar features because they had similar aims and similar prompts. China's reform endeavours were driven by successive military defeats at the hands of various powers. Defeats at Russian hands in 1828 and 1877–8 were vital in the Ottoman case. The loss of the Crimean War and the 1905 defeat to Japan explain Russia's drive. The fear of the Chinese or Ottoman fate of neo-colonial subordination inspired Japanese reforms, and the last major Ottoman reform movement, that of the 'Young Turks', was in turn inspired by Japanese success against Russia. Each of these cases underlines the truth in the words of one scholar of politics that 'the concept of tradition gives a poor picture indeed of the amount of inventiveness, innovation, and conscious dexterity which is needed for any state to survive at all'.[54] Nothing is to stop one focusing on the differences in the programmes of reform or their success, but that cannot occlude the similarities in 'situation' and innovation.

---

[53] An example from Steven Lukes, *Moral Relativism* (New York: Picador, 2008), 37–8.
[54] Bernard Crick, *In Defence of Politics* (London: Penguin, 1964), 120, 121. For similar sentiments in Oakeshott, see his 'On Being Conservative', in Oakeshott, *Rationalism in Politics*, 168–96. See also Claudio Cioffi-Revilla, *Politics and Uncertainty* (New York: Cambridge University Press, 1998).

Let us now move away from the relationship of cultural and functional thought and towards the relationship of values and interests within the confines of any given culture, in the loose sense of a way of life. What follows is not an extensive discussion of how the play of values and interests relates to the play of cultural and functional explanations, or of the extent of what Geertz calls 'intrinsic characteristics' and cross-cultural 'commonalities in mental functioning'. All that is sought here is to establish the moral relevance of the fact that values and interests, while not necessarily in opposition, are not entirely dissoluble into each other. As such, apprehending the relationship of values to interests in any given instance is vital for the matter of taking actors 'on their own terms'.

It is an absolutist or moralist fallacy to suppose values and interests must necessarily be at loggerheads,[55] but they can be, and while values can shape interests it is eminently possible for values to be the servant of or the camouflage for interests. For all the neo-historicist preoccupation with the difference between humans across time and space, one may still hazard that there is a general human capacity to lie to oneself as well as others or to sustain an undeserved sense of piety, even if different social arrangements channel and constrain these tendencies in different ways.[56] Consider Hungarian Holocaust survivor Imre Kertész's semi-autobiographical novel *Fatelessness*, as the subject encounters a baker in his home town who was known to dislike Jews.

That was also why the bread he pushed at me was a good half pound short. I have also heard it said this is how more leftovers from the ration stayed in his hands. Somehow, from his angry look and his deft sleight of hand, I suddenly

---

[55] Indeed, it is a reasonable historical assumption that morality had origins in social functionality, the need for cooperation and the shared rules that would govern cooperation. The need for mutual understanding and assurance that is essential to cooperation will issue in presumptions in favour of truthfulness. The need for internal protection and group reproduction will issue in strictures against arbitrary forms of violence and in favour of more-or-less ritualized forms of dispute resolution. This goes for relations between groups as well as within them: without customs governing feud, or delineation between the state of war and non-war, intergroup commerce would be impossible. Discerning where morality meets functionality and prudence is difficult in principle because of the issues of reciprocity and cooperation. To be sure, a resolutely 'deontological' account of morality depends upon the distinction: Kant keenly distinguished his categorical imperative from the biblical injunction to do unto others as you would have done unto you because of the implicit contract of reciprocity in the latter. It is not surprising, though, that 'golden rules' equivalent to 'do unto others as you would have them do unto you' recur across a wide range of times, places, and cultures. One could say that prudence and reciprocity have moral valence whatever the Kantian absolutist has to say of them. Alternatively, one could say that it is what philosophers call a genetic fallacy to allow the origins of a practice to colour it for evermore, and to suggest that if morality emerged out of interest then it is not really morality. We could say that a practice effectively becomes moral in an absolutist rather than functional sense precisely at the point when its initial instrumental justification is forgotten. We do this because it's just what we believe it to be right to do, not for any pay-off. In any case, even if at one point the presumption against lying or arbitrary killing was functional, in the permanent now of considering whether to lie or kill, it will not be the idea of the ban that is under debate so much as its terms. Only negotiation will bring forth alterations to what is a permissible sort of calculation and after negotiation outer limits of some sort will still exist—they will just be different.

[56] D. Livingstone Smith, *The Most Dangerous Animal* (New York: St Martin's Press, 2007), 107, 109.

understood why his train of thought would make it impossible to abide Jews, for otherwise he might have had the unpleasant feeling that he was cheating them. As it was, he was acting in accordance with his conviction, his actions guided by the justice of an ideal

The account illuminates the way in which cognitive dissonance can be reduced not by changing behaviour, but by justifying behaviour through realigning values.

Montesquieu was thinking along similar lines when he parodied the 'right' to enslave Africans: 'The peoples of Europe having exterminated those of America had to reduce the peoples of Africa to slavery in order to use them to clear so much land. Sugar would be too dear if the plant which produces it were not cultivated by slaves.' As to the slaves who therefore must be used: 'We cannot suppose that such folk are men, because, if we suppose them to be men, people might begin to think that we ourselves are not Christians.'[57] Even when slavery was well established, and racism a given part of the value system for many whites, many slave-owners who benefited from the doctrine that their slaves were inferior beings suitable for enslavement nonetheless felt them sufficiently human to rape them. A fine balance indeed: how fortunate for all the beneficiaries and perpetrators that values and interests were in such pinpoint harmony. Montesquieu's approach is not illegitimate: the norm that ultimately came to underpin the practice was racism, but racism does not necessarily lead to slavery; material interests at the very least reinforced the norm as the norm legitimated that method of furthering the interests.[58]

As ever, it may be impossible to establish whether what is under consideration in any given case conforms to the economist J. K. Galbraith's definition of 'one of man's oldest exercises in moral philosophy'—'the search for a superior moral justification for selfishness.'[59] But it matters nonetheless whether, say, the idea of purity that has long been central to Indian social stratification is a fundamental religious principle from which all else springs or whether 'the value relating to purity' exists 'thanks to certain economic and power relations...which [the value] is summoned to justify.'[60]

---

[57] Montesquieu, De l'esprit des lois, bk XV, ch. 5, cited in John Plamenatz, Man and Society, i (London: Longmans, 1969), 295.

[58] Two older articles that take different positions on the slavery-racism chicken-egg question are: Carl N. Degler, 'Slavery and the Genesis of American Race Prejudice', Comparative Studies in Society and History 2 (1959), 49–66; Oscar Handlin and Mary F. Handlin, 'Origins of the Southern Labor System', William and Mary Quarterly 7 (1950), 199–222. More recently: Davis Eltis, 'Europeans and the Rise and Fall of African Slavery in the Americas: An Interpretation', American Historical Review 98 (1993), 1399–1423. Thanks to Paul Quigley for pointing me to these pieces.

[59] J. K. Galbraith, 'Stop the Madness', interview with Rupert Cornwell, Toronto Globe and Mail, 6 July 2002.

[60] Ruth Prince and David Riches, 'The Holistic Individual: Context as Political Process in the New Age Movement', in Roy Dilley (ed.), Context and Social Anthropology (New York: Berghahn, 1999), 167–86, here 168–9.

Kertész's baker returns to mind legion beneficiaries and accomplices in sundry genocides. These people do not fit the model of true believers, yet nevertheless end up with the jewellery of the dead, the businesses of the evicted, the daughters of the murdered—forced marriage within the 'enlarged family' saving a dowry in some cultures, let us not forget. Those ordinary Germans who used denunciation to the Gestapo for personal ends, even as they indirectly bolstered the control of the regime, were not ideologues but were akin to those who used the wider context of the Greek civil war for local score settling, those conquistadores who Montaigne saw using their convictions as a cloak for their greed, or those crusaders motivated to massacre in and en route to the Holy Land by prospect of plunder.

In every society so far as we know, significant acts are justified and explicable in reference to significantly shared meaning systems, ideas of the good, the beautiful, and the true, and beyond that the ontological sense of what is real in this world and perhaps worlds beyond. Societies work by prompts by which the individual pursues certain aesthetic or moral or prudential courses. For the most cynical actions the relationship of interests and values is encapsulated in the aphorism that hypocrisy is the tribute vice plays to established virtue.[61] If an individual transgresses a regulatory norm of the moment, she may meet with disapprobation, loss of social standing, impoverishment, or physical punishment. Such outcomes work insofar as they reinforce the general *value* system by playing on the *interests* of the transgressor—i.e. her concern about the likelihood, magnitude, and nature of disapprobation or punishment. If she does something that is not transgressive, we cannot know why she did it without evidence other than her self-testimony, because whatever the actual motive, actors tend to justify their actions according to prevailing value systems. If one focuses, *pace* the sociologist Talcott Parsons, on the 'normative structure' that provides 'value orientation' for a society, then one is apt to see the causal arrow pointing in one direction only, out from societal meanings to individual interests and then action. Not least of the problems of running too far with structural-functionalist sociology, or with Michel Foucault's concept of discourse (see p. 118), is that once one has entirely reduced the social to the socialized, one loses the tools to distinguish whether someone is acting because of coercion, consent, or ulterior motive.[62]

Put differently, the values that purportedly govern in a social system can influence *intent* towards certain goals but without dictating the *motive* for achieving those ends. In a highly religious society, an ostentatious act that is associated with religiosity might spring from fervent belief but it might also spring from the desire to be seen to be adhering to a dominant norm with special commitment, in

[61] Pierre Bourdieu, *Practical Reason* (Cambridge: Polity Press, 2001), 98.
[62] Dennis Wrong, 'The Oversocialized Conception of Man in Modern Society', *American Sociological Review* 26 (1961), 187–93.

order to maintain social capital. It is scarcely beyond human intelligence to discern rationalizations that seem appropriate to the moment. Quite the opposite: such divination is exactly what it means to be a knowing participant in a cultural sphere. Sometimes people lie and contrive to get away with it just because it seems to chime with 'reasonable' expectations of what would motivate in similar situations, as with those British paratroopers who for a long time got away with claiming that they shot Irish republican protesters on 'Bloody Sunday' because they felt under threat. Security services regularly invoke security considerations to justify their actions—given their social function, what else are they likely to invoke?—just as the military are apt to plead military necessity and politicians *raison d'état*; it is up to everyone else to work out whether the justification works.

Turning from the question of value to that of *meaning*, in accordance with the influential conception of culture as a shared system of intelligibility, we might say that certain options are cut off because they are incomprehensible within that meaning system. But we would be better saying that if culture provides the framework within which human acts can be made intelligible, then if an act cannot be intelligibly described from within that culture, inhabitants of the culture would not be able to *recognize* it as a deliberate act. In any case the unintelligible 'options' are *not* those that are proscribed, since proscription entails acknowledgement of the possibility. Were this not the case, there would be no need for the punishments which exist in all societies to deter people from transgressing local norms; without choice there could be no taboo, no possibility of transgression, and no need for deterrent. One point of distinguishing between values and meanings in the sense of intelligibility is that given something is intelligible within a culture, its position on the spectrum of values is not fixed. One need only reflect on how in the Anglo-Saxon countries the cultural meaning of what it is to be a Christian has changed from when it implied disavowal of earthly goods and veneration of the poor, to see that few 'truths' within a tradition remain constant or are given equal stress across time.[63] The Quran can be quoted against suicide bombers as well as in support of them; Adam Smith would not have approved of the economic philosophy of London's Adam Smith Institute. Far from being an iron cage, cultures would not be able to survive over time, unless, like languages, they combined flexibility with their depth.[64]

The valence of meanings themselves can change too, and quickly, as long as some point of reference remains. In another example associated with wartime defeat, consider the development of the concept of 'proper place' within

[63] Sharon Farmer and Barbara H. Rosenwein, 'Introduction', in Farmer and Rosenwein (eds), *Monks and Nuns, Saints and Outcasts: Religion in Medieval Society* (Ithaca, NY: Cornell University Press, 2000), 1–15, here 4, show how the deployment of different doctrinal strands and emphases was dependent upon the needs of society and its most influential institutions in medieval Europe.

[64] Loretta Fowler, *Shared Symbols, Contested Meanings: Gros Ventre culture and History, 1778–1984* (Ithaca, NY: Cornell University Press, 1987), 236, 242, and *passim*.

Japanese culture. In the 1930s and early 1940s, this concept was bundled up with presuppositions about status, morality, and race to legitimate Japan's claim to leadership amongst the peoples of East Asia. After defeat the rhetoric of 'proper place' paved the way for acceptance of Japan's more modest status in the family of nations.[65]

The speed of the Japanese transition reminds us of a matter as important as changes over the long term, namely disagreement in the moment. If we take the definition of culture as a shared system of intelligibility, all that that necessarily means is that people within the culture understand better than anyone outside the culture what they are disagreeing about and are best placed to manipulate the available resources of that culture in their own cause. As to self-interested behaviour, that only needs to have been imaginable within a culture and to the advantage of enough of the right people for it, over time, to gain candidate status as 'part of the way we do things', even if that time is much longer than the lifespan of its original pathbreakers. Every 'time' in every culture has its amoralists who stand subjectively neutral to values while transgressing them. Every time has its equivalent of the cannabis smoker who smokes in private, accepting the law and hoping not to get caught breaking it. But some cannabis smokers deliberately do it in public: existing meanings can be changed—deliberate and repeated transgression of the acceptable is a well-tested way of revising what is considered unacceptable—and purpose-driven action, whether its salient consequences are intended or not, is one of the engines of historical change. Consider events in the era of the 'English Reformation'. These included massive sequestration of land and other wealth from the ecclesiastic institutions by a monarch—Henry VIII—happy to divide the booty with his supporters in the Tudor administration. Under the name 'enclosure', the landed classes had already increased their holdings, this time at the expense of the commons. In response to claims that the poor rebels of 1549 were engaged in sedition, against a backdrop of sixteenth-century unrest caused by the development of English agrarian capitalism, the English poet Robert Crowley (b. 1517) attributed the real sedition, the overturning of mores and transgression of boundaries, to serried nobles, knights, lawyers, and merchants, 'men that haue no name because they are doares in al things that ani gaine hangeth vpon'. 'Men that would haue all in their own hands: men that would leaue nothyng for others; men that would be alone on the earth; men that been neuer satisfied. Cormerauntes, gredye gulles: yea, men that would eate vp menne, women, & children, are the causes of Sedition.' Greedy gulls: a term quaint to contemporary ears but damning in the context of a society in which voracious acquisitiveness was not yet a general characteristic. For while Crowley has been characterized as having a 'medieval' (read: outdated) concept of the

---

[65] John Dower, *War Without Mercy: Race and Power in the Pacific War* (New York: Pantheon, 1986), 211, 259.

commonwealth, perhaps because of his recently rather unfashionable view that the poor were heard especially loudly in heaven, it seems that his view was shared by 'most of his mid-Tudor contemporaries'.[66] Most of what the 'gulls' did was quite legal, and lawmakers were among the beneficiaries. Yet it would take a long time for their agenda to become normative in the sense of being widely accepted as legitimate.

The interrogatory work that 'bad faith' does at the personal level by exposing the relationship between espoused values and interests is performed at the systemic level by 'immanent critique'. That is the grand name for assessing whether something lives up to its own account of itself, for instance assessing whether unfettered capitalism comes good on justifications like trickle-down wealth enhancement. The foregoing studies of Bloch and Robinson and Gallagher were instances of immanent critique applied to works of History, though in the latter case they provided some evidence for immanent critique of official Victorian imperial justifications, too. If, in that case, all we are ultimately saying is that Victoria's colonial officials were only consistent at pursuing interpretations of national interest as narrowly defined, then we are already saying they were rather less than they might have liked to claim. We certainly should not today make the mistake of repeating their more grandiloquent self-projection as if that represented the relevant reality. It will perhaps be enough for their defenders then and now to say that the Victorian elites were good at looking after national interest, especially in a world where now, as then, the national interest provides a powerful justification. But being satisfied with a pared-down claim to virtue when acting effectively as judge in one's own national case will leave many others unconvinced. For all the stock placed in high-minded British imperial intentions then and still now in some empire scholarship, we would do well to recall that label applied by various Europeans at points, and implied by American diplomats who sought to escape the 'whirlpool of old world diplomacy'. That label, with all its intimations of bad faith, was 'perfidious Albion'. Naturally those applying the label were not disinterested observers, but as soon as the defender of the Victorian officials utters a rejoinder to the effect 'well Britain's competitors would say that, wouldn't they?', then that defender is making an argument, however unsophisticated, about the way that value judgements serve interests and this argument can be turned upon their own clients and indeed themselves.

In cases of especially egregious behaviour, scholars who wish to respect the ground rules of historical contextualization while not resiling from moral comment may criticize historical actors for their infringement of their own espoused

---

[66] Tom Betteridge, *Literature and Politics in the Tudor Reformation* (Manchester: Manchester University Press, 2004), 109–10; Andy Wood, *The 1549 Rebellions and the Making of Early Modern England* (Cambridge: Cambridge University Press, 2007), 35, 102. I thank Colin Richmond for alerting me to the 'greedy gulls'.

values. In his *The Origins of Indian Removal, 1815–1824* Reginald Horsman was clear that one should only ever criticize according to the prevailing standards of the actors' times and went on to show how those standards were routinely transgressed.[67] Other works have done more or less the same thing, such that we now have quite an inventory not just of atrocity but also of what one might call bad faith: making treaties with Native Americans then breaking them, or deceiving the indigenous population into inequitable compacts while talking the language of honour; encouraging religious and/or cultural conversion on promise of consideration as equals, then failing to provide said consideration, even, sometimes, to the point of murdering converts as cuckoos in the white nest; laying claim to land on the doctrine 'terra nullius', then taking land even if it was being used for the productive purposes that taking it was supposed to justify; not to mention the many points at which systemically exploitative relations tipped over into actual violence against individuals and populations on grounds of greed just as much as racist acculturation. In the contrast between action and stated belief, or the juxtaposition of incompatible self-justifications, the results of historical investigation open up these historical actors to a host of criticisms that one suspects some of their contemporaries would have acknowledged as fair. That is an achievement in historical inquiry, but it is, again, an achievement in orthodox historical investigation in the sense of (moral) contextualization. The only reason it might seem otherwise is the presumption against evaluation in which any criticism is deemed as anachronistic or the agenda by which evaluation is only considered as illegitimate when it is negative.

With a view to future arguments in this book, it is worth pondering what happens if one puts all one's eggs in the immanent critique or bad-faith basket and yet bad faith is not demonstrably present. What, for instance, when good faith issues in bad outcomes, or when we encounter a Nazi who genuinely believed he was doing the right thing—that sincere Nazi who posed a problem for Jean-Paul Sartre's existentialism?[68] The philosopher Berel Lang claims that the Nazis knew that what they were doing was wrong, by which reasoning the prevailing value system becomes morally and contextually irrelevant.[69] The Holocaust historian Saul Friedlander also refuses to allow that the leading Nazis may have acted in accordance with the values of their own moral world. He described the Holocaust as the product of 'an amorality beyond all categories of evil'. Such arguments

---

[67] Reginald Horsman, *The Origins of Indian Removal, 1815–1824* (East Lansing, MI: Michigan State University Press, 1969). I thank Claudia Haake for pointing me to this work.

[68] The fundaments of the Sartrean argument as to why an authentic Nazi was a contradiction in terms—an argument that has not been universally seen as persuasive—appear towards the end of his 1945 lecture 'Existentialism is a Humanism', first published in France in 1946 by Nagel, and appearing along with other pieces in Jean-Paul Sartre, *Existentialism Is a Humanism*, trans. John Kulka (New Haven: Yake University Press, 2007). See also *Anti-Semite and Jew* (New York: Schocken, 1948).

[69] Berel Lang, *Act and Idea in the Nazi Genocide* (Syracuse, NY: Syracuse University Press, 2003), 25–32.

appear to be related to his opposition to the general historicist potential for 'relativization of the political sphere; cancellation of [ie. by chronological] distancing; historical evaluation of the Nazi epoch as if it were as removed from us as sixteenth-century France'.[70] Whether Friedlander's and Lang's characterizations of Nazi morality are accurate is not the point, and there is more to be said about moral contextualization and the Nazi case (see pp. 54–5). The point for the moment is that by some moral contextualist reasoning there can be no such thing as bad outcomes, only outcomes *simpliciter*, because the only aspect of the historical drama on which the historian feels it legitimate to make evaluative comment is motivation and the matter of good or bad faith. This situation is curious, since the salient outcomes-of-action by colonialists or slavers or *génocidaires* are evidently what the scholars who appeal to bad faith are often trying to criticize, however indirectly they feel they have to render the criticism.

On Ideology

The strand of philosophy called virtue epistemology aids critical purchase on the idea of 'good faith'. Philosopher James A. Montmarquet argues for the allocation of what he calls 'doxastic responsibility', which includes the idea of an actor's responsibility for the acceptance of the belief to which she was subsequently faithful. The clearest instance of doxastic responsibility is that in which one wilfully adopts a certain belief from a menu of alternatives, and knowingly, therefore, accepts possible consequences pursuant to acting on that belief. Montmarquet argues that doxastic responsibility exists even in instances of less forthright decision-making, though that must remain moot—or perhaps we can say it is determinable only on a case-by-case basis.[71] The utility of this line of thought is in scrutinizing subjectivisms of the type 'that's just what I believe' or 'that's just how I live my life', as if all beliefs and ways of life were merely imposed on people and they could never reflect on their ways. Consider George Orwell on two objects of William Thackeray's satire:

> Major Pendennis is a shallow old snob, and Rawdon Crawley is a thick-headed ruffian who sees nothing wrong in living for years by swindling tradesmen; but what Thackery realizes is that according to their tortuous code they are neither

[70] Saul Friedländer, ' "The "Final Solution": On the Unease in Historical Interpretation', in Peter Hayes (ed.), *Lessons and Legacies: The Meaning of the Holocaust in a Changing World* (Evanston, IL: Northwestern University Press, 1991), 23–35, here 27; Martin Broszat and Saul Friedländer, 'A Controversy about the Historicization of National Socialism', *New German Critique* 44 (1988), 85–126, here 93.

[71] James A. Montmarquet, *Epistemic Virtue and Doxastic Responsibility* (Lanham, MD: Rowman and Littlefield, 1993); Montmarquet, 'Culpable Ignorance and Excuses', *Philosophical Studies* 80/1 (1995), 41–9; Montmarquet, 'Zimmerman on Culpable Ignorance', *Ethics* 109/4 (1999), 842–5.

of them bad men. Major Pendennis would not sign a dud cheque, for instance; Rawdon certainly would, but on the other hand he would not desert a friend in a tight corner.... yet one sees, better than any diatribe could make one, the utter rottenness of that kind of cadging, toadying life[72]

The thinking characteristic of virtue epistemology also works well in highlighting those areas that are consciously pushed from mind at one point, hopefully never to return. The Victorian prime minister Lord Melbourne dismissed Dickens's *Oliver Twist*: 'It's all among Workhouses, and Coffin makers, and Pickpockets...I don't like those things; I wish to avoid them; I don't like them in reality, and therefore I don't wish them represented.'[73] Perhaps an unfortunate stance for a figure notionally charged with the well-being of the whole polity, Melbourne's attitude was nonetheless a useful way of pre-empting dissonance. Today's equivalents might be the politicians who too willingly accepted the assurances of tobacco lobbyists, and now imbibe the bromides of climate-change deniers; or anyone who does not avail themselves of the accessible knowledge about factory farming or unregulated labour because such information would make it harder to justify continuing to buy the salient products. We might also consider the fate of title VII of the 1964 US Civil Rights Act, which addresses not only intentional discrimination in employment but also 'disparate impact', meaning the adverse consequences of employment decisions irrespective of their ostensibly fair intent.[74] That doctrine has recently come under attack from elements of the American Right and has been weakened by Supreme Court decisions.[75] The reaction against it is consistent with the governing American myth that anyone can make a fortune with enough effort and failure is a purely personal shortcoming rather than the outcome of structured disadvantages. Undermining title VII means the system's beneficiaries will find it easier to continue to believe what they want to believe about their own virtues.

The motivation in weakening title VII overlaps with what Orwell called 'protective stupidity' but we might rephrase as 'protective ignorance'. This expression denotes the refusal, out of self-interest, conformity, opportunism, or the desire to retain the emotional or cognitive solace offered by a coherent view of the world, to think counter to that view's precepts, to let experience of the infinite complexities of the world in, let alone to consider alternative interpretations. The expression also encapsulates the sort of thinking Sartre evinced, in neglect or (worse?) in consciousness of his own existentialist call—that yes or no that one ought

---

[72] George Orwell, *Critical Essays* (London: Secker and Warburg, 1946), 25.

[73] Cited in Gertrude Himmelfarb, *The Moral Imagination: from Adam Smith to Lionel Trilling* (Lanham, MD: Rowman and Littlefield, 2012), 57.

[74] The Act was in 1964. A key Supreme Court decision shaping disparate impact doctrine was *Griggs* v *Duke Power Co.* (1971).

[75] Girardeau A. Spann, 'Disparate Impact', *Georgetown Law Journal* 98 (2010), 1133–63.

constantly issue to the world when it might be convenient to abrogate responsibility and describe oneself as being swept up by events—when he wrote that 'To keep hope alive one must, in spite of all mistakes, horrors and crimes, recognize the obvious superiority of the socialist camp.' Nikolai Tolstoy noted the implication that 'it is better for millions of Russians to suffer "horrors and crimes" than that he, Sartre, and his friends should have to abandon their illusions'.[76]

If some level of belief-choice is central to the concept of doxastic responsibility, even if the choice is to stay with what you know, then the concept presupposes belief-options that were recognizable as such. Here, and we arrive at the central argument of this section, there is utility in a distinction between explanations to 'culture' in some broad sense on one hand and on the other hand explanations to 'ideology' in a narrower sense of one of a range of competing theories of why the world is as it is and what, if anything, needs to be done to change it for the better. Using this distinction between culture and ideology, one can identify moments at which they are distinct and moments at which they come together. It is perfectly possible to have both an imperial culture and a political ideology of imperialism, a culture or an ideology of racism, a 'bottom line' of communitarian order which none within the order can gainsay and an internal faction that is self-consciously yet more communitarian than the norm. Religion provides a useful way of approaching the question, because it is bound to culture, and indeed may be purely cultural as opposed to metaphysical (in the way that an atheist could be described as culturally Christian), yet it can also be the subject of 'revivalist' or 'extremist' movements that are manifestly ideological. The Islamic State movement and the American Evangelical Right both play on cultural and metaphysical symbols as they seek to shape social norms anew. This need not be a matter of interests exploiting values; as with the fundamentalist's reading of sacred texts, or the neo-liberal who runs with a selective interpretation of classical economics, it may be a matter of special emphasis on particular extant values reshaping the wider climate of values and interests. A new ideology successfully propagated for long enough will become woven into the (modified) culture from which it emerged. Ideology can survive its most zealous, initial proponents, and may subsequently be embodied by people within structures who do not necessarily reflect on what it is they are enacting, and why.

Ascertaining of any act at any moment whether it expresses a culture or an ideology will not provide an answer that is necessarily generalizable to others even in the same processes at other times, and yet it is important in terms of contemplating the actors as subjects. Consider the different moral valences of the propositions: 'Julius Caesar was a man of his times'; 'Fidel Castro was an ideologue'. An extreme example illustrates further. The Nazi leaders fall into the

---

[76] All cited and contextualized in Erika Gottlieb, *The Orwell Conundrum: A Cry of Despair or Faith in the Spirit of Man?* (Ottawa: Carleton University Press, 1992), 122–4.

category of revolutionary ideological actors. Hitler felt himself intervening in the historical process in order to change its direction, as did some of the OUN-B leaders examined by Snyder. The very present-changingness of Nazism means that so much about it would be missed were one just to present it as a cultural phenomenon. War, genocide, and the reshaping of state and society were *system-atic*, conscious, and transformative rather than *systemic*, automatic, and repro-ductive. The idea of revolutionary conviction based on prior *self*-persuasion helps explain why the conventional historian who distinguishes in principle between 'the man of his times' and the 'ideologue' has much in common with the moral relativist who argues 'different but equal', or 'incommensurable', yet rejects the hostile, anti-relativist *argumentum ad Nazium.*[77]

To develop the argument about the moral valence of contextualizations, con-sider three statements: (1) The ancient Babylonians tortured for (given) cultural reasons; (2) The British in Kenya in the 1950s tortured because of (imposed) proximate circumstance; (3) The Khmer Rouge tortured for (self-imposed) ideo-logical reasons. Assuming that the relevant facts of torture are accepted by all par-ties, what present-day defenders of Britain's name fear is that (2) is not the case, i.e. that they cannot appeal sufficiently to some widely accepted if vaguely defined concept like immediate 'military necessity' to justify the extent and nature of the action against the Kikuyu population. If the argument to (2) is inadequate, as it clearly is when one links the nature of British actions to pejorative ideas about Africans and a concern for imperial prestige in crushing rebels, then (1) (culture) is a more attractive alternative than (3) (ideology) because it is the basis for his-toricization, which, satisfactorily performed, may also put the matter to bed given prevailing neo-historicist sensibilities. Some examples suggest that while histor-ians rarely phrase the contextualizing contest in terms of 'culture versus ideology',

[77] The *argumentum ad Nazium* runs that relativism cannot work because if it did we would have no grounds to judge Nazism. This anti-relativistic argument is complicated when we refer, as suggested here, to 'political/ideological' as opposed to 'cultural' contextualization. Such considerations could fruitfully be factored in to the work of Richard Rorty, *Objectivity, Relativism and Truth* (Cambridge: Cambridge University Press, 2008), 42, and Hilary Putnam, *Reason, Truth and History* (Cambridge: Cambridge University Press, 1998), 167–8, as both scholars discuss the thought of John Dewey. By extension, such considerations could take some of the sting out of Elizabeth A. Clark's criticism of Putnam in her *History, Theory, Text: Historians and the Linguistic Turn* (Cambridge, MA: Harvard University Press, 2004), 219 n. 74. My distinction between 'ideological' and 'cultural' contextualization should not be taken to imply that I think relativism does any practical work; indeed I shall elaborate the argument that it does not in Part 3. It merits underlining, though, that the (reasonable) determination to rebut real and imagined 'relativist' arguments against judging Nazis merely exhibits that the judge-ment on the Nazis has already been made. It is the grounds of justification to pronounce judgement, rather than the judgement itself, that is in question, and in that sense Nazism is by no means pecu-liar—it is just that in its extremity it brings a general issue into particular relief. What I have to say about distinguishing Nazism as an ideology from the culture within which it was born has little rele-vance for the arguments of Parts 2 and 3 about external judgement—it is only relevant to the issue of moral contextualization that preoccupies this Part of the book. After all, the historian who constrains herself to moral contextualization implies that the only legitimate evaluative standard comes from contemporaries of the Nazis who did not share their agenda, and thus is a standard internal to the period under contemplation, rather than external to it.

that is often precisely the battle that is joined, and there are significant political stakes for the historian-combatants.

The distinction between the ideological and the cultural has been at issue in debates over the retrospective evaluation of slavery in antebellum USA. As David M. Potter noted in 1962, anti-slavery historians could be reluctant to take Confederate claims to nationhood seriously because granting the Confederacy status as a nation was a 'valuative' act which might ultimately condone slavery.[78] Put into the terms of the present argument, granting the Confederacy the status of a nation would allow it separate internally legitimate national-cultural values that could then be invoked by way of contextualizing slave-ownership as something that 'They' just did because that was Their way. Denying nationhood meant that the debate over the rights and wrongs of slavery were kept in the ideological arena. Parenthetically, in a distorted mirror image of this sort of thinking, immediately after the Civil War and up to the 1950s white Americans and many of their historians pushed the slavery issue to the margins of the collective memory of the conflict in the name of the re-formation of the all-USA white national-cultural community. 'Even-handedness' in the historical treatment of two valiant warring foes was now the order of the day, detached from consideration of an obvious reason for their fighting. In the interests of healing the wounds between northern and southern white communities, and stressing their basic commonality, southern racist ideology rather triumphed, with romanticized accounts of slavery, and recriminations against the supposed redistributive and egalitarian 'excesses' of the reconstruction era of 1863–7.[79] Black memories were subjugated.[80]

In 2011 one of Spain's leading new 'revisionist' historians of the Spanish Civil War era, Manuel Alvarez Tardío, joined another contextualization battle. He wrote of the rise of the Spanish Republican regime from 1931 that 'arguments emphasizing structural factors which stress [...] the extremes of wealth and poverty [...] are effectively justifying the radical political project of left republicans and socialists, their political intransigence and even the violence emanating from political and union organizations representing the "disinherited"'. Put aside the question of just how 'radical' the 1931–3 projects of socialists and allied republicans were. Clear is that those who seek to outlaw critical emphasis on structural factors for fear of leftwing 'justification' wish themselves to delegitimate the leftist project, rather than aspiring to some discursive state beyond legitimation and delegitimation. As well as (re)legitimating the social order that the leftists sought to change, such arguments can also be deployed to (re)legitimate, or at least

---

[78] David M. Potter, 'The Historian's Use of Nationalism and Vice Versa', *American Historical Review* 67 (1962), 924–50.

[79] David W. Blight, *Race and Reunion* (Cambridge, MA: Belknap Press, 2001). The book is mostly about public memory but there are key connections to professional historiography. Thanks to Paul Quigley for the reference.

[80] Charles Mills, 'White Ignorance', in Shannon Sullivan and Nancy Tuana (eds), *Race and Epistemologies of Ignorance* (Albany, NY: SUNY, 2007), 11–38, here 30.

provide mitigating argument for, the Franco regime that overthrew the Republic on the tacit basis that the Republic was a partisan 'ideological' interlude in the life of the supra-political Spanish cultural order. Tardío may reasonably be read as suggesting that long-standing arrangements, however unequal, comprise some sort of hallowed given whose normative weight trumps that of any mere political contestation. Putatively monolithic cultural 'value' trumps 'ideology', and it should not, one supposes, enter into the equation that the Restoration order was so obviously partisan in the interests it served.[81]

A similar bid to claim the mantle of 'culture' for one particular ideology against others was made in 1859 at the founding of the *Historische Zeitschrift*, one of the most influential historical journals of the nineteenth century. The editor, Heinrich von Sybel, described it as

> a historical periodical, not an antiquarian or political one. On the one hand, it is not our aim to discuss unresolved questions of current politics, nor to commit ourselves to one particular political party. It is not contradictory, however, if we indicate certain general principles, which will guide the political judgment of this periodical. Viewed historically, the life of every people, governed by the laws of morality, appears as a natural and individual evolution, which—out of intrinsic necessity—produces the forms of state and culture, an evolution which must not arbitrarily be obstructed or accelerated, nor made subject to extrinsic rules. This point of view precludes feudalism, which imposes lifeless elements on the progressive life; radicalism, which substitutes subjective arbitrariness for organic development; ultramontanism, which subjects the natural and spiritual evolution to the authority of an extraneous Church.[82]

Edmund Burke's reflections on the French Revolution of 1789 and the English Peasants' Revolt of 1381 likewise sought to assert *the* normative parameter in the form of the givenness of some social order, as if normative parameters and the character of the social order were not precisely what was under dispute.

> When great multitudes act together, under [the] discipline of nature, I recognise the PEOPLE. I acknowledge something that perhaps equals, and ought always to guide the sovereignty of convention…But when you disturb this harmony; when you break up this beautiful order, this array of truth and nature, as well as of habit and prejudice…I no longer know that venerable object called the people in such a disbanded race of deserters and vagabonds…The mind owes to them no sort of submission. They are, as they have always been reputed, rebels. They may be lawfully fought with, and brought under, whenever an advantage offers.[83]

---

[81] Tardío quote from Helen Graham (ed.), *Interrogating Francoism* (London: Bloomsbury, 2016), 23-4.
[82] Trans. and repr. in Fritz Stern (ed.), *The Varieties of History* (New York: Meridian, 1956), 171-2.
[83] Reproduced in R. B. Dobson (ed.), *The Peasants' Revolt of 1381* (London: Macmillan, 1970), 292-3.

Any rejoinder to these partisan cultural contextualizations ought not go to the other extreme and claim that what is taken for an expression of normative culture is really ideology, but the blurred border between the two is conceptually and evaluatively important. On one hand even ideologies as revolutionary as Nazism were not entirely novel phenomena—elements of Nazi thought were shared by other non-Nazi right-wingers and can be traced to earlier romanticism, so they fell into some fertile cultural soil. On the other hand, and more importantly for the present discussion, it is impossible, without remainder, to dissolve social action into culture as culture as conceived in this section, and that is true whether the social forces in question are more associated with continuity or change. The best way to illustrate this point, which is ultimately a point about what we might call conservative ideological agency, is to return to the conceptualization of 'context' and work from there.

As soon as one deconstructs the distinction between context and cause (as on p. 30), one also deconstructs the distinction between context and process. Remember that a context is just a name for a cause, and processes are caused. We generally associate the idea of process with the idea of change but continuity is also processual: indeed it helps to think not of change versus continuity but of social transformation versus social reproduction, since this emphasizes processual elements ('reproduction') in what can sound like stasis when under the label 'continuity'. Both continuity/reproduction and change/transformation are caused, so the question is not of the absence of causes in a situation of continuity, but of the prevalence of continuity's causes over the causes of change. There are proactive agents of continuity, be they individual, collective, or institutional.

As an ongoing, active process, social reproduction requires not just consumers and recipients but also 'cultural warriors', gatekeepers, enforcers. The warriors may be members of functional elites, like Orwell's reactionary 'hanging judge, that evil old man in scarlet robe and horsehair wig, whom nothing short of dynamite will ever teach what century he is living in, but who will at any rate interpret the law according to the books and will in no circumstances take a money bribe'.[84] Or like the Guardia Civil who in Restoration Spain protected the interests of the latifundistas more than rural Spaniards in general. But equally, like those white Americans who lynched African Americans until well into the twentieth century, cultural warriors may be lower within the social system, keen to sustain such social capital as they have by ostentatiously policing the social boundaries separating them from the very lowest, in just the way that has so often prevented solidarity between subaltern groups like successive waves of immigrant workers. Analogous dynamics may also play out within the family, as, say, patriarchy is coercively maintained. A husband physically asserts his domestic dominance—he

---

[84] George Orwell, *Facing Unpleasant Facts: Narrative Essays*, ed. George Packer (Boston: Mariner, 2009), 118.

beats his wife—in a way that, while perhaps 'regrettable', possibly illegal (though rarely prosecuted), is nevertheless important in perpetuating a particular social organization. Obviously enough it is not just revolutionaries who bring violence. Sometimes the violence of what passes for the status quo may be less dramatic, visible, and intensive than revolutionary violence, being more akin to what the sociologist Johan Galtung called 'structural violence'.[85] But the sociological study of overt ethnic violence, up to and including grand massacre, has also shown that one of the most common conditions of its occurrence is when superordinate groups feel their social power to be eroding and they fight to sustain their privileged dominance.[86] Such massacres are manifestations of conservative ideological agency, extreme instantiations of the general phenomenon that one theorist of politics had in mind when writing that sometimes 'it is not merely necessary "to reform in order to preserve" as Burke's great maxim had it, but actually to create in order to preserve'.[87]

Projecting purposively to the future—even if with the determination that the future be as much like the present or the past as possible—is not just a necessary element of any willed human action (see p. 37). It is an essential element of anything meaningfully called political. In other words, conservatism, whether of the Left, the Right, the religious, or anything else, is not a passive disposition but as active a stance as is anti-conservatism. After all, in a system of complete and enduring 'natural' social consensus, there would be no need for a conservative agenda, because there would be no anti-conservative agenda.

Politics presupposes disagreement about the desirability of the way things are at any moment. More than an institution called congress, the witan, or what have you, the political sphere is the arena of articulation of competing social projects, competing views of the desired, against the backdrop of whatever is given in the moment. The adviser to President George Bush Jnr was only exaggerating a central political idea when he said that the American leadership was creating its own reality rather than tailoring its policies to address analysed reality.[88] As much as being the art of the possible, politics is the art of making possible the conditions

---

[85] Johan Galtung, 'Violence, Peace, and Peace Research', *Journal of Peace Research* 6/3 (1969), 167–91.

[86] Susan Olzak, *The Dynamics of Ethnic Competition and Conflict* (Stanford, CA: Stanford. University Press, 1992).

[87] Crick, *In Defence of Politics*, 121.

[88] Karl Rove: 'We're an empire now, and when we act, we create our own reality. And while you're studying that reality—judiciously, as you will—we'll act again, creating other new realities, which you can study too, and that's how things will sort out. We're history's actors.' Reported in Ron Suskind, 'Faith, Certainty and the Presidency of George W. Bush', *New York Times Magazine*, 17 Oct. 2004. Hannah Arendt used her studies of totalitarianism to show that an assumption underlying 'consistent action can be as mad as it pleases; it will always end in producing facts which are then "objectively" true. What was originally nothing but a hypothesis, to be proved or disproved by actual facts, will in the course of consistent action always turn into a fact, never to be disproved.' I do not believe this phenomenon to be in any way limited to totalitarianism. Arendt, *Between Past and Future* (Harmondsworth: Penguin, 1985), 87–8.

for the desirable, and preventing the conditions for other possibilities from coming into existence. The radical Brazilian educator Paulo Freire described strategy as asking the question 'what can we do today, so that tomorrow we can do what we are unable to do today?'[89] He was perhaps thinking of Marx's *Theses on Feuerbach*, wherein 'it is essential to educate the educator himself because 'the materialist doctrine that men are products of circumstances and upbringing...forgets that it is men who change circumstances....The coincidence of the changing of circumstances and of human activity can be conceived and rationally understood only as revolutionising practice.'[90] Obviously enough, these dynamics cannot be fully accounted for by contextualizing reference to 'structure' or 'culture', whether the actors in question subscribe to present-transforming ideologies or present-reproducing ideologies.

As a general reflection, it helps to conjure up a sort of sliding scale where, for different acts, explanations to 'culture' and its attendant systemic characteristics vary in relation to explanations to 'ideology' and its systematic characteristics, with an admixture of explanations to more proximate functional 'situation'. If, as is the case in this part of the book, the priority is taking a historical actor on his or her own terms, every case must be considered in its own particularity. This means balancing what was taken as given with what was more consciously chosen; and when it comes to what was chosen, at issue is the relationship between what was simply assumed to be right and what was pursued because it was advantageous to the agent.

Political Morality and Special Roles

An attempt to take people on their own terms must remain sensitive to roles, because roles shape terms. Withholding information from the authorities might be an act of heroic solidarity or criminal complicity for us ordinary people; for a psychotherapist it is known as patient confidentiality and stands up there as a vocational principle with the Hippocratic oath of the medic. When one stands *in loco parentis* to a child, one assumes greater responsibilities to that child than to others, however much one might believe in the equal worth of all. The role-holder will never stand isolated from a 'cultural' context. At the same time, a role constitutes a 'functional' context, with the pertinent 'situation' obtaining for as long as the person occupies the role.[91]

---

[89] Paolo Freire, *Pedagogy of Hope* (London: Continuum, 1998), 108.

[90] This is from Marx's 'Theses on Feuerbach': see Karl Marx and Friedrich Engels, *Karl Marx and Friedrich Engels—Selected Works in Three Volumes*, i (Moscow: Progress, 1966), 13.

[91] The following works have been especially influential on my thought throughout this section: Coady, *Messy Morality*; Thomas Nagel, *Mortal Questions* (Cambridge: Cambridge University Press, 1979), chs 5 and 6; Michael Walzer, 'The Problem of Dirty Hands', *Philosophy and Public Affairs* 2/2

This section has some general relevance given that all societies feature some role differentiation. It has special relevance for occidental historiography in that a significant proportion of historical scholarship has focused on the actions of special role-holders, notably political and military 'great men'. The roles it considers are political leadership roles, which explains the 'political morality' of the section title, and functionary roles such as those of the warrior or bureaucrat. In each case it identifies potentials for misunderstanding the nature of the roles, and thus for misplaced criticism, praise, or exemption from evaluation. It also shows how the particular obligations and legitimations of the roles nevertheless do not put role-holders in completely separate moral universes to everyone else.

In any evaluation of the actions of role-holders, one needs to avoid two poles. One pole, defined and discussed later, is 'heroic realism' (pp. 69–70). The other is the dogmatic moralism that is blind to any variation in context. Moralism's hard-and-fastness means, for instance, that it cannot see that what is just bad faith in a private capacity might be necessary subterfuge in a public or representative role.

Political or executive morality in the sense furthest removed from familiar forms of interpersonal morality is an amalgam of partiality (to one's own polity or group), impersonality (polities and groups are suprapersonal entities), and possibly selflessness (disregard of one's own purely personal interests and commitments, insofar as they can be separated from one's special role). Note that this account of political morality is defined in a maximally contrastive sense for heuristic purposes. The idea is to bring the underlying issues into sharpest relief rather than to capture every possibility. Thus, for instance, stress on the matter of a leader's partiality to his or her group as a very common feature of human history should not be taken as denying the possibility of a cosmopolitan political morality or its actual existence at this or that point in time. The boundaries of 'groups' are also themselves objects of political contestation.

Considerations of political morality under the above-stated conditions sometimes entail measures on behalf of the collective that might be illegitimate in an interpersonal capacity. Recognition of this fact may help us to contextualize political theorist Hans Morgenthau's claim that 'Man's aspiration for power over other men, which is of the very essence of politics, implies the denial of what is

---

(1973), 160–80; Arthur Isak Applebaum, *Ethics for Adversaries: The Morality of Roles in Public and Professional Life* (Princeton: Princeton University Press, 1999). Most of all, however, I have benefited from the advice of Jonathan Leader Maynard. It is also pursuant to his promptings that I should clarify that this section is not an attempt to define all of the boundaries of political morality. My focus on the notion of delegated/representative/vicarious roles should not be taken to deny other relevant features. Within political theory, scholars have proposed quite a number of different features of politics that might make it some kind of distinct domain from other areas. Aside from the notion that leaders act on behalf of others, other possibilities could include: a need to respect reasonable intercommunal disagreement; a need to legitimate political policies to some degree within the community; a greater priority of certain values such as order or justice; a greater concern with the determination of membership and communal identity; especially high stakes outcomes, intergenerational or otherwise; and more besides.

the very core of Judaeo-Christian morality – respect for man as an end in himself. The power relation is the very denial of that respect; for it seeks to use man as means to the end of another man.'[92] He could perhaps have added Kantian to Judaeo-Christian morality, since one iteration of Immanuel Kant's categorical imperative was always to treat individual others as ends in themselves, never as means to another end—though the interpretation of Kant's imperative remains the subject of great debate.

The public conscience of leaders and representatives cannot just or always be an enlarged version of the individual conscience, as Thomas Jefferson thought it could. It certainly may not be possible to heed the unqualified 'thou shalts' and 'thou shalt nots' associated with religious commandments or the dictates of Kantian moral reasoning about the right thing to do irrespective of outcomes. Making a martyr of oneself is different to martyring those for whom one speaks, even in the improbable event of the entirety of the collective backing the same purpose with the same strength of purpose. Equally, it may be necessary to subject or expose individual members of the collective—even quite large numbers—to harm in the interests of the good of the all. Such considerations are familiar to consequentialist theories of morality, of which utilitarianism is a well-known sort and 'the greatest happiness of the greatest number' a well-known expression. Consequentialist theories are results-orientated theories, being concerned less with what must be done for its own sake than with the balance of outcomes. The coexistence of competing moral doctrines, when set alongside necessary subterfuge and dissembling, provides ample space for leaders and politicians to leap opportunistically from one sort of moral justification to another, whilst lying when it is just convenient rather than necessary. They also pave the way for moralistic misunderstanding of political leadership under particular circumstances, which brings us to Machiavelli.

Whatever the opprobrium heaped on Machiavelli around his time—in fact this probably explains the opprobrium, since he exposed hypocrisies—he reasonably saw himself as bringing out underlying principles of existing political comportment. In clarifying those principles, he had to contest what were sometimes almost wilful absolutist misunderstandings of political morality. When Machiavelli urged that as a prince the good man had to learn to be evil, 'good' and 'evil' were oriented to absolutist ethics of the 'thou shalt (not)' sort. One of the implications of the idea that one had to learn to will evil for reasons of higher good was the Christian conceit that evil was otherwise a temptation to which the weak succumbed, something that in the ordinary run of things was not desired as such, unlike the good to which one had to be strong to cleave but with which one

---

[92] See Hans J. Morgenthau's introd. to Ernest Lefever's *Ethics and United States Foreign Policy* (New York: Living Age Books, 1959), p. xvi.

was automatically acquainted.[93] (As it happens, from the outset Christian thinkers found ways of accommodating the need for earthly rulers to get their hands dirty.[94]) Equally, if it is important that a prince not be 'too good' to do what is sometimes necessary, it is also important that he be 'good enough' as to register the moral weight of his necessary actions. That awareness serves as a check on unnecessary ruthlessness or deceit, which might be counter-productive in a specific political crisis or more generally by weakening faith in the projects and polities that leaders purport to embody and encouraging unbridled cynicism deleterious to the necessary minimum of trust required for the conduct of political affairs.[95]

When pondering different sorts of moral theory, whether in the private or the public realm, it is important to recognize that people's moral doctrines very often blend elements of consequentialism and absolutism. Sometimes people do things because they believe them intrinsically right, sometimes because they see them as a price worth paying, and sometimes they fudge the principles. Sometimes, too, it is possible to have both absolutist and consequential concerns about the same action and for both concerns to point in the same direction. Furthermore, absolutists and consequentialists have refined their positions in response to critiques coming from the other side, such that it can be difficult to tell the positions apart based on what they prescribe doing in most cases even though the principles of derivation remain different: compare Kantian deontology with rule-utilitarianism rather than act-utilitarianism.[96] There is also a theory of 'elite utilitarianism' whereby consequentially oriented leaders perceive utility to flow from the inculcation of deontological stances amongst the masses—the idea that on the whole it is best if people do believe in absolute, intrinsic rights and wrongs, even if their leaders have an eye to balances of outcomes more than anything else. At the same time, while consequentialism may be competent as regards certain forms of moral 'method'—the calculus of means as against ends, ends as against competing ends, and so forth—it cannot establish what is valuable or good *simpliciter* and what, therefore, is fit to serve as a basis of those calculations. Here we come to the non-relative rather than the relative element of thinking about 'the greater good'. Consequentialism is always based on a pre-consequentialist conception of what counts as the good, success in working towards which counts as a positive consequence. The precise character of this good varies for political leaders, though it is apt minimally to include the survival of the relevant group(s) and, less minimally, the relative thriving of the group(s). Let us leave open who gets to describe what

---

[93] Walzer, 'Dirty Hands'.

[94] Joan D. Tooke, *The Just War in Aquinas and Grotius* (London: SPCK, 1965), ch. 1; and see here, Part 3, History I.

[95] Walzer, 'Dirty Hands'.

[96] On varieties of consequentialism, see Michael D. Bayles (ed.), *Contemporary Utilitarianism* (New York: Anchor, 1968).

'thriving' means. What is clear is that for political leaders, it is their group(s), however defined, that constitutes the primary community of obligation: group members are the ones whose goods the leaders take solely or primarily into account in moral reasoning. For leaders like Bismarck, Machiavelli's prince, and a vast, vast number of others besides, past and present, the primary community of obligation is some subset of the globe and/or its human population, not the entirety of either. When it comes to intergroup affairs the partisanship of such leaders towards their community of obligation complicates any talk of conse-quentialism as well as (say) of Kantian absolutism, as we shall now elaborate.

Partiality towards a subset of the world explains a lot about the character of political morality that has been displayed historically and presently, whilst pro-viding some with grounds for proclaiming that political morality is no morality at all. In recent times, the 'national interest', however interpreted, has been an espe-cially important name for the basic good that political leaders seek to maximize, but we should think of it as a placeholder for a concept of 'group interest' that has much broader historical applicability. It is not that 'national interest' and its off-shoots like *raison d'état* are not themselves partisan concepts (they are), but because claiming to act in the national (or group, etc.) interest is claiming legit-imacy for acting in a way that would not apply in other contexts and for other, 'lesser' interests. One cannot, yet, claim the same sort of legitimacy by claiming to act in the interests of the military-industrial complex or accountancy firms, because the latter seem to imply some interest that is no more than extended per-sonal self-interest, whereas acting in the national interest has the ring of 'service' about it. Indeed, where 'interests' are often opposed to 'values', this is not the case with the national interest or its functional equivalents: very many people believe that the national interest is a good and furthering it the right thing to do. Obviously enough, the leader-servant's acting pursuant to projects of national (etc.) interest might bring her polity onto a collision course with the projects of another polity, which presents another moral problem. Such conflicts can occur internally too, most blatantly in the forms of civil wars and revolutions, but since some of that terrain is covered in Part 2 under the rubric of legitimacy contests, this section will keep the focus on relations between polities.

Morgenthau also wrote that the 'denial' of respect for 'man' as an end in 'him-self' is 'particularly flagrant in foreign policy; for the civilizing influences of law, morality, and mores are less effective here than they are on the domestic political scene'.[97] (Note that in light of Morgenthau's whole oeuvre, statements like this appear ambiguous as to whether he was merely making a descriptive claim about common practice in international affairs, or a normative claim about the actual or potential applicability of moral rules in international politics. Such ambiguity is

---

[97] Morgenthau's introduction to Lefever, *Ethics and United States Foreign Policy*, p. xvi.

not altogether rare in International Relations—'IR'—debates.) Let us say that there is a polity in which the egalitarian utilitarian formula 'each to count for one, none for more than one' is observed. Unless that polity is coextensive with the globe, its leaders and representatives will only be able to apply the principles of equality internally. When acting externally they will obviously be thinking of the consequences of their actions, but they cannot be said to be thinking in terms of the application of consequentialist moral principles where every person everywhere counts as equal, since they are only acting on behalf of some of the global population—the part whose overall well-being constitutes their primary community of obligation—whilst potentially affecting other parts. Sacrificing others has generally been preferable to sacrificing one's own, and that has not changed in the present, whatever the rhetoric of universal human rights. However the sociopolitical order may be configured within the boundaries of a polity—whatever its internal hierarchies, whether inside its borders it is individualist or communitarian, liberal, fascist, etc.—when that order confronts another order it still tends to be projected by its representatives as a corporate individual, and its representatives may indeed act in ways that seem entirely at odds with its prevailing internal political philosophy. This is, in fact, one of the major thrusts of key IR theories. The argument goes that even were leaders interested in a broad range of moral values, and even if these were part of their 'role' domestically, they would find themselves constrained in their ability to adhere to/pursue those values by the anarchical structure of the international system.

Morgenthau was a 'Realist' IR theorist, and his words need to be understood against the backdrop of a widespread Realist assumption that an honest reckoning with the realities of politics, especially international politics, is a precondition for the existence of a domestic social order in which morality could play its full part. Furthermore, despite some of his categorical pronouncements on the irrelevance of moral considerations to international politics, Morgenthau tried to modify some of the amoral assumptions of other thinkers within the broad Realist church.[98] As a Realist—the IR school whose longest-standing theoretical counterpart is 'Idealism' (a pejorative term developed by realists) or 'Liberalism'— Morgenthau was pessimistic about the possibilities for harmonization of international relations, or harmonization of ends and means.[99] Nonetheless he was concerned, for instance, to conceptualize ways in which the pursuit of the corporate individual's self-interest vis-à-vis others need not result in omni-destructive competition between polities. This aspect of his work has led to some scholars calling him an Ethical Realist,[100] a label that has nothing to do with the sorts of

---

[98] Anatol Lieven and John Hulsman, 'Ethical Realism and Contemporary Challenges', *American Foreign Policy Interests* 28/6 (2006), 413–20.

[99] For general Realist assumptions on this point, see Norman E. Bowie and Robert L. Simon, *The Individual and the Political Order* (Lanham, MD: Rowman and Littlefield, 2008), 208–9.

[100] Lieven and Hulsman, 'Ethical Realism and Contemporary Challenges'.

'moral realists', alluded to in Part 3 of this book, who consider that there are such things as mind-independent moral facts. There is certainly a prescriptive, as opposed to purely descriptive, element to Morgenthau's thought. Ethical IR Realists prescribe that states *should* act according to what they consider their interests rather than according to more abstract values, lest faith in values distort true understanding of the way of the world and thus be self-defeating concessions to an illusory moral order. Further, like other Realists they would argue that an absolutist-moralistic approach to international relations is itself dangerous, being so sure of itself that it is not subject to the judgement of prudence about the necessity of compromise. But while they might prescribe the subordination of means to ends in dealing with other polities, then—as with the laws of war, which derived from pragmatism at least as much as principle—Ethical IR Realists would be most prominent among Realists in proposing some limits on means, wary as they are of creating a precedent for extreme measures, for spiralling retribution and counter-retribution.

A focus on prudence, caution, and so forth, leaves significant areas of political action unaccounted for, morally speaking, by Realists of any stripe. The conduct of much nineteenth-century European foreign policy had a great influence on the development of theories of Realism but let us consider more specifically the Berlin Conference of 1884–5 at which the major European powers decided how much of Africa would be carved up. The point of deciding to decide on how to divide Africa, rather than engaging in a free-for-all, was to make sure that carving up the relatively weak didn't disturb relations between the relatively powerful. We can infer that if Africans had been more powerful, their agendas would have had to be factored in, up to the point at which dividing Africa would never have been a realistic option for the Europeans. Since Africans were not powerful, one of Thucydides' Melian propositions seems confirmed: the strong do what they can while the weak suffer what they must. Now the Ethical IR Realist might well just shrug and state how this proves that the bottom line of international affairs is indeed power. But let us not forget that the pessimism accompanying this shrug itself connotes a value judgement, if not necessarily on any particular statesperson (though it could be), then on the exercise of power. It is not a value-neutral position—and for what it is worth, a number of key Realists who have addressed normative considerations have reached conclusions tantamount to that of the Realist and historian E. H. Carr, namely that 'it is an unreal kind of realism which ignores the element of morality in any world order'.[101] Again we will note the ambiguity between descriptive and evaluative terms in many such verdicts.

---

[101] Carr quoted in Jack Donnelly, *Realism and International Relations* (Cambridge: Cambridge University Press, 2002), 186. See also Donnelly's analysis of tensions in the pronouncements of George Kennan at pp. 163–4, 166–7. With other relevant thinkers in mind, including Thucydides, whose work Donnelly analyses extensively in ch. 6, see p. 187: 'For all their appreciation of the force of realist arguments, Thucydides and Machiavelli, along with Carr, [Reinhold] Niebuhr, and [the 'Realist Liberal'

Forms of Realism developed in recent decades do tend to claim to be purely explanatory theories, neutral as to value, and these merit some mention, if for nothing else than that political leaders may still infer prescriptions for action from such accounts. Even if relevant Realist theories are value-neutral, that does not mean that all 'real-world' choices that embrace a particular Realist precept exist in a separate realm to that in which moral evaluation is appropriate. Like military necessity, *raison d'état* is an implicitly moral argument that certain unpleasant means can sometimes be legitimated in pursuit of certain ends. As with the concept of the lesser evil,[102] to recognize the normative weight of the means is not to declare them a non-evil, or there would be nothing to 'balance'. Whatever its conclusions, the argument can only be had on moral terrain. Indeed, even in the event that a certain leader refused to recognize any moral consider- ations save that of his own ends, this scarcely renders moral thought irrelevant because there will be any number of observers and peer-leaders who might think differently.

While there is no space here to do justice to the diversity of all species of Realism,[103] it may help to think of them on the whole as conceiving leaders as fulfilling the role of representative in an 'adversarial system'—though this is not a common metaphor in IR scholarship.[104] The Anglo-American courtroom is a paradigmatic adversarial system. There are lawyers whose obligation it is to act in the interests of their clients. Only by representing those partisan interests zeal- ously, so the logic goes, does the adversarial system work, and any client would have reason to feel aggrieved at a lawyer who did not represent her vigorously. At

John] Herz, suggest an approach to international politics that is much more "realistic," in the ordinary sense of that term, because it refuses to be confined to the narrow and ultimately inhuman realm defined by so-called realist laws.'

[102] The lesser evil, like the greater good, is an intriguing concept because it compounds relative and absolute elements. On one hand the lesser evil implies that some evils are greater than others, and thus that the lesser one can be justified to ward off the greater: this is the relative element. On the other hand it implies that an evil of whatever scale is still an evil, which means good and evil are not just different points on the same spectrum, like higher as opposed to lower speeds. Accordingly, harming someone in the name of preventing a greater evil may still be wronging that person, even if the harmer has good or politically- or militarily-legitimate reasons for inflicting the wrong. At the very least, from the perspective of any actor who subscribes to the concept, there is still a normative weight attached to the act and consequences comprising the lesser evil. More than by Michael Ignatieff, *The Lesser Evil: Political Ethics in an Age of Terror* (Princeton: Princeton University Press, 2005), my thoughts on the matter are influenced by Thomas E. Hill Jr, 'Moral Purity and the Lesser Evil', *The Monist* 66/2 (1983), 213–32 and Hill, 'Making Exceptions without Abandoning the Principle: Or How a Kantian Might Think about Terrorism', in R. G. Frey and C. W. Morris (eds), *Violence, Terrorism and Justice* (Cambridge: Cambridge University Press, 1991), 196–229. For a hard case, see C. A. J. Coady's disagreement with Frances Kamm, in Coady, *Messy Morality*, and Applebaum, *Ethics for Adversaries*, 147–8.

[103] For the significant differences in Realist positions, see for instance the contrast between two influential positions: the Defensive Realism of Kenneth N. Waltz, *Theory of International Politics* (New York: McGraw Hill, 1979) and the Offensive Realism of John J. Mearsheimer, *The Tragedy of Great Power Politics* (New York: W. W. Norton, 2001).

[104] I borrow it from Applebaum, *Ethics for Adversaries*.

the same time, the analogy to the courtroom is imperfect, because there are less well-codified procedures for the advocates (i.e. leaders) to adhere to in international affairs, and no non-partisan and sufficiently powerful superordinate authority (like a judge) to adjudicate on procedural breaches or to enforce judgement on any and all parties. It is the absence of this referee that has coloured many Realist portrayals of the nature of international affairs, with polities supposedly behaving, in the absence of a superordinate power, in the same way that individual people supposedly behave in a Hobbesian state of nature—a very influential metaphor in the field. This is a disputable account of individuals and international affairs, based on an erroneous assumption implication that morality is no more than a function of enforceable higher law, and an accompanying caricature of innate and untrammelled human selfishness that can be traced to deep strands of thought in the occidental tradition from which so much Realist thinking derives. Besides, even if we assume that a claim about the polity's interest constitutes the primary normative consideration for the polity's leaders, that does not mean that those leaders cannot also consider other normative concerns to be relevant.[105]

Clearly we are not bound to swallow this or that Realist theory whole, and, more to the point of the present work, we should not think as if any historical actor carried around an international relations textbook to consult in tricky situations. Leaders can lurch unconsciously or consciously from acting roughly in accordance with the descriptive tenets of one of the IR doctrines to acting roughly in accordance with the tenets of another. Furthermore, as with absolutism and consequentialism in ethics, so with Liberalism and Realism in the study of relations between polities: in their practical elaboration the outcomes of Liberal and Realist thought can converge despite the divergence in their founding assumptions. One might find that one's group's interests are best served by establishing relations of trust with other groups, replacing beggar-thy-neighbour competition with mutually beneficial commerce. Fostering shared values might further mutual understanding and harmony. Some polities might even bind themselves formally to other states by alliances, thus ceding some sovereign prerogatives in exchange for other advantages. Treaties, confederations of islands and tribes: none of these is a novelty. Polities can also form relations with non-state international actors like corporations, the first of which in the occident were established in the Middle Ages, or like the UN and NGOs. So even when the obligation to the group or the territorial unit remains primary for its leader, honouring that obligation may involve honouring other obligations that ultimately become difficult to distinguish from the primary normative obligation.

---

[105] See Donnelly, *Realism and International Relations*, 161–7 on the points made in the final two sentences, and, on influential Hobbesian concepts of 'human nature' Marshall Sahlins, *The Western Illusion of Human Nature* (Chicago: Prickly Paradigm Press: 2008).

The IR theory of Constructivism comes in to criticize the sharpness of the interest-value distinction in principle as well as practice. Along with Liberals, Constructivists would say that at the very least interests can become bound to the values that they invoke, however cynically, in legitimation—hypocrisy, again, being the tribute that vice pays to virtue. Even in destabilizing action we see the trace of common value as polities try to justify aggression by some principle other than just self-interest; the self-defensive pretext for war is as old as recorded history. Constructivists observe that interests are never just given, outside value contexts, and even if we need not accept that 'all the way down', in the sense that the meeting of some interests is a condition rather than a criterion of value, we can still accept the thrust of the Constructivist point. By extension, Constructivism, like Liberalism, questions the sharp Realist distinction between the internal and external realms. External forces and developments clearly influence internal orientations. Conversely, internal debates about values, identities, interests, and the boundary of the primary political community of obligation on whose behalf leaders act, will all have knock-on effects on external comportment.

One can adopt descriptive elements from the Liberal and Constructivist accounts without subscribing to any of the optimism that accompanies some Liberal visions of greater harmony or even value-convergence between polities. The point of invoking these competing theories from the perspective of the present book is not to provide substitutes for moralism in the form of hard-and-fast yardsticks against which past behaviour can be measured. While theorists from each camp draw often extensively on historical evidence, they also abstract from cases in the interests of lawmaking. Historians with their taste for the specific may find the approach problematic. Yet, as ever, they must consider whether, while supposedly disavowing all theories, they are actually subscribing unawares to a theory, and what such a theory implies for their own stance towards particular historical actors. Above all, self-declared neutral historians must be careful that, in their desire to be 'realistic' about the exercise of power, they do not unwittingly adopt some version of Realism as a true account of power's exercise rather than a contested theory of power (and even of human nature), and adopt a series of assumptions about the nature of political morality without questioning or perhaps even recognizing them. Academics in their role as armchair warriors can be as susceptible as anyone else to the desire to be seen as 'hard-headed', 'tough-minded', and so forth, and can thereby replace moralism with heroic realism.

Heroic realism moves from acknowledging the moral quandaries of those in special roles to an infatuation with the hard 'necessities' of power. For the historical actor, the sometime need for 'dirty hands' becomes a pride in 'doing the dirty work', a test of mettle. When they are not lecturing on the impossibility of making omelettes without breaking eggs, you will hear some heroic realists incanting that the ends justify the means, without necessarily showing that the ends are themselves justified or that the chosen means are the only (as opposed, say, to the most convenient) way of attaining the ends. The heroic realist tends not to think of the 'lesser evil' as an evil at all, while 'greatness' tacitly assumes its own particular moral aspect, as when tabloid journalists talk of putting the Great back into Great Britain. For the actor, so too, sometimes, for the observer: in *La Renaissance* (1877), by the racist social Darwinist Joseph Arthur de Gobineau, Pope Alexander VI advises Lucrezia Borgia that 'For the kind of person whom destiny calls to dominate others, the ordinary rules of life are reversed and duty becomes quite different. Good and evil are transferred onto another and higher plane.'[106] Note: 'higher' rather than just 'different' and 'reversed' as opposed to 'sometimes altered.' Friedrich Meinecke's teacher and Bismarck's sometime cheerleader, the nineteenth-century historian Heinrich von Treitschke, was more nuanced but nonetheless tended towards the heroically realist when he wrote:

> No man ever went through life with absolutely clean hands and no clashing of duties. In any case there is no walk of life more moral than the statesman's, who on his own responsibility guides his country through quicksands....No higher or harder moral task can be set for any man than to spend the whole strength of his personality in the service of his people. We must not belittle or conceal the tragedy of guilt which sometimes clings to great names, but neither should we examine the leaders of the State with the eyes of an attorney....The statesman has no right to warm his hands with snug self-laudation at the smoking ruins of his fatherland, and comfort himself by saying 'I have never lied'; this is the monkish type of virtue.[107]

As to 'greatness' as a value, ponder the pseudo-moral calculus hinged around the 'but' in this sentence from a History of England's Plantagenet dynasty:

> It is undeniable that during the Plantagenet years many acts of savagery, butchery, cruelty and stupidity were committed, but by 1399, where this book ends, the chilly island realm [*sic*] which had been conquered by William, the bastard of Normandy, in 1066 had been transformed into one of the most sophisticated and important kingdoms in Christendom.[108]

Heroic realism, the term that seems so apt in contradistinction to monkish virtue, was adopted by the Nazi Werner Best, one of the architects of the SS's police and intelligence organization, as he averred that the 'principle of recognition for each people and its right of existence applies equally to the relationship with all other

---

[106] Michael Biddiss, 'History as Destiny: Gobineau, H. S. Chamberlain and Spengler', *Transactions of the Royal Historical Society* 7 (1997), 73–100, here 77.
[107] Heinrich von Treitschke, *Politics*, i (New York: MacMillan, 1916), 103-104.
[108] Dan Jones, *The Plantagenets* (London: Harper, 2013), p. xxviii.

nations. In times of conflict we will of course pursue the vital interests of our people even to the extent of annihilating the opponent—but without the hatred and contempt of any value judgement.' He also claimed that anti-Semitism was 'not a world view but a political, economic and cultural defence'.[109] This we might call 'objectivity' and objective necessity relative to the hard parameter of some sectarian position, which was in this case extreme, paranoid nationalism.[110] You will guess from the loaded choice of example that it is just as easy to take this line of thought too far—to run a very long way with subjective judgements of what is necessary in the group interest, and also to meet 'threats' with the most extreme violence—as it is to ignore its real salience. Historians will not perhaps be convinced by Best but they might well evince their own versions of heroic realism, which can tell us as much about their own pet theory of roles as about the historical object of inquiry.

As if in reflection on Alexander VI's idea of a higher plane of morality, Bloch once observed of his occidental present that even 'when to die for one's country has altogether ceased to be the monopoly of one class or one profession, the [feeling persists] that a sort of moral supremacy attaches to the function of professional warrior—an attitude quite foreign to other societies, such as the Chinese'.[111] We can see this feeling at work in another of our military historians. He concludes his analysis of the British 'saturation' bombing campaign in the Second World War with an apparent abrogation of judgement: 'Easy judgements were my birthright because so many made difficult ones.'[112] Another writes in the context of 'passing judgements' that 'Those of us who have never been obliged to participate in a great war seem wise to count our blessings and incline a bow to all those, mighty and humble, who did so.'[113] Such conclusions—whose subtext is actually to endorse heroic realism as if that were the only alternative to 'monkish' moralizing—get things the wrong way around. 'Difficult' judgements are the ones that most need serious moral reflection, and, like 'complexity', 'difficulty' is not a synonym of ambiguity. The more serious the situation in which they were made, the more important is reflection on these judgements. Assuming that we historians are already trying to take people on their own terms, we may even take another step and give them the benefit of the doubt for being in a difficult position, as

---

[109] Ulrich Herbert, 'Ideological Legitimation and Political Practice of the Leadership of the National Socialist Political Police', in Hans Mommsen (ed.), *The Third Reich Between Vision and Reality* (Oxford: Berg, 2002), 95–108, here 105.

[110] Eckart Menzler-Trott, *Gentzens Problem: Mathematische Logik im nationalsozialistischen Deutschland* (Basel: Springer, 2001), 139.

[111] Bloch, *Feudal Society*, 451. Note that he was writing in the late 1930s.

[112] Mark Connelly, *Reaching for the Stars: A New History of Bomber Command in World War II* (London: Tauris, 2001), 163.

[113] Max Hastings, *Nemesis: The Battle for Japan, 1944-1945* (London: Harper Perennial, 2008), introd. Another military historian quotes precisely this passage by Hastings: Nick J. Guevara Jnr., *West Point, Bataan, and Beyond: Santiago Guevara and the War in the Philippines* (Silver Spring, MD: Garfield Street Publishing, 2016), 116.

Butterfield was prepared to.[114] But that scarcely concludes the matter, and it certainly does not remove it from the realm of moral evaluation, since we are talking here about principles like mitigation or lenience, or charity in judgement, or suspending judgement pending further consideration of the evidence.

We need not always agree with Butterfield, given the relationship between power and responsibility and given that power can be enjoyed as well as endured: think how unenjoyable it is to be powerless (see p.120). Of Louis XVI, Edmund Burke wrote in 1790 that 'misfortune indeed it has turned out to him that he was born king of France. But misfortune is not crime.'[115] Louis was obviously not always as powerless—as 'unfortunate'—as he became after the Revolution. And what of the many who may have perceived themselves the victims of misfortune to be born into an ill-run state? Here we have a form of charity distributed solely among a circle of the elect by chroniclers of the elect. Better words than charity for such beneficence might be deference or, more strongly, collusion; it is not neutrality or impartiality.

When thinking evaluatively about a political actor, one does not just adopt the political standard she sets herself, even when one is thinking as a moral contextualist. There is also the standard that the actor must implicitly subscribe to if the system which she purports to uphold is not to be threatened by the outcome of her actions. Further, even in the unlikely event that a leader acted as if no moral considerations of any sort applied, this would not stop evaluation of her rule according to standards held within her moment, as judged, say, against the behaviour of earlier leaders or leaders of other polities. It is one thing to claim that a politician acted in the name of some definition of group interest, and quite another to say that hers was regarded as a good interpretation of that interest or that she pursued it prudently as opposed to counter-productively. Finally, whatever the heroic realist might think, while *some* different moral considerations obtain in leadership and executor roles than in private or personal morality, that is a far cry from the claim that *all* of the moral considerations differ from one to the other.

If anything, the historian's study of specificities will reveal just how little the dictates of interest and value each point unambiguously in set directions. Were that not the case, there would be little need for leaders, who could be economically replaced with a political sliderule. The requisites of power or the 'national interest' are not just given; they have to be interpreted and applied at contextual nexuses that are never precisely repeated. One of the descriptive strengths of IR Constructivism is that it assumes neither 'liberal' convergence nor a permanent, rather atemporal situation of 'realist' power politics in which the fundamentals

---

[114] Herbert Butterfield, 'Moral Judgments in History', in Hans Meyerhoff (ed.), *The Philosophy of History in Our Time* (New York: Doubleday, 1959), 228–49, here 236–7; C. T. McIntire, *Herbert Butterfield: Historian as Dissenter* (New Haven: Yale University Press, 2004), 221.

[115] Edmund Burke, *Reflections on the French Revolution*, ed. W. Alison Phillips and Catherine Beatrice Phillips (Cambridge: Cambridge University Press, 1912), 83.

remain the same even when the players shift places. Instead, Constructivism deals in unpredictable conversation. Once we consider the different layers of this conversation, and the different parties to it, we must also take into consideration that individual element that cannot be reduced to the functional contextualization of the special role.

Conversation occurs not just across the porous boundaries of internal and external affairs but also between public and private personae, between the person-as-roleholder and the person-in-herself, as it were. Lord Salisbury (1830–1903), twice British secretary of state for India, later foreign minister and later still prime minister, was a devout Christian who nevertheless claimed to maintain a distinction between public and private morality in pursuing British interests.[116] We are not obliged to agree with Salisbury on this neat division of moral labour. That he came up with the formula may tell us that he found it convenient to accept at face value the proposition *gesta Dei per Anglos*, such that the division was largely formal for him. Or it may tell us that he was adept at justifying things to himself, which scarcely distinguishes him from many of us as we strive to minimize cognitive dissonance in all areas of life. Most importantly, it is questionable where he managed the total separation of personae anyway. In later reflection on the 1866 Orissa famine which occurred early in his first stint as India secretary, Salisbury wrote:

> The day I took office in that year [1866] Lord Ellenborough wrote to me warning that there were indications of a terrible Famine, and urging me to take measures in time. I was quite new to the subject—and believed that if any precautions were necessary the local Government was sure to take them. I did nothing for two months. Before that time the monsoon had closed the ports of Orissa—help was impossible—and—it is said—a million people died. The Governments of India and Bengal had taken in effect no precautions whatsoever...I never could feel that I was free from all blame for the result.[117]

As it happens, Salisbury's recollection is itself inaccurate in a self-serving fashion,[118] but the major point is that if he had genuinely managed to separate public and private morality, he would only have felt this guilt in his public capacity, not in his private one. To state the distinction is to undermine it. Whatever he thought, Salisbury the person was still the arbiter of the morality of Salisbury the statesman: the former entity had a hand in the interpreting of which interests to pursue, how, and how far.

---

[116] Peter Marsh, 'Lord Salisbury and the Ottoman Massacres', *Journal of British Studies* 11/2 (1972), 63–83, here 65–6.
[117] Michael Bentley, *Lord Salisbury's World: Conservative Environments in Late-Victorian Britain* (Cambridge: Cambridge University Press, 2004), 232.
[118] For reasons provided in Bentley, *Lord Salisbury's World*, 232.

Were there a political slide-rule that told one what to do in any given situation, one might be able to convince oneself that the role demanded that one obey the slide-rule, but that would mean that one was not really making any decisions within the role, only a decision about accepting the role. As soon as decisions are to be made within the role, things must be weighed. These things do not just include the facts of any given case but the counsel one receives. Few leaders are without counsellors, however unwanted. The modern democratic leader may for instance listen to the voice of her own convictions about the way the world should be made to work, her own understanding of the best interests of the electorate as things stand at that moment, or what the opinion polls or the newspapers tell her about what the voters want, whatever she believes about voter-wisdom.[119] How she chooses is a matter for her, the person at the nexus of a specific set of contexts. Where there is choice there is responsibility, and where there is responsibility there can be evaluation.

The case to which we now move, that of the administrator or order-receiving soldier, is different in some ways to that of the leader and order-giver, similar in others. It is similar insofar as both are special roles with accompanying moral permissions and restrictions. It is different insofar as within the official or sol-dierly role there is less discretion in setting ends, more emphasis on finding the best way to achieve the ends set by others, in a form of what Weber called 'instrumental rationality'.[120] When reflecting on the moral issues at stake, here again one needs to navigate between two extremes of which a decontextualizing moralism is one.

Consider a notorious case: the 'Nuremberg defence'. The obloquy directed at the plea 'I was just obeying orders' is based on the idea that obedience, like loy-alty, sincerity, or courage, is a secondary virtue when the individual conscience stands before its own sovereign tribunal or god. What matters more in this view is the choice of cause to which one stakes one's obedience. But such reasoning over-looks the fact that bureaucrats, soldiers, police, and others, may commit to the role before they commit to any of the particular things that the role demands of them. That is, they make a general 'initial' moral choice that can be construed as a choice of principle about forgoing specific moral choices in the subsequent enact-ment of the role. This is a service ethic, one variety of what Weber called an 'ethic of responsibility', and it is expressed by those agents acting as if what to others are the secondary virtues of obedience, etc., are primary virtues to them. Functionaries can claim that they are enacting the will of the leader in his or her role as expres-sion of the group's identity (or embodiment of divine right), or that they are enacting the will of the group itself as constituted through some consultative or

---

[119] Applebaum, *Ethics for Adversaries*, ch. 9.
[120] For the sake of idealizing the discussion, I will ignore the fact that it can be practically difficult to separate the question of how-to-implement from that of what-to-implement.

representative process. More than this, functionaries may congratulate themselves on their moral *self*-sacrifice at forgoing what they might think of as their normal, 'civilian' prerogatives of moral discernment in order to work in the higher cause of the collective whose needs impel them to act in ways that they might not as 'civilians'. If pride is not opportune, they might go for self-pity—just the sort of self-pity displayed by some former perpetrators of Nazi genocide as they bemoaned having been put in the position of 'having had' to kill. After all, in discharging that responsibility to kill they had, at least so they could tell themselves, been *selfless* in a higher cause—the cause not being genocide, or at least not necessarily, but rather service to their state whatever it demanded.

With Nuremberg in mind, one does not wish to be understood as sanctioning apologia for sundry mass murderers: the reasoning provided above is not exhaustive and there are legitimate objections to it, just as there is evidence that many Nazi functionaries did what they did enthusiastically, not just because they were ordered to. At the same time, let us not forget that it is often necessary for individuals in certain roles—warriors, police, administrators—to act in ways that may be contrary to their personal convictions. Alongside self-defence, many significant cooperative human activities would be rendered impossible without a service ethic; whether we talk of 'obeying orders' or 'implementing policy', such an ethic is essential for an anti-welfarist who in her capacity as civil servant nonetheless equitably administers social security payments. Furthermore, we happily fall back on legitimation roughly along 'Nuremberg' lines in other cases. One of Britain's most famous historians wrote reassuringly of the aircrews that bombed German cities in the Second World War that, unlike Nazi perpetrators, 'their intent [*sic*] was not dishonourable'. This claim does not do the work that our historian wishes, and his terminological muddle underlines the conceptual problem, for it is actually the bombers' *motives* that he must mean to address, not their intent.[121] The substantive activities of the bombers are not the same as those of the SS (though there were still consequences in terms of great civilian death toll) but the explanations to motive, i.e. the explanation for why they did things that they would probably not have done outside of their special roles, is not *necessarily* different.

At the other extreme from a decontextualizing moralism that ignores matters like the service ethic, one ought to avoid the assumption that the demands of and commitment to a service role mark the end of the matter, evaluatively speaking. At Nuremberg and other post-war trials, 'I was just obeying orders' was often supplemented by something like 'and I had no choice', with accompanying evocation of the coercive nature of the totalitarian state. *Notwehr* was the legal name for the claim, or, when it transpired that terrible consequences had not actually been

---

[121] Niall Ferguson, *The War of the World: History's Age of Hatred* (London: Penguin, 2009), 571.

threatened for non-compliance, *Putativnotwehr*, the idea that such consequences were subjectively perceived as likely. Whatever the sincerity of the claim, it suggests that 'I was just obeying orders' *simpliciter* was by no means always in practice seen as sufficient to justify participation. Even if it was strictly more in the way of mitigation than justification, the spectre of sanctions for disobedience was supposed to be seen as generally understandable in producing obedience. Indeed there are cases like the Rwandan genocide and the Stalinist purges in which bureaucrats and others much more obviously did participate out of fear to life and limb; in such cases a role loses its moral specialness in the measure that the agent's actions were dictated by purely personal existential interests.

In further evidence that the special role does not hermetically seal the role-holder from his or her person outside the role, some officials do object to specific policies, and a characteristic expression of dissent is resignation from the role. Resignation is actually consistent with the idea of general commitment to the role, in the sense that when one finds oneself unable to justify (to oneself) enacting a specific policy within the role, then rather than picking and choosing between policies whilst remaining within the role, one resiles from the general commitment to the role, perhaps with appropriate advertisement of the whistle-blower variety. After all, while in some sense the general decision to commit to the special role came prior to any of the specific things demanded by the role, in another sense that general decision is constantly being tacitly reaffirmed by the act of staying in post, and as such may at any point be countermanded.[122] When resignation from the role is not an option, objection to the specific task is then all that is left if the opposition is strong enough. That may or may not mean refusal to enact the task, given countervailing commitments, but, again, the choice about weighing one commitment against another cannot be immune from judgement.

The Importance of Hindsight

Richard Evans encapsulates some grounds for reticence about such judgement when he writes that the historian ought not 'issu[e] arrogant verdicts on complex moral issues based on the luxury of hindsight'.[123] Now the moral complexity that Evans invokes is only relevant in a context where moral issues are recognized as salient, and the same goes for the concept of moral ambiguity that some people wrongly treat as a synonym of moral complexity. If we remove the word 'moral' from Evans's sentence, we have a decent description of what most historians do. Whether a historian deserves the label 'arrogant' can only be judged on a case by case basis. Evans's main warning about hindsight is, however, clearly reasonable.

---

[122] Which is a point Sartre made about the soldier.   [123] Evans, 'What Is History?', 5.

The concern about hindsight is sometimes subsumed under the general fear of anachronism, so some clarifications are in order. As the application to the study of the past of after-the-fact knowledge, hindsight *can* constitute one strain of anachronism. Another strain of anachronism is the application of after-the-fact values. At the moment the focus is on matters that might but need not fall under the ambit of the first strain, including matters that are central to so much of what historians do, whatever they say about what they do. This section builds from showing the importance of hindsight in any historical explanation to showing that hindsight can be deployed for evaluative purposes without contravening the perceived imperative to assess historical actors on their own terms.

It is amazing what fear of anachronism can do to the historian's judgement, as evidenced in the soldier and historian Mungo Melvin's recent biography of the Second World War German Field Marshal Erich von Manstein. Given the severity of some of the crimes in which Manstein was implicated, including the mass murder of Jews, it is impossible for Melvin to avoid the normative element in his concluding summary of the soldier's deeds. Yet he repeatedly justifies his inability to call a spade a spade with intimations that whoever would use that designation is somehow guilty of presentism. He tells us that the story is 'complex: over time, "good" and "bad" can never look in opposite directions from one single, fixed position in history'. It is unclear what this means even if one ignores the prob-lematizing inverted commas around good and bad. The picture is yet more blurred given that by 'bad' Melvin denotes Manstein's conviction as a war crim-inal, which seems straightforward enough, while by the balancing 'good' he refers to Manstein's record as 'the most gifted German operational brain of the Second World War', which is more a matter of competence than morality.[124] Melvin refers twice to Manstein's 'alleged war crimes' (he was convicted on several counts).[125] He concludes that with 'twenty-first-century hindsight and with the benefit of detailed research, of course, it is easy to cast doubt on the veracity of Manstein's evidence at Hamburg and condemn him for his failure to protect the lives of Jews and others in the Soviet Union', which might reasonably be translated as saying that Manstein lied under oath and was complicit in the murder of Jews and others. And again: 'From today's perspective of exposure and recrimination against the Wehrmacht, a much less rosy picture of the individual emerges', as if the pejorative 'recrimination' were unrelated to the evidence 'exposed'. Melvin does not spell it out but the reader might reasonably infer him to be saying that because the research was conducted at a later point in time than the deeds researched, then its conclusions are tainted by 'hindsight' and a particular 'per-spective'. The corollary is that the criminal somehow becomes less guilty in pro-portion to the time it takes to piece together evidence of his deeds, or, conversely,

---

[124] Mungo Melvin, *Manstein: Hitler's Greatest General* (London: Weidenfeld and Nicolson, 2010), 505.
[125] Melvin, *Manstein*, 504, 505.

that the further back we go in time towards Manstein's deeds, the less morally problematic they are to someone who understands history properly.[126]

As with 'relativism', the fear of 'hindsight' is such that historians tend not to reflect on it even when it touches integral parts of their activity. In one obvious way the historian is bound in most of what she does by hindsight in the sense of after-the-fact knowledge. Historical patterns only become evident when they have already established themselves, i.e. when they are viewed partly or wholly in retrospect. Whatever the likes of Melvin might feel to be ethically appropriate or contextually sensitive, it is only possible to investigate things when they have occurred. Equally, some sorts of 'significance' vary with subsequent occurrence, as is the case with the reinterpretation of texts across time. The memory of insulting another person ten years ago gains more significance to me, here, now, if I happen to have just been made the victim of his long-burning desire for revenge than if I have not. Aftermaths can dictate some of the things that can be said about what preceded them.[127] Manifesting a new interest in something in the past because it seems to prefigure a present-day phenomenon is one of the things that keeps the historical profession alive. New historical interests, stimulated by the new articulation of social forces, may also be read back into the past in a way that may be relevant to the present without necessarily being distortive of the past, as all manner of social History shows. The causes of any eventualization are only identified as causes in light of what it is they are held to have resulted in. To inquire after the causes of the First World War is to depend upon a perfectly proper form of hindsight, since without the advent of the war we could hardly talk of 'the causes of the First World War'.

This account of the relationship between causal explanation and hindsight might seem to be challenged by elaborated 'counterfactual History', but the impression is illusory. Counterfactual History is based on the recognition that all of the things that are normally accounted for in explanations of, say, the war might have come to pass, barring just one, and the war would not have happened, or not in the way or at the time it did, and so on. My objection, it should be

---

[126] Melvin, *Manstein*, 505, 506. Further, if anyone can make sense of what Melvin is trying to say on the moral and legal front in the second paragraph of p. 506, I should be keen to know, especially as concerns the claim about the 'apparent severity' of Manstein's sentence and Melvin's torturous pronouncement that 'Notwithstanding the judgements at both the International and American tribunals at Nuremberg, Manstein became the very personification—if not a scapegoat—of the Wehrmacht under trial for its cruel misdeeds'.

[127] The statement 'Napoleon Bonaparte was born in Corsica' was true from whatever point he was born on 15 August 1769 and remains true today. 'Napoleon Bonaparte, later emperor of the French, was born in Corsica' is true today but only became so after he became emperor; it was not true on 15 August 1769. 'The emperor of France, Napoleon, was born in Corsica', was true for a time-limited period from some point on 2 December 1804. 'The spur to later European nation-state formation, Napoleon I, was born in Corsica', could only become true, if it is true, at some point after his reign. 'The inspiration for some twenty-second-century leaders of France, Napoleon I, was born in Corsica' will only if at all become true in virtue of events yet to transpire. Arthur C. Danto is the source of such ruminations.

reiterated, is to *elaborated* counterfactual History because it will be a part of many historians' thinking to try to put themselves in the position Bloch recommended before a past event, in order that one might 'gauge its chances' of materializing;[128] if one is interested in some event's confirming or refuting a general assumption, then one will base some of one's judgement on speculating how the world of assumptions would have looked without the event's having taken place. But this is just a matter of recognizing contingency in history and writing so as not to make what materialized seem inevitable. It is misleading to lay out what one thinks would have occurred but did not.

What makes any elaborated counterfactual misleading is that it builds on that single recognition of contingency a superstructure that is determined in the new scenario. One factor is changed in a moment frozen in time, and then the future interaction of other factors predicted as if there were no such thing as the fortuitous interaction of yet other hitherto unforeseen factors, and as if the new interaction of the included factors was perfectly predictable. This undermines the counterfactualist's sensible insistence on the contingency of History. Consider John Lewis Gaddis:

> counterfactual reasoning can help to establish chains of causation: to argue that the Japanese might not have attacked Pearl Harbor *if* the American oil embargo hadn't been imposed; or to claim that the Americans might not have chosen to cut off the oil flow *if* the Japanese hadn't moved into French Indochina—these are perfectly legitimate positions for historians to take.[129]

'Might not' is the salient formulation here; 'might' is its counterpart—and the reader of any account would have been able to make either inference for herself insofar as the historian had established some connections between Japanese expansion, American oil embargo, and Japanese attack. To take Gaddis's thinking to its conclusion would be not just to ask about the specific non-occurrence of Japanese expansion and US oil embargo but also to hypothesize about what might (/not) have happened at some other point absent those events. Perhaps Japan would have expanded a little earlier or later, or not to quite such a degree, or to a greater degree; perhaps the US response would have been more vociferous than an embargo, and so on. If we simply replace the given facts of Japanese expansion and US embargo with nothing at all, then we might—or might not—be hypothesizing about the US and Japanese state regimes being different in outlook than they were, which would open up yet further counterfactual thinking retrojected into the prehistory of the 'events' in question, with no end to where we might stop the process.

---

[128] Cited in John Lewis Gaddis, *The Landscape of History* (Oxford: Oxford University Press, 2004), 100.
[129] Gaddis, *The Landscape of History*, 102.

To dwell on historical counterfactuals is to dwell on the non-causation of non-events, which is different to the important study of the 'causation' of non-events. One does not, one cannot, go about with an infinitely long list of spatio-temporally non-specific non-occurrences and inquire of all of them *what and what if?* Let us clarify. In thinking of war-causation, it is perfectly proper to ask why in this or that historical instance war did not occur when some of the omens seemed to have been in view. But that inquiry would still require a specific state of affairs (the non-occurrence of war *there and then*) as a focus for the establishment of prior causal chains for war's non-occurrence, involving positive causal factors that forestalled conflict. Once the historian inquires only of the non-causation of specific things, then she is in the fraught but useful business of trying to isolate variables in causation, which she cannot do with a no-variance study of war-causation that only contemplates scenarios that did produce war. In that case, however, the 'counterfactualist' is not really that at all: she is just acting as a comparative historian interested in different outcomes. Insofar as the counterfactualist does that which is peculiar to counterfactual History, i.e. fleshing out a vision of new scenarios had certain things transpired differently, then she is dealing with neither the causation of events nor the 'causation' of non-events. She is doing something that claims knowledge of all of the spatio-temporally non-specific 'occurrences' of the future from her chosen point of manipulation onwards (and possibly hinting at a different past, too, as in Gaddis's Pearl Harbor example), and discarding them all except one. She is free to do this because she is no longer constrained by evidence or by having to take account of causal indeterminacy. It becomes clear why historians have so often limited themselves to asking why what actually happened happened, and to the further consequences of those happenings.

Contemplation of consequences and outcomes brings us to consider the way in which historical *evaluations* can legitimately depend upon hindsight. Evans's reference to 'moral complexity' could mean the complexity of choice—as in situations where it was unclear as to what was the morally correct thing to do in accordance with governing values—or it could mean the complex relationship between intentions and outcomes. It seems that Evans means the former, but before getting to that, we need to address the latter given the interest many historians have in causation.

Causation in human affairs is so complex that there will very often be intervening factors that magnify, thwart, or refract human intentions. Where an intention bears no fruit in outcomes it may still be of concern to historians interested in the character of the historical actor; other historians might be drawn to the forces and intentions that did the thwarting as they investigate the causation of non-events just described. Where intentions are realized in outcomes, or are even magnified, there is relatively little complexity in the relevant sense, and as such we may proceed to inquire into the nature of the intentions that have shaped the historical outcomes, including its moral aspects. Where intentions bear fruit, but not of the sort intended, then the human actor has still involved herself in a causal chain, co-producing an outcome that would not have been the same without her contribution. This is perhaps where moral complexity is most obviously manifest, but that complexity does not necessarily mean that we withdraw from moral evaluation.

The idea that unintended consequences can affect our moral assessment of the state of affairs that brought them about only seems peculiar, if it does, in the abstract. One obvious qualifier is that some unintended outcomes are more predictable than others, which means that an unforeseen outcome might just be the result of the actor's failure to foresee it, where no superhuman perspective was needed to envisage its possibility. To render a judgement on the predictability of an unforeseen outcome is, if that outcome happens to have moral implications, to render a judgement that touches on the morality of the actor. Here, we are apparently not being anachronistic because, like Bloch, we are trying to place ourselves in the position of actors contemplating possibilities from a situation prior to the act and its possible outcomes. But the nature of the outcome is, again, important to the nature of the assessment, which is where why we need to return to our thoughts about causation and hindsight.

Given concrete examples, it becomes intuitively obvious that consequences often must be taken into account in moral evaluation. If I promise to do something, then the promise itself can only be assessed in light of future events, i.e. whether or not I come good on it. Even if it could be shown that I had definitely intended to fulfil the promise at the time of making it, that will not be the only thing in the balance if I nevertheless do not fulfil it: my mind might have changed in the interim, or I might not have tried sufficiently hard to fulfil my obligation, or I might have wrongly made a commitment that I was always likely to be unable to fulfil, irrespective of my determination. If, in full possession of my faculties, I throw furniture into the street from my second-floor window as a shortcut to clearing out my house, I may or may not kill a passer-by. If I do not, then my actions may be judged reckless, but they will certainly meet with greater disapprobation if I do, and the legal punishment that ensues will be an approximate quantum of that added moral weight. Now an example of the sort more likely to appear in a History book: the general who takes a risk in battle may end up winning thereby, or he may see slaughtered the battalions he dispatched on the risky manoeuvre. The first outcome will bring him acclaim, the second will not. His judgement will work to maximize the chance of success, but chance is still an operative word. The name philosophers have given to this sort of moral problem is, appropriately enough, *moral luck*.[130]

Moral luck can obtain before the act as well as during or after it. A child of wealthy parents may never be confronted with the moral dilemmas that regularly

---

[130] Bernard Williams, *Moral Luck* (Cambridge: Cambridge University Press, 2012); cf. Nagel, *Mortal Questions*, ch. 3.

present themselves in violent areas beyond his gated community. The moral (good) luck that allows him to preserve his moral purity, because he does not have to use violence to repel an assailant or does not have to ingratiate himself with local thugs to avoid being assaulted in the first place, lies in the circumstances of his upbringing. If a queen has to choose between war and surrender, then she may be choosing between certain bloodshed and an uncertain military outcome on one hand and probable humiliation and the servitude of her people on the other. Whether or not she provoked the confrontation, she is presented with a choice with moral consequences in either direction and it may just be her moral (bad) luck that that is so.[131]

The queen's dilemma perhaps encapsulates what Evans meant by a moral complexity that forbids with-hindsight judgements. Indeed, there *will* be some dilemmas that do not seem to admit of even one less terrible outcome among more terrible ones, whether those are viewed after the fact or with the greatest effort of understanding about the perspective of the decision-maker. But identifying such dilemmas is the result of moral inquiry into them, not of having such moral inquiry already ruled out of court. Equally, moral inquiry will reveal many instances where the moral issues are more clear-cut than they may first appear.

It would be a strange queen who did not think that her actions needed to be assessed in terms of consequences as well as motives. As a rule of thumb people who make decisions hope to see themselves vindicated by events. Many historical figures have explicitly appealed to the verdict of posterity above the head of contemporary criticism. The philosopher Benedetto Croce described this rather forcefully: 'the feigned indignation which the accused often display in order to cover their action, frequently take[s] the form of...an appeal to history'.[132] 'Let History judge' illustrates the extent to which decisions are bets on how things look from the future. It would be hard to make sense of them otherwise, since the future is what they hope to influence, and one of the reasons leaders get to leadership positions is on the back of some special claim to be able to lead into that future. Divine right, martial prowess, age-seniority, or manifesto-based election are all justifications for leadership based on some alleged qualification to lead, and 'leading', in whatever political direction, must entail moving from one situation to another future situation. Yet some bets do not come off, some predictions are just wrong, some terribly wrong, and some more predictably so than others. This is true in ordinary life, and it is true there that our opinion of someone who makes decisions with significant consequences will be affected positively or

[131] Note that my observing of these situations that 'that is just the way it is' is not pursuant to a contention that nothing should be done about e.g. the sorts of circumstances that lead to great inequality, gated communities, and so forth. It is just that these are matters to be arbitrated at the level of social policy, and any moral critique is a critique at the level of the social system. Further to this point, see p. 207.

[132] Benedetto Croce, *History as the Story of Liberty* (Chicago: Regnery, 1970), 208.

negatively in line with those consequences. Had the 2003 invasion of Iraq resulted in swift harmonization there, the debate around the invasion's motivations would be less heated.

Clearly these are arguments involving reference to consequences, but they are not necessarily consequentialist in the philosophical sense of a particular moral theory, any more than is the expression 'all's well that ends well'. One of the oddities of so many consequentialist thought experiments, like 'would you kill one innocent person to save two more from certain death?', or 'would you torture a suspected terrorist if this produced information that saved the lives of potential bomb-victims?', is that they assume certainty about outcomes, presenting the decider with the actual occurring results as a way of helping her choose. In real life, as it were, one rather assumes that very often the decision will be made without certainty as to outcomes.[133] Whatever information one gathers, there is often still an element of a leap in the dark, with varying degrees of probability as to outcome. We can well imagine some governmental policy, say of taxation or public expenditure, which, after some time in train, has produced quantifiable changes to what went before. If the new distribution of gains and losses is deemed more desirable than what went before, the policies are continued. But clearly the decision to continue A when it has a track record of inducing outcome B is different to the enactment of novelty X in the hopes that it will induce outcome Y. Saying that the deed is justified by the outcome (which Richard Nixon may have said at some point) is subtly different to, because more conditional than, what we tend to understand when saying that the end justifies the means (which Nixon definitely said). It is more open to the vagaries of the future. At the same time, it underlines the significance not of slide-rule utilitarian calculations for action but of prudence.

'Prudence' derives, via *prudens/prudentia*, from *providens/providentia*, meaning foresight, and it connotes the reflective application to unique new situations of general principles gleaned from experience. The degree of alignment of one's foresight with the way things actually turn out will influence others' assessment of one's prudence, as, by extension, will the success of one's contingency planning, i.e. risk anticipation. The medieval theologian Thomas Aquinas felt that imprudence was not itself a sin since no one would be consciously imprudent, and imprudence could not be erased by repentance. Nonetheless, if prudence is considered a virtue, as Aquinas also believed, it might make sense to conclude that failure to cultivate where possible the qualities we dub prudential is a shortcoming.[134] Either way, imprudent action may bring down consequences of considerable

---

[133] I think Bernard Williams a point along these lines, but I cannot locate the reference.

[134] Thomas Aquinas, *Summa Theologica*, trans. the Fathers of the English Dominican Province (Raleigh, NC: Hayes Barton Press, 2006), 2555–6, 2576, and 2548–96 more generally.

normative weight, in connection with political as well as personal morality.[135] The CIA invented the term 'blowback' for the unexpected (but not necessarily unpredictable) and deleterious consequences of self-interested intervention in the affairs of others.[136] Butterfield invoked blowback *avant la lettre* when he pointed his readers to the geopolitical legacy of Britain's encouraging Prussia into the Rhineland in order to contain post-Napoleonic France.[137] Once one is aware of the possibility of blowback, one can try to factor it in to one's prudential calculations, though only time will tell how successful one's prognostications were. Henry Kissinger's successor as US National Security advisor, Zbigniew Brzezinski, was interviewed in 1998 about the wisdom of US support for Afghan Mujahideen religious extremists *before* the Soviet invasion of Afghanistan, as a device to increase the probability of Soviet invasion and thereby overstretch Soviet power. He announced: 'What is most important in world history? The Taliban or the collapse of the Soviet empire? Some agitated Moslems or the liberation of Central Europe and the end of the cold war?'[138]

There are, of course, limits to the role of hindsight in moral assessment. The serial killer is not redeemed for the murder of three people if evidence subsequently comes to light that one of the victims was a terrorist intending to blow up a passenger ferry. Nor do we applaud the inventor of mustard gas because a derivative later became a chemotherapy agent. Once we travel too far down the chain of causation away from the salient decision that—along with other factors—shaped the outcome, once we begin commenting on entirely unpredictable (as opposed to just unpredicted) outcomes, we are in the realms of causal explanation that has no ramifications for moral evaluation.

The upshot of this section thus far: (1) there is no such thing as decision unconditioned by some sort of context over which actors have no control—having to make a decision itself presupposes an assumption about the necessity of deciding; (2) there is rarely a frictionless realization of the desired object of a course of action; but (3) issues of responsibility are not thereby necessarily rendered irrelevant, because of the potential for prior insight into possible outcomes and the relative power inherent in the capacity to decide, irrespective of the pressure to decide. Whether they are public or private, decisions are activated claims about what is the right or good thing to do. 'Right' here can mean either or both of 'morally right' or 'correct for the attainment of a given goal'. If the decision ultimately fails according to either criteria, or if it succeeds but at relatively high

---

[135] For a discussion of the relationship between prudence and morality, Coady, *Messy Morality*, 21 ff.

[136] Chalmers Johnson, *Blowback: The Costs and Consequences of American Empire* (New York: Henry Holt, 2001).

[137] Herbert Butterfield, *Christianity and History* (London: G. Bell and Sons, 1949), 140.

[138] Interview with Brzezinski in *Le Nouvel Observateur* (Paris), 15–21 January 1998, trans. in David N. Gibbs, 'Afghanistan: The Soviet Invasion in Retrospect', *International Politics* 37 (2000), 233–46, here 242.

human cost, then it must be legitimate to interrogate the failure, or the means–ends calculus, lest we fall into one of two traps.

The first trap is the heroic realism already addressed; the second awaits those who proclaim 'that is just how things were', and proclaim that asking why things were not otherwise is anachronistic, equivalent to empty wish-fulfilment, or moralism in the guise of 'writing history as it should have happened'.[139] A good example is William D. Rubinstein's self-explanatory *The Myth of Rescue: Why the Democracies Could Not Have Saved More Jews from the Nazis* (1997). The book begins by claiming that

> no Jew who perished during the Nazi Holocaust could have been saved by any action which the Allies could have taken at the time, given what was actually known about the Holocaust, what was *actually proposed* at the time and what was realistically possible. If there are any exceptions at all to this statement, their numbers may be measured in the dozens or hundreds rather than in some higher figure. *All* of the many studies which criticise the Allies (and the Jewish communities of the democracies) for having failed to rescue Jews during the Holocaust are inaccurate and misleading, their arguments illogical and ahistorical.[140]

The book is replete with accusations of hindsight against historians who disagree with its author. In keeping with a number of other prominent reviews, one notice declared the book 'an antidote to moral fantasy'.[141] Rather than engaging with Rubinstein's often reasonable discussions about policy specifics, let us address the sort of thinking laid out in the passage above.

In claiming that nothing more could have been done, Rubinstein claims that everything plausible was done given the relevant contexts. He claims to know to an impressive degree of precision how many more Jews might have been saved in the event that his calculations were incorrect that no more could have been saved. It is indeed a remarkable insight into History As It Might Have Been that he not only knows that nothing more could have been done in a number of directions but also knows the margin of error of his certainty. This is another species of counterfactual thinking—it is inverted or negative counterfactualism in which what occurs is accorded the honour of being the only thing that could 'realistically' have occurred.

---

[139] For this accusation, see John Conway, review of Tom Lawson's *The Church of England and the Holocaust: Christianity, Memory and Nazism* (Martlesham: Boydell, 2006), in *Reviews in History* online at http://www.history.ac.uk/reviews/review/559. Tom Lawson's response to the review is available at the same address.

[140] William D. Rubinstein, *The Myth of Rescue: Why the Democracies Could Not Have Saved More Jews from the Nazis* (London: Routledge, 2000), p. x. Emphases in original.

[141] *The Observer*, quoted on the cover of *The Myth of Rescue*.

Focusing on one aspect of Rubinstein's argument helps make my point. In his determination to limit the scope of available possibilities to those actually vocalized at the time, Rubinstein ignores some alternative lines of inquiry that are just as legitimate. He goes to one level of the hypothetical but not the next, which is the level at which we ponder why what was not proposed was not proposed, and why the circumstances were not different such that certain things not proposed could have been proposed. We might speculate that, since some British and American officials are on record as fearing that action on behalf of Jews might spawn domestic anti-Semitism, these officials actively did not wish to give more thought to possible means of rescue or intervention.[142] What ideas might they have come up with had they been prepared to put their heads together and think harder? Would they have thought harder, or expended more resources, had it been British POWs, or the Gentile population of France, being systematically murdered? No certain answer can be forthcoming save the answer that just as one cannot know that other developments might have occurred, one is in no position to claim that what did occur was the only thing that could realistically have occurred. The points just suggested are not elaborated counterfactuals but counter-pre-emptive arguments against elaborated counterfactuals. They are designed to show that, while no historian can claim the truth about what might have been but was not, no historian can cover all counterfactual bases in the attempt to shore up a claim about what must have been. Just like positive counterfactualism, Rubinstein's negative counterfactualism entails evoking alternative worlds, whether to embrace or in this case dismiss them, in a way that is at best a waste of time, and at worst a self-confirming exercise in pick 'n' mix from the past's real and imagined offerings.

Another pundit wrote that Rubinstein had 'established incontrovertibly the terrible inevitability of the Holocaust',[143] which is the sort of claim that always brings to mind A. J. P. Taylor's saying nothing is inevitable until it happens. The assertion shows that negative counterfactuals can produce more deterministic accounts than non-counterfactual Histories need to. None other than the conservative historian Geoffrey Elton observed that hindsight can make the historian 'into a tedious defender of accomplished fact'.[144] Elton was criticizing a disposition that seems like the opposite of the anachronistic moralizing that Evans rightly fears and the what-if?-ery that Rubinstein derides, but which actually contains elements of both tendencies in mirror image.

---

[142] On official attitudes, see Louise London, *Whitehall and the Jews* (Cambridge: Cambridge University Press, 2001).

[143] 'Enigma of Survival: What Bletchley Learned of the Holocaust—and When', *Daily Telegraph*, 18 April 1999.

[144] G. R. Elton, *The Practice of History* (Sydney: Sydney University Press, 1967), 99.

PART 2

WRITING HISTORY: PROBLEMS OF NEUTRALITY

Introduction

Underlying most of the arguments against evaluation is the belief that it is possible to write non-evaluative historianship in the first place, or the conviction that non-evaluative historianship is a good, even if unattainable, standard to hold as an ideal. This Part of the book considers both positions. It challenges the assumption that, where it matters, it is either desirable or possible to avoid value judgements and the sorts of evocative descriptions that imply or could reasonably be expected to prompt such judgements. Unlike Part 1 it is not primarily concerned with the moral contextualization of past actors according to the standards of their time. It is concerned with the historian's role in characterizing and explaining past forces, actors, and developments within an integrated historical account. It shows that such accounts often and legitimately introduce 'external' evaluations—i.e. evaluations that need not accord with the governing 'terms' of the actors whose behaviour is under explanation.

The first section makes some distinctions between History and particular traditions within the social sciences, with the aim of showing why the 'rules' about evaluation can be different in these differing endeavours. The second section establishes the widespread existence of evocations and evaluations in the very labelling and description of many historical phenomena. It suggests not just how peculiar works of History would look in their absence of these evocations and appraisals, but that their absence would often distort what is being reported. These arguments are key to the distinction made in the third section about rejecting value neutrality as a governing ideal while insisting on truthfulness as a historian's primary duty. The fourth section highlights the nature of most historical accounts as composites of a range of perspectives, as it considers questions of context, agency, outcome, and experience. The composition gives rise to the overall impression, evaluative or evocative, provided by works of History. The fifth section brings together a number of the chapter's themes as it examines an important case of the historian's judgement—judgement about the legitimacy of power in past worlds where legitimacy could be as contested as often today.

History versus Social Science

The sociologist Max Weber (1864–1920) is associated above all others with the imperative of scholarly neutrality. Along with his contemporary, the philosopher Heinrich Rickert, he observed the distinction between subjective judgements about social or historical values and the scholarly task of relating those facts to values in an explanatory sense. For Rickert, 'Valuations must always involve *praise* or *blame*. To refer to values is to do neither.' For Weber:

> the investigator and teacher should hold as unconditionally separate the estab-lishment of empirical facts (including what he establishes as the 'value-oriented' conduct of the empirical individuals whom he is investigating) and his own practical evaluations of those facts as commendable or reprehensible (including among such facts the evaluations made by empirical individuals that are the object of an investigation).[1]

Before investigating the practicalities of such a separation it is worth reflecting on the nature of Weber's and Rickert's distinction. They seem to be insisting that the distinction is logical, but Weber also claimed to be able to show, by reference to historians like Heinrich von Treitschke and Theodor Mommsen, how the introduction of value judgements by historians interfered with the understanding of 'the facts'.[2] On the face of it these are complementary positions, but there is a tension between them. If establishing facts (including facts about past values) and making value judgements are two logically separate things, then it is possible to do both without the latter harming the former, as long as one makes it clear which of the two operations one is engaged in at any given moment. If, conversely, judgements *must* prevent understanding of the facts then the two things are not logically separate after all, and so whatever the supposed problems of doing both it is not a category error to do both.

As it happens, Weber never went on to show why historians' value judgements *must* interfere with historical understanding, as opposed perhaps to showing that, in the wrong hands, value judgements *might* hinder such understanding. It is no

---

[1] Rickert cited in Rudolf A. Makkreel, *Dilthey: Philosopher of the Human Sciences* (Princeton: Princeton University Press, 1992) 41; Weber quote from Max Weber, 'Der Sinn der "Wertfreiheit" der soziologischen und ökonomischen Wissenschaften', in Weber, *Gesammelte Aufsätze zur Wissenschaftslehre*, ed. Johannes Winckelmann (Tübingen: Mohr, 1985), 489–540, here 499.
[2] Max Weber, 'Wissenschaft als Beruf', in *Max Weber: Schriften 1894–1922*, ed. Dirk Kaesler (Stuttgart: Alfred Kröner, 2002), 474–511, here 498.

proof in either direction, but merely suggestive that there are judgements of different qualities, to note that one of the last British 'Whig' historians, G. M. Trevelyan, contrasted Mommsen and Treitschke unfavourably with Albert Sorel. Unlike the work of the Germans, Trevelyan claims, Sorel's *L'Europe et la Révolution française* was 'impartial', not because it forswore judgement but because it engaged in 'the just distribution of blame for the foolish and wicked deeds by which men are perpetually destroying the hopes of mankind'.[3]

As to the basic principle at stake in at least one of his positions, Weber was contending that evaluation is antithetical to understanding. Richard Evans took a step in the same direction when he claimed that 'The historian's job is to explain; it is for others to judge', and that a moral approach to the past was 'unhistorical'.[4] The historian George Kitson Clark had earlier made the same distinction.[5] Ginzburg agreed unequivocally: he saw the two concepts of 'judging or under-standing' as presenting a 'dilemma', as if they were antonyms. Much the same thinking is present in a work on collective violence that describes 'the dual and conflicting need to both understand and judge' as an 'aporia'—a fundamentally irresolvable clash of principles.[6] The claim is wrong. Exercising judgement in any non-arbitrary sense of the concept presupposes some understanding, but nothing in the concept of understanding precludes judgement.

Nor is it possible to sever explanation from evaluation by fiat like that of Bloch as he observed that 'value judgment has a *raison d'être* only as preparation for an action',[7] 'whereas'—and here the false dichotomy again—'the historian's sole duty is to understand'.[8] Oakeshott distinguished between the 'practical' use of the past as it might obtain for politicians in the realms of will and value, and the academic interest, which was categorically different. These are just assertions and prescriptions without guidelines as to how to turn off one's evaluative faculties and render one's prose value-neutral. With the Weberian distinction between reportage and evaluation in mind alongside the arguments elaborated in Part 1, we might ask which operation is in play when the historian establishes that a historical actor met or fell short of a moral standard of her time. The answer is that here, as in other cases to be examined below, the reportage and the evaluation cannot be disentangled, any more than they would be disentangled by my saying that a contemporary of mine has met or fallen short of a moral standard of today. To say that some act was in accordance with or transgression of some standard just is to imply a judgement on the act. The difference between the assessment of past acts and the acts of my contemporary is not whether they can be judged according to standards but the different nature of the standards by which each can be assessed.

---

[3] G. M. Trevelyan, 'Bias in History', *History* 32/115 (1947), 1–15, here 6.

[4] Evans, 'What Is History?', 4–5.

[5] George Kitson Clark, *The Critical Historian* (London: The History Book Club, 1968), 209.

[6] Ginzburg, *The Judge and the Historian*, 15; Leonhard Praeg, *The Geometry of Violence* (Stellenbosch: SUN, 2007), 152.

[7] Bloch, *The Historian's Craft*, 139, 142.   [8] Bloch, *Feudal Society*, 318.

Weber might well have been correct to distinguish between reportage and evaluation in the matter of, say, recording the laws of some foreign civilization past or present. One can easily imagine History as a sort of retrospective ethnology whereby historians just seek to establish the governing norms of particular pasts alongside mores, aesthetics, and epistemologies. Weber's own conception of an ideal-type social model was of a part with that sort of ethnographic exercise as it abstracted from a complex reality to generalize about the nature of governing values and institutional relations at any moment in time. Clearly historians are not constrained by these concepts of inquiry. (Nor, for that matter, are the social sciences: it is only from this limited sense of 'social science' that the arguments of this section distinguish History.) Where Weber's ideal-types and structuralist accounts (see pp. 215–6) create simplified cross-sections of societies at any one moment, and where Durkheimian *représentations collectives* focus on what is shared by a society rather than what divides it, historians are apt to investigate change and its causes, to address matters like conflict within and between societies, to consider agency and acts as opposed to abstractions, and even to consider the human costs of particular social arrangements. Each approach has strengths and weaknesses, but the latter sorts of approach will involve the historian in some evaluations or evocations whether she likes it or not.

Finally, for all this talk about actors and actions, humanistic-historical thought need not be individualistic, and by extension the evaluative element of the thought need not pertain to individuals. Many human relations are indirect and fundamentally economic: they are products of situations in which individuals recursively act in accordance with aggregated patterns that are themselves the impression of multiple, accumulated individual actions. But identifying impersonal causation is not necessarily the same as claiming natural causation, as in a freak weather incident. When we call a famine 'man-made' the human element may be the impersonal but nonetheless human-made mechanisms of distribution, hoarding, export, and pricing that prevent food getting to where it is most needed. Structural inequality, while an impersonal condition at the point at which it is encountered, i.e. at which it shapes individual life-prospects, as well as at the point of its production, is not the same as the naturally-produced physical inequality brought about, say, by a genetically inherited disability. Structural inequality is the product of established social arrangements that tacitly favour one part of humanity over another; arrangements that might include, for instance, unintended but practically significant discrimination against those with genetically inherited disabilities. Competing philosophies past, as still now, debated the justifiability of such social arrangements. As now, in the past it was perfectly coherent to contend, with wrong (or right) in mind as well as harm (or benefit), that such-and-such a structured arrangement or systemic logic was unjust (or just) while not, or not necessarily, or only to an attenuated degree, criticizing (or praising) those whose daily labour upheld the structures and systems.

Evaluative and Evocative Language

Words like 'enslavement' or 'killing' evoke particular responses. Depending on circumstances one justifies, approves, or disapproves of killing, but, as on the question of the right to choose, it is not something towards which one is neutral. That may be a problem for the neutralist, but the neutralist needs to recognize that neutral-sounding language can be just as deceitful as misplaced evaluative language. The use of the word mistress to describe Sally Hemings's relationship to Thomas Jefferson's obscures, and is meant to obscure, the fact that she was his slave, his property, with all the associated implications of power asymmetry and exploitation. Much the same goes for the 2015 Texas social studies curriculum that described enslaved Africans as 'immigrants' and 'workers'.[9] Such evasions are not remotely new. The King James Bible delicately deploys the terms 'servant' and 'maidservant' when the Hebrew and Greek words clearly denoted 'slave', and this verbal tradition was maintained in the American South, where 'warranteeism' was also used in lieu of 'slavery'.[10] Historians of Britain and its colonial offshoots may refer to the Norman conquest of Britain and are scarcely chary of using 'invasion' in other contexts but tend to prefer the gentler-sounding European *settlement* of the Americas or Australasia; conversely, they may refer to the 'Indian mutiny' of 1857 rather than the 'Sepoy uprising'. Henry VIII's *dissolution of the monasteries* strikes a milder tone than the suppression of same. Various regimes and leaders have advocated *population transfer* when meaning mass expulsion or ethnic cleansing, while *pacification* remains one of those terms beloved of military historians as much as media commentators and soldiers. Like the others italicized in this paragraph it is not a euphemism—each of them works in the sense it is intended to. But they are pre-emptive of evaluation; they are attempts to command the tone. 'Neutralization' is in play, i.e. the attempt to render non-neutral situations neutral.

Certain things cannot be described in non-evocative terms if one wishes to describe them accurately, which makes one wonder how George Kitson Clark reconciled his anti-judgemental stance with his dictum that historians 'must not gloze over ugly things, or avoid calling them by their proper names'.[11] Consider rape, specifically the matter of *droit de seigneur*, the 'right of the first night'. This may be a myth, though it is so interculturally widespread a trope that the question cannot be said to be definitively settled. Even if just a myth it serves analytical

---

[9] On these cases, see Britni Danielle, 'Sally Hemings Wasn't Thomas Jefferson's Mistress: She Was His Property', *Washington Post*, 10 July 2017, https://www.washingtonpost.com/outlook/sally-hemings-wasnt-thomas-jeffersons-mistress-she-was-his-property/2017/07/06/db5844d4-625d-11e7-8adc-fea80e32bf47_story.html?utm_term=.dceb32eeda3a.

[10] David Brion Davis, 'Reflections: Intellectual Trajectories: Why People Study What They Do', *Reviews in American History* 37/1 (2009), 148–59, here 157.

[11] Kitson Clark, *The Critical Historian*, 208.

purpose, not least because the cultural 'memories' of the practice are marked by resentment of it, rather than acceptance of the lord exercising the 'right' in question, namely the right to sexual intercourse with a woman prior to consummation between the newly-weds. Given resentment and its predictability, then whatever else it might be, a commitment to exercise *droit de seigneur* would be a commitment to the probable necessity of coercion, on the principle that even outward compliance from the victim ('victim' being an evocative term that is also descriptively appropriate) likely stemmed from fear of the consequences of refusal. The 'right', is, amongst other things, a right to coerce. That does not make the coercion disappear, and coerced sex is reasonably described as rape, whenever in human history it occurred. Whether the actual word rape is used or not, the only way a description of the situation could avoid an element that lends itself readily to negative evaluation would be if it avoided the coercive element of the sexual encounter, which would be significantly to misdescribe what is entailed in the exercise of the picturesquely named *droit de seigneur*.

Now let us consider the concept 'anti-Semitism' as it appears in the work of Steve Rigby, one of the most accomplished historians at blending empirical and theoretical approaches. Rigby's *English Society in the Later Middle Ages: Class, Status and Gender* excels in testing social scientific theories of stratification against the evidence of this particular national case. One of the 'status-groups' he considers is Jews in the thirteenth century, up to their expulsion by Edward I in 1290, through the lens of growing anti-Semitism. His inquiry as to whether enhanced hostility can be attributed to the Crown, the Church, or popular sentiment concludes on all three, as it interweaves political, religious, economic, cultural, and social factors at a particular conjuncture.[12] During the explanation he uses the term 'anti-Semitism' repeatedly, as defined 'in the broad sense of anti-Jewish sentiment'. Like 'racism', 'anti-Semitism' describes an outlook that no reader regards neutrally. There is no neutral alternative: possible formulations like 'the belief that Jews as Jews were inferior, or sinful, etcetera' are just different ways of making the point that anti-Semitism is a blanket belief about a particular people, and it is precisely this blanket belief that non-anti-Semites reject as problematic, however sincerely it is held. Putting aside the question of whether it is possible, would it be desirable in the interests of understanding for us not to have some evaluative attitude towards anti-Semitism? This is doubtful on the face of it and it would be unnecessary anyway since, again, evaluation is not antithetical to understanding. It is perfectly possible to hold in one's head an explanation as to why someone espoused anti-Semitism and a belief that anti-Semitism is wrong— or right, if one is an anti-Semite.

---

[12] S. H. Rigby, *English Society in the Later Middle Ages: Class, Status and Gender* (Manchester: Manchester University Press, 1995), ch. 8; all quotes in this discussion from pp. 284–90 of the book.

When Rigby talks of the general thirteenth-century regnal 'onslaught', as against a twelfth-century 'halcyon period for the Jews in England', he reveals the existential stakes in evocative language that, again, seems perfectly appropriate. There is a general tendency, in the absence of justificatory argument to the contrary, to prefer halcyon days to onslaughts, and even among those who prefer things the other way around, the predilection is not a consequence of disinterest. As to the explanation for the intensification of anti-Semitism, in one of Rigby's thematic strands we read of Edward's 'impoverish[ing] the Jews by punitive taxation'. Then, having availed himself of other sources of credit than Jewish money-lenders, Edward saw no advantage in continuing to give Jews legal protection. Early on in the thirteenth century King John had already shown that protections and privileges were 'extremely tenuous and...likely to be ignored according to the convenience of the Crown'; he had engaged in 'persecution' and 'extortion'. These explanations to venality are apt to put John and Edward in a negative light, and well might that be the case if the evidence points to their venality.

Some evaluations just can be warranted by the evidence without fear of anachronism. Take the concept of a deceitful act. Since every culture (or society, etc) has standards, every culture will have a concept of failing to meet those standards and of better and worse reasons for failing to meet those standards. Even where criteria and types of truthfulness vary across cultures, the claim that someone has been deceitful stands or falls purely on the evidence of transgressing that norm. Accordingly, one can have evidentiary warrant to describe someone in the past as having acted deceitfully—it is a legitimate, bona fide 'research finding', as they say—but the description as to deceit will colour the impression of the historical actor. Now 'cowardice'. Standards and types will vary—compare ancient Greek martial concepts of honour with some contemporary sense of moral cowardice—but the idea of failing to live up to some standard in relation to a pressure on one's interests (say fear) is general. While a specification may be needed as to the standard of courage/cowardice at issue, it is as legitimate to use the word 'cowardly' to characterize the actions of a Homeric Greek who shies from battle as it is to describe the behaviour of some academic who fails to defend a junior colleague against the bullying faculty-head.

The cases of deceit and cowardice encapsulate an obstacle to 'quarantining' the evaluative valence of certain historical judgements to the historical period under investigation via the 'moral contextualism' discussed in Part 1. 'Deceit' and 'cowardice' illustrate the point in a different way to the way in which it is illustrated by the discussion of anti-Semitism. We can understand that anti-Semites might find themselves justified in their actions and beliefs, i.e. that some anti-Semites might be perfectly sincere in their anti-Semitism and would reject the negative connotations of the term. This is rarely the case with 'deceit' or 'cowardice'. When we deploy such terms, as when we identify King John's venality, we are making evaluations in light of standards that we have reason to believe that those transgressing the standards would recognize. But even in these cases the evaluation in some way exceeds the cultural context of the deceitful or cowardly act. The fact that some actor, let us call her Helen, transgressed the extant values of system 1 for reasons that were non-virtuous by the light of those values is scarcely going to put Helen in a good light from the perspective of any other moral system, since all moral systems perforce imply the restraint of certain interests in the light of certain values, and consistency in adherence to values.[13] This reasoning holds even if Helen's act, while transgressive in system 1, happens not to be transgressive in system 2 and even praiseworthy in system 3.

Rhetoric and Truthfulness

One need not use the actual words 'deceit' and 'cowardliness' (etcetera) to produce the evocative effect that their deployment elicits—the implicit judgement on King John's motives is present even though Rigby does not use 'venal'. Richard Evans is getting at something like this point when he writes that

> a historian who uses terms like 'wicked' and 'evil' about a person or persons in the past will only succeed in looking ridiculous. It is perfectly legitimate, however, to point out in factual terms when people in the past, such as monks and nuns, behaved in private in a manner quite different to that which they advocated for other people, and boasted of themselves, in public.[14]

The second sentence is clear and unarguable but the first requires analysis in order to reflect on what exactly Evans is ruling out and why.

Let us consider three possible reasons for Evans's rejection of labels like 'evil' that are also rejected by the fifty-eight Oxford scholars mentioned in the Introduction (pp. 4-5). These reasons are: objection to any sort of evaluation per se; objection to specifically moral forms of evaluation; or objection to words like evil and wicked on grounds particular to those words. If the objection is to evaluative language of any sort, whether aesthetic, prudential, or moral, then the words 'lazy', 'foolish', or 'blinkered' are just as objectionable as 'evil'. If the objection is only to moral forms of evaluation, then alongside 'wicked' it is not acceptable to use words like 'callous', 'avaricious', or 'oppressive'. (By his own lights, Kitson Clark should perhaps not have deployed the adjective 'ugly'—see p. 91—which is a case of an aesthetic term adopted for moral purposes.) While less extreme labels than evil, none of these is any less judgemental, and each probably

---

[13]   On e.g. truthfulness and reciprocity, see Bernard Williams, *Truth and Truthfulness: An Essay in Genealogy* (Princeton: Princeton University Press, 2002); Sarah F. Brosnan and Frans B. M. de Waal, 'Evolution of Responses to (Un)fairness', *Science* 346/6207 (17 October 2014).

[14]   Evans, *In Defence*, 45, 44.

has wider applicability. Moving from the language of criticism to that of praise, it is equally untrue that historians who deploy *positive* language, even highly positive language, are perforce deemed ridiculous. William Hague's biography of a slave-trade abolitionist concludes with the sentence 'In the dark historical landscape of violence, treachery and hate, the life of William Wilberforce stands out as a beacon of light, which the passing of two centuries has scarcely dimmed', yet that did not prevent the author winning the 2008 *History Today*–Longman Trustees' Award for History.[15] There are few biographies of Winston Churchill or John F. Kennedy that hide their authors' feelings about their man. In sum, judgemental language of both the moral and non-moral sort is acceptable as judged by widespread practice. Of the three sorts of objections enumerated, the third seems to have most force, perhaps because of the quasi-theological nature of terms like 'evil'; though even then a number of academic works pertaining to Nazism have 'evil' in their title, as does the collection entitled *The Problem of Evil: Slavery, Freedom, and the Ambiguities of American Reform* (2007). 'Evil' and 'wicked' differ importantly from some of the other terms of disapprobation here in that they do little descriptive work. They are purely, and thus imprecisely, evaluative, and have the air of unhelpful, generalized pronouncement. In that sense they are not representative of the majority of evaluative terms that carry with them some indication of why they are being used. But Evans does not make the distinction between sorts of evaluative terms, and so rather casts all of them out together.

As to one of the major concerns of this section, namely rhetoric, Evans writes:

> Historians have far more powerful rhetorical and stylistic weapons at their disposal than mere denunciation: sarcasm, irony, the juxtaposition of rhetoric and reality, the factual exposure of hypocrisy, self-interest, and greed, the uncommented recounting of courageous acts of rebellion and defiance. All of this can be achieved without the direct application of the transient moral vocabulary of the society that the historian is living in.

Again, there is much to agree with here, but there are also some tensions and some implications that need drawing out. Putting aside the potential conflation of 'denunciation' with the use of any and all evocative terms, this passage does not provide an argument against evaluation, and so sits slightly askance to other things Evans has written against value judgement—here his argument is only against explicit evaluation. Further, the objections to explicit evaluation seem to be split between the point that it would be embarrassing for the literary sophisticate and the point that it would be 'transient'. But if transience is a concern, along

[15] William Hague, *William Wilberforce: The Life of the Great Anti-Slave Trade Campaigner* (London: Harper Perennial, 2008), 515.

with its relationship to anachronism, then it is a concern for implicit judgement just as much as explicit judgement, unless, that is, one intends to leave things ambiguous by one's implicitness. Evans does not appear to be espousing ambiguity, but one does need to dig deeper into the various functions 'rhetoric' can fulfil, recognizing that it can dilute, and obscure, but also that, in Meinecke's words (p. 10) it can have an effect 'more profound and moving than if the evaluation were to appear directly in the guise of moralizing'. In other words, rhetoric can be a good tool for surreptitious evaluation as well as for implicit evaluation.

An elegant analysis of the techniques of the surreptitious judge is provided by the historian of science Robert A. Richards in his discussion of 'the moral structure of narrative grammar'.

> The historian can orchestrate outrage ... by cutting quotations from an actor into certain vicious shapes. Or, like Gibbon, the historian can evoke feelings of moral disdain with little more than the magical mist of antithetic possibilities. As a result, readers will have, as it were, a sensible, even an olfactory understanding: the invisible air of the narrative will carry the sweet smell of virtue, the acrid stench of turpitude, or simply the bittersweet of irony.

Of Gibbon, Richards cites that part of *The History of the Decline and Fall of the Roman Empire* that addresses Julian's motives while his soldiers were advocating his accession to the imperial throne still occupied by Constantius II. From Gibbon:

> The grief of Julian could proceed only from his innocence; but his innocence must appear extremely doubtful in the eyes of those who have learned to suspect the motives and the professions of princes. His lively and active mind was susceptible of the various impressions of hope and fear, of gratitude and revenge, of duty and of ambition, of the love of fame and of the fear of reproach. But it is impossible for us to ascertain the principles of action which might escape the observation, while they guided, or rather impelled, the steps of Julian himself. ... He solemnly declares, in the presence of Jupiter, of the Sun, of Mars, of Minerva, and of all the other deities, that till the close of the evening which preceded his elevation he was utterly ignorant of the designs of the soldiers; and it may seem ungenerous to distrust the honour of a hero, and the truth of a philosopher. Yet the superstitious confidence that Constantius was the enemy, and that he himself was the favourite, of the gods, might prompt him to desire, to solicit, and even to hasten the auspicious moment of his reign, which was predestined to restore the ancient religion of mankind.[16]

---

[16] Richards, 'The Narrative Structure', 3.

While agreeing with Richards's general points one could make a strong case that Gibbon's evaluations in this particular excerpt are neither surreptitious nor unconscious, merely implicit.[17] As a general principle, the literary theorist Marshall Gregory suggests that 'every work of literary art extends to its readers at least three invitations', of which one is indeed the invitation to *feel* and the third and final the invitation to *judge*, but there is also the invitation to *belief*.[18] One might pretentiously translate this into the terms of the classical rhetorical tradition, where to evoke feeling is to use *pathos*; to evoke belief, *logos*; to evoke judgement, *iudicium*. For Gregory's second and third invitations to be accepted, substantiation is required. The question for Gibbon is whether he had empirical warrant for his insinuations. If he did, then his evaluation should be acceptable to whoever understands that rhetoric can mean communicating well, rather than deceit.

Depending on the case, disguised evaluative elements may feature in prose that lacks any of Gibbon's purple colouring and avoids the everyday dramatizations achieved by hyperbole, aposiopesis, paradiastole, or simple descriptive vividness.[19] One such instance is the sparser prose of the 'realist' if that minimizes troublesome elements via 'full disclosure' hastily mentioned then discarded, or provides summary justifications passed off as self-evident in the real world of tough decisions, or merely avoids the trickiest questions in the hope that the reader does not know to ask them. Here, 'realism' functions more like rhetoric understood as legerdemain.

The ancient Greek historian Thucydides is one scholar whose qualifications as a realist vary depending upon whether that epithet applies to his mode of historical writing or his view of international relations. Either way, his scholar Walter Robert Connor commends the Thucydidean use of straightforward reportage as artifice. There is, Connor writes, nothing wrong with 'using objectivity as an authorial stance rather than as a principle or goal'. Connor invokes the journalist and historian of the Vietnam War, Jonathan Schell, who opened one essay with the avowed intention of recording 'what is happening to Vietnam—to the people and the land—as a result of the American military presence. I shall not discuss the moral ramifications of that presence. I shall simply try to set down what I saw and heard first hand.'[20] The student of evaluation is, however, bound to inquire after the similarities between what Schell did and what historians can legitimately

---

[17] For Gibbon's inconsistencies, his difficulty in dealing with changes in character over time, and his tendency to make overall judgements on people as well as motivations in specific instances, see Charlotte Roberts, *Edward Gibbon and the Shape of History* (Oxford: Oxford University Press, 2014), 27 ff., which focuses in particular on Julian.

[18] Marshall W. Gregory, 'Redefining Ethical Criticism: The Old vs. the New', *Journal of Literary Theory Online* 4/2 (2010), 273–301, http://www.jltonline.de/index.php/articles/article/view/287/879

[19] Stefania Tutino, *Shadows of Doubt: Language and Truth in Post-Reformation Catholic Culture* (Oxford: Oxford University Press, 2014), 69–70.

[20] Connor, *Thucydides*, 7.

do, and thus whether Connor is correct to deploy them together in support of his contention. There are good grounds for believing him to be incorrect.

Despite disavowing moral comment, Schell was aware of the contexts in which he would be read; his words would provide moral ammunition in the Vietnam debate. He was trying to establish awareness in order to shift the centre ground of the field of common sense on which arguments about Vietnam were conducted. Rather than being pre-emptive, trying to establish the terms of debate by getting in first, he was being counter-pre-emptive.[21] Not a political or moral argument as such, and more reportage rather than analytical contemporary History, his piece was a preliminary to such arguments. It was legitimate in that capacity insofar as it helped correct a presumptive balance of official or popular opinion that down-played the consequences of the American military presence for Vietnam by the ever-useful device of simply ignoring them. Schell's was a provision of evidence to be taken into account in a future reckoning. Historians are not in the same situation, however. On the whole they deal more in integrated explanations than prolegomena or polemic, as elaborated below in the discussion of Histories as compositions (pp. 102–113). For the historian to deploy 'objectivity as an author-ial stance rather than a principle or goal', is to enter that terrain of ambiguity between implicit and surreptitious judgement into which Meinecke strode when he commended 'abstain[ing] from value judgements ... as an artifice'. At worst it is to pronounce at the reckoning without even alerting the reader that a reckoning had occurred.

Ultimately, when making explicit judgement or deploying rhetorical devices from the romantic to the 'realist' varieties, the question is of authorial responsibil-ity, but responsibility to what? The answer must prioritize some conception of shared scholarly standards, but that does not get us too far since some think neu-trality should be a standard. If we define neutrality as precluding any explicit or implicit value judgements of any sort, then for reasons already provided that standard is ill-conceived. It seems unobjectionable to state instead that whatever else the historian's responsibilities are thought to include, they must include and indeed prioritize a commitment to truthfulness.

Truthfulness is an ethical commitment. It does not guarantee locating the truth, however truth is defined, but it is a commitment amongst other things to rigour in making inferences from evidence, and because it is therefore also a commitment to taking account of thesis-challenging evidence, it is a commitment to acting without fear or favour in coming to conclusions. This is not to say that everything can be judged according to the rubric of truthfulness, and certain value judgements cannot be, but it is to say that when there is a clash between the principle of truthfulness and another principle, truthfulness must win out.

---

[21] To use the term 'counter-pre-emptive' in the sense deployed by W. G. Runciman, *A Treatise on Social Theory*, i (Cambridge: Cambridge University Press, 1993), 339.

In order to fulfil the commitment to truthfulness, historians have to be careful to establish legitimate and illegitimate meanings of concepts like 'balance', 'impartiality', and 'fairness'. An illegitimate meaning is that to which critics of the British Broadcasting Corporation rightly gesture when they invoke the BBC's 'fairness bias' or 'balance bias'. Concern to air a 'balance of opinions' can result in the scientific expert in the study of climate change being paired off with a corporate climate-change denier. One way to improve the situation would be for the BBC to 'balance' opposing opinions from authorities of roughly equal relevant intellectual stature and commitment to investigative principles, but the sort of 'playing off' involved there is more akin to what the textbook-writer tries to achieve as she summarizes and juxtaposes key arguments in some debate for her readers. When the historian is engaged in her own research project or work of synthesis, neither of these sorts of 'balance' pertain. For the historian in the mode of original investigation, 'balance', like 'impartiality', relates to treatment of whatever is considered to be the evidence—it makes no sense to talk of 'balancing arguments' in a way that is separate from the processes of inference from evidence that lead to the production of the argument.

'Even-handed' may or may not be a synonym for 'impartial' in that final sense. When the historian Geoffrey Wheatcroft wrote of David Cesarani's *Major Farran's Hat: Murder, Scandal and Britain's War Against Jewish Terrorism 1945–1948* that Cesarani tried to be 'even-handed' despite having 'Zionist sympathies',[22] Wheatcroft did not elaborate upon the grounds of his conclusion. What we may say is that the only legitimate grounds on which Wheatcroft could accuse another historian of being un-even-handed was in contrast to Wheatcroft's own evidence-based idea of what a really even-handed treatment of the historical issues would look like. Having decided, presumably, that Cesarani's account fell short in this respect, and that the shortcomings were sufficiently consistent in one direction, Wheatcroft attributed the situation to Cesarani's political views, as opposed to some accidental oversight of research or shortcoming in understanding. The reason it would have helped if Wheatcroft had been clearer is that expressions like even-handedness are so often used in relation to interactions between humans. Even other historians who should be more alert to the potential pitfalls may read 'even-handedness' as pertaining to: the interests of concerned parties in the present; the behaviour of the relevant parties in the past; or the evidence of the behaviour of the relevant parties in the past. The last sort of even-handedness is the only sort to which historians should aspire as historians.

Even-handedness, fairness, balance, and so forth, must pertain to the historian's truthful treatment of evidence, without regard to historical parties or audience. The imperative of truthfulness might involve stating that as far as one can

---

[22] Geoffrey Wheatcroft, 'On Trying to be Portugal', *London Review of Books* 31/15 (6 August 2009), 32–3.

infer from the evidence, historical character or interest group X was responsible for inciting a race riot against ethnic group Y. Since we tend to view such incitement as bad whenever or wherever it happens, this will colour contemporary perceptions of X. Political implications may flow from the findings, but insofar as political considerations consciously shape the historical claims from which political implications might be drawn, the historian needs to relabel herself a propagandist.

The historian is exposed to many influences in the present, and those influences may push in various directions. While presentism is considered to be a major problem with historical value judgements, the demands of the present can equally conduce to the partisan *withdrawal* of certain historical phenomena from evaluative consideration. To make the point from the reverse direction, consider Evans's statement that especially 'in periods of mass destruction such as the years 1914–45, it is difficult for the historian not to take a moral stance'.[23] The statement itself is just honesty: what would it say about us if devastating war, genocide, and totalitarian dictatorship did not arouse some moral response? But questions remain about the implied threshold that needs to be passed for a moral stance to be non-controversial, and the nature of that threshold may tell us more about the present than the past.

To take but the most obvious candidate from the 1914–45 period, Nazi Germany and its deeds, it is not just a matter of the level of 'destruction' but the nature of and unquestioned responsibility for some of that destruction. While some scholars have deployed, unscorned, terms like 'evil' in discussing Nazism, it is also possible to discuss some of the historical issues in an understated way precisely because of widespread knowledge about and disapprobation of Nazism, because the moral stakes are taken as given, and because no mainstream voices speak to the contrary. (Exemplary in its understated power is the work of the historian Christopher Browning on the evolution of Nazi policy and the motivation of perpetrators of the Holocaust.[24]) Once the principle of value judgement is admitted, however, it is strange to restrict it to instances such as the Nazi case, where judgement is obviously merited to anyone who is not an extreme racist. Such a restriction would tie the historian to the state of popular consensus, and scarcely coheres with the principle of her acting without fear or favour, letting the chips fall where they may once one she has exercised due rigour in making inferences from evidence.

If a value judgement on the past is deemed controversial, that may just mean that it is an unwelcome intervention in some present context, not that the warrant

---

[23] Evans, *In Defence*, 45.

[24] Christopher Browning, *Ordinary Men: Reserve Police Battalion 101 and the Final Solution in Poland* (New York: Harper Collins, 1993); Christopher Browning with Jürgen Matthäus, *The Origins of the Final Solution* (Lincoln, NE: University of Nebraska Press, 2005).

for the judgement was questionable. By the same token, writing in such a way as to cause no ructions in the present can be distinctly loaded, perhaps overtly ideological.[25] The tendency may bespeak a conscious desire not to please or displease some constituency in the contemporary audience. Or it may reflect a less conscious disposition, which in turn is the product of a general socialization whereby certain practices have become so normalized—'neutral'—in the present that they seem perfectly normal in the past too, seeming to warrant no comment. Treatment of them as neutral in the past reinforces their normalization in the present. (See Part 4.)

In yet other cases the appraisal may be less categorical or extreme, but that does not mean it is any the less necessary or legitimate or evaluative. It may suggest that evaluation is relatively complicated, and thus requires more qualification and insight. In such instances someone who has spent much time getting to grips with the historical particulars is singularly well placed.

If the issues are more balanced or fundamentally irresolvable, in the terms under discussion the balanced or unresolved arguments would still be moral ones, and a conclusion as to such balance or unresolvability could only arise as the result of applying evaluative thought in the first place. Consider the 'standard-of-living debate', which concerned arguments about improvement or decline in the life conditions of workers during Britain's Industrial Revolution, especially the period 1790–1840. The social theorist W. G. Runciman pointed out that while it was possible to come to some general agreement on changes in real wages during that period, such agreement was unlikely to be reached in other areas, given the contestedness of concepts like life conditions and the varying ways in which the revolution affected different people. But the absence of agreement is not a denial of the stakes, as reflected in Runciman's own evocative prose.

Is it or isn't it an 'improvement' for the agricultural labourer of the late eighteenth century to exchange lower wages and the relatively better sanitation of the countryside for higher wages but a greater chance of the death of a larger proportion of infant children in the town?…How far should the presumptive improvement in well-being reflected in the statistics for increased per capita consumption of beer and spirits be offset by evidence for the need to have recourse to alcohol to assuage feelings of exhaustion, degradation, and despair?…Can the improvement in the welfare of a half-starved crofter's son living on potatoes in a hovel in a rain-swept Highland glen who has become a skilled cotton operative living in a four-roomed house in Glasgow and eating meat every Sunday be said to compensate for the decline in the welfare of a hand-loom weaver of the previous generation from a once-prosperous Yorkshire

[25] Gerard J. Libaridian, 'Objectivity and the Historiography of the Armenian Genocide', *Armenian Review* 31/1 (1978), 79–87, here 83.

dale who ended up coughing his lungs out in a filthy cellar in Leeds after being driven to pawn the tools of his only available livelihood?[26]

Once one reflects on the intimate relationship in a humanistically inflected discipline between description and the sort of evocative language that encourages or is tantamount to evaluation, one appreciates how much effort must go in some cases into avoiding evaluation, and how question-begging that activity itself is.[27] Emphasizing the characteristics of language, and the relationship between description and evaluation, is not to suggest we are in thrall to evaluations beyond our control. When we use evocative nouns, adjectives, and adverbs we must acknowledge that they are apt to evoke particular sentiments and 'own' the connotations of the verbal choices we make. We also need to think harder about deploying evaluations consistently and with a determination to ignore the demands (say) of 'balancing' sensibilities in the world of the historian's readership. There is no necessary relationship between being controversial or non-controversial in the present, or between seeming gauche in one's explicit judgement or suave in one's rhetorical insinuations, and being a procedurally sound historian who uses language that she deems appropriate to communicate truthfully something that she infers about the past.

Combining Perspectives

The argument of this section is that a work of History provides an overall impression whether or not the historian admits it and, depending on topic, this impression will have evocative or evaluative implications. The historian's authorial choices as she creates her composition will not remove the impression; they will only influence what sort of impression it is. The choices include where to begin the story, how to contextualize, which perspectives to invoke, and when to move from an internalized, actor's perspective to one or more external perspectives. The way that the historian relates to outcomes caused by the historical actors on whom she focuses is another element of the composition.

When Jonathan Schell reported the American impact on Vietnam (pp. 97-8), he substantiated the assertion of the historian Agathias of Myrina (536/7–c.582 CE)

---

[26] Runciman, *A Treatise on Social Theory*, i. 325–6.

[27] Isaiah Berlin contended in his *Historical Inevitability* that were the historian to succeed in expunging from her prose the nouns, adverbs, and adjectives that connote evaluation, the final result would not be a neutral tale since the very act of expurgation would be so obviously unnatural that it would arouse the suspicion of the reader. For similar points, see Cracraft, 'Implicit Morality'. See also Robert J. Richards, 'The Moral Grammar of Narratives in History of Biology—the Case of Haeckel and Nazi Biology, in David L. Hull and Michael Ruse (eds), *Cambridge Companion to the Philosophy of Biology* (Cambridge: Cambridge University Press, 2007), 429–51, and Richards, 'The Narrative Structure of Moral Judgments'.

that the 'physiognomy of events suggests praise or blame'.[28] Whatever rhetorical skills may be used to present events in a way that minimizes their evocative effect, or channels it in favourable directions, it remains the case, as Orwell pointed out, that it is sometimes easiest just to sideline certain matters altogether.[29] Polybius (200–118 BCE) exemplified this approach in his attempt to 'frame the debate', i.e. control the evaluative tone. Polybius was critical of the earlier historian Phylarchus, whose purpose he deemed to have been 'to emphasize the cruelty of Antigonus and the Macedonians and also that of Aratus and the Achaeans' in the action against the Mantineans in 233 BCE. 'In his eagerness to arouse the pity of his readers and enlist their sympathy through his story', writes Polybius, Phylarcus 'introduces graphic scenes of women clinging to one another, tearing their hair and baring their breasts'. While mixed with a call for a sort of dry analytical History, as against Phylarcus' 'ignoble and unmanly' account, this is Polybius' attempt to control the cause in which the reader's blood is stirred by the simple device of not talking about one thing and instead talking about something else.[30] Polybius goes beyond explaining things according to the perspective of a set of actors past, here Antigonus, the Macedonians, etc. He agrees with their perspective. He is suggesting that the Mantineans had it coming in virtue of their earlier treachery, and as such that their suffering merits no sympathy, nor, therefore, the coverage that might lead to sympathy. He enters the game of evaluation himself, and whatever we might think of his tactics, he is at least open about what he is up to.

Much less open are those scholars who adopt the official position of the Turkish state on what befell the Ottoman population of Armenian Christians in 1915. These scholars are clearly involved in a blame game. They seek to blame the population that was deported and attacked by focusing solely, and exaggeratedly, on factors that they think justify the policies of the Ottoman regime of 1915, such as Armenian secessionism and wartime disloyalty, as opposed to the increasingly chauvinist ideologies of the Ottoman rulers. Under the name of 'balance' against 'Armenian propaganda', the clearest favouritism is evinced towards a historical party and a particular present-day statist agenda, which helps explain how little of this 'scholarship' makes an impression in scholarly citation indices outside Turkey. The first thing to say is that the defences do not even work in their own terms. To claim that the 'Young Turks' believed that the entire Armenian community constituted a security threat—or, the same thing more artfully phrased, that for the

---

[28] Agathias, *History of His Own Times*, preface, repr. in Arnold Toynbee, *Greek Historical Thought* (New York: Mentor Books, 1952), 87–92, here 91.
[29] Orwell, *Critical Essays*, 17: 'the apologists of any revolution generally try to minimize its horrors', and that goes for other objects of historical inquiry too.
[30] Polybius, *The Rise of the Roman Empire*, trans. Ian Scott-Kilvert (London: Penguin, 1979), bk II, §56. For this not-uncommon feature of Greek and Roman historianship, Victor d'Huys, 'How to Describe Violence in Historical Narrative', *Ancient Society* 18 (1997), 209–50.

regime 'security' was conceived in ethno-religious terms—is really to say that the Young Turks were after all prejudiced against Armenians, since the harbouring of beliefs about the collective agenda of an ethno-religious group is just how ethno-religious prejudice manifests itself. But with a mind to Schell and Polybius, the whole process of trying to shift the normative focus is much easier if one minimizes or just ignores what was actually done by tens of thousands of perpetrators from Ottoman Muslim state and society, as Armenians were robbed, knifed, drowned, sawn, cudgelled, shot, crucified, abducted, raped, mutilated, disembowelled, immolated, and left to starve or die from disease. Further, that these things were inflicted on women and infants, often after their menfolk had already been killed, and were inflicted systematically in a pattern that reproduced itself across a vast area, much of it far beyond any war zones, are facts that have to be downplayed lest the whole narrative of 'realistic' security measures against dangerous insurgents is compromised. At the very least, readers might ask whether anything could really have justified the outcomes in question.

The Turkish case raises in stark terms the general issue of exclusion and inclusion in any historical account. What is and ought to be in a work of History? This is a difficult area. Focusing on A rather than B for explanatory reasons is clearly different to following Polybius' lead by avoiding B for fear that it will influence evaluations of A. Nonetheless the effect on the overall impression provided by the historical work might be the same in either case and those emulating Polybius are more likely to appeal to the principle of freedom of inquiry than to advertise their partisan tactic. Finally, even if historians wish to, they simply cannot look at everything, far less look at everything from every perspective. This selectivity cannot be regretted intellectually since it is a condition of completing any significant project of inquiry.

While taking freedom of focus as given, the rest of this section is effectively a reflection on the responsibility attending that freedom and the legitimate criticisms that may follow from certain uses of it. The aim is to highlight the potential intellectual and moral problems of exclusive concentration upon the perspectives and motivations of particular causal actors. The focus of criticism hereafter is by no means just bad-faith scholarship of the Turkish denialist sort, because bad-faith scholarship implicitly recognizes the intellectual and moral stakes. A more important audience comprises those who refuse to admit the evaluative stakes and just want to get on with providing what they see as valuation-free historical accounts. Within that broader audience, particular confusion is created by those who believe in good faith that historical explanation is coextensive with seeing through the eyes of their chosen historical actors. One even encounters thinkers whose highest goal is adopting the perspective of their historical actors, as if blind to the fact that such an approach itself prejudices the issue of justification that cannot be separated from explanation in morally salient matters.

We have already seen that the opposition between understanding and judgement is a false one, but manifestly we also need to avoid equating the two things under a title like 'empathy' (further discussed at pp. 260–1). Tolstoy approached such an equation in *War and Peace*, when he wrote 'il faut se mettre à la place de chacun: tout comprendre, c'est tout pardonner'—'one should put oneself in the place of each other person: to understand all is to forgive all'. The polymath Gustave le Bon (1841–1931) went further. Commenting on the historiography of the St Bartholomew's Day massacre of Hugenots in 1572, which had been characterized by enthusiastic participation, le Bon wrote that 'When time had somewhat cooled religious passions, all the historians, even the Catholics, spoke of St. Bartholomew's Day with indignation. They thus showed how difficult it is for the mentality of one epoch to understand that of another.'[31] Indignation was equated with misunderstanding, and understanding with enthusiasm for the massacre, as if understanding the motivating passions was the same as sharing them. A host of homespun wisdoms point in broadly the same direction. The anthropologist Bronisław Malinowski was simply wrong that 'to judge something, you have to be there'.[32] What system of evaluation, from the courtroom examination of acts conducted elsewhere in the dead of night to the study of the moral philosopher to the citizen's probe into secret official malfeasance, could ever function under such a principle?[33] Only if metaphors like walking a mile in another's shoes retain their metaphoricity can they retain their force. We cannot be swayed by Kitson Clark. Arguing against 'judgements on dead people', he wrote that it is impossible 'to know enough of the circumstances of those on whom they are to be pronounced'.[34] This is true of living people too, but judge their acts we nevertheless do, and routinely.

Returning from the empaths to the self-professed neutralists, the likes of Robinson and Gallagher do not themselves want to think as Victorian officials thought: reasonably enough, they want to portray to their readers what they infer the officials thought in order to help their readers understand the officials. But understanding historical actors involves more than understanding their own account of themselves. In certain respects historians can understand past actors better than those actors did themselves, and past societies better than their inhabitants did. This is not because of inherently superior capacities of insight. It is because the historian has an external perspective, which means that she can observe some of the conditions of the actors' beliefs that were invisible to the actors. As part of their explanations we expect historians to provide such external insights, which is one of the things we are getting at when we talk of establishing the contexts of actors' lives.

---

[31] Gustave le Bon, *The Psychology of Revolution* (1913; Sioux Falls, SD: NuVision Publications, 2010), 25. 'Ils montrèrent ainsi la difficulté de comprendre la mentalité d'une époque avec celle d'une autre.'

[32] Bronisław Malinowski, *Argonauts of the West Pacific* (London: Routledge and Kegan Paul, 1922), cited in Ryszard Kapuściński, *The Other* (London: Verso, 2008), 88.

[33] Arendt makes similar points to those of the two sentences preceding this footnote in her postscript to the revised edition of *Eichmann in Jerusalem* (Harmondsworth: Penguin, 1994), 295–6.

[34] Kitson Clark, *The Critical Historian*, 209.

Identifying matters that were not considered by contemporaries is not necessarily the same as treating them anachronistically or imperially. Anthropologist Mark Hobart puts a great burden on the 'may' when he writes that in choosing 'contexts in preference to those used by the participants themselves, we may be guilty simultaneously of an act of distortion and a subtle kind of epistemological domination'.[35] The historian's access to evidence that was not available to contemporaries enables her to discern agendas or patterns or actions that may have been hidden at the time, which is why the time machine that deposits us at the same spatio-temporal point as the actor would not solve all the historian's investigative problems. The anarchist Pierre-Joseph Proudhon wrote that one should not look to the actor for the meaning of her acts, but 'to the acts themselves'. In any society, many relations are indirect, 'economic' in the previously specified sense (p. 90). Acts may embody some systemic logic that is lost on individual actors. The quest to understand systemic or otherwise institutionalized power relations will not necessarily be furthered by listening to what individuals from past societies might have believed. The historian may be interested in interrogating things that seemed mundane or given in their historical context, and while this new interest may issue in tales of the marginalized (e.g. females in male-dominated societies), it will also issue in greater understanding of the marginalizers, since one learns a great deal about a social order by that which it takes, unquestioned, as given. The nature and function of social structures is often more easily discernible from beyond those structures than from within them.

The combination of external and internal perspectives is one of the hallmarks of the composition created by the historian. Collective memory illustrates the amalgamation of different elements, as when, for instance, impressions of Winston Churchill interpenetrate with what the British are apt to call Dunkirk spirit, or the actions of Roosevelt fuse with impressions of what Americans are apt to call the greatest generation. This fusion happens all the time in works of professional History too. A proverbial historian of Germany in the eighteenth century might write on the Enlightenment in general and the thought of Kant specifically, yet the book as a whole will not leave the reader with an impression of two entirely separate entities; rather, students of the German Enlightenment will recognize the interpenetration of the 'spirit of the times' and one of its most innovative manifestations as they chart the uncertain, interactive relationship of agent and context.[36] It is not that historians cannot establish the volition and

---

[35] Mark Hobart, 'Introduction: Context, Meaning, and Power', in Mark Hobart and Robert H. Taylor (eds), *Context, Meaning and Power in Southeast Asia* (Ithaca, NY: Cornell University Press, 1986), 7–19, here 8.

[36] The point about combining different perspectives was made in embryonic form by John Dewey, 'Historical Judgments', in Meyerhoff (ed.), *The Philosophy of History in Our Time*, 163–72, here 168. It has been elucidated elegantly in Jörn Rüsen, *Rekonstruktion der Vergangenheit. Grundzüge einer Historik II: Die Prinzipien der historischen Forschung* (Göttingen: Vandenhoeck und Ruprecht, 1986), ch. 2.

motivation of actors and set those things in relations of tension or harmony with structures of social function, meaning, and value. Given appropriate evidence, all such discriminations are possible within a work of History, and they influence individual choices of words and phrases. Rather, the overall impressions of events, periods, places, etcetera, that are created by a History cannot be distilled to just one side of any of the duos subjective vs objective, internal vs external, human vs structural, motive vs outcome, etcetera. Well might this be so, as is illustrated by contrast with a hypothetical alternative.

Imagine a historical actor, Ivan, and an exclusively internalist account, by the end of which we readers have come to understand why, by Ivan's thinking, he performed morally significant act X. Does such an account fulfil the criteria of neutral explanation? Well, explanation of what? If what is supposed to be explained is Ivan's beliefs themselves, then even if we say neutrality has been achieved, what is produced by the internalist account is a description of elements of his beliefs and only a peculiarly aetiolated explanation of them: an explanation of someone's beliefs is at best only partially available from within those beliefs. If what is supposed to be explained is the act X, we have a peculiarly aetiolated explanation of X for the same reasons that we have a peculiarly aetiolated account of Ivan's beliefs; furthermore, the only view of X's justifiability that we readers will be exposed to will be Ivan's. If that is what a neutral account involves then it is not desirable on intellectual or moral grounds. The account will not have addressed questions like: how did Ivan's agenda compare to those of others in Ivan's position?; were the Freemasons really in a conspiracy against the State when he decided to launch a campaign against them?; was the girl really 'asking for it' by her behaviour? Had the text addressed such questions, then it would have betrayed the principle of internal explanation by tacitly characterizing Ivan's behaviour by standards other than Ivan's; standards, wheresoever they might come from, pertaining to the justifiability of X. As things stand we have no idea of whether Ivan is deluded, unusually prejudiced, cynical, and so on.

A heuristic purpose of this extreme thought experiment is to stress that what is left out of a historical account is as important as what goes into it if the excluded material would have changed the impression given by the content. This rather banal-sounding claim gets its importance from the fact that on the whole we do tend to prioritize what historians and other pronouncers say rather than what they do not say. Part of the explanation for that tendency is surely that we recognize that pronouncers cannot say everything, but another part is that it is more difficult to make positive inferences about what they 'mean' by exclusions than by those things that they do attend to. It is easier to engage with what is said and, when one has prose to refer to, one can point positively to the grounds for one's inferences, rather than speculating as to the reason for and character of omissions. Nonetheless a rich history of hermeneutic reading techniques and rhetorical argumentative techniques reminds us of the structuring role of absences as well as presences. The expression 'constitutive silences' encapsulates the point.[37] Historians can write what they wish, given empirical warrant, but that is not the end of the matter. They may still be held accountable by readers who recognize that the written account is constituted as much by what it omits as what it includes, and who may find certain exclusions bewildering, suggestive, or downright suspicious.

The intellectual problems arising from a focus on particular agent perspectives have a moral element insofar as they pertain to justification in its moral sense. *Mein Kampf* is, we can infer, an expression of Hitler's world-view, and since it is in his own words it is a particularly important document. Yet while it is important to transmit the content of Hitler's views on 'Jewish conspiracy' or social Darwinism because it helps explain what he did when in power, it would be strange indeed were the historian of Hitler's beliefs effectively just to precis the relevant parts of *Mein Kampf* as opposed to providing some additional, externalized perspective on why Hitler subscribed to such beliefs—an account which could not but highlight that some of his beliefs were not justified. In *The European Civil War* (1987), the conservative scholar Ernst Nolte depicted Germany's invasion of the USSR in 1941 as a sort of pre-emptive strike, effectively a self-defensive action, and in the way he related Soviet crimes in the 1930s with the Holocaust, he gave the impression of assimilating his perspective as investigator to that of Hitler, or of Nazism.[38] Nolte seemed not just to be saying that the Nazis felt themselves justified in their actions—which scarcely distinguishes them from most warmongers and mass murderers and anyone else—but that in some sense they were justified, objectively. This is what the Turkish justifiers do in the Armenian case, alongside their denial.

One needs to be clear about whose perspective is whose, and on that front Robert J. McMahon's generally excellent *History of the Cold War* has a problematic passage:

> When the Soviets dispatched military equipment and technicians to support the fledgling regime of Patrice Lumumba, the Americans dispatched an assassination team in an unsuccessful attempt to dispose of the embattled Lumumba, an ardent nationalist whom they wrongly tagged as a wild-eyed radical and Russian stalking-horse, In 1961, pro-American Congolese forces murdered Lumumba...at the same time, Joseph Mobuto, America's favoured candidate, emerged as the dominant figure in a new Congo government. The United States thus managed temporarily to thwart Soviet ambitions in central Africa, if at the cost of imposing Cold War geopolitics on an impoverished, strife-torn former colony.[39]

---

[37] The name most recently and famously associated with reading for absences is Jacques Derrida.
[38] Ernst Nolte, *Der europäische Bürgerkrieg 1917–1945* (Berlin: Propyläen, 1987).
[39] Robert J. McMahon, *The Cold War* (Oxford: Oxford University Press, 2003), 85, 88.

In the first sentence McMahon establishes the 'internal' American perspective of the time on Lumumba whilst applying an external perspective that suggests the inaccuracy of that American view. By the first clause of the final sentence McMahon brings the external perspective into line with the internal American perspective, implying that the internal perspective was accurate, and thus that the US successfully thwarted an actual threat. But then in the second clause of the final sentence McMahon returns to the corrective form of the external perspective, as he states that the US, not Lumumba or the Soviets, 'impos[ed] Cold War geopolitics' on Congo. Knowing what really went on here is not unimportant in understanding the Cold War, the course of Congolese history, and subsequent attitudes to US neo-imperialism. Knowledge of CIA perspectives is a contribution to historical knowledge but so is the contention that those outlooks were incorrect, if we have evidence to believe that they were. Both the understanding of the perspective and understanding of the mistakenness of the perspective contribute to the historian's composite and give it a different tint to that which it would have had were the matter explored no further than to the point of claiming that American actors believed themselves justified in trying to assassinate a foreign leader and then supporting his overthrow.

The relationship between causal explanation and assessment of moral responsibility is always close to the surface in the historiography of the Cold War and its origins. Given that so much of the debate revolves around each superpower's understanding of the other's intentions and actions, it is incumbent upon historians to be maximally clear about what they are claiming in any given instance. 'Was it justified?' is a different question to 'did the relevant actors feel it was justified?' In principle historians can make the relevant distinctions as they deploy internal and external perspectives; in practice it may well be difficult to make those distinctions given the role of perception, but under such circumstances the historian must not muddy the water even further. In another generally excellent study, this time of superpower confrontation in South East Asia, Steven Hugh Lee alternates between invoking an objective 'communist threat' or 'Soviet threat'[40] and a more subjective 'perceived [US] need to undermine the bases of Soviet power', culminating in a confusing blend of the objective and the subjective: 'a perceived need to counter the increasing global threat of the Soviet empire'.[41] The problem for the reader is not understanding what American actors perceived, but rather understanding what Lee is claiming in explanation and justification of those perceptions.

The competing influence of two old historiographical traditions can still be detected in the 'debate' about perspectives. Embodying one tradition we have the

---

[40] Steven Hugh Lee, *Outposts of Empire: Korea, Vietnam and the Origins of the Cold War in Asia, 1949–1954* (Liverpool: Liverpool University Press, 1995), 3, 4, 5.
[41] Lee, *Outposts of Empire*, 8, 9.

likes of Agathias of Myrina with his conviction that the very 'physiognomy of events suggests praise or blame'. Agathias was writing in the spirit of the major Greek and Roman historians before him and many medieval historians afterwards as they recorded worldly events with a view especially to the exemplary quality of notable deeds that would ring down the ages. Let us call this a more externalist tradition. The other tradition we may call internalist. It was the hermeneutic tradition of interpretation developed by theologians as they read sacred texts in pursuit of religious meaning. Over time the hermeneutic approach was applied to a much wider range of actual texts and human activities and then the texts of other cultures and their other creative objectifications, like art and architecture. Hermeneutics was vital in shaping traditions of historical source criticism and indeed the techniques of interpretative anthropology. Worldly objectifications of meaning are the starting point of the inquiry, and the hermeneut then works backwards inferentially to the minds or cultures which produced them.

The two traditions are not quite opposites, but tensions may arise between them in virtue of their significantly different priorities. We may detect the influence of the 'internalist' hermeneutic tradition in the thought of the historically minded philosopher Martin Heidegger as he denigrated the 'ocular' perspective.[42] In Collingwood's influential account of the historical discipline, the historian's investigation 'may begin by discovering the outside of an event, but it can never end there; he must always remember that the event was an action, and that his main task is to think himself into this action, to discern the thought of its agent'. Since 'all history is the history of thought', the object must be the 'inside' or 'thought-side' of events rather than the 'outside' in the sense of things that might be 'described in terms of bodies and their movements'. For the hermeneutic philosopher Wilhelm Dilthey, the key was 'the movement of understanding from the external to the internal', to 'what is inaccessible to the senses and can only be experienced inwardly', away from the 'outer clamour of history'.[43] Historical events were 'a manifestation of the mind in the world of the senses', but the quest was for the mind beyond the world of the senses.[44] The medievalist R. J. W. Southern described 'the valuable deposit of the past' as comprising people's 'thoughts and visions, moods and emotions and devotions'.[45] The contemporary historian of emotions Susan J. Matt enjoins recovering 'the history of subjectivity', uncovering 'intention, motivation, and values that might be invisible if only external behav-

---

[42] Martin Heidegger, *Sein und Zeit* (Tübingen: Niemeyer, 1967), 400: the expression 'okularen Bestimmung', ocular ascertainment, was that of Count Paul Yorck von Wartenburg.

[43] Parts of Collingwood and Dilthey cited in Mark Salber Philips, 'Distance and Historical Representation', *History Workshop Journal* 57 (2004) 123–41, here 134. Other Collingwood citations and context from Collingwood, *The Idea of History*, 213, 315–20.

[44] Esteve Morera, *Gramsci's Historicism: A Realist Interpretation* (Abingdon: Routledge, 1990), 16.

[45] R. W. Southern, *History and Historians: Selected Papers of R. W. Southern*, ed. R. J. Bartlett (Oxford: Blackwell, 2004), 100.

iors...are traced'.[46] All well and good, but there is a rub if the preoccupation is with accessing the inner meanings of authors, actors, and architects: the rub is that objectifications of motives and meanings may be inscribed on other people's corpses as well as landscape, canvas, or vellum. A worker's crooked spine is an objectification of a particular system of labour. Acts may structure the existence of other parties: one man's internally stimulated behaviour is another's experience of a blow received; one group's quest for resources to sustain itself is another group's eviction or servitude. A victim of domestic violence might be one of patriarchy's objectifications. She is also a subject with her own interiority, conceptualizations, and capacity for suffering and ascribing meaning to her experiences. Just how problematic indenture to some authorial or internal perspective can be varies with the sort of History in question.

Let us create another heuristic distinction, this time between historians who focus more on change and its causes and those who focus more on the texture of life at any given point in the past. We might parse the distinction as that between Histories of doing and Histories of being. Histories of doing/cause and of being/lived texture cover most if not all historianship. Given the focus on texture, the relative importance of actors disappears. Any person or group, no matter what their relative power status, is as eligible for consideration as anyone else in terms of how they lived and experienced bits of life, how they felt about their situation, and so forth. To put it differently, once one is concerned with texture and the experience thereof, one may be concerned with subjectivity or internality purely for its own sake. It jars, however, if the historian of cause restricts her interest entirely to the subjective realm of relatively powerful agents, given that we tend to be interested in such agents in the first place because of what they brought on others through their power.

Event-oriented historians work back inferentially from an event in order to locate its causes, in a way that is analogous to hermeneuts contemplating the meanings that drove the creation of their texts, but the endeavour is only given its impetus by some sense of the significance of the event under explanation, just as the inquiry into the 'mind' or milieu of the artist begins with the painting she produced. Where does this sense of the event's significance come from? There are many sources: if the sense is not provided in the selfsame History that examines the causes, it may issue from other works of History, or from collective memory which may be informed by anything from films to memorials to educational curricula. Some events are well known, and accorded significance in the public sphere, others not. We have suggested that one can find books that address the causes of the First World War with little reference to the slaughter of the Somme, or the legacy of the war in international relations, but it is the fact of battles like

---

[46] Susan J. Matt, 'Current Emotion Research in History: Or, Doing History from the Inside Out', *Emotion Review* 3/1 (2011), 117–24, here 118.

the Somme, or the war's legacy, that fires so much interest in the causes and invests them with such significance, moral and otherwise. By the same token a great deal of antiquarian inquiry into the minutiae of the conflict stems from a belief in reflected significance, and this is if anything even more true of the Second World War. In any given historical inquiry that discusses some outcome or the causes of that outcome, the historian will need to establish a claim on the outcome's significance unless she assumes an existing appreciation of its significance among her audience. Perhaps she will wish to assert a certain significance as opposed to a pre-existing estimation of significance. Any assertion of significance, whether from scratch or corrective in nature, and whether deflationary or inflationary in its evaluative implications, will have to deploy its own externalized evocative terms to describe the event and/or to orchestrate its own evocative illustration of the impact of the event on parties in the past by deploying the 'voices' of those parties. And whether asserting or assuming significance, the historian is already 'in the significance game'; she is trading on significance, whether she recognizes it or not.

Let us say that an attribution of historical causal responsibility takes into account, as it should, the contexts within which this responsibility was accrued. Depending upon the assumed or asserted character of the event caused, or act authored, such contextualization might be tantamount to justification, mitigation, or aggravation of the actor's behaviour according to certain inferable local standards, in accordance with the practice of moral contextualization. But it does not follow in principle or in widespread practice that descriptions of the acts themselves, or their consequences, are aligned evocatively/evaluatively to the 'terms' of the authors of the acts, any more than the imputed significance or appreciation of a work of art is necessarily aligned to an understanding of the artist. Take the sentence: 'For reasons now to be explored heretics were persecuted by Church and State in the high Middle Ages.' It would be hard to argue that 'persecution' was not an appropriate term for what the authorities embarked upon and the heretics were exposed to—they were targeted collectively on grounds of their beliefs. As such, we can say that labelling something as persecution catches something inferable about the past. But 'persecution' is manifestly evocative of evaluation: nobody, including those who think it a good thing, stands neutral to it. Perhaps the sentence could be supplemented by: 'Heretics were persecuted by Church and State in the high Middle Ages because the authorities viewed the heretics as a threat to Christian society and suspected that if the tables were turned the heretics would have engaged in their own persecution.' Here we have a mitigating, in some eyes justificatory, contextual explanation of the Church's actions. That explanation could further be modified to make reference to the centralizing, regulating agenda of the Church and of various States at the time. Each modification enhances the understanding while giving a different tint to the explanation of motivation, but either way the descriptive-evaluative word 'persecution' remains to attribute a particular character to the Church's actions against the heretics, as in the perfectly appropriate adjective in the title of R. I. Moore's *The Formation of a Persecuting Society: Authority and Deviance in Western Europe 950–1250* (1987).

Legitimacy Contests in the Past

'Legitimate', like 'illegitimate', is one of those concept-terms that is at once descriptive and evaluative. Like all such terms it can be used directly or its meaning can be alluded to, so the coming discussion is not limited to cases where the word is deployed.[47] McMahon's *History of the Cold War* exemplifies the allusive route in a tacitly evaluative and eminently justifiable conclusion, as it distinguishes 'between a Soviet empire that was essentially imposed on much of Eastern Europe and an American empire [in Western Europe] that resulted from a partnership born of common security fears and overlapping economic needs'.[48]

The concept of legitimacy has far broader reach than the sense of modern democratic legitimacy, as Montesquieu observed against the conceits of the European social contract theories of his age.[49] In medieval Europe the concept of the just king was associated with the king's executing his mandate to rule in a spirit appropriate to someone acting as God's trustee. Later on, monarchs claiming the divine right of kings were still at least notionally constrained by the precepts of divine or natural law. In China the concept of the 'Mandate of Heaven' has existed for about 3,000 years and is related to the concept of a just ruler rather than inhering in the person of whoever happens to be ruling. To be sure, the doctrine served the instrumental interests of successful insurgents who wished to claim legitimacy for their fait accompli and imply possession of a divine mandate to rule. But such legitimacy claims are always double-edged: the very implication that power could legitimately be wrested under certain circumstances tied rulers to certain precepts. When the concept of the Mandate was established, as the West Zhou dynasty (1100–771 BCE) supplanted the Shang dynasty, the Zhou leaders claimed 'heaven does not favour anybody; only morality makes heaven trust you'.[50]

---

[47] The historian David M. Potter was making a closely related point about the relation between description and evaluation in this connection when he wrote: 'it is a paradox not generally recognized that the historian cannot make a simple descriptive observation about the degree of group cohesion among an aggregate of people without inadvertently registering a valuative judgment as to the validity of the powers that this aggregation may assert for itself. If he were applying a standard of ethics, it would be recognized at once as a valuative standard, but since he seemingly applies only a measure of relationships, it is easy to overlook the valuative implications.' Potter, 'The Historian's Use of Nationalism and Vice Versa', *American Historical Review* 67 (1962), 924–50, here 929.

[48] McMahon, *The Cold War*, 33.

[49] A point made and nuanced in Plamenatz, *Man and Society*, i. 262–3. See also John Macmurray, *Persons in Relation* (London: Faber and Faber, 1995), ch. 9.

[50] Yanqi Tong and Shaohua Lei, *Social Protest in Contemporary China, 2003–2010: Transitional Pains and Regime Legitimacy* (Abingdon: Routledge, 2014), 28.

As with concepts like deceit or cowardice, historians will be aware that different standards of legitimacy obtained at different times, and, given evidence as to the nature of the standards, historians will be able to make the relevant adjustments in assessing its presence or absence. This section reflects on the conditions by which a historian might infer that a given dispensation was legitimate or not. As with 'deceit' and 'cowardice', the conclusion will still have an evaluative quality whose valence is not quarantined to the past in question. As with 'persecution', the conclusion as to legitimacy cannot just be a function of what the powerful party felt was appropriate. With its emphasis on the contestation of standards within the past, this section serves as a conclusion to Part 2 and a segue into Part 3.

It is understandable that those who wish to downplay the evaluative nature of their undertaking or have just not considered the evaluative implications will assert or assume legitimacy and then move on swiftly to discuss other matters 'neutrally' against that tacit backdrop. Sometimes they will surely be correct in their assertions or assumptions. Yet at other times they might be subscribing to what we can call the historicist fallacy, which is one of two almost opposing errors in the consideration of legitimacy in societies past. The historicist fallacy is that tendency whereby referring to some act or arrangement in the context of its time is effectively an injunction to understand it as being *legitimated* by its authorship there and then, rather than its merely being conceivable, which is axiomatic.

There was an appropriation of Darwin that assumed moral improvement over time, by which logic the latest form of life must be morally superior to its predecessors. This book does its bit towards further discrediting that idea (see pp. 234–6). But there was an equally problematic competing appropriation of Darwin that played on the concept of niche adaptation. This appropriation can be traced back at least as far as the nineteenth-century historian and critic Hippolyte Taine.[51] For a more recent version of the position, take *The Evolution of English Justice* (1999) by Anthony Musson and W. M. Ormrod. They applaud the 'neutral stance which judges change by its success or failure in adapting to new environmental conditions'. Quoting biologist Stephen Jay Gould, they ask rhetorically, 'if an amoeba is as well adapted to its environment as we are to ours, who is to say that we are higher creatures?' They describe their stance as one of 'moral neutrality' for the historian. They do not address why it might not be appropriate to treat human social arrangements in the way that one might treat amoebas' evolutionary adjustments.[52] Far from being 'neutral' as to values, this sort of niche-thinking

---

[51] Martha Wolfenstein, 'The Social Background of Taine's Philosophy of Art', *Journal of the History of Ideas* 5/3 (1944), 332–58, here 339–40.

[52] In fact there are a number of tensions in their words, which make it hard to identify any underlying philosophy except a standard rejection of judgementalism. They find that 'moral neutrality has particular advantages for the study of later medieval English law, since fourteenth century political rhetoric was often preoccupied with a perceived deterioration of public order and the apparent

can lead to an almost naturalistic legitimation in the sense of saying that values and arrangements X were *ipso facto* appropriate for place-time Y because they evolved there. Durkheim took this position when claiming: 'History has established that, except in abnormal cases, each society has in the main a morality suited to it, and that any other would not only be impossible but also fatal to the society which attempted to follow it.'[53] Likewise the American social scientist W. G. Sumner (1840–1910) in his classic *Folkways*: 'Everything in the mores of a time and place must be regarded as justified with regard to that time and place.' 'Hence our judgments of the good or evil consequences of folkways are to be kept separate from our study of the historical phenomena of them, and of their strength and the reasons for it. The judgements have their place in plans and doctrines for the future, not in a retrospect.'[54]

Ranke partook of a version of this niche-thinking: when he described every epoch as 'immediate unto God' and each as equidistant from eternity,[55] at the same time as validating other ways of life in the past, he was effectively giving absolute sanction to his social order in its actions in the present. To remove the self-serving element while staying true to the more inclusive side of Ranke's prescription, let us replace the idea that all social orders are perforce divinely approved with the idea that no given social arrangement was/is privileged in and of itself just by virtue of existing. Unless we historians believe in divine warrant for this or that social arrangement, we need to avoid any implication that, for instance, negative attitudes towards acts or dispositions that we now term homosexual, or positive attitudes towards chattel slavery, just are appropriate to a certain time or place. These attitudes never 'just' existed—they were brought into being out of situations in which they were only one possibility among others.

---

reduction in the will, or the capacity, of the crown to deliver justice to its subjects...It has been accepted for some time, however, that increasing public criticism is no real measure of the supposed failure of the late medieval judicial system: indeed, as K. B. McFarlane pointed out, it can actually imply the exact opposite, by signifying that society had higher expectations of that system and was more conditioned to working with, rather than against, it. Evolution theory here allows us to avoid assumptions about whether the judicial system became either "better" or "worse" in the course of the fourteenth century, and instead calls for a more objective assessment of the extent to which the law and its agencies, as social institutions, adapted successfully to the environmental changes going on around them.' Despite the authors' disavowal, their language in the final sentence is shot through with tones of evaluation according to standards of 'success': how is success to be judged other than by better and worse approximations to whatever the standard in question? They equate moral neutrality with the possibility of 'objective assessment' of whether such standards are attained, which is not obviously a stance of neutrality. Prejudicially, they equate moral non-neutrality with 'assumptions' instead of with substantiated reasoning. Indeed, whilst combating negative evaluation they open the door to positive evaluation with an example of McFarlane's sophisticated evaluative reasoning. Musson and Ormrod, *The Evolution of English Justice: Law, Politics and Society in the Fourteenth Century* (Basingstoke: Macmillan, 1999), 4–5.

[53] Émile Durkheim, *Sociology and Philosophy* (1906; New York: The Free Press, 1953), 56.
[54] W. G. Sumner, *Folkways* (1906; New York: Dover Publications, 1959), 58–9.
[55] Daniel Fulda, *Wissenschaft aus Kunst: Die Entstehung der modernen deutschen Geschichtsschreibung, 1760–1860* (Berlin: de Gruyter, 1996) 183–4.

Lord Acton (1834–1902), a historian often dismissed as a moralist, was alert to the problem of automatically privileging successful dispensations. If all value is relative to local, historical, norms then is it just a matter, as Lenin put it, of *ktokogo?*—who (rules) whom?—and gets to determine the prevailing norms.[56] The philosopher of science Karl Popper called it moral positivism, or 'the theory that there is no moral standard but the one which exists; that what is, is reasonable and good'.[57] Popper might as well have had in mind the historian Thomas Carlyle, who wrote that 'all goes by wager of battle in this world' and 'strength, well understood, is the measure of all worth. Give a thing time; if it can succeed, it is a right thing.'[58] E. H. Carr sometimes echoed Carlyle from a very different political position.[59]

Knee-jerk legitimation, stemming from an undiscriminating fear of anachronism, can produce entertaining results. In autumn 2008 the British justice secretary was petitioned to grant posthumous pardons to the women and men executed for witchcraft in Britain between the sixteenth and eighteenth centuries. Two years before, the British Government had created a precedent for such action by granting posthumous pardons to British soldiers executed during the First World War for cowardice, when some may well have been suffering from neurasthenia ('shell-shock'). The historian Geoffrey Alderman provided what he must have assumed to be an authoritative historian's perspective on an illegitimate politicization of History. He objected to the principle of posthumous action, asserting that all of 'those executed for desertion remain guilty as charged'. As to the witches: 'whatever the outcome of the petition invoked on their behalf, [they] remain, in historical terms, as guilty as hell'. What was 'then' considered ' "right" may now be considered very wrong', he argued, and such pardons amount to the use of contemporary 'law to rewrite history'.[60] At one level the debate revolves around what we understand by 'guilty'. If we mean guilty in the eyes of the law or the State then of course these 'witches' and oft-shell-shocked soldiers were guilty. But the same would be true today of someone successfully framed for murder by corrupt policemen. If, however, we mean 'guilty because they did what they were accused of', whether that be desertion because of cowardice or the practising of witchcraft, then, along with our framed 'murderer', some of the soldiers and most if not all of the 'witches' were not guilty. It may well be that some of the soldiers were simple deserters, and Alderman is correct that in these cases the men did what was charged of them and with the appropriate *mens rea*, or guilty state of mind. All that that illustrates, however, is the existence, on one hand, of a fact of

---

[56] Lord Acton, *Historical Essays and Studies* (London: Macmillan, 1908), 436–7.

[57] Karl Raimund Popper, *The Open Society and Its Enemies*, ii (London: Routledge, 2003), 227.

[58] Thomas Carlyle, *Heroes and Hero Worship*, repr. in Carlyle, *Sartor Resartus, Heroes and Hero-Worship, Past and Present*, ed. G. T. Bettany (London: Ward, Lock and co., 1892), 105.

[59] For a nuanced treatment, see Jonathan Haslam, *The Vices of Integrity: E. H. Carr, 1892–1982* (London: Verso, 1999), ch. 8.

[60] Geoffrey Alderman, 'The Witching Hour Has Passed', *The Guardian*, 3 November 2008.

the matter, namely whether people had practised witchcraft or deserted through fear. On the other hand, there are only competing beliefs about that fact of the matter, some of which were and are correct and some of which were and are not. What happened in the past, as far as we can tell, is that courts sometimes found people guilty for things that they had not done or had not done with the *mens rea* that the courts claimed. No harm is done to the past to acknowledge that, as if it were anyway possible to change the past. No one proposed to deny that the courts made the decision they did, or to locate seventeenth-century trial manuscripts in the British National Archives, cross out guilty verdicts, and replace them with the opposite. This is not the same as Stalinists airbrushing murdered former colleagues out of photographs to pretend that they had never been comrades in the first place.

The path to Alderman's conceptual misunderstanding was paved not just by a misplaced fear of anachronism but also by an equally misplaced sense of what 'proper' historical understanding must involve in the sphere of moral discourse. In Alderman's failure to distinguish a fact of the matter from one perspective on the matter, he adopts the view of dominant forces in the past. We are left with a peculiar legal-moral positivism retrojected: if a state once declared that Catherine was an artichoke, then Catherine was indeed an artichoke, and must be remembered as such. What the dominant power decreed was ipso facto correct.

While it would be bizarre to pretend that every society had the same set-up and values, and pointless to suggest that they should have done, that does not mean one needs to opt for Darwinian niche-thinking or Alderman's peculiar legal positivism, and nor ought it lead to embracing a roughly opposite error. That faulty alternative is the vulgar Marxism that sees all claims to legitimacy as the camouflaged expression of some sectional interest. Such Marxism carries with it the tacit allegation that legitimacy is/was not real legitimacy and accuses those masses who accept the claim to the legitimacy of an order of suffering from false consciousness. This line of thought suffers from at least one of two significant problems, one empirical, the other conceptual. Insofar as the Marxist makes a claim about false consciousness, or an inauthentic 'second nature', he must have some claim on what real consciousness or an 'authentic' outlook would look like, but such a claim has no empirical grounding since humans are not available for interrogation in a pre-socialized state. The claim may merely reflect the Marxist's own preferences. When the vulgar Marxist makes a claim to the effect that social orders are held together by a species of moral propaganda for governing material interests, then he is cutting off the branch on which he sits insofar as he tries to make the case for a truly legitimate new order. He has already undermined the idea of there being any such thing as true legitimacy to which to appeal. This self-undermining is a problem of 'crypto-normativity'.

Crypto-normativity is also a characteristic of the work of the philosopher-historian Michel Foucault. In his descriptive mode he differed from the early

Marx in denying the existence of a real consciousness that is subverted by false consciousness. There was, he claimed, no given nature of the human, only varying conceptions of what it is to be human that were produced by historically contingent ways of conceiving the human. In many ways this was just a restatement of a sociological commonplace that humans are products of differing societies, but Foucault gave a particular character to his discussion of subjectivity by relating it to the workings of power. He conceptualized power in a specific way, especially by relating it to a web of interlocking knowledge-claims in the human sciences from psychiatry to economics, claims that he called 'discourses'. In his best-known conceptualization he also attributed power a dispersed, impersonal, invisible character. (Towards the end of his life Foucault implied a more commonplace conception of power that militated against the impression of his work on power-knowledge.[61]) This Foucauldian power is cryptic: it doesn't chain you to a galley bench or have you beheaded but it speaks through you and makes you, eliciting consent and creating the conditions for you to be free—which may, again, just be a way of stating the banal truth that freedom presupposes a structure within which it can be exercised. For Foucault at that stage of his work, all we are left with is power-effects. For the individual whose subjectivity is constituted by 'discourse', or 'power-knowledge', those effects quite simply comprise reality and its social features like morality. Yet while he made these descriptive claims Foucault also manifested a marked distaste for modern regimes of power, both in his historical work, in which for instance he took sides with those individuals subjected to new psychiatric and institutional regimes when the asylum was born, and in his later prescriptive work on resisting regimes of power-knowledge and engaging in liberationist acts of self-creation. His crypto-normativity is manifest in the way his prescriptive views and his evocative historical accounts undermined his claim to be presenting a view of power as disinterested and neutral. His concern with the subjectivity-creating effects of power raised the unanswered question of the justificatory basis of his own critical stance towards that power, which left him in this respect in the same conceptual dilemma as the vulgar Marxists.[62]

At the descriptive level one may contest Foucauldian claims about the cunning and subtlety of power, for instance by reference to James C. Scott's work on the failure of sundry centralized state 'modernization' projects.[63] Power may be blind, even foolish, getting away with those shortcomings only because in the last

---

[61] See the distinctly 'old-fashioned' connotations of Foucault's account of power in Michel Foucault, *Ethics: Subjectivity and Truth*, ed. Paul Rabinow (New York: The New Press, 1997), 296–9.

[62] On crypto-normativity, Jürgen Habermas, *The Philosophical Discourse of Modernity* (Cambridge, MA: MIT Press, 1990); Nancy Fraser, 'Foucault on Modern Power: Empirical Insights and Normative Confusions', *Praxis International* 1/3 (1981), 272–87. Jonathan Hearn, *Theorizing Power* (Houndmills: Palgrave, 2012) 91–2, 104–5 on domination and on Steven Lukes's claim that Foucault often really just deployed ordinary sociological concepts in radical-sounding ways.

[63] James C. Scott, *Seeing Like a State: How Certain Schemes to Improve the Human Condition Have Failed* (New Haven: Yale University Press, 1998).

instance it just can, simply in virtue of its coercive capacity and the prohibitive costs of challenging it. For those nobles and English churchly chroniclers who could only conceive of the mobilized peasantry of 1381 as an animalistic rabble instrumentalized by a devious leadership, the unappreciated truth of the sophistication of the movement made no difference to its quashing. And that is not just a medieval challenge from before the age of sophisticated modern power-discourse: think of the 'shock therapy' visited upon the transitioning Soviet Russian economy at the end of the Cold War. The 'shock and awe' campaign inflicted on Iraq in 2003 was by name tribute to what Foucauldians would call a premodern theatrical display of power, overt rather than covert, and is appropriate to that least subtle instantiation of force, the bomb.[64] The invasion was 'justified' in a way that was manifestly half baked, and it was succeeded by a murderous chaos that many a specialist had warned of but no one in power cared to hear about. Iraq prompts two deflationary retorts to the self-appointed speaker of truth to power, and while one is in some sense Foucauldian—what makes you think that power doesn't already know?—the other is: what makes you think power cares?

Sometimes power cares, and sometimes not, but explaining that distinction is impossible without a subdivision of power's instantiations. What of power that is wielded openly, either because its wielders hope that their main constituency is not sufficiently troubled to protest too long and loud or because the wielders have some mandate, i.e. some legitimacy, predicated on 'authority' in political philosopher Hannah Arendt's sense as something conceptually prior to power?[65] Without a concept of legitimacy, which Foucault gave little attention to, one cannot make any critique of, say, the invasion of Iraq as illegitimate, because the concept of illegitimacy is parasitic on that of legitimacy.

Basic questions to be asked of any distinctly Foucauldian conception of power must pertain to the possibility of resistance worthy of the name—i.e. resistance that is not itself already subsumed or inevitably to be subsumed by the power regime it seeks to challenge.[66] Such questions must, by extension, address not just power's production or self-representation, but its consumption, rejection, or manipulation by its putative objects. Think of some of the subjects of Scott's work, who lead us to the conclusion that it is not a matter of fighting *against* some omnipresent but intangible 'power', but fighting *with* power and *for* it, against

---

[64] On 'shock and awe', and other relevant examples, Raewyn Connell, 'Northern Theory: The Political Geography of General Social Theory', *Theory and Society* 35/2 (2006), 237–64, here 261.

[65] Arendt, *Between Past and Future*, ch. 3.

[66] The Foucauldian formula that power implies resistance (Foucault, *Ethics: Subjectivity and Truth*, 292–3) does not do the work often claimed for it in Foucauldian rejoinders to allegations of the irresistibility of power in Foucault's best-known conceptualization of it. It is true that, as opposites in some discursive settings, power and resistance each imply the existence of the other, as is true of legitimacy and illegitimacy, night and day, and so forth. But while saying that one concept implies the existence of its opposite works at the level of conceptual possibility, this does not mean it works in any given empirical case. Thus if I say that someone is dead, I am implying the concept of life of which the dead person is bereft, but I am not saying that the person is actually still slightly alive.

other instantiations and possessors of it, however asymmetric such battles can be.[67] Such work also reminds us, in the face of any crypto-normative critique of power as such, that the state of *powerlessness* is scarcely desirable. While the possession of power is not a criterion of the good it is a condition of achieving the good in the world beyond the mind.[68]

Among what Scott calls the 'weapons of the weak' is the ability to use established norms and rules against those who seek at any moment to bend them too far for their own purposes, on the basis that all political systems carry with them some constraint of power, whether axiomatic or customary. On resistance more generally, Scott's work reveals a 'secret dossier' of transactions in which subaltern groups seek the best way to mitigate the impact of regimes of power on their lives, and even to exploit the small opportunities for criticism and subversion. Study of medieval carnivals shows that the authorities who allowed these festivals as ways of permitting the peasantry to let off steam ultimately had to clamp down on the unusual freedom of expression thus permitted; the upshot was yet further manoeuvring by the peasantry as part of an unequal but ongoing conversation about the prerogatives of official power.[69] Legitimacy's dual-edged character is apparent in the vocabulary to which authorities had to subscribe to justify their actions, and in their furious attempts to delegitimize the most serious challenges to them, as, say, in 1381. Authorities could stretch and modify the vocabulary of legitimacy but not overstretch or discard it. The very idea that the vocabulary could be contested presupposes competing interests that acted upon it rather than the nature of interest simply being dictated by it.

An alternative to knee-jerk legitimation à la Alderman or Sumner and to crypto-normative delegitimation à la Foucault is to consider dispensations of power and systems of value as contested social matters. However people view their society, they tend not to view it neutrally. As long as social power has existed, thus throughout the history of human societies, so has the scope to use it in different ways, and so have contemporary perceptions about whether it is used more or less well and more or less justly, and whether its underlying principles are agreeable or objectionable.[70] It is not an invention of the contemporary world to distinguish between fairer and more corrupt officials, more and less equitable rules, more and less exploitative or capricious leaders.

The alternative position adopted here incorporates some of the thought of the Marxist Antonio Gramsci, although it accords more attention to legitimacy in the

---

[67] James C. Scott, *Weapons of the Weak: Everyday Forms of Peasant Resistance* (New Haven: Yale University Press, 1985).

[68] Hearn, *Theorizing Power*, makes this point about powerlessness.

[69] Scott, *Weapons of the Weak*; C. Humphrey, *The Politics of Carnival: Festive Misrule in Medieval England* (Manchester: Manchester University Press, 2001).

[70] Colin Richmond, 'Mickey Mouse in Disneyland: How Did the Fifteenth Century Get That Way?', in Linda Clark (ed.), *The Fifteenth Century*, v. *Of Mice and Men: Image, Belief and Regulation in Late Medieval England* (Woodbridge: Boydell Press, 2005), 157–70, here 166.

way already characterized. Gramsci believed that there are always at least two hegemonies actually or incipiently in conflict. By hegemony, he meant not just domination by hard power, but rule by control of the moral tone, which puts him at a point on the road between the Marxists who talk of false consciousness and Foucault's sociology. Gramsci did not use 'hegemony' consistently, seeing it some-times as dependent upon consent and at other times on coercion; but his point was its instability, and here is where this section's interest in legitimacy contests kicks in.[71] Morality and would-be hegemonic dispensations are rarely coexten-sive. Things change, morality, laws, economic practices, ruling factions, etc., and not always in the same rhythms, so even in the event that at any moment the logic of the dominant social dispensation overlaps morality entirely, it is yet more unlikely that that situation will last. The society with consistently perfect overlap we would call the fully integrated society. It may be that there is a tendency towards full integration. There are good functional reasons for the tendency: pre-dictability, replicability, and harmony of social behaviour. Yet the completely inte-grated social system that possesses no internal potential for conflict is an ideal model not a reality. The same goes for the feared state of anomie at the other end of the spectrum.[72]

The best-integrated orders, one might expect, are to be found in societies of relatively small scale in relative isolation—those which figure less in occidental historiography than in anthropological inquiry. But complete integration still has to be substantiated rather than assumed, and such assumptions have often been shown to be the product of a rather orientalist assumption about certain peoples living in a timeless stasis, rather than deep acquaintance with such societies.[73] Some of the same stereotypes have also been applied to the pre-modern, aka 'traditional', occident. Consider the following from the social historian Edward Shorter:

> By 'traditional' I refer to European rural and small-town society between 1500 and 1700. It was a period of cultural homogeneity in which all popular strata behaved more or less the same, having similar social and sexual values, the same concepts of authority and hierarchy, and an identical appreciation of custom and tradition in their primary social goal, the maintenance of static community life.[74]

---

[71] Perry Anderson, 'The Antinomies of Antonio Gramsci', *New Left Review* 1/100 (1976), 5–78.

[72] John Rex, *Key Problems of Sociological Theory* (London: Routledge, 1961), 102–5.

[73] 'If social and cultural distinctiveness and mutual separation were a hallmark of humankind, one would expect to find it most easily among the so-called primitives, people "without history," suppos-edly isolated from the external world and from one another.' Thus wrote the anthropologist Eric Wolf, before going on to show how much this expectation, which is related to the assumption of complete integration, was thwarted by the empirics. Eric Wolf, *Europe and the 'People Without History'* (Berkeley and Los Angeles: University of California Press, 2010), 4.

[74] Shorter, 'Illegitimacy, Sexual Revolution and Social Change in Modern Europe', in Theodore K. Rabb and Robert I. Rotberg (eds), *Marriage and Fertility: Studies in Interdisciplinary History* (Princeton: Princeton University Press, 1980), 65–120, here 88.

This vision of social History with politics replaced by herd mentality may be contrasted with the accounts of rural discontent in one European country in that period by the historian Andy Wood, whose titles are self-explanatory: *The 1549 Rebellions and the Making of Early Modern England* and *The Politics of Social Conflict: The Peak Country, 1520–1770*.[75]

The inconstancy of values across time and place is held to be one of the main arguments against moral evaluation across time and place. The most powerful argument in that direction, the argument of relativism, will only be fully addressed in Part 3. For the moment let us note that a complication at least for some of the most influential relativisms is the contestedness of values *within* any given time and place. Even if some of the bases of morality might gain general recognition at any given time, emphases and applications may be in tension.

In the past, as now, the only thing needed to judge some arrangement as good, bad, just, or unjust, and thus potentially to stimulate a challenge to it, is some standard. That standard can come from any place, or any time. Perceptions of relative beneficence or justness may be shaped by (1) contrast with other communities, (2) contrast with the history of the same community, or (3) contrast with an imagined future. (The corresponding denunciations of the contrasters are (1) 'traitors!'; (2) 'nostalgiacs!'; (3) 'utopians!'.)[76] The historian Christopher Hill encapsulated the attitude of many Protestants in English society at the time of the Reformation when he wrote that the 'appeal to conscience against authority is an appeal to the present against the past. For the society in which men live forms their consciences, whereas authority gets fossilized in a set of institutions or writings'. But equally one could invoke the prerogatives of the past against the impositions of the present, as was the case with the miners of England's peak country in the mid-seventeenth century or the insurgent peasants of 1381 and 1549.[77] The economist Friedrich Hayek remarked at a very different historical juncture that the path was still blocked 'by the most fatuous of all fashionable arguments, namely, that "we cannot turn the clock back"', expressive of 'the fatalistic belief that we cannot learn from our mistakes'.[78]

In the past, as now, in the words of one social scientist:

Right and wrong, good and evil, justice, duty, conscience, are operational concepts, gripped into social action. Morality, then, is that system of rules and

---

[75] Published by Cambridge University Press in 2007 and 1999 respectively.

[76] I think Terry Eagleton made this point before me.

[77] Christopher Hill, *Reformation to Industrial Revolution* (London: Penguin, 1969), 199; Andy Wood, *The Politics of Social Conflict: The Peak Country, 1520–1770* (Cambridge: Cambridge University Press, 1999).

[78] F. A. Hayek, *The Constitution of Liberty* (London: Routledge and Kegan Paul, 1960), 284.

standards which gives significance to the activities of individuals in relation to one another in society.... It justifies conduct, even in opposition to major structural principles. Associated with the perception of inconsistencies in action, it may even set the seal on opposition as one of its social functions.[79]

Compare those words with Sumner's (p. 115):

For the men of the time there are no 'bad' mores. What is traditional and current is the standard of what ought to be. The masses never raise any question about such things. If a few raise doubts and questions, this proves that the folkways have already begun to lose firmness and the regulative element in the mores has begun to lose authority. This indicates that the folkways are on their way to a new adjustment.[80]

In Sumner's account impersonal forces have the agency and people follow where they lead. 'The times' mysteriously change, and with them people, rather than people (say, civil rights protestors) changing 'the times', which really means challenging what was considered to be acceptable at any given 'time'.

Knowledge of the contestation of principles and of legitimacy is necessary to the explanation of repression, but also of reform and revolution. If the once-influential theory of structuralism (pp. 215–6) proposed something like a biopsy of social order freeze-framed at any moment in time, then it perforce could not gauge which elements might be emergent, ascendant, or declining. It might give a false picture of harmony, mistaking a wrestling match for an embrace without the before and after of the snapshot, or it might imply complete success for some regime of power that was actually under imminent threat. The sociologist Pierre Bourdieu was in principle as alive as Friedrich Nietzsche had been to the problems of separating 'sociology and history', by which he meant synchronic and diachronic study. One 'cannot grasp the dynamics of a field ... without a historical, that is, a genetic, analysis of its constitution, and of the tensions that exist between positions in it'.[81] It is instructive that Foucault was weak at explaining change, whatever his avowed rejection of structuralism.

The philosopher Stephen Toulmin once provided his own thumbnail sketch of a development of morality whose function is 'to reconcile the independent aims and wills of a community of people' as that community emerges from a prior state

---

[79] Raymond Firth, *Elements of Social Organisation* (London: Watts, 1963), 213.

[80] Sumner, *Folkways*, 59.

[81] Pierre Bourdieu and Loïc Wacquant, *An Invitation to Reflexive Sociology* (Cambridge: Polity, 1992), 90. For an assessment of the way Bourdieu and Foucault dealt with the issue in practice, see Michel de Certeau, *The Practice of Everyday Life* (Berkeley and Los Angeles: University of California Press, 1988), ch. 4. Further on Foucault, Neil Brenner, 'Foucault's New Functionalism', *Theory and Society* 23 (1994), 679–709.

in which the motto is 'every man for himself'. In the communal arrangement, all 'the principles, which together make up a moral code, can be related to some institution within the society'. Every institution from the family to representative assemblies comprises a subsystem of duties and privileges, leading to actors within those institutions referring to things like 'My station and its duties'. One possibility is that 'those in effective control' of any of these institutions tries 'to "freeze" the moral code and institutions: to assert their absolute authority, to legislate for every possibility', to 'discourage independent speculation and the airing of grievances, and to provide a communal aim which the citizens must like— or lump'. Such an arrangement might well lead to disaffection from that particular idea of community and associated moral code: the very communally oriented 'development which first takes us from "Every man for himself" to "My station and its duties", leads us later to criticize the "duties" and "stations" as at present established, and to suggest changes'. This criticism may indeed lead to changes in moral codes and social institutions, but it might also lead to the hardening of the power-response. If that hardening process prevails over the desire for change, then it cannot be justified as a legitimate claim of the powerful, since it is 'the outcome of mutually contradictory desires'. The rulers 'want to insist on the citizens' fulfilling absolutely a set of "moral obligations" towards them, which, at the same time, they want to be excused from respecting towards the citizens—thus presenting in the guise of "morality" a collection of privileges without foundation in ethics'. Here it is the separation of a moral code from the social interactions that necessitated the code in the first place that render the code no longer moral in the sense its contemporaries claimed, if moral at all.[82]

This skeleton argument hints at the truth that might does not in and of itself make right. If only as a self-justification, power seeks the support of interpretations of the right and the good and so pays them vice's tribute to virtue. We lack evidence of a polity in which might alone, i.e. utterly arbitrary might, wielded in disregard of all rules and conventions, was equated with right by all affected parties. Some decisions will favour some inhabitants of the social order more than others, as in matters of resource exploitation and allocation, rights, and so forth, but beyond a point differential treatment will bring into question the idea of the order as an embodiment of any collective interest and shared values and threaten its existence. Beyond a point the dependence on force to sustain a social order invalidates the adjective 'social'. It marks the point where politics has either failed to sustain integration or succeeded in 'othering' potential or erstwhile members of the community of obligation so that they may be dealt with by extra-political

---

[82] Stephen Toulmin, *The Place of Reason in Ethics* (Cambridge: Cambridge University Press, 1950), 170–1. Note that 'My Station and Its Duties' was the title of a relevant essay by the philosopher F. H. Bradley.

means like civil war, mass expulsion, or genocide.[83] Where hierarchies are sustained more by overt force than anything else, as for instance with Greek and Roman slavery, or the slavery of the old American south, the situation, which is effectively a perpetual, one-sided warfare, approximates more closely Gramsci's idea of straightforward domination than his idea of hegemony. That is, the slave-owners might have tried to justify slave-owning to themselves, as Aristotle tried and failed to,[84] but they were not concerned with persuading all the slaves of its legitimacy. Any consideration of what was actually entailed in sustaining such systems of incarceration and repression cannot but cast negative light on the architects, upholders, and beneficiaries of those systems—unless the reader is of a very particular disposition.

Whatever the variable content of any social understanding of legitimacy, legitimacy only makes sense if it is conferred as much as presumed. In any society legitimacy can be retracted or argued about irrespective of the desires of the most powerful, even if the argument ends up with the wholesale slaughter of the weaker party. Even the historian who takes care to establish the legitimacy of some practice at some point in the past has to be careful not to assume that its legitimacy endured, or she may end up embracing the same historicist fallacy as the historian who automatically legitimates every act of power with reference to some supposedly general 'standard of those times'. If some historical actors or interest groups presumed to embody legitimacy, the historian ought not take them at their word. When historians intimate legitimacy and illegitimacy they are making a judgement that is at once empirical and evaluative.

Could the historian circumvent the evaluation issue by just referring instead to a stew of competing legitimacy-claims? That approach would run into much the problems described above for any attempt to provide a purely internal actor's perspective in lieu of a more integrated causal explanation: any given legitimacy-claimant could be radically deceived. The approach would also duck the fact that legitimacy is a matter of perceptions, but not just the perceptions of those who claim it. All perceptions have a subjective element, but we may distinguish between perceptions that are purely relative to individuals and those that may be relative to certain contexts but are intersubjective or shared within those contexts. Contentedness can fall into the first category. If someone feels content, we may reasonably say that they are content, whatever we might think about whether they should feel content. Legitimacy is not like this. The perception of legitimacy must be shared to some degree beyond the circle of those claiming the power to act with it, which may well mean other historical parties than the party that constitutes the historian's major focus.

---

[83] My thinking here is informed by Bernard Williams, *In the Beginning Was the Deed* (Princeton: Princeton University Press, 2005), 3–6.

[84] On Aristotle, see Bernard Williams, *Shame and Necessity* (Berkeley and Los Angeles: University of California Press, 1993), ch. 5.

To be sure, it will not always be a question of establishing the legitimacy of one party versus the illegitimacy of another. There may genuinely be multiple candidates with powerful claim. We may also talk of diminished, enhanced, or challenged legitimacy. But these are all matters of nuance in judgement, and from the fact that one set of cases are finely balanced or equivocal it does not follow that all will be so. We will not be able to distinguish one class of cases from the other without engaging in a form of thought that is suitable to reflection on entities who are capable of forming an opinion on the nature of demands made of them, sometimes unto death.

PART 3

JUSTIFYING JUDGEMENT ON THINGS PAST

Introduction

Since it is impossible to justify all of this book's arguments in accordance with the prevailing standards of historianship, those standards have to be challenged. Mounting a challenge would be difficult enough were the standards the product of purely specialist consensus within the confines of an academic discipline. The task is greater still when the specialist standards cohere with popular thought. There is indeed a link between a popular orthodoxy in Western moral thought and orthodoxy in an academic historiography that bears the hallmarks of the culture from which its norms evolved. That link is the reason for the occidental focus of this Part of the book. Hereafter the common orthodoxy will be refered to as 'internalist', whether it refers to the interior mental/spiritual world of an individual or that of a cultural group.[1] These internalist positions, while different, have a common origin in strands of religious thought that retained their hold amid secularization.

However entrenched the academic convention that historians refrain from moral evaluation, it is contestable in principle as well as being undermined by commonplace practices. Accordingly, revising the standards in question is less a quixotic tilt than a matter of showing the standards to be unfit for purpose while underwriting some features of historianship that exist in disregard of the standards. The clarifications provided here will also imply guidelines on what sorts of judgements ought to be resisted.

---

[1] I use the term 'internalist' in a slightly different but nevertheless related way to the way it is often used in ethical theory. In that ethical theory it is common to talk of 'motivational internalism', 'judgement internalism', etc., which refers to the supposedly necessary connection between moral judgements and moral motivation—if I judge that X is the right thing to do, then I am immediately motivated to do X (I don't need an additional desire to motivate me as I would when I judge that e.g. Y would be beneficial to my career, fun, expensive). In the present book I use 'internalism' to denote the idea that individual or collective actions can only be judged according to standards that the individual or collective accepts as appropriate. The close relationship between the two sorts of 'internalism' is elaborated at p. 247, n. 320.

The basic issue when thinking about the past (and this goes for the present too) is again contextual understanding and some of the injunctions that have arisen around it. Beyond their surface instruction these pronouncements hint at some underlying philosophy, because taken literally 'you have to understand these people in context' may, given the many meanings alloted to 'context', mean nothing more than 'you have to understand these people'. Part 1 of this book addressed the literal instruction, working through the evaluative connotations of the historian's commitment to take her chosen historical actors 'on their own terms'. The underpinning philosophies are less clear: for instance what do those historians who echo cultural theorist Fredric Jameson's imperative 'always historicize!' think that will achieve?[2] Clarification would be desirable even if it set one historian against another, because while 'historicization' can just mean contextualization it can also have relativist valence.

Encapsulating one interpretation of Jameson's dictum, historian Dan Stone writes that 'history is the most radical of all the disciplines': 'history destabilizes everything precisely by historicizing it'.[3] Stone does not reckon with Ranke and theorists of niche-adaptation (pp. 114–15) who intimate that particular arrangements are validated precisely because of their historical specificity. Each historian points in his own ways towards relativism, nonetheless: Ranke in the 'positive' sense of according each group and time its own truths; Stone in the 'negative' sense of dissolving universal truths in the ether of time's passage and cultural variation. Ranke's classical historicism and Stone's secular neo-historicism (see pp. 40–41) correctly hint that the discipline of History has indeed contributed to the rise of relativism, moral relativism included, at least as much as having been shaped by relativism.

While some trends in History and the social sciences have enhanced the conceptual problems at issue, historical explanation can also serve clarificatory purposes, and that is the task of the three Histories comprising the first three sections in this Part of the book. Now we need to be clear at the outset about what exactly historical accounts can and cannot achieve in the sphere of social or intellectual critique. Historical contextualization-cum-explanation may *destabilize* existing arrangements, but it need not; it does nothing necessarily to *legitimate* or *delegitimate* any given view or claim. One cannot prove or discredit the coherence, logic, or critical purchase of a belief just by explaining its historical origin or development. Far, then, from deploying 'contextualization' or 'historicization' to do surreptitiously critical or crypto-normative work, many of the arguments hereafter address head-on the shortcomings of 'internalist' moral thinking. They show that when we judge consistently with internalist models, we are unable to do justice to

---

[2] Fredric Jameson, *The Political Unconscious* (London: Routledge, 1983), p. ix.
[3] Dan Stone, 'Surviving in the Corridors of History or, History as Double or Nothing', in Jeffrey R. Di Leo (ed.), *Federman's Fictions* (Albany, NY: SUNY, 2011), 203–13, here 205.

many of the consequences of individual or collective action for other individuals or collectives. At the same time, the historical investigations in which the moral arguments are embedded do serve to *defamiliarize*; illustrating the thoroughly contingent origins and development of 'our' internalist beliefs helps to bring those beliefs under the scrutiny they rarely receive because we take them for granted. These historical investigations also show how alternative models of thought were never entirely banished in internalism's rise. We already often act, and configure our social arrangements, in ways that implicitly justify non-internalist models of morality, hereafter called 'relational' models, even while we continue to stress the internalist models in our self-idealizations. Attending to those partly obscured 'relational' elements helps us to make sense of some of our activities in the world, including in the sphere of evaluations in historical scholarship.

History I charts the rise and problems of a Western preoccupation with the *interior of the individual person* as a final court of appeal, with particular reference to the development of Christian theology.[4] The problems include the sort of thinking involved in what the sociologist Edvard Westermarck called 'that beautiful modern sophism which admits every man's conscience to be an infallible guide'.[5] History II addresses the rise and problems of a justificatory focus on the *collective interior*, especially the cultural and national interiors. History III charts relations between individual and collective internalism to the present.

To be sure, different levels of 'internality' may pull in different directions. The emphasis on collective internality tends to heteronomy, with the person's values and choices conditioned from outside, by cultural norms, say. The argument to individual internality can point in the direction of moral autonomy of the Kantian sort, with the person determining her own path. However, the tension between individual and collective internality can be illusory since individual freedom cannot operate without structures that facilitate it and culture is one such structure. And when we move from the *logical* relations between individual and collective interiors to *analogical*, *genealogical*, and *metaphysical* relations between them, the two levels of internality can complement one another, as examples from occidental history show.

On the matter of *analogies* between the individual and the collective, Plato modelled his ideal society on a well-ordered soul: different social classes should act in union just as the parts of the soul do. A medieval illustration of the relationship of individual to social whole was John of Salisbury's *Policraticus* (*c*.1159), depicting a literal body-politic, with its image of the prince as head, peasantry as feet, senate as

---

[4] On different sorts of individualism, see Koenraad W. Swaart, '"Individualism" in the Mid-Nineteenth Century (1826–1860)', *Journal of the History of Ideas* 23/1 (1962), 77–90. Swaart identifies three sorts of individualism: economic, political, and romantic. The sort on which I primarily focus has more in common with his romantic type, but I am much more interested in its religious origins and character.

[5] Cited in Timothy Stroup, 'Westermarck's Ethical Relativism', *Ajatus* 38 (1980), 31–71, here 39–40.

heart, judges and regional governors as senses.[6] In the modern period nationalism began as a liberal doctrine, even if it developed illiberal traits. The analogy from the individual and her self-determination to the collective and its self-determination maps onto the analogy between liberalism and nationalism.[7]

One can actually only think of collective identity in certain ways given certain conceptions of the individual, which is a claim that brings us to *genealogical* linkages between different levels of internality. The historicist historian Gustav Droysen (1808–84) wrote that 'Insofar as I consider the past from my standpoint, from the thoughts of my nation and state, from my religion and past, I stand high above my individual ego. I think, as it were, from a higher ego, in which the slag of my little persona has been melted away.'[8] Droysen's idea of an individual ego needing consciously to be transcended presupposes the idea of the individual ego that really does stand separate to culture, society, past, etc., in the first place. Droysen's case suggests how the individualist tendencies of so much popular thought share origins with the impersonal contextualisms of so many historians, even while the stances seem to be opposed, with historians generally scornful of the failure of 'ordinary people' to appreciate how much their own lives are shaped by historically evolved norms and structures. While History II and History III are more obviously relevant to historians because of their attention to collective, group-level interiority, History I, which addresses individual interiority, is the foundation on which connections between different levels of interiority are established.

What of the *metaphysical* linkage between different levels of internality? A brief survey of relevant ideas will prepare the ground for what is to come in the first three sections. Linking individual people to a worldly community and to God, Matthew's Gospel (18:20) tells us that 'Where two or three are gathered together in my name, there am I in the midst of them.' The same thought was expressed in the Jewish oral tradition, with which Jesus was probably familiar.[9] Paul's First Letter to the Corinthians (10–15) uses 'the body of Christ' for the eucharistic invocation of Christ's body on the cross, the Corinthians as a community, and the resurrected body that all shall receive at the end of days.[10] This was perhaps the earliest written conception of the *universitas fidelium*, the earthly body of the faithful that comprises the assembly of God and represents the new society. Individual Christians

---

[6] Martin Loughlin, *Foundations of Public Law* (Oxford: Oxford University Press, 2010), 29.

[7] See also Samuel Fleischacker, *Integrity and Moral Relativism* (Leiden: Brill, 1992), 170–1, 207–10.

[8] Frederick C. Beiser, *The German Historicist Tradition* (Oxford: Oxford University Press, 2011), 307.

[9] It was later recorded in the Talmud: 'If two are sitting and studying the Torah together, the Divine Presence is with them' (*Berakhot* 6a). Thanks to David Patterson for this information, as for much else of relevance.

[10] On the Corinthians, see Conrad Leyser's introduction to Ernst H. Kantorowicz, *The King's Two Bodies: A Study in Medieval Political Theology* (Princeton: Princeton University Press, 2016), p. xxii.

were brought together by their beliefs, thus conjoining two senses of liturgy, each derivable from the root of 'communion': the sense of liturgy as forging a vertical connection with the divine from within each individual and the sense of it as establishing a horizontal community of values between individual liturgists.

Developments and tensions within the Christian community are a key part of both the History I and History II sections. When Christianity rose to the religion of state in Rome, 'the juridical person of the Roman *respublica* became transformed into the mystical person of Christian society'. Subsequently, the *respublica christiana*, Christendom, transcended state boundaries, though each state could comprise a different sort of *universitas* in its own right, as John of Salisbury illustrated. At the head of Christendom was the pope, microcosm of the whole, at once representative and embodiment of the corporation.[11] At a time of doctrinal and political strife within Christendom, Nicholas Cusanus (1401–64), sought to establish harmony within the institutional Church and, within the *universitas fidelium*, harmony between temporal and spiritual power, using models of hierarchy and equality that drew on analogy between the human body and soul.[12] Drawing on Cusanus and the classical concept of the monad, Gottfried Wilhelm Leibniz (1646–1716) provided the groundwork for an especially influential way of conceptualizing the link between different levels of unique interiority—from the individual soul through confessional units and polities to, in principle at least, the entirety of humanity—after western Christendom's religious unity had been broken by Protestantism, and after Protestant teaching had emphasized inner dispositions rather than external deeds.

History II establishes the relevance down the centuries of the tradition of thought to which Leibniz made such a contribution. His metaphysics, ethnography, and linguistics manifest a linkage between the Lutheran focus on individual internality and the later Lutheran-tinted concern with uniqueness and cultural-linguistic self-expression. Cultures constitute the sort of collective singular that preoccupied major 'early Romantic' thinkers like Johann Gottfried Herder and likewise nineteenth-century historicists. Leibniz's influence may be traced in the anthropological models of the late nineteenth and early–mid twentieth century created by Franz Boas and his students Margaret Mead and Ruth Benedict.[13] There is an affinity, for instance, between the 'patterns' in Benedict's 1934 *Patterns*

---

[11] Loughlin, *Foundations of Public Law*, 29–32, quote from 29.

[12] Marica Costiglielo, 'Organic Metaphors in "De Cordantia Catholica" of Nicholas of Cusa', *Viator* 44/2 (2013), 311–22.

[13] Fleischacker, *Integrity and Moral Relativism*, 168–9, 207–9, 217; Jürgen Trabant, 'Humboldt et Leibniz: Le Concept intérieur de la linguistique', in Tullio De Mauro and Lia Formigari (eds), *Leibniz, Humboldt and the Origins of Comparativism* (Amsterdam: Benjamins, 1990), 135–56; Matti Bunzl, 'Franz Boas and the Humboldtian Tradition', in George W. Stocking, Jnr. (ed.), *Volksgeist as Method and Ethic: Essays on Boasian Ethnography and the German Anthropological Tradition* (Madison: University of Wisconsin Press, 1996), 17–78; Hans F. Vermeulen, *Before Boas: The Genesis of Ethnography and Ethnology in the German Enlightenment* (Lincoln, NE: University of Nebraska Press, 2015).

of Culture and the self-sufficient, unitary wholes that Leibniz called monads.[14] Boas and his students were known as historical particularists or historicists, after the eponymous nineteenth-century intellectual tendency. The 'structural historicism' of Marshal Sahlins also fits this pattern, with its conception of the cultural 'unity' that 'defines all functionality',[15] and there are family resemblances in the work of Geertz (pp. 216–18).

It is key for the story as it unfolds that, as well as being a contribution to religious harmony, Leibniz intended his thought to be politically irenic at a moment threatened by inter- and intra-state strife. In that sense it was of a part with Ruth Benedict's wartime anti-racist pamphlet *The Races of Mankind*, which celebrated the union of culturally diverse peoples in fighting the racist Axis,[16] and with the anthropologist Claude Lévi-Strauss's *Race and History* (1952), which was written at a time of decolonization and anti-colonial warfare. So far so good for the Leibnizian tradition. But what of Benedict's 1946 book *The Chrysanthemum and the Sword*? In considering the Japanese, 'the most alien enemy the United States had ever fought in an all-out struggle',[17] Benedict contrasted what she thought was a Japanese 'shame' culture with an occidental 'guilt' culture.[18] The book sought to explain Japan to Americans in the name of tolerant understanding of difference. However, its elements of caricature and misunderstanding about shame and its relationship to guilt (see pp. 139–42) did little to combat the belief of those who perceive themselves to belong to conscience-based guilt cultures that shame cultures are inferior. Indeed Benedict bolstered a sense of superiority when she associated the very intercultural tolerance that she purported to promote with a trait—individualism—that was supposedly connected to the subject-internality of the western 'guilt' culture. In the end some cultures just were more desirable than others.[19] Benedict's works at once explain the appeal of a certain sort of 'monadic' thinking and suggest its problems. A doctrine developed to celebrate difference, possibly with a view to higher unity, may end up constructing or exaggerating difference, hardening the Us–Them divide and homogenizing the

---

[14] Fleischacker, *Integrity and Moral Relativism*, 168–9; George Gurvitch, 'Is the Antithesis of "Moral Man" and "Immoral Society" True?', *Philosophical Review* 52/6 (1943), 533–52, here 548.

[15] Cited in Li, 'Marshal Sahlins and the Apotheosis of Culture', 219.

[16] Ruth Benedict and Gene Weltfish, *The Races of Mankind* (New York: Public Affairs Committee, 1943).

[17] Ruth Benedict, *The Chrysanthemum and the Sword: Patterns of Japanese Culture* (1946; Boston: Mariner, 2005), 1.

[18] Benedict, *The Chrysanthemum*, 222–4 on matters of variable balance between 'guilt' and 'shame' across different cultures, and for her summary characterizations of the differences between the two sorts of culture. See also p. 14 against the argument that cultural differences are superficial.

[19] On the relationship between individualism and tolerance, see Christopher Shannon, 'A World Made Safe for Differences: Ruth Benedict's *The Chrysanthemum and the Sword*', *American Quarterly* 47/4 (1995), 659–80, here 670–6. For criticisms of Benedict's characterizations, John Lie, 'Ruth Benedict's Legacy of Shame: Orientalism and Occidentalism in the Study of Japan', *Asian Journal of Social Science* 29/2 (2001), 249–61; Clifford Geertz, 'Us/Not-Us: Benedict's Travels', in Geertz, *Works and Lives: The Anthropologist as Author* (Stanford, CA: Stanford University Press, 1988), 102–28.

Them, if not also the Us—and there is no way of guaranteeing that the differences thus portrayed will actually be celebrated. Thinking at the political level, and to the hundred years or so before the publication of *The Chrysanthemum and the Sword*, such is the story of nationalism, as the idiom of self-determination for peoples with unique cultural characteristics morphed into that of cultural narcissism, paranoia, and existential struggle between groups.

Monadic thinking, as we might call it, could never do the political work hoped of it. In particular we must distinguish between religious conscience and moral conscience, and between tolerance of belief and tolerance of action. If, as is contended in History I, a certain modern concept of individual autonomy developed from the paradigmatic basis of tolerance of conscience in the sense of internal orientation towards a deity, then that concept has little significance for the development of conscience-as-morality in the sense of acting towards others in this world. As part of showing that certain concepts of culture and the nation developed analogously to the development of thinking about freedom of individual conscience, History II shows that these concepts pertained to collective systems of belief and value in a purely internal sense, with the national-cultural spirit—*Volksgeist*—being emblematic. It is precisely this self-contained, 'monadic' cultural model on which influential moral relativisms draw, and insofar as relativists claim any practical significance for their doctrine it is hard to see how the claim is borne out when cultures and their physico-political vessels collide, or when 'a people' turns out to be internally heterogenous, its culture a battleground rather than a common script for internal harmony. The doctrine of freedom of religious conscience was an important achievement in a world when, as sometimes now, people might be killed purely on grounds of what was going on inside their heads. But the considerations remain different as regards moral conscience, individual or collective, when the beliefs of one person or group issue in acts affecting other people and peoples.

Discrepancies between religion and morality, and between 'personal morality' and the law, have done nothing for conceptual clarity in the matter of moral evaluation. Key terms and concepts are multivalent. Consider that resort to religious vocabulary when one appeals to 'good faith' or 'good conscience' even when one is not talking about religion. 'Right', *Recht*, *droit*, may ground the moral sense of rectitude, the idea of a just or merely given order of things as something that can be appealed to (objective right) and the idea of having a personal right to some particular (subjective right). Then there is 'guilty' which, as in the case of Alderman's deserters (pp. 116–17), can refer to a subjective feeling or an objective legal pronouncement. Whatever the clarity achieved by some moral philosophers, there is no consensus over choice or blend of theories in their guild either. For the rest of us, and likely the philosophers too when they are not philosophizing, moral thought is a hotchpotch of only partly congruent factors, owing something to our immediate interests and at least as much to our history as to any process of systematic thought. How different, though, would be the balance of historiographical common sense at the level of collective life, and so much occidental moral 'common sense' at the level of individual life, if the broader cultural environment had been more shaped by other strands of Christian thought than those that did gain ascendance, or indeed by Jewish thought? The difference is in the relationship between exteriority and interiority. Judaism is a religion of the deed more than the creed, which is why Judaic other-facing morality and 'inner' faith are inseparable, while since Luther at the latest, and arguably since Paul, it has been possible to separate the corresponding elements of Christianity and to prioritize faith and the world of the spirit (*pneuma*, *Geist*).

While the three Histories help substantiate my claims about the moral problems of internalist moral, the fourth section summarizes the conceptual differences between internalist and relational thought. That section and the following one are of a less historical, more purely analytical nature. The fifth section brings relational precepts to bear on moral relativism and prescriptions like a blanket tolerance in one's consideration of foreign countries past, or indeed present. The sixth section constitutes a segue from the concerns of Part 3 of the book to those of Part 4.

A 'relational' concept of morality in the way it is presented here is not a theory in the sense of something that purports to provide criteria for judging any given thing as right or wrong. Such criteria are just what is in question: the variety of often clashing moral theories helps promote relational thinking in the first place. Relational thinking is just moral thinking insofar as we take morality to pertain to relations among people, however indirect or distant, rather than between any given person or group and some actually non-separable entity called their conscience, their beliefs, their faith, their culture, or the *Volksgeist* of which they partake.[20] Once one adopts a relational model one heads towards evaluation on the principle that no one is an island, and only the powerful have ever been in a position to act as if they were. Relational thought, which can rarely be escaped in practice whatever we are told in principle, legitimates a range of evaluations across cleavages of belief and identity while reminding the judge that she cannot insulate herself from the judgement of external others by a philosophy of spiritual self-certification or moral relativism. Judge and be judged, as it were.

History I: By Faith Alone

When Herbert Butterfield warned against evaluation, issues of context were important, but also the recognition that the historian could never know whether

---

[20] To be precise I should say that morality pertains to relations among people, but not everything that pertains to relations among people involves moral considerations.

one person or another 'made the most of the opportunities heaven gave to each'. Once near the 'intimate interior' of historical personalities, 'we are inevitably brought to a halt before those final recesses which the technical historian cannot reach'.[21] For Butterfield, as for Kitson Clark when he opposed 'judgements on dead people', the idea seems to be that all evaluation must be of the form of Gibbon or the Roman biographer Suetonius forming a verdict on the person as such, as if they were allocating individuals to heaven or hell. The equation of evaluation with something like divine judgement explains the experiences of the moral philosopher Claudia Card, who recalls being interviewed and asked whether Saddam Hussein was evil as opposed to whether what he had done was wrong.[22] The idea of judgement on the soul as either separate from or more important than evaluation of the soul-bearer's comportment is characteristic of the problematic dualisms that Christian civilization has specialized in.

On trial in Jerusalem in 1961, the former SS officer Adolf Eichmann relied on precisely the defence that his acts of wrongdoing said nothing about who he really was. Whatever he had done in administering genocide, he had not followed his 'innerer Schweinehund'—he had not compromised himself at the deepest level of interiority.[23] Eichmann was trying to explain his outer conformity precisely by disowning actions that in his account were never authentically 'his' to begin with. Eichmann the spiritual or inner being was divorced from what Eichmann the actor did. However sincere or insincere the appeal was, and no one could ever know, it was nonetheless an appeal to a real cultural trope, a version of the thing quietly dissenting Germans invoked when they referred to their 'inner emigration' during the Nazi period. Apparently inner emigration had also been commonplace in the turmoil created by the Thirty Years War (1618–48), which gives an indication of its cultural depth. Certainly, decades before the Nazi assumption of power the philosopher Wilhelm Dilthey had applauded and Nietzsche criticized what each saw as a particularly German concern with the internal mental-spiritual world, with Nietzsche invoking 'the German' who 'cannot be judged at all by an action and remains hidden as an individual even after this deed. He must, as is well known, be measured by his thoughts and his feelings.'[24] Such inwardness is not a solely German speciality, though: there is evidence from the wider West in the present of a religious emphasis on 'the inner experiences of isolated individuals, cultivated and evaluated largely by those individuals', and this helps to

[21] Butterfield, *Christianity and History*, 45, 43, 18, 110.

[22] Claudia Card, *Confronting Evils: Terrorism, Torture, Genocide* (Cambridge: Cambridge University Press, 2010), 5–6.

[23] Arendt, *Eichmann in Jerusalem*, 25–6.

[24] Isaiah Berlin, *Four Essays on Liberty* (Oxford: Oxford University Press, 1969), 139; Wilhelm Dilthey, *The Formation of the Historical World in the Human Sciences*, ed. Rudolf A. Makreel and Frithjof Rodi (Princeton: Princeton University Press, 2002), 117, 199–204. Nietzsche, *On the Advantage and Disadvantage of History for Life* (Indianapolis: Hackett, 1980), 24–30, quote at 26.

explain attitudes towards 'spirituality' as a widespread source of personal gratification.[25]

Erstwhile British prime minister Tony Blair once justified his role in bringing Britain into the invasion of Iraq in 2003. 'Do I know I'm right? Judgments aren't the same as facts. Instinct is not science . . . I only know what I believe.'[26] When an official inquiry criticized all of his major judgements, and rejected his claim that the violent chaos pursuant to the invasion had been unpredictable with reference to actual predictions, Blair took solace in the fact that the inquiry had not impugned his 'good faith'.[27] Let us ignore the fact that the good faith defence constituted a major change of tack from Blair's pre-invasion appeal to history—i.e. to the way he predicted that events would unfold—as his judge.[28] Again, the major point of interest is the trope of self-certification: invoking integrity as a final court of appeal. Not long after the publication of the war report, a British athlete who had taken medicines with known performance-enhancing side effects clarified that he had sought no advantage, as if that rendered evaluatively irrelevant the question of whether he had, predictably, gained advantage.[29] Like Eichmann, Blair and the athlete allude to some sort of self-justificatory inner purity that morally superseded whatever they had predictably brought about. A related phenomenon is manifest in those cases today where someone in the public eye makes a racist or sexist remark and then defends themselves on the basis that that remark 'is not who I am'.

As if in supportive preparation for these self-justifications, in the *Discourse on Inequality* the eighteenth-century philosopher Jean-Jacques Rousseau wrote of 'social man' who 'lives always constantly *outside himself*, and only knows how to live in the opinions of others'.[30] By the later twentieth century, by the offices of the likes of the anthropologist Benedict, the 'social man' thus characterized had become restricted to a certain sort of 'traditional' society, one now called an honour or shame society. Of shame/honour societies, the sociologist Bourdieu wrote: 'the point of honour is the basis of a moral code of an individual who sees himself always through the eyes of others, who has need of others for his existence'.[31] How the alchemical change away from honour societies had occurred in the West is a good question. Rousseau would likely have claimed that it had not

[25] Cited in Robert C. Bishop, *Philosophy of the Social Sciences* (London: Bloomsbury, 2007), 111.

[26] Catherine Bennett, 'Never Mind the Facts, Trust Tony's Faith', *The Guardian*, 30 September 2004; Jamie Whyte, 'Is Tony Sure he Exists?', *The Times*, 1 October 2004.

[27] e.g. *Independent* staff, 'Chilcot Report Published: Read Tony Blair's Statement in Full', *The Independent*, 6 July 2016.

[28] Jackie Ashley and Ewen MacAskill, 'History Will Be My Judge', *The Guardian*, 1 March 2003.

[29] Owen Gibson, 'Bradley Wiggens Tells Andrew Marr "I Did Not Seek an Unfair Advantage"', *The Guardian*, 25 September 2016.

[30] Rousseau, *The Social Contract and the Discourses* (London: Dent and Sons, 1973), 116.

[31] Bourdieu, cited in Douglas Cairns, 'Honour and Shame: Modern Controversies and Ancient Values', *Critical Quarterly* 53/1 (2011), 23–41, here 23.

actually occurred, and there are grounds to agree on that score. What had happened was that the ideal of the person whose opinion of himself was grounded entirely in his pristine interior—an ideal Rousseau helped foster—had become more profoundly emphasized. The seed of this ideal was planted far before modernity or the Enlightenment. It was nourished by Christian theology before, as a flower in bloom, its scent infused theories of relations between individual, God, state, and society.

We begin with early Christianity, which may not be insulated from non-Christian influences. Some of the metaphysical structures Christianity inherited can be traced back at least to Plato. As to morality, the Roman Stoic of the first century BCE, Marcus Tullius Cicero, and Jesus' contemporary Seneca, elaborated ideas of guilt, sin, and expiation, including the Latin term *conscientia* itself. *Conscientia* corresponds precisely to the Greek *syneidêsis* (συνείδησις). It was the word used by Jerome to render *syneidêsis* when he translated Paul's letters from the Greek in the production of the Vulgate in the fourth century. Conscience and consciousness share a root, connoting knowledge (*scientia*), in this case of good and evil. The *syn/con* part of the term connotes 'with' or 'together'. It can indicate a human community of customary value in the sense of inherited, shared precepts, but the 'relationship' can also be reflexive—it is knowledge that one has of oneself, and that one shares with oneself as if in inner conversation.[32] A further element was stressed in Seneca, though it was not original to him: as with Socrates, the inner voice can be associated with a higher voice. In the Stoic tradition, following this voice is a way of coping with external vicissitudes with equanimity, more than imposing oneself on the world.[33]

Despite such debts, some cardinal Christian virtues were set with varying degrees of strength at different moments against representations of some of the cardinal Graeco-Roman virtues, and 'Jewish' virtues too. The 'pagan' ethics of achievement of Achilles, Alcibiades, and Caesar, celebrated in poetry, prose, and at the forum, promoted egoism and elitism. And had not Plato disparaged 'effeminate' lamentation and empathizing? 'Pharisaic' morality, meanwhile, allegedly promoted blind obedience, being apparently a merely external matter. What of conscience, humility, inner disposition, the good heart?[34]

---

[32] Paul Strohm, *Conscience: A Very Short Introduction* (Oxford: Oxford University Press, 2011), 8–10; Anders Schinkel, *Conscience and Conscientious Objections* (Amsterdam: Pallas, 2007), 172. Thanks also to Douglas Cairns for discussions on this point and many others of relevance in this section.

[33] Gabriele Thome, 'Crime and Punishment, Guilt and Expiation: Roman Thought and Vocabulary', *Acta Classica* 35 (1992), 73–98; Matthew B. Roller, *Constructing Autocracy: Aristocrats and Emperors in Julio-Claudian Rome* (Princeton: Princeton University Press, 2001), 82–8. See also pp. 21 ff. of the same book on the social dominance of more externalist conceptions of ethics in the world in which Seneca made his intervention.

[34] For these juxtapositions in a sharp form, see Bob Zunjic, 'The Sermon on the Mount: An Outline' at http://jakavonyte-philosophy.yolasite.com/resources/Zujnic%20on%20Sermon%20on%20 the%20Mount.pdf , here pp. 3–5.

Christian views of Hebrew morality have been dogged since the beginning by misunderstanding, not so much of the prominence of *Halakhah*—the body of law—in much Judaic teaching, as its function in that teaching.[35] Augustine, author of that seminal document of 'internality', the *Confessions*, contributed to the depiction of literalism as being a result of Jews' failure to understand the spiritual meaning of Scripture, their having been blinded by God in order that their blindness might serve as witness to Christianity's truth. 'Like the donkey in the sacrifice of Isaac (Genesis 22), they carried all that was necessary for the mystery of salvation, but they themselves did not comprehend that mystery.'[36] Augustine was unaware of the oral traditions laid down in Talmud, Midrash, and Kabbalah, which were still in the process of being recorded when he was alive. Many centuries later Kant had no such excuse when writing that the Ten Commandments were 'given with no claim at all on the moral disposition in following them (whereas Christianity later placed the chief work in this) but were rather directed simply and solely to external observance.'[37]

Rather, if the law is an expression of God's will, then acting in conformity with it is following God's example, acting as God would want rather than you might choose. This is an end in itself. It is also intimately associated with the sustenance of human community, with relationships to other flesh-and-blood beings. A commandment is a *mitzvah*, a word that derives from the Aramaic *tzavta*, which means connection. To observe a commandment is to make a connection with God and with fellow human beings at once. There is no relation to God without the human relation.[38] Of the Decalogue, the Utterances on the first tablet that Moses brought down from Sinai listed human duties to God, while those on the second tablet enumerated responsibilities to other people. For Jews, rather than strictly being commandments, these ten declarations are more like classificatory headings for more detailed individual commandments, of which there are, by the most conventional count, 613 in the Torah.

> That combination of seemingly antithetical ideas—that we always and everywhere think about what it is that we're doing, that we always and everywhere think beyond what we're doing—lies at the heart of a religion so dedicated to the extraction of the sacred from the profane, of locating the sacred within the profane, that it encircles human action with 613 commandments, lest any moment or gesture of a Jew's life be without thought of God.[39]

---

[35] E. Owen and Barry Mesch, 'Protestants, Jews and the Law', *Christian Century*, 6–13 June 1984, 601–4.

[36] Frans van Liere, *An Introduction to the Medieval Bible* (Cambridge: Cambridge University Press, 2014), 118.

[37] Immanuel Kant, *Religion Within the Boundaries of Mere Reason and Other Writings* (Cambridge: Cambridge University Press, 1998), 131.

[38] I thank David Patterson for this information.

[39] Corey Robin, 'The Trials of Hannah Arendt', *The Nation*, 1 June 2015.

The outside moral world is not separable from the inside one, which makes Judaism necessarily a social theory as well as a religion, and a religion of the deed more than the creed. Indeed, the caricatured transcendent *impersonality* of the Hebrew god may be a condition of 'his' societal valence, in the sense that God remains distinctly 'other', non-assimilable to the individual human ego, and therefore stands as a reminder as to how other humans should be treated. As in the thought of the philosopher Emmanuel Levinas, it is not a matter of comprehending God but of 'enacting God through responsibility to the other through justice'.[40] Putting aside the religious element (though that would make no sense to a devout Jew) there is psychological and sociological sophistication to all this. As Aristotelian virtue ethics and psychology both tell us, developing patterns of behaviour can shape one from the outside inwards. In Judaism, following the law is itself a form of betterment by ongoing self-creation through accumulated righteous behaviour which accustoms one to acting rightly.

We might add that one of the great strengths of an abiding emphasis on justice rather than love—to stereotype the chief virtues of the Jewish and Christian traditions respectively—is that love can only be given, whereas justice, whether interpreted in either Aristotelian sense as law-abidingness or as equitability, can be demanded by the aggrieved.[41] Justice is more egalitarian, as also manifest in that traduced doctrine of 'an eye for an eye',[42] the *lex talionis*. The convention enshrined general reciprocity in order to forestall personal, disproportionate retribution (two eyes for one) and grudge-holding, and was not necessarily literal, in the sense that material compensation (e.g., in a later, early medieval setting, *wergeld*) could substitute for non-material loss, as it still can today under civil law. Martin Luther King misunderstood the doctrine when claiming it tended to universal blindness.

If Christianity sometimes defined itself against a Jewish faith that supposedly kept its transcendent-cum-social externality external, then Homeric Greece, or at least the Greece of Homeric description, may be characterized by its more purely social externality. In the 'progressivist' strand of classical scholarship, with its Christo-centric leanings, the Homeric age was characterized as a shame culture lacking in a mature sense of agency and responsibility and was thereby

---

[40] Section 2.4.5 of Bettina Bergo, 'Emmanuel Levinas', in Edward N. Zalta (ed.) *The Stanford Encyclopedia of Philosophy* (Fall 2019 edn), https://plato.stanford.edu/archives/fall2019/entries/levinas/. Note that Judaism is repeatedly used hereafter, heuristically, as one contrast to Christianity. I am conscious that the image of Judaism that I present thereby may appear to be homogeneous and unchanging, which does scant justice to the reality. For some relevant continuities in Jewish thought over the long term through Levinas, see David Patterson, *Genocide in Jewish Thought* (Cambridge: Cambridge University Press, 2012), ch. 1.

[41] Macmurray, *Persons in Relation*, 188.

[42] For some of the roots of this traducing, see Augustine, *Contra Faustum*, bk XIX §3, at Augustine, *The Works of Aurelius Augustine: A New Translation*, ed. Marcus Dods, v (Edinburgh: Clark, 1872), 328–9.

exaggeratedly distinguished from its successor civilizations. Like other 'shame cultures' in the present and recent past, which equally stood in contrast to the modern Western way of course, it was given an air of undesirability by its link to hierarchic status-consciousness, conceptions of distinctly male, probably martial honour and, often by extension, a sexist preoccupation with female chastity.[43]

One preliminary way of balancing the picture is to show how unattractive the nominal opposite of externalist thinking can be. Let us say that the internalist 'ideal' of the 'guilt culture' is, improbably, achieved in its purest form; would the outcome be desirable? It requires prodigious self-confidence, not to say egotism bordering on sociopathy, to ignore the outside world completely—people's reactions to one, one's standing in social contexts, and so forth—in forming an estimation of oneself, shaping one's life decisions, and ascertaining what, if anything, one should feel guilty for.[44] Consider that incorruptible man of conscience, the Rousseau aficionado Robespierre, or the French-educated Suong Sikoeun of the genocidal Khmer Rouge: 'Robespierre is my hero. Robespierre and Pol Pot: both men have the same quality of decisiveness and integrity.'[45]

In any case, whatever we might like to think, most of us have not discarded all of the 'hang-ups' of the stereotyped shame culture anyway, even though we tend to use words like 'esteem' now rather than 'honour'. Do you believe that your ethos is entirely autonomous, your self-esteem purely self-generated? Does it feel that way when you have been demoted (i.e. when someone else has told you you are not good enough), or your colleague promoted over you (i.e. when you have lost in a competition)?[46] The so-called individualism promoted by liberal capitalism is anything but: the emphasis might be on the self in the sense of pursuing self-interest, but insofar as that is self-interest in monetary enrichment, the definition of the interest is set by 'the system' not the individual, and the whole system is predicated upon competition and consumption, which are other-conscious through and through.

If esteem and disesteem just do matter, then it is important to get beyond bandying around prejudicial cases from the 'shame' or the 'guilt' side of things. More dispassionate reflection reveals that esteem and disesteem have key structuring roles but do not determine content. In other words, there is no set thing that 'shame cultures' produce shame about.[47] They can produce chauvinism but also great social sensitivity. A further key point is that the binary shame–guilt

---

[43] Williams, *Shame and Necessity*; Cairns, 'Honour and Shame', 23; Geertz, 'Us/Not-Us'; Eiko Ikegami, 'Emotions', in Ulinka Rublack (ed.), *A Concise Companion to History* (Oxford: Oxford University Press, 2011), 333–53, here 344.

[44] Which is roughly Williams's point in *Shame and Necessity*, 98–100.

[45] Cited in Eric Weitz, *A Century of Genocide: Utopias of Race and Nation* (Princeton: Princeton University Press, 2009), 147.

[46] Cairns, 'Honour and Shame'.

[47] Cairns, 'Honour and Shame', 30; Williams, *Shame and Necessity*, 92: 'we, like the Greeks, can be as mortified or disgraced by a failure in prowess or cunning as by a failure of generosity or loyalty'.

does not work. Just as it would be wrong to think that certain Christian and/or modern cultures supplanted exteriority entirely, it would be wrong to think that there is no element of internality in the other systems outlined here. It is just that in those other models internality is more explicitly a product of *internalization* rather than some internal immaculate conception to which one cleaves on pain of 'inauthenticity', that buzzword of twentieth-century existentialist philosophy. Internality as a product of internalization is simply the logic of the individual as social animal—as an entity that is individuated in the process of socialization. In each social case subjects try to mould themselves to the demands of external standards which cannot in the first instance touch on anything like guilt/conscience. When the message of external standards and their external interpreters is positive, for the subject they have the structure of something like honour or esteem as measured by gauging how others see one—more sophisticatedly, one uses one's reflective judgement to imagine how others might see one. When negative, they have the structure of shame. Shame may arise from any comportment which does not cohere with the self-image that one has developed as a particular person, a self-image which is based in part on cognizance of how others might in principle expect such a person to behave. This is the terrain of personal ethos. As to interpersonal matters, and consideration of the (in)appropriate treatment of others, consultation of Homer suggests that 'obligations to behave honourably and to respect the honour of others can be internalised and generalised . . . Characters regularly observe that one should not oneself do things that excite one's own nemesis [indignation] when others do them.' In either set of cases, when the mature individual lets herself down, she feels ashamed under the gaze of her own internal(ized) guide, which is neither just an objective standard mindlessly adopted nor a decontextualized conscience welling up from the depths of the soul.[48] If all of this sounds rather alien, just consider the father of liberal economics, Adam Smith, and his talk of an ideal 'impartial spectator' as the imagined authority whose standards we seek to uphold.[49]

For, say, the 'Homeric Greeks' the function of shame ultimately comes to subsume some of the functions of guilt, rather than standing separately to it as is supposedly the case in distinctions between shame and guilt cultures. Under Judaism, ethics and morality are tightly related, if by ethics—in the sense of an ethos—we understand how one styles or generally comports oneself and by morality we mean what one owes to others. One difference between either of

---

[48] Cairns, 'Honour and Shame', with quote about Homer's characters at p. 30; Williams, *Shame and Necessity*, ch. 4; Ikegami, 'Emotions', 344–6; Kwame Anthony Appiah, *The Honor Code: How Moral Revolutions Happen* (New York: Norton, 2010), 61–5.

[49] Smith, *The Theory of Moral Sentiments* (6th edn, London: Cadell, 1790), 128–9: 'The man of real constancy and firmness . . . has never dared to forget for one moment the judgment which the impartial spectator would pass upon his sentiments and conduct. He has never dared to suffer the man within the breast to be absent one moment from his attention. . . . He does not merely affect the sentiments of the impartial spectator. He really adopts them.'

these set-ups and that which supposedly prevails today is that under neither dispensation would it make sense to appeal to what one 'really' was inside as having any priority over, or separation from, what one had actually brought about in the world.[50] Even with the changes in Greek philosophical thought from Plato onwards, this emphasis on the public dimension of behaviour remained, and it endured into Hellenized Roman civilization, forming the context in which the Roman Stoics made their modificatory intervention.[51]

The latter-day conception of a hermetic, punctal, or self-enclosed self is related to the ideas of a soul and a 'personal' (Christian) god. Naturally, balances between internal and external desiderata have changed over time in Christianity as this or that doctrinal strand achieved dominance and as the *ecclesia* metamorphosed from a band of believers to a state after its adoption by Rome, and thence to a civilization. This first essay dwells more on contrasts than commonalities in the developing ideals of Christian versus non-Christian orders, especially insofar as Christianity, in distinction to Judaism, claims that 'law is not what religion is really about'.[52] But let us not forget that Jesus himself was a great exemplar, a doer as well as a preacher who likely saw himself as renewing Jewish verities rather than supplanting Judaism—though much hinges on what Jesus is taken to have meant when he talked of fulfilling the law.[53] Thus when he announced two apparently new commandments—to love God and to love others—he was summarizing the precepts of the first and second tablets of the Decalogue respectively.

Parts of the New Testament (e.g. Galatians 3:24, 'The Law was our teacher unto Christ'; Matthew 5:17–20 and 7:12) reflected the 'Jewish' heritage of a focus on adherence to 'the law'. Other parts (e.g. Galatians 2:16, and 3:13 on the 'curse of the law') focused less on the good works that followed from obedience to the law, and more on the internal disposition of faith, and indeed grace, i.e. undeserved and unpredictable divine favour (e.g. Romans 5:20, 6:14, 7:5–25; John 3:16). Paul, the converted Jew who was also a Roman citizen, wrote that cardinal manifesto of creed-based thinking, 'man is justified by faith apart from works of the law' (Romans 3:28), a doctrine that moved the focus to the interior from the outside world. Rarely, though, did the contending doctrines of law versus faith confront each other in unadulterated form. 'Moderate' proponents of each tradition might find as much to dislike in 'extreme' versions of their own position as in iterations of the opposite tradition, though after a point in time few Christians anywhere

---

[50] Cf Nietzsche, *On the Advantage and Disadvantage of History*, 26.

[51] On Aristotelian philosophy, Hannah Arendt, *Responsibility and Judgment* (New York: Random House, 2003), 64–5.

[52] Alexander Murray, *Conscience and Authority in the Medieval Church* (Oxford: Oxford University Press, 2015), 10.

[53] On the Jewishness of the teachings of Jesus, see Alan L. Berger and David Patterson, *Jewish–Christian Dialogue: Drawing Honey from the Rock* (St Paul, MN: Paragon House, 2008), ch.3.

For attempts to distance Jesus from Jewish tradition, see Augustine, *Contra Faustus*, bk XIX §§1–4, in *The Works of Aurelius Augustine*, v. 326–9.

had much good to say about Jews. 'Antinomian' was the name given by the institutional arbiters of faith's order to those irritations—from second- and third-century Gnostics through the twelfth-century Joachim of Fiore to sundry Nonconformists and Protestants in the early modern period—who developed the emphasis on the internal-subjective element most extensively at the expense of the *nomos* or given law. Elements of both doctrines could be found in the vast literary corpus of Augustine (354–430 BCE). His treatise 'On the Spirit and the Letter' of 412/413 CE, reflected on Paul's claim that 'the letter kills, but the spirit gives life' (2 Corinthians 3:6) and insisted that the letter of the law and spirit had to go together. In the absence of spirit, the letter apparently 'causes sin to be known rather than avoided, and therefore to be increased rather than diminished', which was why Augustine believed Paul was right 'to commend the grace which has come to all nations through Jesus Christ, lest the Jews should extol themselves at the expense of the other peoples on account of their having received the law'.[54] At the same time simple obedience was important, for while Augustine talked of human hearts being grasped by grace, and imbibing the spirit behind the law, he was suspicious of giving free rein to a potentially faulty, passion-driven human moral reasoning.[55]

Another influential strand of Augustine's moral theory is eudaemonist in character, oriented to the moral agent's happiness.[56] The point was pursuing the road that led to true happiness, not the pseudo-happiness of instant gratification. True happiness might best be served by working towards an earthly kingdom—*civitas terrena*—of love and peace, though the highest and most perfect peace was to be found in the kingdom of god, or as Augustine called it in the title of his best-known work, the city of god: *Civitas Dei*. In this element of Augustinian thought we detect an influential strand of social theory that would retain currency through the Middle Ages and beyond, whether or not in its explicitly Christian form. It was a social theory in that while the agent's overarching concern in deciding on action was fear/hope for her soul, those actions were also apt to produce socially favourable outcomes in the earthly kingdom.

A problem for Augustine was reconciling measures that might be necessary for the maintenance of the *ecclesia* on earth when they seemed to go against the peaceful teaching of Christ and the principles of inner religious sincerity. How could earthly coercion of schismatics like the Donatists lead to sincere religious faith—sincerity being a condition of salvation? Only late in life did Augustine

---

[54] Augustine, *A Treatise on the Spirit and the letter*, chs 8 and 9[vi]; further to the Jews' 'boasting', see chs 13[viii] and 21[xiii]. (Arabic numerals indicate the version that is split into 66 parts, Roman numerals the version with 36 parts.) Treatise repr. in Augustine, *St Augustine's Anti-Pelagian Works*, ed. Philip Schaff (Woodstock, Ont.: Devoted, 2017), 170–201.

[55] Mark Ellingson, *The Richness of Augustine* (Louisville, KY : Westminster John Knox Press, 2005), 135; Michael Bryant, *A World History of War Crimes* (London: Bloomsbury, 2016), 52–3.

[56] Anthony Kenny and Charles Kenny, *Life, Liberty and the Pursuit of Utility* (Exeter: Imprint Academic, 2006), 21–4.

conclude that it might be legitimate to force people into the fold. *City of God*, meanwhile, was concerned not just with spiritual matters but with responding to physical, 'barbarian' threats manifested in the sack of Rome (410 BCE). Relevant here is Augustine's theory of the unavoidability of evil in the mundane realm: it is an ineluctable dilemma of life in the earthly city in the time between the Fall and the Last Judgement. As applied to the specific situation in hand, Augustine demanded soldierly obedience in the face of superior orders rather than exercise of individual and potentially faulty moral discretion. Soldiers had to kill.[57] This doctrine gave impetus to that dualism that has features of a theory of special roles (see pp. 60–76), but which gained purchase well beyond the bearers of particular roles. Christ's words were only to apply to the inner disposition of the warrior, not to his acts in the external world. Such reasoning was repeated by the great twelfth-century canon law jurist and theorist of just war, Gratian. In the words of *Causa* 23 of Gratian's *Decretum*, 'it is not a sin to wage war . . . [Christ's] precepts of patience must be observed in the preparation of the heart, not the conduct of the body.'[58] Mind–body dualism was not a precise analogy to Church–State dualism, but both highlighted the problematic relation not just between the demands of the earthly and the heavenly city but also between the inner and outer world of the individual person, between the material realm of *physis* and the spiritual realm of *pneuma*.

Church–State tensions had already been highlighted when Constantine (r. 306–37) intervened in ecclesiastical affairs. If, to the emperor, interventions were an expression of the bond between politics and theology, then, with the advent of any doctrinal dispute in the Church the bond meant that the emperor had to take sides and risked antagonizing the losers. Especially important was the Arian controversy that resulted in the Nicene Council and Creed of 325 CE, which is often seen as marking the terminal point of 'early Christianity'. (Arianism, the adopted religion, inter alia, of the Goths who sacked Rome in 410, was ruled a heresy.) The redivision of the Roman Empire between Constantine's sons portended the later and more permanent division of the empire at the close of the fourth century. There is some truth to the cliché that the eastern part of the empire, today remembered as Byzantium, retained a greater harmony of Church and State under 'Caesaro-papal' emperors, emblematically Justinian, while in the West an uneasy dualism persisted. From the fifth-century fragmentation of the western Roman Empire, the bishopric of Rome remained a religious focal point and centre of power, albeit often in tension with the patriarchate of Constantinople. With the expansion of Christian influence in Europe over ensuing centuries, Rome sought to reassert its spiritual power over the secular forces on which it had had to rely. The best-known high medieval battles between regnal and sacerdotal

---

[57] Bryant, *World History*, 52–3; Tooke, *The Just War*, 7–12.
[58] James J. Megivern, *The Death Penalty: An Historical and Theological Survey* (Mahwah, NJ: Paulist Press, 1997), ch. 2, sect. V pt D; Tooke, *The Just War*, 13, 29.

institutions would occur precisely where the relationship between pope and monarch had been closest in previous centuries, in the 'Holy Roman Empire'. But this is to jump ahead. First, we need to address how the inhabitants of what came to be known as the Holy Roman Empire, and other northerly polities, became Christians, which is a story of further inner–outer tensions.

Conversion was generally a top-down affair, beginning with chieftains, and an outside-inwards affair, beginning with the adaption of existing festivals, practices, icons, and places of worship to Christian purposes. Christian propagandists seeking to play on the prestige of Rome were distinctly ambiguous about the Judaic heritage of their religion, yet it did not escape their notice that convertible warrior tribes were more impressed with the fighting capacities of the ancient Hebrews, and the severe god of some of the legal and historical books (though not the prophecy and poetry) of the Old Testament than with certain New Testament teachings about humility and forgiveness.[59] Correspondingly, the Christ that was deployed in proselytization was often the martial victor over Satan, not the martyred apostle of love who came to be emphasized in the second millennium CE: *Christus victor* rather than *Christus crucifixus*, as it were. The hope was that all this emphasis on externality and worldliness was the first step in the conversion of inner states, but as the Franks converted from the late fifth century—Anglo-Saxons followed in the seventh century, and other populations to the north and east of the Frankish realms through the twelfth century and in some cases even the fourteenth—they shaped Christianity as much as it shaped them. In trying to make Christianity appealing, missionaries presented the supposed this-worldly benefits of Christianity at least as much as the next-worldly connotations. Many of the prosyletized barely knew what it was that they had signed up to and poured the old wine of their established belief systems into new skins. Far from producing Stoic internalism, 'world-rejecting and soteriological', as befitted the early underground, multi-ethnic Christian community, the result was a 'heroic, folk-centred', 'sociobiological' 'interpretation of Christianity'. Owing to the strength of the Frankish Carolingians and Ottonians, which were the first two dynasties of the Holy Roman Empire, this syncretism greatly influenced the character of Christendom. It was precisely the rejection of that sort of 'compromised' Christianity—with its accompaniment in what Ruth Benedict would have called a 'shame culture'—in favour of the *ecclesia primitiva* and a more internal spirituality that encouraged the great papal reform projects of the early second millennium CE, and even the Lutheran Reformation.[60]

---

[59] Charles F. Briggs, *The Body Broken: Medieval Europe, 1300–1520* (London: Routledge 2011), 284; on the testaments, Joseph H. Lynch and Phillip C. Adamo, *The Medieval Church* (London: Routledge, 2014), 206–7.

[60] James C. Russell, *The Germanization of Early Medieval Christianity: A Sociohistorical Approach to Religious Transformation* (Oxford: Oxford University Press, 1996), *passim* but esp. ch. 7 and conclusion, with the quoted passages at pp. 209 and 212.

The growth of a new order of states in the first centuries of the new millennium, after the fragmentation of the Carolingian Empire characterized in Bloch's discussion of the 'first feudal age' (pp. 19–20), enhanced some of the centralizing tendencies that had been present in the Carolingian polity and Anglo-Saxon England. Monarchs of the era shared with the Papacy the agendas of pacifying militarized societies and hierarchically organizing large earthly realms, even as royal and ecclesiastical claims to authority sometimes conflicted. From around the year 1000 the 'peace of god' movement sought to constrict privatized violence within the Christian polities, even if that meant channelling violence outwards through crusade in a way that actually enhanced a sense of shared Christian civilization in the face of non-Christian others. In the name of the 'king's peace', Angevin England saw an intensified attempt to establish a royal monopoly on the legitimate use of force by making private violence a public offence.[61] The principle of compensation for harm to individuals was increasingly replaced by that of retribution for harm to the sovereign's order, though this process, which had started earlier, was gradual and uneven:[62] *wergeld* lasted in some places through the Middle Ages and in Ireland its equivalent for homicide (*éraic*) into the early seventeenth century. Royal authorities took increasing responsibility for prosecution of certain sorts of offence, even if many would continue to be dealt with through manor or city courts and other such enduring features of a more localized power structure.

Another way of putting matters is that the concept of justice as *righteousness* was consolidated alongside and sometimes at the expense of the idea of justice as *satisfaction* that was associated with the payment of compensation or private

[61] On the peace of god, Tomaž Mastnak, *Crusading Peace: Christendom, the Muslim World, and Western Political Order* (Berkeley and Los Angeles: University of California Press, 2002); on the king's peace, Karl Shoemaker, *Sanctuary and Crime in the Middle Ages, 450–1500* (New York: Fordham University Press, 2011), 114.

[62] Eugene J. Chesney, 'The Concept of Mens Rea in the Criminal Law', *Journal of Criminal Law and Criminology* 29/5 (1939), 627–44, here 627–8, including the judgement that 'early English law grew from a point bordering on absolute liability'. Chesney's article relies heavily on Francis Bowes Sayre, 'Mens Rea', *Harvard Law Review* 45/6 (1932), 974–1026. On the blend of emendable and unemendable offences (i.e. the most serious outright murders, meriting capital punishment) in Anglo-Saxon criminal justice that supposedly prevailed up to and even for a century after the Norman Conquest, see Thomas A. Green, 'The Jury and the English Law of Homicide, 1200–1600', *Michigan Law Review* 74 (1976), 413–99, here 416–17. Conversely, on the 'marked switch in later Anglo-Saxon law from amendment to penalty', and the accompanying change, from the early tenth century, in the meaning of *bót* from 'redress of wrong to an injured kin' to 'a fine for damaging society as a whole', see the more recent Patrick Wormald, *Legal Culture in the Early Medieval West* (London: Hambledon, 1999), 60–1. Wormald observes that 'most commentators on early medieval law' contend 'that its dominant notion was one of tort as opposed to crime', then goes on, with respect to the English case, and reference to the Anglo-Saxon tenth century, to problematize the idea of a caesura at the Norman Conquest of 1066. Wormald is not, of course, denying the significance of the tort–crime distinction, merely backdating, with respect to one kingdom, the period of the shift in 'dominance' from one concept to the other.

vengeance.[63] The residue of the concept of justice as satisfaction may be detected in the German word for guilt, *Schuld*, which is also the word for debt.[64] This rise of the concept of justice as righteousness meant the augmentation of concrete grievances with the idea of offences against an abstraction that might also go by the name 'morality' or 'the state'.[65] Indeed behaviour might in principle be prosecuted that had not resulted in any reported harm against any person.

This gradual conceptual shift created an increasingly conducive environment for the pursuit of heretics and the stigmatization of Jews and lepers and indeed the high medieval State was a more enthusiastic persecutor even than the Church, as would often be the case in the witch-hunts of the early modern period. The Fourth Lateran Council of 1215, whose credal tenets defined the conditions of membership in the western Christian community and stipulated distinctive clothing for Jews and heretics, was the culmination of many previous ecclesiastical and royal decrees in these directions. The quest for uniformity was a bedfellow of the demand for submission and was driven with a violent vigour disproportionate to any threat.[66]

As to the law for those within the universe of obligation, the bureaucratic expansion of the central Middle Ages brought great codifications and treatises. From the mid-twelfth century Gratian became synonymous with canon law, in the next century Bracton with English common law. The 'Roman law' culminating in the sixth-century code of the Byzantine emperor Justinian became a touchstone of the legal revolution in continental Europe after the rediscovery of Justinian's *Digest* in the late eleventh century, though it served more as inspiration than template over the next few centuries as it influenced the *ius commune* or common law of the western and central European states. One overall development in western Christendom was an increasing emphasis on the subjective/internal/mental element of what we would now call crime.[67]

[63] For such a distinction, Bryant, *World History*, 52.

[64] Which is a point of which Nietzsche made much: *On the Genealogy of Morality*, ed. Keith Ansell-Pearson (Cambridge: Cambridge University Press, 2006).

[65] See Wormald, *Legal Culture in the Early Medieval West*, 61, claiming that from the early tenth century in England *bót* generally 'meant compensation to God, Church, king or community at large', thus giving it the more abstract, less interpersonal character that we tend to associate with the public law, as opposed to the interpersonal character of wergeld and private law.

[66] Moore, *Formation*, 6–10, 158–69; and (which is also relevant to subsequent paragraphs) Manfred Schneider, 'Forum Internum–Forum Externum: Insitutionstheoriem des Geständnisses', in Jo Reichertz and Manfred Schneider (eds), *Sozialgeschichte des Geständnisses: Zum Wandel der Geständniskultur* (Wiesbaden: VS, 2007), 23–42, here 24 ff.

[67] Chesney, 'Concept of Mens Rea', 629–32; Virpi Mäkinen and Heikki Pihlajamäki, 'The Individualization of Crime in Medieval Canon Law', *Journal of the History of Ideas* 65/4 (2004), 525–42. (Note that Gratian's *Decretum* was scarcely confined to matters of canon law.) On the other side of the ledger, on the endurance of elements of absolute liability in the influential *Leges Henrici Primi*, and thus the not entirely representative nature of the *mens rea* clause that appeared in it, see Sayre, 'Mens Rea', 978–83.

We know that interest in the subjective element of action was not original to Christian civilization, far less second-millennium Christendom. Thus we must disregard much of the 'progressivist' orthodoxy that purports to identify a late medieval 'moment of transition from the primitive emphasis upon *actus reus* or externalities to the modern focus on internal or subjective culpability', and the partially backdated version that gives Justinian all the credit, even as we can allow that the subjective element did become more pronounced in the first half of the second millennium than, say, under Frankish law, owing to aforementioned reasons of sociology, state, and religious reform.[68] Subjective disposition—*mens rea*—came to be a key criterion in distinguishing crimes/felonies from torts and delicts, i.e. harmful failures of due care.[69] The law of torts and delicts—or the law of obligations, as it is more suggestively called in some quarters—falls today under the remit of civil law, as opposed to criminal law.

The argument of legal historian Penny Crofts requires some qualification but nevertheless captures an important truth. She observes that modern law's 'regime of subjective culpability' is more individualist and internalist than its more socially minded predecessors, and as such 'pushes negligence, strict and absolute liability offences to the side as awkward exceptions, and constructs [for instance] categories of constructive homicide as archaic offences that have not as yet caught up with the regime of *subjective* culpability'.[70] The qualification—and to such matters the present section will return near its conclusion—is that rather than anachronistic residues of an earlier age, perhaps concepts of negligence, gross negligence, and recklessness constitute enduring counterbalances to an excessive emphasis on a particular mental state. Further, mention of absolute liability offences reminds us that we ought to attend to civil law as a paradigm of broader culpability and obligation than that presented by criminal law.[71] The truth in Croft's position lies in the significance that tends to be attached to the criminal-civil distinction, a distinction marked not least by the differing sorts of penalty

---

[68] For the 'primitive' quote, which represents a position with which the author of the quote disagrees, Penny Crofts, *Wickedness and Crime: Laws of Homicide and Malice* (London: Routledge, 2013), 33, 258. On the salience of the mental element, especially under ecclesiastical jurisdictions, 'even' in the early medieval Latin West (under Charlemagne and his successors), see Murray, *Conscience*, 10–14. For exaggerations of the innovations of Justinian's code on the matter of animus (will/intention), see Adolf Berger (ed.), *Encyclopedic Dictionary of Roman Law* (Clark, NJ: The Lawbook Exchange, 2004), 362. On Cicero's important views, see Chesney, 'The Concept of Mens Rea', 630. On relevant legal concepts in the classical Roman period: Eric Descheemaeker and Helen Scott (eds), *Iniuria and the Common Law* (Oxford: Hart, 2014), chs 5 and 6. Israel Drapkin, *Crime and Punishment in the Ancient World* (Lexington, KY: Lexington Books, 1989), 241, shows that later Roman penal law, while not as influential subsequently as Roman civil law, clearly distinguished between subjective and objective elements. Yet further back, see Aristotle, *Ethics*, trans. J. A. K. Thompson (Harmondsworth: Penguin, 1966). bk V, ch. 8 (pp. 155–6) on state of mind in the sense of motive.

[69] In addition to preceding notes on *mens rea*, on the origins and changing meaning of the word 'felony', see Wormald, *Legal Culture*, 62.

[70] Crofts, *Wickedness and Crime*, 28–33 and *passim*, quotes from pp. 33 and 258.

[71] Williams, *Shame and Necessity*, 64–5.

that can accrue in each sphere. We might hazard that there is an enduring general association of crimes, as opposed to torts and other breached obligations, with sinfulness of a particular order. Certainly the Latin *crimen* could denote 'sin', and while it has probably never been maintained that all sins are also crimes,[72] a great overlap has long been assumed, and our conception of what is really wrong, and why, continues to be shaped by religious categories even as the law itself has adopted more secular terms. ('Punishment' shares a root with 'penance', and 'penitentiary' is the name still used in the USA for 'prison'.) Furthermore, given the prioritization in 'progressivist' thought of justice as righteousness over justice as satisfaction between individuals, it is significant that criminal law better fits the former category and civil law the latter. Perhaps, then, the major critical point here pertains to broader culture, rather than to the law.

Thinking to cultural 'common sense', another indication of the ongoing influence of the religious heritage pertains to the original sin. That was a sin of what Augustine called *concupiscence*, hurtful desire, unbound. In legal parlance, deliberate action to achieve a desired goal is known as direct intent. It is distinguished in morality, 'common sense', and to some extent in law from simply allowing something to happen, but also from bringing something about in a way that was predictable even if not desired. This implicitly normative distinction helps explain why we routinely consider genocide, say the intentional massacre of a million people, as morally worse than creating for other reasons the conditions in which a million people will predictably starve, and not intervening when they do starve. The term collateral damage serves to insert a moral distinction between the pursuit of the direct ends of, say, military bombing, and the often-predictable side effects of the same. The famed doctrine of double effect—in many influential iterations—is based on the idea that we bear less moral responsibility for that which we indirectly intend than that which we directly intend and it has influenced just-war theory as much as debates about the distinction between voluntary-active and voluntary-passive euthanasia.[73] The moral hierarchy is not axiomatic.

---

[72] On *crimen*, Murray, *Conscience*, 26. Further on the significant though not total overlap between *crimen* and sin, including the relationship of *crimen* to 'mortal sin', see James Gordley, *The Jurists: A Critical History* (Oxford: Oxford University Press, 2013), 73.

[73] The law itself does have ways to circumvent some of the potential problems here, which is why I stress the general cultural aspect. On the legal side, see Jeremy Horder, 'Intention in the Criminal Law—A Rejoinder', *Modern Law Review* 58/5 (1995), 678–91; specifically on the origins of the concept of oblique intent and its partial incorporation in British legal thought on intent, see Mohamed Elewa Badar, *The Concept of Mens Rea in International Criminal Law* (Oxford: Hart, 2013), 48–9. On overstatement of the significance of the difference between direct and oblique intention in traditional just-war theory and international law, especially on the matter of 'collateral damage', see Michael A. Newton and Larry May, *Proportionality in International Law* (Oxford: Oxford University Press, 2014), 218; on the euthanasia issue, A. M. Begley, 'Acts, Omissions, Intentions and Motives: A Philosophical Examination of the Moral Distinction between Killing and Letting Die', *Journal of Advanced Nursing* 28 (1998), 865–73.

Let us now move more fully to the development of moral theory in and beyond the Middle Ages, while bearing in mind moral theory's overlaps with law and theology. As opposed to acting from fear of hell and hope for heaven, one could emphasize the honouring of god's law solely for its sake. This duty-based philosophy, like Kant's later version, is most clearly associated with the thought of the late medieval theologian Duns Scotus (1266–1308).[74] From the functional perspective of rulers, this sort of self-policing appears institutionally attractive, 'conscience control' being a more advanced form of social control than preference-shaping by threat. Yet there were potential costs for Church and State. For the Church, the problem was that were such thinking taken to one conclusion, morality was entirely detached from prospects for salvation, which might be to detach it from faith. Equally if social control was the goal, that was always threatened by the risk, which Augustine had recognized, that not everyone's conscience or reason would take them in the same direction in the interpretation of God's law. Finally, there is the question of whether God and State should judge the individual by the same criteria. Addressing that question requires us to engage with the thought of Peter Abelard, from whom we shall work forward to the Reformation and its stipulations on the relationship between faith and morality.

The difference between Abelard (1079–1142) and some of his predecessor philosophers was one of degree. He expanded the equation of sin with mental acts—mental acts being those things that transformed into sins otherwise ordinary dispositional vices that one might not be able to help, or sensuality that one could not help but 'feel'. He made the rightness or wrongness of the external act contingent on the preceding mental act.[75] By extension, works or acts in themselves do not merit praise or condemnation of the actor, rather the actor's mindset does. This brought the focus not just to intention but to motive. One must, however, recognize Abelard's particular distinction between crime and sin. Crime was punishable by earthly justice whose important exemplary function necessitated dealing only with externally visible signs of interior motive states, whereas only God had direct access to the sinful mind. Nor was Abelard a pure subjectivist who adverted in the last instance to the authenticity of the individual conscience. His talk of divine natural law suggests it was possible to discern what is intrinsically good and bad, and indeed the possibility of such discernment is central to the

---

[74] Anthony Kenny, *A New History of Western Philosophy* (Oxford: Clarendon Press, 2010), 463–5.

[75] John Marenbon, *The Philosophy of Peter Abelard* (Cambridge: Cambridge University Press, 1999), ch. 14, with discussion of some potential confusions and inconsistencies on Abelard's attempts to restrict his own subjectivism at pp. 293–5; Linda Hogan, *Confronting the Truth: Conscience in the Catholic Tradition* (Mahwah, NJ: Paulist Press, 2000), 73–5; Ralph McInerny, *A History of Western Philosophy from St. Augustine to Ockham* (Notre Dame, IN: University of Notre Dame Press, 1963), pt III, ch. 3; David Knowles, *The Evolution of Medieval Thought* (Baltimore: Helican, 1962), 128 ff.; Michael Bertram Crowe, *The Changing Profile of The Natural Law* (The Hague: Nijhoff, 1977), 114. Paul Tillich, *A History of Christian Thought* (New York: Touchstone, 1968), 170–1 on the contexts of reception of Abelard's thought.

individual's striving for purity of heart. It was thus of paramount import, as Abelard put it, to 'know thyself'. One could thereby align the subjective element with objective, God-given desiderata, in order that subjectivism might not run riot. (Like Augustine, he believed that the value-determining centre was outside himself.) Yet it was also possible for those, such as the crucifiers of Christ, not to know what they were *really* doing, and thus not to merit blame in the sense of guilt for a sin. Given such examples, Abelard's thought was not taken up unreservedly in theological circles. However the enhanced subjective element could no longer be avoided, and this was especially true after the early thirteenth-century Latin rediscovery of Aristotle's *Ethics*.[76] It is in the area of moral thought that Abelard found his major legacy, not least on Gratian.

Abelard, like Gratian after him, was also important in the incubation of the distinction in canon law between matters of the *forum internum* and the *forum externum*, as they would be called in post-Tridentine Catholicism. In the decades after Gratian's *Decretum* of.1140, the *forum internum* was called the *forum conscientiae*, or court of conscience, as opposed to the more formalized, 'external', compulsory ecclesiastical court, which was concerned solely with 'manifest and public' transgressions of the Church's law or of the divine law. Where the ecclesiastical court could hand down orthodox punishments of a 'negative' kind, the outcome of confession in the court of conscience tended to be penance, i.e. more 'positive', compensatory acts to God and/or the community. The court of conscience was not just concerned with 'public and manifest' sins—and confession of those could not safeguard the penitent from prosecution in a public court—but also with inner or hidden sins. The external court was based on argument and external examination, but in the internal court (which, to be clear, involved more than one person, and was thus not completely internal to the mind of the penitent), while the confessing penitent could be prompted and guided by a trained confessor, the penitent herself was at once accuser and accused. The confessor saw himself as caring for the health of the penitent's soul; the penitent was encouraged to provide a detailed account of sins by way of encouraging self-reflection. Confession, that blend of introspection in a dialogic setting, was made mandatory for laypeople on an annual basis by Lateran IV, by which time too the legal confession—the baring of the conscience by the only person who could really testify to it—in criminal ecclesiastical cases had been crowned 'queen of proofs'.[77]

---

[76] Aristotle's first commentators in the early thirteenth century downplayed the civil and political dimensions of ethical life in favour of the contemplative side. See Irene Zavattero, 'Moral and Intellectual Virtues in the Earliest Latin Commentaries on the *Nicomachean Ethics*', in István Pieter Bejczy (ed.), *Virtue Ethics in the Middle Ages* (Leiden: Brill, 2008), 31–54.

[77] On Abelard, sin, crime, *forum internum* and *forum externum*, and confession, see Mäkinen and Pihlajamäki, 'The Individualization of Crime', 531 ff., including 537 on 'queen of proofs'. Further on *forum internum* and *forum externum*: W. Trusen, 'Zur Bedeutung des geistlichen Forum internum und externum für die spaitmittelalterlich Gesellschaft', *Zeitschrift der Savigny-Stiftung*, Kanonistische

One contribution by Thomas Aquinas (*c*.1225–74) was to develop a distinction between *syneidêsis* and *conscientia*. Prior to the work of Peter Lombard (*c*.1095–1160) these things had been considered identical, as in Jerome's translation of the Vulgate. Aquinas held *syneidêsis*, now widely known as *synderesis* after a twelfth-century mistranscription, to be the innate, God-given knowledge of the fundamental principles by which to distinguish good from evil, whereas *conscientia* was a matter of judgement in the application of these general principles to particular situations. It is easy to get confused here, but note that the concept of conscience as it was developing at this point comprised both *synderesis* and *conscientia*—they were two elements of conscience. As for Aquinas, whatever the allowances he felt that one might make for the errant *conscientia* that still bound its owner, and thus the lack of blame that should attach to her whose judgement has gone astray in applying the principles given by *synderesis*, proper goodness must cohere with rationality. But he also insisted on a separation between things that were to be judged by God alone and those judged by man, and by 'man' he seemed to include confessors.[78] He rendered the canon law distinction between the *forum conscientiae/forum internum* and the *forum externum* into something more like an opposition. In his *Summa Theologica*, the 'court of conscience' is reduced to conscience itself—it is on the way to becoming a purely conceptual forum, completely internal to the individual's head or heart. Conscience is a matter for the 'relationship' between the person and God, without the mediation of any agent of the Church. The internal forum was for Aquinas akin to an untouchable inner sphere.[79]

These musings were more important for the high doctrinal conflicts that would later lead to schism in the western Church than for social history in the three centuries from Lateran IV. After all, by 1500, confession 'had become so efficient, so well-fortified with literature and theology, and so nearly universal that, far from being scandalously inadequate, it threatened to exceed the other way and become a tyranny'.[80] But perhaps the most important crack Aquinas created in theological orthodoxy was his contention that while God was immediately

Abteilung 7/6 (1990), 254–85; P. Petkoff, '*Forum Internum* and *Forum Externum* in Canon Law and Public International Law with a Particular Reference to the Jurisprudence of the European Court of Human Rights', *Religion and Human Rights* 7 (2012), 183–214, here 201–2; Schneider, 'Forum Internum–Forum Externum: Insitutionstheoriem des Geständnisses', 24 ff.; and most important for the above analysis, Joseph Goering, 'The Internal Forum and the Literature of Penance and Confession', *Traditio* 59 (2004), 175–227, with 'manifest and public' at 183 and Gratian's influence at 211–12.

[78] Kenny, *A New History of Western Philosophy*, 457–60; Hogan, *Confronting the Truth*, 76–8; Tobias Hoffmann, 'Conscience and Synderesis', in Brian Davies and Eleonore Stump (eds), *The Oxford Handbook of Aquinas* (Oxford: Oxford University Press, 2012), 255–64. On the mistranscription, Schinkel, *Conscience*, 172, and 174–5 on *conscientia* and *synderesis* as part of conscience and on the theological and historical context (including the Abelardian background and the prescriptions of Lateran IV) that conduced to this shift in the understanding of *conscientia*.

[79] Petkoff, '*Forum Internum* and *Forum Externum*', 208–9.   [80] Murray, *Conscience*, 53.

certain for himself, he was not immediately certain to humans.[81] In compound with the legacies of Abelard and others, such contentions provided an important starting point for the 'nominalist' challenge of the later Middle Ages.

Nominalism brought epistemological, metaphysical, and moral questions together. In an answer to questions that had some echoes of one of Plato's dialogues—(1) do the gods will what is just/reasonable/good or (2) is the just/reasonable/good what the gods happen to will?—the metaphysical 'realists' like Duns Scotus banked on the certainties of (1), meaning that the earthly doer of duty could follow reason, morality, and God simultaneously. In reconciling Christian doctrine with Aristotle Aquinas also rendered god's reason anterior to 'his' will. William of Ockham (1288–1347) reversed the order of priority, on the principle that only if will were supreme could God's power be truly unlimited, truly free.[82] Nominalists also dissented from the related theologically 'realist' claim that one could know the natural and historical world objectively as the manifestation of a divine, hierarchical order. For nominalists, the human mind was left with articulating its own systems on the fragmentary evidence of experience or reason. Logic of thought and grammatical logic of written and spoken language were the only reliable tools for comprehending the world at human disposal, but they were uncoupled from metaphysics, i.e. from entities of the sort that Plato had called eternal 'forms'—entities that for prior theologians had vouchsafed the interlinked order of the natural world, that 'book of God'. The emphasis on the inner states and human tools of comprehension also suggested that religious hierarchs were in no better position to determine the higher meaning behind the literal word of the Scriptures than any other literate person proficient in the use of reason. Everything else was at God's unknowable disposition, leaving the human with faith alone, and while William provided some reasons as to why God would not suddenly change the rules of the world that he had contingently chosen to create, certainty about there being things that were right in themselves received a significant blow. Save at those moments at which God might choose to intervene in the world, concrete, mundane individuals existed on their own, albeit in virtue of God's omnipotence and in some way in his image, certain only of their own situation as creatures free to will.[83] One result was a sort of moral intuitionism that by no means did away with the idea of conscience but

---

[81]   Paul Tillich, *The Protestant Era* (London: Nisbet, 1955), 71.

[82]   Jörg Dierken, *Selbstbewusstsein individueller Freiheit: Religionstheoretische Erkundungen in protestantischer Perspektive* (Tübingen: Mohr Siebeck, 2005), 203 ff.; Lauri Haikola, *Gesetz und Evangelium bei Matthias Flacius Illyricus: Eine Untersuchung zur Lutherischen Theologie vor der Konkordienformel* (Lund: Gleerup, 1952), 32 ff.; Schinkel, *Conscience*, 179, 430.

[83]   Janet Coleman, *Ancient and Medieval Memories: Studies in the Reconstruction of the Past* (Cambridge: Cambridge University Press, 2005), 530–6 and *passim*; Gordon Leff, *William of Ockham: The Metamorphosis of Scholastic Discourse* (Manchester: Manchester University Press, 1975), 54–5.

still left it as a rather formal category, bereft of the substantial contents of certain, objective right, that a 'realist' metaphysics claimed to be able to identify.[84]

The Reformation owes to nominalism the doctrine of divine voluntarism and the challenge to institutional interpretative authority. The Lutheran belief that salvation comes not from the commission of good works on earth but from the meeting of human faith and God's grace, stems additionally from elements of Pauline thought and aforementioned developments in moral theory, in which good deeds were at most just uncertain evidence of inner dispositions. In his commentary on Paul's Letter to the Galatians, Luther described 'papists' as 'our Jews'; 'Papists' had perverted the sacraments and fallen into what Paul had dubbed 'works righteousness'.[85]

While Luther added 'papists' to the list of those traduced for lacking the relevant philosophy of internality, the trend towards subjectivism and reliance on inner faculties may be detected across new confessional boundaries and in many areas of inquiry. A Catholic was the author of the most famous subjectivist motto of them all, *cogito ergo sum*. Where Augustine had reasoned 'I doubt, therefore I am', Descartes's (1596–1650) update, 'I think, therefore I am', moved the focus from truth as a property of the objective world to certainty as a product of the inquiring mind.[86] This mind, as a 'thinking' thing, was categorically separate from the body that housed it and was capable of forming 'clear and distinct ideas' as the basis for systems of philosophical knowledge. The body was characterized by 'extension' rather than thought and was part of the natural order just as much as was any non-human animal. Such mind–body separation recast the familiar two spheres model of *physis* and *pneuma* (p. 144). The doctrine also complemented dualisms in other areas of social and religious thought. In fact in principle it dug a broad ditch between the inner existential certainty of the thinker and everything else, other minds included.

Luther's understanding of the importance of faith alone and its supposed complement, original sin, was based on a reading of Paul that Luther wrongly assumed was the sole basis for Augustine's doctrine.[87] Luther underpinned a specifically spiritual doctrine, as separate from a theory of social justice or revolution in earthly kingdoms. His insistence on God's pure transcendence, God's existence in another realm, was the warrant for secular governance and hierarchy

---

[84] Schinckel, *Conscience*, 179, 430.

[85] Martin Luther, *Commentary on Pauls' Epistle to the Galatians* (Lafayette, IN: Sovereign Grace, 2001), 206; Mark U. Edwards, *Luther's Last Battles: Politics and Polemics 1531–1546* (Minneapolis: Fortress, 2004), 116, 129.

[86] On Descartes and the nominalist inheritance, and the way in which interior self-certainty of thought becomes the 'measure' of method, see Robert B. Pippin, *Modernism as a Philosophical Problem* (Oxford: Blackwell, 1999), 23–4.

[87] John M. Rist, *Augustine Deformed: Love, Sin and Freedom in the Western Moral Tradition* (Cambridge: Cambridge University Press, 2014), 174, 184–7 and ch. 7 more generally.

in the earthly sphere, even as Luther rejected earlier 'sociobiological', this-worldly systems of faith. The Church, meaning the institutions of the Church, was of the external world just as much as was the State, and in that world the State must stand supreme, contrary to certain papal ambitions.[88] That is the common wisdom about Luther's thought and with a contested degree of qualification it stands.[89]

Luther's not-always-consistent distinction between spiritual and mundane spheres became categorical in horrified response to the 'peasant' rebels, who in the war of 1524–5 followed what they saw as the logic of his attacks on immoral Church and misuses of power. Luther's settled view marked him off radically from those medieval antinomians like Joachim of Fiore and the Brethren and Sisters of the Free Spirit. These people believed in God's immanence as well as transcendence, and so in the possibility of a genuine union with God on this earth—a union that came to be called indwelling. By this union, matters of good and evil were transcended, and earthly hierarchies rejected alongside the idea of private property. Early modern successors of the Brethren were to be found in Calvin's Geneva under the name 'spirituals', and in Civil War and Commonwealth England under the attribution 'Ranters'. All three groups were subject to intense vilification, as in Calvin's *Contre la secte phantastique et furieuse des Libertins qui se nomment Spirituelz* (1545). The propaganda makes it difficult to establish how coherent and numerous they were, let alone what they actually did. The violence of the reaction against them, as against the insurgents of 1524–5, tells us a great deal about the phobias of the prevailing orders about the diffusion into the mundane world of too much of the spirit of some people's interpretation of the Reformation.[90]

---

[88] While Luther's two kingdoms model clearly draws on Augustine's two cities model, differences between them are elucidated in Rist, *Augustine Deformed*, 176 ff. The mention of 'sociobiological' belief systems is to make the contrast with the vision of Christianity elucidated on p. 145.

[89] One qualification is that as the institutions of the Church lost direct authority in Protestant states, there was a further infusion of religious precepts into the secular sphere of law and order. The decline in ecclesiastical courts was matched by secular courts (thus the State) expanding their remit and in the process becoming more explicitly 'moralized' in their concerns. Public ordinances addressed matters of family law, antisocial behaviour and moral torts, school curricula, and so forth. See Elizabeth Zoller, *Introduction to Public Law: A Comparative Perspective* (Leiden: Martinus Nijhoff, 2008), 67–8; Edgar J. McManus, *Law and Liberty in Early New England* (Amherst, MA: University of Massachusetts Press, 1993), 3. However, for a debate as to how 'Lutheran' was the major legal development of the Germanic 1532 Carolina penal code, see Harold J. Berman, *Law and Revolution, the Formation of the Western Legal Tradition* (Cambridge, MA: Harvard University Press, 1983), 28–9, 196 and Berman, *Law and Revolution II: The Impact of the Protestant Reformations on the Western Legal Tradition* (Cambridge, MA: Belknap Press, 2003),144 ff., as opposed to Heikki Pihlajamäki, '*Executor divinarum et suarum legum*: Criminal Law and the Lutheran Reformation', in Virpi Mäkinen (ed.) *Lutheran Reformation and the Law* (Leiden: Brill, 2006), 171–204, here 177, who finds traces of Protestantism difficult to find in the Carolina.

[90] Philip Schaff, *History of the Christian Church*, viii (Grand Rapids, MI: Eerdmans, 1969), 494–500. On Ranters and related matters: Christopher Hill, *The World Turned Upside Down* (London: Penguin, 1991).

Luther's social thinking was still shaped by those organic philosophies of society where each part of the earthly *universitas* had its place, higher or lower, in a coherent whole. Individual uniqueness went together with acceptance of one's allotted social role, as also in Calvin's teaching about being true to one's 'calling'. Were St Paul correct that master, slave, and the 'earthly prince' were equal in the eyes of God, their unequal standings for a while on earth mattered little. Besides, in Luther's outlook, as in Augustine's, real Christians were thin on the ground, and the anarchy that would ensue from secular instability would provide even more fertile terrain for the Devil. Luther relied heavily on Paul's Letter to the Romans (particularly Romans 13) in distinguishing between heavenly and earthly laws, though one wonders how the thought of Paul, who died between 64 and 68 CE, would have been modified had he written after the onset of Nero's persecution of Christians in 64 CE. Luther, himself having enjoyed the Elector of Saxony's protection much as the nominalist William of Ockham had earlier enjoyed Emperor Ludwig of Bavaria's protection from the Church, interpreted the fifth command of the Decalogue as an injunction to obey one's political father.

Luther was obviously concerned with good and evil and was obviously not trying to encourage immorality; yet the route to *divine* forgiveness was ultimately through faith, rather than reparational acts, and even, if we are to be cynical about it, rather than much consideration of any earthly victim. In truth, the institution of confession had already encouraged the latter tendency, by providing a hermeneutic for the sinner with no parallel hermeneutic for the victim of sin.[91] (A historiographical expression of the same principle is *The Constitutional History of England* by the historian and later Anglican bishop William Stubbs, which closes in tribute to 'that highest justice which is found in the deepest sympathy with erring and straying men'.[92]) Furthermore, scriptural justification existed for the focus on sinner and forgiveness in Luke 15:7: 'there will be more rejoicing in heaven over one sinner who repents than over ninety-nine righteous persons who do not need to repent'.

What Luther achieved was undermining the central tenets of sacramental confession in the process of separating 'private conscience and the institutional church'.[93] Out went the priest's power of absolution, and his concomitant power to prescribe penitential works. In came the belief in the individual's essential powerlessness, and the conviction that faith was the only hope. All were sinners, unable to fulfil the demands of biblical law, but belief in forgiveness of sins through the grace of God was inextricably associated with the prospect of such forgiveness. (Contrast this stance with Jewish confession wherein God's

---

[91] For which point I thank Jürgen Manemann, in conversation.
[92] William Stubbs, *The Constitutional History of England in Its Origin and Development*, iii (Oxford: Clarendon Press, 1890), 639.
[93] Murray, *Conscience and Authority*, 87.

forgiveness is sought for sins against God, but forgiveness for sins against other humans must be sought from them.) The 'peaceful conscience, which is a product of the firm belief that one is forgiven, is a prerequisite of forgiveness. One of Luther's favorite ways of dramatizing this paradox was to insist that if we do not believe we are forgiven—if we do not find peace in the promise of forgiveness— we make God a liar.' Good works ensue from the state of believing oneself justi- fied, though those works are not themselves relevant for salvation. Equally, no human is perfect, or godlike, and as the faithful Christian cannot but continue to sin, it is rather important that, as Luther wrote in 1520, no amount of sinning will lead the Christian to 'forfeit his salvation . . . unless he decides not to believe'.[94] On another occasion he declared that 'it is solely by impiety and incredulity of heart that a man becomes guilty, and a slave of sin, deserving condemnation; not by any outward sin or work'.[95]

The lawyer and Seneca scholar Calvin was not prepared to subordinate the Church to the State, nonetheless he endorsed a 'two kingdoms' dualism of his own. Increasing social authority in his Geneva was vested in the Consistory, which was founded in 1541–2 but effectively gained theocratic power in 1555. It did not distinguish between religious and moral precept and provided the institutional discipline that in Calvin's view fickle conscience could not be trusted to bring to bear on the earthly comportment of bodies. Bodies was a keyword here, as it had been for Augustine and Gratian, since bodies, like active works, were phenomena of the temporal, political world, rather than the world to which faith pertained. Calvin wrote of twofold government, the 'spiritual and temporal jurisdiction'. 'The former has its seat within the soul, the latter only regulates the external conduct.'[96] The 'visible Church', i.e. all the institutions of religion, is, like the State, confined to the temporal realm, and does not mediate between the two worlds as it had earlier via the institution of confession. For Calvin, the mistake of the antinomian *spirituels* was to conflate the two realms. They had confused the genuine freedom of the soul, in the realm in which earthly morality was as little relevant as any other

---

[94] Thomas N. Tentler, *Sin and Confession on the Eve of the Reformation* (Princeton: Princeton University Press, 2015), 349 ff., with quote about Luther at 355—the point made by that quote is at the centre of Paul Hacker, *The Ego in Faith: Martin Luther and the Origin of Anthropocentric Religion* (Chicago: Franciscan Herald Press, 1970), wherein Luther's quote on forfeiting salvation is at 136; Schinkel, *Conscience*, 198; Lyndal Roper, *Martin Luther: Renegade and Prophet* (London: Bodley Head, 2016), 167–8, and 208 on Luther's stress on faith *alone*. It is worth reiterating that Luther was at least as much a polemicist as a systematic theologian, so his writings are by no means consistent. For relevant resistance to some of the connotations of his own proclamations, see e.g. Harry Loewen, *Luther and the Radicals* (Waterloo: Wilfrid Laurier University Press, 2010), ch. 6.

[95] Philip Hughes, *History of the Church*, iii (London: Sheed and Ward, 1947), 518.

[96] Jean Calvin, *Institutes of the Christian Religion* (Woodstock, ON: Devoted, 2016), 371 (*Institutes* bk III, ch. 19, §15).

earthly concern, with a world in which the body and the moral conscience were heteronomous, subject to external authority civil and religious.[97]

Calvin's doctrine, like Luther's, effectively involved a subdivision of the purely internal version of the *forum internum* between a forum of conscience about right and wrong as worldly concerns and a forum of pure belief and individual spirituality pertaining to a soul that was entirely separate from the temporal world. Luther sharpened the distinction, there in principle in Duns Scotus, between conscience-as-faith and conscience-as-morality. Faith was conceptually separated from morality, and in the sense that heaven was more important than earth, the soul more important than the body, faith was promoted above morality in a way alien to Judaism, which has relatively little to say about the next world because of its preoccupation with the sacredness of this one, and its belief that the relationship to God works through relations with other people.

The cultural influence of this sort of thinking should not be understated, and as with all cultural diffusion Calvin's and Luther's distinctions could be adapted. The division of the soul from the worldly moral conscience, and accompanying doctrines of *solefideism* (by-faith-alone-ism) and Calvinist double predestination, must be the origin of that peculiar all-or-nothing, saved or damned, outlook whereby instead of considering whether actor X's act was wrong, one addresses what actor X 'was'.[98] As to the emphasis on the internality of the actor, rather than the world outside, consider the nineteenth-century Lutheran and existential philosopher Søren Kierkegaard. He wrote: 'it is true of the religious man who goes astray by reason of his pristine passion that this puts him in a kindly light'. Concerning other sorts of people he also wrote: 'By reason of the infiltration of the State and social groups and the congregation and society, God can no longer get a hold on the individual.' Then, polemically: 'So let us rather sin, sin out and out, seduce maidens, murder men, commit highway robbery—after all, that can be repented of, and such a criminal God can still get a hold on.'[99] Kierkegaard's rumination was far from the first indication of the social ramifications of doctrines whose primary concern was the state of one's own soul rather than, say, the mutilated body of another soul-bearer. Indeed one assumes that Kierkegaard had in mind Luther's extremizing assertion to Philip Melanchthon in 1521 that 'sin

---

[97] Torrance Kirby, 'A Reformed Culture of Persuasion: John Calvin's "Two Kingdoms" and the Theological Origins of the Public Sphere', in Richard R. Topping and John A. Vissers (eds), *Calvin@500: Theology, History and Practice* (Eugene, Oregon: Wipf and Stock, 2011), 52–66; cf. Matthew J. Tuninga, *Calvin's Political Theology and the Public Engagement of the Church: Christ's Two Kingdoms* (Cambridge: Cambridge University Press, 2017), 184, stressing that 'for Calvin the fundamental difference between the two kingdoms is not that one is inwards and the other is outward, but that one is spiritual and eternal, and the other is temporal and political'.

[98] For an element of this, Schinkel, *Conscience*, 196–7.

[99] Søren Kierkegaard, *Kierkegaard's* Concluding Unscientific Postscript, trans. David F. Swenson and Walter Lowrie (Princeton: Princeton University Press, 1961), 484–5.

will not tear us away' from God, 'even if thousands and thousands of times a day we fornicate or murder'.[100]

Wherever Luther wished to set the forum boundaries at various points, his words contributed to this-worldly conflict, and the rest of this section charts enduring dualistic tensions. The religious, military, and political strife of the sixteenth and seventeenth centuries were amongst other things battles over the nature of conscience, faith, and god, in which rulers tried to co-opt subjects and subjects sometimes rebelled. Faith was politicized more than ever. Combat settled little concerning the relationship between conscience and morality or that between the prerogatives of the individual and the needs of society and political order.

Few contemporaries are on record as having agreed with the philosopher Thomas Hobbes (1588–1679) that conscience was as trivial as mere opinion and that *conscientia* only had real meaning as public and shared, even if there was clear logic to his conviction about the 'repugnan[ce] to civil society' of the doctrine whereby 'whatsoever a man does against his conscience, is sin'.[101] Even if one was not a *solefidian*, the cat was out of the bag as far as a heightened self-consciously subjective orientation was concerned. At the same time, the very reinforcement of different State religions in successive sixteenth- and seventeenth-century peace treaties encouraged scepticism as to claims on the one true way, and thus the potential to foster doctrines of tolerance of different beliefs. Some thinkers sought a set of minimal principles to which any Christian could subscribe. The legacy of Calvin's intransigence found a counterpart in the legacy of the tolerant Erasmian Sebastian Castellio (1515–63).[102] Moral reason rebelled against the inequity of arbitrary salvation, the idea of the will's bondage, and the accompanying doctrine of original sin. Against Luther's 'lopsided Augustinianism'[103] it was recalled that Augustine had had quite a lot to say about love as well as faith. The argument that God's goodness governed 'his' will rather than being mere expression of it had a long 'realist'—as opposed to nominalist—history that was easily recovered.

Then there were tensions between different levels of individual in the mundane sphere. On one hand, at the highest political level, the drive to accommodate the confessions and remove some of the causes of violence within Christendom reinforced the power of 'Caesaro-papist' princes as against the international forces of the Papacy and the Holy Roman Empire. Ending the Thirty Years War, the Westphalian treaties of 1648 built on and amended the 1555 Peace of Augsburg, which had established, with exceptions, the principle that each state's religion correspond to that of its ruler: where Augsburg recognized Lutheranism as a religion

---

[100] Hughes, *History of the Church*, iii. 518.
[101] Schinkel, *Conscience*, 209–10; Strohm, *Conscience*, 90–1.
[102] On Castellio's importance, Perez Zagorin, *How the Idea of Religious Toleration Came to the West* (Princeton: Princeton University Press, 2005), ch. 4.
[103] Rist, *Augustine Deformed*, ch. 7.

of state alongside Catholicism, Westphalia added Calvinism. On the other hand, significant concessions were made to the consciences of subjects too. The signatory rulers committed themselves to permitting religious minorities in their states to practise their faith under certain restrictions. Furthermore, under both the Augsburg and the Wesphalian dispensation, subjects who did not wish to live in a state of a different confession were granted freedom to emigrate—in other words they were granted some choice over their sovereign.

If the State was increasingly a private individual from the perspective of the international system, how were individual people to conceptualize themselves qua individuals in relation to the state in other spheres than the religious one? Descartes's contemporary Hugo Grotius (1583–1645) turned on its head the doctrine of the theorist of absolutism Jean Bodin (1530–96), while concurring with Bodin on the need for religious tolerance. Where Bodin had made state sovereignty the source of law, Grotius determined that 'just as every right of the magistrate comes to him from the state, so has the same right come to the state from private individuals'. He saw that 'the right of chastisement was held by private persons before it was held by the state'. In principle the individual had sovereign attributes: hence the emphasis on *subjective* right as the primary fount of legal order.[104] Private law was the mechanism for asserting subjective rights, rights whose salient conceptualization can, by the way, be traced to canon law debates of the twelfth century. The rough allocation of remits between public and private law that endures today dates from the sixteenth–seventeenth centuries.[105]

There was more than a grain of contract theory in Grotius' *The Law of War and Peace* (1625), and while fuller versions of contract theory had been devised earlier,[106] Grotius differed from them in hinting at the sort of more individually initiated contract that was influentially propounded by Hobbes and Locke (1632–1704). Locke's contemporary Samuel Pufendorf (1632–94) and Locke's personal experiment in education, the third Earl of Shaftesbury (1671–1713), were concerned in turn to bring the social dimensions of morality into harmony with individual subjectivity. For Pufendorf, individuals combine through *socialitas*, sociability, by enacting their God-given capacity for knowledge of the good, in order to further the common interests of a God-given humanity. Like Grotius, he saw humans as having tendencies towards both selflessness and selfishness. The

---

[104] Ruben Alvarado, *Common Law and Natural Rights* (Aalten: Wordbridge, 2009), 30–2 for the principle and the limits on it, as well as the Grotius quotes.

[105] Zoller, *Introduction to Public Law* on the sixteenth and seventeenth centuries. Note that the public–private distinction was prefigured in Roman law, but the basis and character of the distinction was different. On that matter and on twelfth-century canonists and subjective rights: Berman, *Law and Revolution II*, 298, 426.

[106] Lee Ward, *The Politics of Liberty in England and Revolutionary America* (Cambridge: Cambridge University Press, 2004), 55–6; James Brown Scott, *Law, the State, and the International Community* (Clark, NJ: Lawbook Exchange, 2003), 460; A. John Simmons, 'Locke on the Social Contract', in Matthew Stuart (ed.), *A Companion to Locke* (Oxford: Blackwell, 2016), 413–32, here 417.

point of institutions was to encourage the sociable tendency.[107] Shaftesbury shared ground with Pufendorf in seeing affections as providing a counterbalance to appetites. A Neoplatonist, he based his 'rational religion' on something like a theory of intelligent design, proposed a close affinity between moral and aesthetic judgement, and tried to ground both in objective features of the world. Natural order and beauty were givens, as was the nascent human capacity to appreciate them; what society and reflection provided was the education in taste to cultivate the faculty. And since God had created the whole, the moral sense, based on affective reactions to the world, must appropriately work towards what is best for the whole, i.e. one's society, then the whole of humanity. Needed is the cultivation of this basic moral sense from its embryonic nature in particular affections towards particular people to the point of recognition that it is 'the private interest and good of everyone, to work towards the general good, which, if a creature ceases to promote, he is actually so far wanting to himself and ceases to promote his own happiness and welfare'. The affinity is clear with what came to be called utilitarianism, as it is in Leibniz, and in Shaftesbury's admirer and Adam Smith's teacher, Francis Hutcheson (1694–1746), who felt that the problem of all contract theories was the grounding assumption that individuality precedes sociality.[108] The enduring strength of such philosophies must be borne in mind as we turn the wheel again to consider doctrines that emerged in competition with them.

As nominalism-Protestantism had eroded the theological basis of medieval social theory, in turn post-Reformation social theories like Pufendorf's and Shaftesbury's met philosophical challenge in the form of Jean-Jacques Rousseau (1712–78) and the German early Romantics. Harmonious conceptions of the universe and accompanying views of a benevolent god had found a conducive political environment in the relatively peaceful decades of the early eighteenth century. From around 1740, when the eight-year-long War of Austrian Succession began, and especially with the Seven Years War of 1756–63—in some ways another conflict of Protestant versus Catholic powers, with the former, a rising Prussia included, prevailing[109]—and the disastrous Lisbon earthquake of 1755, greater pessimism

---

[107] Kari Saastamoinen, 'Pufendorf on Natural Equality, Human Dignity, and Self-Esteem', *Journal of the History of Ideas* 71/1 (2010), 39–62.

[108] On Leibniz and Hutcheson, Joachim Hruschka, *Kant und der Rechtsstaat: Und andere Essays zu Kants Rechtslehre und Ethik* (Freiburg: Karl Alber, 2015), 41. On Hutcheson, Gordon Graham, 'Francis Hutcheson and Adam Ferguson on Sociability', *History of Philosophy Quarterly* 31/4 (2014), 317–29. For the Shaftesbury quote on private interest and general good, Shaftesbury, 'An Inquiry Concerning Virtue and Merit', in Laurence E. Klein (ed.), *Shaftesbury: Characteristics of Men, Manners, Opinions, Times* (Cambridge: Cambridge University Press, 1990), 163–230, here 230. On Shaftesbury's philosophy and relations between Leibniz and Shaftesbury in the (Neo)Platonic connection, E. E. Kleist, *Judging Appearances: A Phenomenological Study of the Kantian* sensus communis (Dordrecht: Springer, 2012), 100. More fully on Shaftesbury: Michael B. Gill, 'Lord Shaftesbury', in Edward N. Zalta (ed.), *The Stanford Encyclopedia of Philosophy* (Fall 2016 edn), https://plato.stanford.edu/archives/fall2016/entries/shaftesbury/.

[109] On interpretations of 1763 as a 'final' victory of Protestantism over Catholicism, David Levin, *History as Romantic Art* (Stanford, CA: Stanford University Press, 1959), 84.

infused the philosophy of the Enlightenment, and stirred reactions to it. At the same time the new scepticism rather fitted with nominalist and Protestant suspicion of the capacities of human reason. The *Sturm und Drang* movement stressed subjectivity, emotion, and turbulence in contrast to the 'objective rationality' of French neoclassical art and theatre. And even if one still accepted the harmonious conception, was that not itself a threat to the individual? What if the Enlightenment's supposed replacement of tradition with reason introduced new determinisms to replace old religious ones? A person in harmony with society might really be a person trapped in society, as the interests of the all were promoted above those of the each, or the interests of one class promoted over those of others.[110]

The Genevan Rousseau was a hugely influential critic of key prevailing presumptions in the French Enlightenment, but how he was read depended very much on how much of him was read and thus when his various works emerged. This periodic Calvinist, who converted to Catholicism but ran into doctrinal problems with the Gallican Church, saw society itself as the problem, not original sin or anything else in human nature. Perhaps not all societies were flawed in principle, but certainly the society in which he lived was, and he prescribed root and branch reform given its hierarchies and superficiality. Rousseau's critique implicated those *philosophes* who, for all of their philosophical innovation, found agreeable at least some of the social arrangements that had produced their advantageous positions. Such arrangements bred a particularly intense and virulent form of competive egotism, *amour propre*, in the way in which they legitimated gross inequalities of wealth, and ultimately private ownership of the means of production by which man owned man. This *amour propre* of the 'civilized man', *l'homme artificiel*, was different to the purely self-referential, almost amoral sort of self-love, *amour de soi*, which was needed to keep *l'homme naturel* alive in the state of nature but which was indifferent to others rather than (as Hobbes claimed) predatory on them. When he was berating 'social man' for living 'constantly outside himself' (p. 136), Rousseau's point of contrast was 'the savage [who] lives within himself', thus effectively reversing the grand narrative whereby civilization had progressed inwards from a primitive state of externality, whilst nonetheless holding fast to an ideal of interiority that we might well see as a secularized Calvinism. Rousseau's prescription was not an eradication of all but *amour de soi*, but its augmentation, as the drive for purely individual self-preservation, was supplanted by the development of structures of human interdependence. At the level of social and political theory, he felt that the very recognition of human interdependence, i.e. the human recognition of themselves as having become social beings, was also the precondition for developing what he saw as a proper moral system. It was the responsibility

---

[110] Norman Hampson's interpretation of the 1740s as turning point in the French Enlightenment has been influential on me, as have other claims of his: Hampson, *The Enlightenment* (London: Penguin, 1990).

of humans on earth, not in the next world, to create such a system, one in which some instinctive concern for others (*pitié*, or compassion) was developed by reason into a genuine concern for the commonwealth. In this context a healthy self-esteem would emerge. The minimum requirement of such an order was that it would be more materially equal, and that the State would not be a mere servant of one class interest but the guarantor of laws that each individual had come to recognize as valid because they bind inwardly rather than by external coercion. The famed 'general will', whose underspecified nature has led to much divergent speculation as to its divination, was at any rate not an arbitrary monarchical one, nor the partisan will of others. It was a higher thing than governance by the passions. Realizing it, was the condition for realizing proper individuality.[111]

Rousseau achieved more immediate popularity in the Germanic lands than in France, though the adoption was partial. The *Frühromantiker* of the *Sturm und Drang* period placed great emphasis on individual character, as in Goethe's *Bildungsroman, The Passions of Young Werther* (1774). They were taken by Rousseau's moral psychology, his engagement with emotion, and his rejection of the illusions of society, first flagged in his 1750 essay 'Whether the Restoration of the Arts and Sciences Has Contributed to the Refinement of Morals'. They were more influenced by the self-centred *homme naturel* of the state of nature in Rousseau's *Discourse on Inequality* (1754) than the later law of the *Social Contract* (1762) and the education in citizenship of *Émile* (1762). Accordingly, they did not have to grapple with the potentially authoritarian implications of the 'general will', and they do not seem to have been overly troubled by the issues of inequality raised in early Rousseau. As with the nineteenth-century Romantics, and unlike the emergent strands of liberal egalitarianism around the same time, there is a certain aristocratic, if also anarchic, element to their thinking about individual uniqueness and self-justification: see for example Schiller's *Robbers* (1781). Violent theatricality and the political conditions east of the Rhine from the 1750s to the Napoleonic Wars help explain why, contrary to twentieth-century stereotypes, Germany was a byword for individualism early in the nineteenth century.[112]

Rousseau's internalism was at least as influential on the thought of Immanuel Kant (1724–1804) as were the British philosophical trends that bulked large around Kant's home of Königsberg. Where Ockham had predicated human dignity on liberty, consciousness of which was gained through experience of

---

[111] Quotes from Rousseau, *The Social Contract and the Discourses*, 116. Relevant scholarship: Frederick Neuhouser, *Rousseau's Critique of Inequality* (Cambridge: Cambridge University Press, 2015); Ernst Cassirer, *The Philosophy of the Enlightenment* (Princeton: Princeton University Press, 2009), 153–8; 260–5; Christopher Bertram, 'Jean Jacques Rousseau', in Edward N. Zalta (ed.), *The Stanford Encyclopedia of Philosophy* (Summer 2017 edn),
    https://plato.stanford.edu/archives/sum2017/entries/rousseau/.
[112] On individualism, Swaart, ' "Individualism" ', 82–3, 86–8; on the partial readings of Rousseau, Cassirer, *Philosophy*, 261 ff., which also considers the authoritarian connotations of the general will. For that and alternative readings, see Bertram, 'Jean Jacques Rousseau'.

causally effective choice, for Kant dignity was based on the free capacity for reason and the attempt to realize reason's dictates, whatever the success. Indeed so unpredictable were the consequences of action in a world of multiple agendas and intransigent contexts that Kant wrote in the *Groundwork to the Metaphysic of Morals* that the only purely good thing in the world was a good will—by which he meant a will that had submitted to the dictates of reason.

Arguably the most important modern philosopher in the Western tradition, Kant sought to elaborate the structure of moral reason in order to provide the social glue and legitimacy that religion had once provided—though as we shall see he had scarcely divested himself of all Lutheran or Augustinian tendencies. In replacing the concept of a God-given objective moral sphere he wrote in the *Groundwork* that 'man' was 'subject to his own, yet universal, legislation'. To act morally was to evince the maturity of self-authorization—appropriate in an era which saw the invention of the modern political constitution. All agents of sufficient rationality could come to locate moral rules for themselves, by virtue of reasoning that they themselves were prepared only to live by norms that they would be prepared to legislate for all rational beings. His theory was aimed at the likes of Shaftesbury and David Hume, with their emphasis on group sentiment, bonds of obligation, and acculturated affective disposition. For Kant, this morality of sensibility was no morality at all, for it subjected the individual to causes outside herself. It kept people in the realm of heteronomy as opposed to autonomy, which explains why Kant had little good to say about Judaism, which embraces heteronomy.

There is much to pick over in Kant's thought. Key elements in the oeuvres of Johann Gottlieb Fichte (1762–1814) and Hegel (1770–1831), and before them Kant's erstwhile student Herder (1744–1803), questioned the identity of the peculiar person who can shed his socialization in order to re-engage society anew. While Kant provided inspiration for those utopians prepared to build an earthly 'Kingdom of Ends' from the ground up, his philosophy was part of the problem. If to be an agent, on Kant's reckoning, requires that someone gives themselves the moral law (autonomy), then it is a mystery how someone could give themselves the law without first being an agent.[113]

Reflecting on that 'Kantian paradox' brings us to the question of formalism. Remember that since Ockham a spectre arising from the absence of certain or innate moral knowledge had been that of a formal rather than a substantive conscience. Kant's categorical imperatives were more like principles for deciding on moral rules than rules themselves. As in the post-Lombard–Thomist distinction between *synderesis* and *conscientia*, they carried no guarantee as to correct application of the rules in complex dilemmas and, more importantly, it is not clear that

---

[113] Terry Pinkard, *German Philosophy 1760–1860: The Legacy of Idealism* (Cambridge: Cambridge University Press, 2002), 59–60, 227.

even a 'proper' application would present only one correct answer in each such dilemma. Hegel went further, charging Kant with 'empty formalism', pursuant to his, Hegel's, wider historicizing argument that in order to give the moral law practical purchase Kant had actually had to smuggle in culturally contingent substantive assumptions that undermined his universal aspirations.[114]

When we place Kant's thought in a longer historical perspective, it is as if elements of the nominalist–realist debate are played out not as regards the nature of God but the relation of different human faculties. If reason just does govern the will, there is no real freedom of the will to begin with and as such will cannot be called good in the sense that Kant means it. If, conversely the will was not subordinate to reason, why should it accept reason's dictates, as opposed to the dictates of 'irrational' passion or egotistical self-interest?[115] Fichte (see p. 188) would suggest that the imperative came from concrete human relationships. In the Kantian vision, though, what is important for the agent is disciplining or resisting desire for its own sake. The source of the imperative to do so is either mysterious or shows the enduring influence of 'irrational' religious concepts, notably the fear of the tendencies that supposedly led to the original sin.

Questions about the relations of the faculties dovetail with questions about formalism when we probe the fact that Kantian moral theory only led necessarily to respect for an ideal-rational process of lawmaking. This led to an existential critique: was freedom really freedom if it meant being bound to reason? Kant's identification of autonomy and rationality begged the question. What if, between Emerson, Darwin, and Freud, one saw humans primarily as emotional, creative, impulse-driven creatures?

Exploring the primacy of the will, as opposed to reason, characterized the philosophy of both Arthur Schopenhauer (1788–1860) and Nietzsche (1844–1900). Schopenhauer dismissively associated Kant's idea of the moral law within us with the perpetuation of the *forum internum–forum externum* divide.[116] It is unclear which iteration of that divide Schopenhauer had in mind, but the point is well taken; whatever Schopenhauer's own concerns, might not all the Kantian talk of ideal structures of reason actually result in an aspiration to demit from the earthly world to a world of perfect forms and intentions, a retreat to one's interior in order, Stoic-like, to preserve one's integrity—the sort of thing that the Marxist Ernst Bloch (1885–1977) called an 'oppositional individual ethics of

---

[114] G. W. F. Hegel, *The Philosophy of Right* (Oxford: Clarendon Press, 1952), 89–90. For an elaboration, Sally Sedgwick, 'Hegel on the Empty Formalism of Kant's Categorical Imperative', in Stephen Houlgate and Michael Baur (eds), *A Companion to Hegel* (Oxford: Wiley-Blackwell, 2016), 265–80.

[115] For problems relating to the origin and nature of reason, and exactly how it legislates, see Susan Meld Shell, *Kant and the Limits of Autonomy* (Cambridge, MA: Harvard University Press, 2009); Arendt, *Responsibility and Judgment*, 60–72.

[116] Gerhard Zecha and Paul Weingartner (eds), *Conscience: An Interdisciplinary View* (Dordrecht: Reidel, 1987), p. vii. For some of Kant's own reflections on the fora, Kant, *Lectures on Ethics*, ed. Peter Heath and J. B. Schneewind (Cambridge: Cambridge University Press, 2001) 88–9.

intention'?[117] Alternatively, might the veneration of the 'good will' tend to moral egotism, a determination to do the internally calculated 'right thing' with no mind to the consequences that were in any case beyond the actor's control? Weber gestured at this option when he described the ethic of conviction, *Gesinnungsethik*, in religious terms: 'the Christian does rightly and leaves the results with the Lord'.[118] Either course is indeed a possibility. Either would fit with the concept of the *pneumatikos* of Paul's First Epistle to the Corinthians (1 Corinthians 2:15), the one who could judge but be judged by no other since he was filled with the spirit, or *pneuma*.

As to more than purely interpersonal conduct, sometimes Kant was as happy as Luther to render unto Caesar that which was his, distinguishing between the realm of morality and those of law/justice and political science. His famous essay 'What Is Enlightenment?' distinguished between the commitments of office-holders to their official duties—see the discussion of special roles in Part 1—and their separate roles as members of the public, free to express their views. There is an overlap here with the sort of distinctions Weber made later on when he juxtaposed an ethic of conviction to an ethic of responsibility and value rationality to instrumental rationality. If the Kantian ideal was to subject the will to reason's control alone, as opposed to desire's control, then for the office-holder with different professional priorities, disciplining oneself to do something—however awful—that purportedly did not conform to one's desire was still a moral achievement of sorts. The outer conformity would, however, be no different than that produced by the Hobbesian subject who acted in accordance with the 'artificial soul' of the sovereign. Perhaps this is the first link of that chain of reasoning whereby Eichmann could invoke the Kant 'for the household use of the little man' in a way that would have horrified Kant.[119] One's inner forum, or at least half of it, remained untouched. Conscience (or at least part of it) on one hand and worldly laws and orders on the other hand might retain their own integrity even when they seemed to point in different directions. Such had been true under obedience to those princes to whom Luther deferred in worldly matters, but the distinction can be traced through Gratian to Augustine and then Paul.

Suffice it to say that an oeuvre as broad and brilliant as Kant's was not without its own internal tensions, and lent itself to selective uptake. One could work through the tensions, as Fichte and Hegel tried to. Alternatively, one could focus on the elements most in tune with conerns of the time, like the basic emphasis on sovereign interiority, which helps explain the reception of Kant's *Critique of the*

[117] Ernst Bloch, *Natural Law and Human Dignity* (Cambridge, MA: MIT Press, 1996), 299. Note that Bloch was actually talking about Christian Thomasius, but the same considerations apply. See also Berlin, *Four Essays*, 138–40.

[118] Max Weber, 'Politics as a Vocation', in *Max Weber: Essays in Sociology*, ed. and trans. H. H. Gerth and C. Wright Mills (New York: Oxford University Press, 1946), 77–128, here 120.

[119] Arendt, *Eichmann in Jerusalem*, 136.

Power of Judgement (1790). Though it actually elaborates key aspects of Kant's theory of 'reflective' judgement, and as such answers some of the criticisms of his earlier work on moral reason, this volume, which was at least as important to nineteenth-century thought as his other Critiques, was largely taken as a work on aesthetics alone. Kant's salience for nineteenth-century romanticism lay in his theorizing of the artistic sublime as a feature not of the artwork itself but of the viewer's or listener's experience of the work. The sublime, as in that which exceeds cognition/understanding, had structural affinities with the unknowable god of the nominalists and with the Lutheran *religious* conscience that was beyond any institutional determination. Intuition and emotion returned to the picture, along with a certain elitism of sensibility to go alongside the elitism of character in, say, Romantic accounts of the French or American revolutions.[120] Romantics also share responsibility for the slanted reception of the work of Fichte, the first great post-Kantian idealist, who was often seen as an extreme egotist, attributing vast authorial powers to subjective consciousness.[121]

On the other side of the Atlantic, the lapsed Unitarian Ralph Waldo Emerson blended romanticism, Neoplatonism, and Protestantism. In December 1834, Emerson, later dubbed the prophet of the American religion, wrote in his journal, 'Blessed is the day when the youth discovers that Within and Above are synonyms.' The unity of 'within and above', the idea of the instantiation of God in the individual soul, and thus the import of religious understanding attained through the self rather than the institutions of religion, was a key theme of his famous Harvard Divinity School address of 1838. In that 'Self-Reliance' lecture, with its Jeffersonian overtones, Emerson declared that 'Society everywhere is in a conspiracy against the manhood of every one of its members.' 'Nothing is at last sacred but the integrity of your own mind . . . What have I to do with the sacredness of traditions if I live wholly from within? . . . No law can be sacred to me but that of my nature.' Many decades later, Martin Buber's *I and Thou* outlined a more characteristically Jewish standpoint to the effect that the real synonyms are not

---

[120] On Romantic historiography and the great man, Levin, *History as Romantic Art*, 50–1.

[121] On this reception among Romantics, see Bernard M. G. Reardon, *Religion in the Age of Romanticism* (Cambridge: Cambridge University Press, 1985), 8. One can see how this view of Fichte developed. While Kant had posited objects as somehow conditioning our judgements on them, Fichte argued that the subject–object distinction itself was subjectively established. The 'I' was primary epistemologically. (Under some of the sorts of aforementioned interpretations of him, interpretations that Fichte rejected, the I was even primary ontologically, in the sense that it somehow created the world beyond the mind.) Ostensibly external checks on the free play of perception (that wall that we have just run into) only become checks in the relevant sense through some activity of the self that processes them or permits them to be accepted as such. We must posit such checks as evidence of a world independent of us, but it is still us doing the positing, not the world. So far so clear and so subject-centred. But much more intersubjective, i.e. social, was Fichte's account of the original, self-authorizing recognition of the self (i.e. the advent of self-consciousness) which underlay all specific consciousness of what we take to be external objects. To that I shall return in my History II section. The account of that element of Fichte's work, as of the elements just described, is based on Pinkard, *German Philosophy 1760–1860*, 105–30.

'within and above' but 'between' and 'above'. As opposed to the first line of John's Gospel, 'In the beginning was the word', i.e. $\Lambda\acute{o}\gamma o\varsigma$, *logos*, meaning also reason or spirit, Buber wrote 'In the beginning is relation'. 'Spirit' was to be found not 'in the I, but between I and Thou'.[122]

Emerson's doctrine of self-reliance was not identical to that of the 'bible of mid-Victorian liberalism', Samuel Smiles's 1859 volume *Self-Help; with Illustrations of Character and Conduct*. Emerson would surely have endorsed Smiles's Shakespearean epigraph 'This above all,—To thine own self be true', but Smiles was a little too oriented towards the worldly, not to say material, contributions of the individual. It is important to make this distinction in order not to confuse 'spiritual individualism' with economic individualism. Equally, though, different sorts of individualism could coalesce, as in 'the Jeffersonian conception of the individual as separate, unique, and autonomous—romantic, utilitarian, focusing on will, rights, and personal traits'. In such a conception 'equality' was merely juxtaposed with European class hierarchies, rather than denoting the equal value of all people irrespective of 'character'.[123]

Romantic and existentialist individualisms reacted against the social aspects of commercial and industrial civilization. Where Marx sought to change the outer world, the same social and economic developments against which he schemed prompted some Romantic artists and poets to turn away from the outer world, or at least the social part of it, in search of the solace that lay beyond the philistine mass. Where Shaftesbury had talked of a disinterested admiration of beauty for its own sake, 'art for art's sake' (Théophile Gautier) was now invoked over against the instrumental calculi of capitalism. The other characteristic responses of romanticism to cultural modernity are the emphasis on continuity amid change, the re-embrace of the medieval, recognition of the solid—the cultural-historical—as opposed to the abstract, of the particular as opposed to the universal society, and of the heroic man of action as opposed to the man of reflection. This produced some questionable, essentialist, sometimes teleological medieval history at the overlap of, say, British Whig history, the historianship of the mid-nineteenth-century Prussian school, and the work of the 'New England' historians portrayed by David Levin.[124] But it also produced appreciation of the medieval period as, in

---

[122] I thank David Patterson for drawing my attention to the 'within and above' quote from Emerson, and for the contrast with Buber. That Emerson quote (and the importance of 'In the beginning was the word') is contextualized in Irena Makarushka, *Religious Imagination and Language in Emerson and Nietzsche* (Basingstoke: Macmillan, 1994), 1–3. The quotes from 'Self-Reliance' are from Emerson, *The Essays of Ralph Waldo Emerson* (Cambridge, MA: Belknap Press, 1987), 29–30. For the Jeffersonian background, including some of the more unpleasant manifestations of an ideology of self-reliance, see Thomas Powell, *The Persistence of Racism in America* (Lanham, MD: Littlefield Adams, 1993), 60–3. Buber quotes from *I and Thou* (Mansfield, CT: Martino, 2010), 18, 39.

[123] The quote and the summary of Jeffersonian world-view in Powell, *The Persistence of Racism in America*, 60, 62.

[124] On the latter, see Levin, *History as Romantic Art*, specifically ch. 4 on the medieval element. On art for art's sake, Swaart, '"Individualism"', 83–4.

Ranke's terms, an epoch that like any other was immanent unto God and had to be taken on its own terms rather than Voltaire's.

Romanticism's influence on nineteenth-century historianship and nationalism is beyond doubt, but more open to question is the efficacy of the Romantic artistic form of inner emigration in the face of socio-economic change. Later in the nineteenth century, and much more so in the twentieth, the artistic sphere would find itself coopted by capitalism through advertising, design, and consumption. Where once consumption had denoted distinctions of class, it came more and more to mark distinctions between 'individuals', though we may also be able to detect the presence here of the 'individualism' that in Balzac's (1799–1850) view had hastened the death of genuine individuality, a trait common among those objects of Flaubert's (1821–88) parodies who fancied themselves as entirely self-determining individuals.[125]

Even if one rejected the theory of capitalism's relationship to the 'Protestant ethic', which one need not as long as Protestantism is seen as reinforcing rather than inventing capitalist tendencies,[126] capitalism has shown itself capable of co-opting a great many things. It fused with existentialism, whose heritage includes romanticism, in the thought of Ayn Rand. She celebrated the 'rational egoism' of the 'trader', as opposed to either the altruist who lives to serve others and the 'Nietzschean' egoist concerned with the satisfaction of 'irrational' desire.[127] In individualistic vein, in 1934 Rand posed what to her were rhetorical questions: 'Is ethics necessarily and basically a social conception? . . . Supposing men were born social (and even that is a question)—does it mean that they have to remain so?' She went on:

'Social life,' said [the anarcho-communist Pyotr] Kropotkin, 'that is we, not *I*, is the normal form of life (in man). *It is life itself.* Good god Almighty!!! This is

---

[125] John Xiros Cooper, 'Modernism in the Age of Mass Culture and Consumption', in Peter Brooker et al. (eds), *The Oxford Handbook of Modernisms* (Oxford: Oxford University Press, 2010), 300–14, here 306–9, 311–14; Swaart, '"Individualism"', 84; Pippin, *Modernism*, 32 ff. Nietzsche wrote in the early 1870s that 'While there has never been such sonorous talk of the "free personality" one does not even see personalities, not to speak of free ones, rather nothing but timidly disguised universal men': Nietzsche, *Advantage and Disadvantage*, 29.

[126] If under Protestantism, industry and enterprise were a way of honouring God, and just possibly oneself at the same time, then it was increasingly difficult to distinguish between self-enrichment as a means and as an end or higher purpose, which was rather Weber's point about the growing dominance of instrumental behaviour in a secularizing world. With the slippage from self-enrichment as means to self-enrichment as the end, so we also witness a slippage towards egotistical justification. Such a slippage was even present in utilitarianism since one of its earliest modern enunciations, in Shaftesbury, for whom (borrowing Alexander Pope's words) 'true self-love and social are the same' (Pope, 'An Essay on Man', epistle IV); see e.g. Edward Cahill, *Liberty of the Imagination* (Philadelphia: University of Pennsylvania Press, 2012), 70. Under this rubric, does one act appropriately to the social system because that is ultimately to one's benefit, i.e., does one ultimately act egotistically, or is one's own benefit merely a happy by-product of action that is justified in the name of others and/or the social whole? John Stuart Mill's cold-eyed assessment of capitalism came down for the former interpretation.

[127] Ayn Rand, *The Virtue of Selfishness: A New Concept of Egoism* (New York: Signet, 1964).

exactly what I'm going to fight. For *the exact opposite is true*. If man started as a social animal—isn't all progress and civilization directed towards making him *an individual*? Isn't that the only possible progress?[128]

Once some set of ideas had 'erased the moral disability with which unlimited capitalist appropriation had hitherto been handicapped',[129] then 'the economy' was free to become another paradigm of justice. It had to become one in order to legitimate the inequalities it produced. It came packaged with concepts of virtue, vice, discipline, laxity, reward, and punishment, and high priests in the form of economists. But whatever the belief of the new social scientists that they were merely describing laws, in their very enunciation of what was rational they influenced the behaviour they purported to describe—for who would rationally choose to act irrationally?

The result was a paradox whereby the freedom of the realm of the economic was just a freedom to obey the laws of that realm, just as Kantian freedom was merely freedom to obey the moral law. Whither freedom of the most expansively antinomian sort, the sort that Nietzsche sometimes felt was the only freedom worthy of the name? Creating a structured economic realm of freedom from certain social precepts was one thing. Equally, a growing freedom of conscience might be permitted providing that this was kept internal, between a person and her god. Abandoning social governance and the property order to the dictates of individual interiority was another matter entirely, as the reaction to Anabaptists in the sixteenth century and Ranters, Levellers, Diggers, and other radicals in the seventeenth century reminds us.

When Levellers and other sects of what E. P. Thompson calls 'the poor man's Puritanism' were done down in the Commonwealth, they sundered their spiritual from their worldly aspirations. In the words of the Digger Gerrard Winstanley, they retreated from the 'kingdom without' to the 'kingdom within'.[130] This was a species of 'inner emigration'. Yet Winstanley's retreat was not absolute; a worldly re-engagement was possible at some unspecified future point. In other words, and this brings us to the conclusion of this section, his was not an absolute dualism.

How many people have lived consistently by such dualisms? Certainly not those subscribing to Westermarck's 'beautiful modern sophism which admits every man's conscience to be an infallible guide', since presumably the people Westermarck had in mind take that guide to pertain to worldly comportment,

---

[128] All emphases in original: Ayn Rand, *The Journals of Ayn Rand*, ed. Leonard Peikoff (Penguin, 1999).

[129] Richard A. Hughes, *Pro-Justice Ethics* (New York: Lang, 2009), 156, quoting C. B. Macpherson on John Locke's role in moving the definition of freedom towards possession (of property) and independence from others.

[130] E. P. Thompson, *The Making of the English Working Class* (Harmondsworth: Pelican, 1968), 32–3.

amongst other things. The twentieth-century phenomologist philosopher Max Scheler was equally scathing. When 'anyone can . . . appeal to his "conscience" and demand absolute recognition of what he says from others', the result is 'moral anarchy'. One can understand Scheler's fears, which are not far from Hobbes's, because the historian of conscience Paul Strohm is surely right about the 'now-regnant view that conscience has a close connection with singularity or exception', and that means exception within a human group, not outside it in another a-human realm.[131]

In its most banal form this pseudo-existentialist 'individualism' leads to the parroting of 'I was just being myself' or 'I was just saying what I think', which may short-circuit reflection on what sort of self one would like to be and on the very conditions and ramifications of identity choices. Moralism is a close relation of such subjectivism, even though it sounds like almost the opposite, because, as with the fiction of equal chances in a free market, both stances tend to disregard the social contexts that mediate and for which individual action has ramifications. Take Ariel Levy's discussion of 'female chauvinist pigs' and Natasha Walter's of 'living dolls'—i.e. girls and women who do patriarchy's work for it—in which, say, generally very young women who strip for magazine photoshoots, or lap dance, often genuinely feel that they have made an empowering, liberating choice. Reinforced thereby are the tendencies of objectification and exploitation that affect not just them but other women too.[132] These women are playing by someone else's rules whilst being encouraged by the rhetoric of individualistic freedom to believe they are not.

Thinking beyond such rhetoric, we have multiple paradigms of rule-bound behaviour available, each with their permissions and prohibitions. The list of paradigms includes those set by custom, economic doctrine, criminal law, civil law, and whatever might be our religion, if we have one. It is not given that these paradigms should be separate, and anyway the terms of one might radiate outwards to influence the others, as religious precepts did to secular law at various points in medieval Europe, and as the mores of the wealthy did to criminal law in eighteenth-century England, where even quite minor crimes against property brought death sentences. In virtue of their rule-boundedness these paradigms each share something with what is often called morality. Some people might feel that one or other paradigm is coterminous with morality; others might pick and mix elements. The truly exceptional may even devise their own code that owes nothing to any of the others. In the limited sense of invention or blending it is possible for individuals to have their own unique moral codes, and some might even have the consistency to live by theirs. Naturally this will not save them from

---

[131] Strohm, *Conscience*, 32, 57.
[132] Ariel Levy, *Female Chauvinist Pigs* (New York: Free Press, 2006); Natasha Walter, *Living Dolls* (London: Virago, 2010).

problems when their unique code clashes with another's unique code or one of the established codes, any more than if someone came up with a private language of their own and then tried to communicate in it. Some of the established codes might also clash with each other, and that tension may ultimately be enough to destroy a community, but the split will not leave atomized individuals each with their own codes. However permissive some codes may be in some directions, however rich in the rhetoric of freedom and individualism, all come with many of their rules always already in place at any one time, and these rules are rarely changed wholesale. With rules come consequences for transgression and adherence. Such has presumably been the case since people first coordinated their activities, and it does not matter much whether we can pinpoint one such code of rules and call it a morality. Easier to say almost tautologically that any code that pertains to relations between people may have some moral element within it alongside other elements as may be present.

It is tautological to say that no social system has ever survived without due attention to deeds and their impact, irrespective, after a point, of any allowances made for the internal drivers of action. Utilitarianism as an administrative doctrine is but one of the most recent theories to underline the point that inhered in the medieval concept of 'common good', or the ancient Greek concept of the miasma, the pollution brought by bloodshed that drives Aeschylus' Orestes mad.[133] The social role of law, or law's functional equivalents, means that across the occidental millennia it could never lose its concern for the external or objective element of behaviour, denoted by the *actus reus*, or 'guilty act', whatever important variations there were across time and type of law in the relationship of objective to subjective, mental element. Some law systems may be individualistic and context-myopic in accounting for the *causes* of crime, as we shall see in the History II section (pp. 206–7), but they are not equally so in contemplating the *fact* of crime. By threat of its coercive capacity law can hope to shape human choice, but in virtue of the very fact that a coercive threat is always there, lawgivers can never know—nor, therefore, legislate on—whether transgression is discouraged by something called conscience or by fear of consequences.

The vestiges of pure objectivism in law are necessary to maintain the order that gives the law its role in the first place. Hence the dictum, enunciated inter alia by Justinian, that ignorance of the law is no defence. Then objective elements of outcome, as opposed to intention, inform the framing of different crimes, say attempted murder as opposed to murder. It is a matter of (moral) luck as to whether dangerous driving results in fatalities, but that result may influence the penalty for the driving and even whether the driving is brought to court at all. In most American states one dollar can make the difference between an act of

---

[133] Robert Parker, *Miasma: Pollution and Purification in Early Greek Religion* (Oxford: Clarendon Press, 1991).

pilfering being characterized as grand theft as opposed to theft. Lucky the thief who accidentally dropped that dollar on the premises before being apprehended. The most obvious objective element is that it is not the actor but some higher authority that decides what is and is not illegal. At the level of individual negligence, recklessness, and so forth we have already touched on the judiciable, objective harm that is caused by an actor's behaviour but not willed by that actor. At the level of the systems that decree laws, consider legislation to increase the freeway speed limit: this is likely to increase road-deaths, but at the same time expedite travel, with attendant, especially economic, benefits. There is a systemically-governed trade-off, as there is with laws governing pollution, food standards, employment conditions, or commercial treatment of animals.

As important as the limits on the subjective factor's relevance is what part of the subjective factor is deemed most relevant. On the whole the emphasis in criminal law remains on intent, in the sense of consciously enacting something that one knows, or should know, to be against the law. Note this is not to say 'that one knows to be wrong' because the issue of the rightness or otherwise of an outlawed act is one that the legal system tries to keep beyond discussion, even as it plays on the ongoing association of sin with crime for those whose behaviour is shaped by conscience rather than fear of consequences. When the subjective element of the crime (*mens rea*) is restricted to intent, then it becomes a matter of cognition and will: of knowing what one wants to do and doing it. Subsidiary points include basic mental fitness to know and responsibly to will. The evaluative question around motive, i.e. the reason for willing the act, plays a secondary role, and in many cases none. To be sure, this is not a clear distinction, not least as regards that old chestnut of desire, where you wish something 'for itself' as opposed to instrumentally. Nonetheless, the contrast reminds us that legal systems develop with interaction between humans as a focus, not only with individuals qua individuals. (An extreme example: one does not consider legally salient the terrorist's belief that he was justified in blowing up a building.)[134] The same goes for moral systems.

When pinpointing tensions between a certain subjectivist 'ideal' and social reality, the basic question is what 'conscience' pertains to, and thus in what senses, and to what extent, it can be respected in its freedom. Obviously not all societies have permitted freedom of religious conscience, with its close associations with faith, and some of the most intolerant such societies have been in the Occident. But even when freedom of religious conscience was established in the face of authority, somewhere on the road from Luther to Locke, acting on that conscience in the world (where the world was relevant) was restricted in principle, thus not just by the fact of established authority. The Reformer William Tyndale

---

[134] e.g. Alan Norrie, *Crime, Reason and History: A Critical Introduction to Criminal Law* (Cambridge: Cambridge University Press, 2014), chs 2 and 3.

pointed out in *Obedience of a Christian Man* (1528), you may be obliged 'first because of thyn own conscience' but you are also obliged 'for thy neighbour's conscience',[135] which is a Christian version of Aristotle's concept of justice, uniquely among the virtues, as concerning the good of another rather than the self.[136] It is also a precursor of Fichte's principle: 'limit your freedom so that others around you can also be free'.[137] Then, from Locke to Mill as it were, the principles of freedom expanded from religious conscience to 'political conscience', e.g. opinion, speech, publication, as against not just Church but also State and demographic majority, and ultimately to matters of 'lifestyle'. This second cluster of freedoms concerns what one *may* do, thus what it is illegitimate for some other agent to prevent. Implicit in what one may do is what one may not do, i.e. ought not do, and Mill's freedoms went up to the point at which the freedoms of others were infringed, which reminds us that whatever else political liberalism is, however much of an emphasis on the individual it has, it is still a political-cum-social theory and as such cannot ignore externals in the way that Romantic individualism or the Lutheran religious conscience can.

Externally derived moral injunctions may be accompanied by threat of formal sanction, but sanction may also be informal and social rather than penal, or it may be purely internal, in the fact of a guilty moral conscience. In the last case it is an utterly subjective matter whether or not the sanction materializes, i.e. whether guilt is felt. Do we really think, though, that a moral conscience untroubled on purely subjective grounds is 'free' in any of the normatively positive senses in which many of us talk of freedom of conscience? This is doubtful. We think of it as mistaken, egotistical, self-serving. We think that the person in question ought to feel guilty and should be assessed as guilty irrespective of how they feel—here we are reliant on the double play of 'guilt' as an internal feeling and/or an external pronouncement. In other words, in the last resort external judgement alone is called for. Thinking of 'guilt' versus 'shame', one way in which this external judgement might be expressed is through some sort of shaming, which is nothing other than reminding that party that they are a part of an external world whether they like it or not.

Anything that is solely internal and/or other-worldly in its ramifications and reference is no code at all, save in the purely theoretical sense of the private

---

[135] Quoted in Strohm, *Conscience*, 89.

[136] Aristotle, *Ethics*, 142 (bk V, ch. I).

[137] This is because 'freedom' is the capacity to be the cause of effects in the world, rather than oneself being an effect of other people's causal behaviour: Pinkard, *German Philosophy*, 123. Note the similarity to Kant's configuration of the categorical imperative such that one should always treat others as ends rather than means, but note also the difference that Fichte is prepared, like the utilitarians, to talk about the necessity to limit freedom morally speaking, as opposed to the Kantian view whereby someone is somehow freest when following the moral dictates of practical reason. Fichte's view here is consonant with his theory, explored in the History II section, about the normative relationship between the 'I' and the 'not-I'.

language, and when we get to worldly dealings only the powerful can act as if in a genuinely antinomian sense, or—functionally the same thing—as if guided by their own unique code. But their capacity to act with impunity—their ability to exempt themselves from punishment in any external forum—does not mean that we should not assess their actions *as if* they had been brought to such a forum. Seneca and earlier Stoics, just like Abelard later, recognized that external judgements and public punishment on earth could be justifiable irrespective of the condition of the individual's conscience.

Stoic *autarkeia*, remember, did not involve making up one's own laws, or discarding worldly laws, so much as not bothering about what others thought of one. One should be prepared to put up with ill-repute, *mala fama*, punishment, even death, provided one has obeyed the dictates of one's conscience.[138] The Stoic point has a corollary, and it is as follows. While, say, Butterfield was right to warn historians not to play God in their judgements, it does not follow that we should act as if each person were her own god. Let us say for the sake of argument that God exists. Leaving 'him' to judge on the state of souls is the best way of taking on their own terms people who orient their behaviour to that understanding of him. Such worldly evaluative conclusions as follow from their behaviour in this world may be of sublime indifference to such people, as to those Stoics who genuinely lived up to the ideal of *autarkeia*. So be it: their integrity is intact, no doubt; but how their deeds ought to be remembered in the world that the deeds affected cannot be dictated by how they think those deeds ought to be remembered.

History II: God Is With Us

This History moves away from anticlerical *sacro egoismo*—the belief that the individual is the final locus of religious interpretation. It moves towards the nationalist *sacro egoismo* propounded by Italian prime minister Antonio Salandra in 1914.[139] It is concerned with the ascription to collective entities of characteristics similar to those attributed to the 'punctal', hermetic individual who is ultimately answerable only to what Emerson called his within/above. That ascription is implicit in the words of the Irish nationalist leader Éamon de Valera, speaking in 1922: 'whenever I wanted to know what the Irish people wanted, I had only to examine my own heart'.[140] The 'heart' was a collective one.

This History sets itself against the assumptions of the historian Jacob Burckhardt as he warned against evaluating collectivities. He suggested leaving 'those who find pleasure in passing sweeping censures on whole nations to do so

---

[138] Roller, *Constructing Autocracy*, 83; Schinkel, *Conscience*, 162.
[139] William Mulligan, *The Great War for Peace* (New Haven: Yale University Press, 2014), 100.
[140] Michael Mays, *The Cultures of Irish Nationalism* (Lanham, MD: Lexington Books, 2007), 97.

as they like', because a 'great nation . . . lives on with or without the approval of theorists'.[141] Note that he did not reject the idea of the essence of collectivities, only that he considered himself incompetent to evaluate those essences. Thus:

> It may be possible to indicate many contrasts and shades of difference among different nations, but to strike the balance of the whole is not given to human insight. The ultimate truth with respect to the character, the conscience and the guilt of a people remains for ever a secret; if only for the reason that its defects have another side, where they reappear as peculiarities or even as virtues.[142]

This talk of 'peoples' and their character from the scholar who claimed of Renaissance Italy that it was the birthplace of individualism! Or perhaps the birth*time*—after all, Burckhardt's name is associated like no other with the concept of the *Zeitgeist*, even if he is talking more about a *Volksgeist* here.

Even as Burckhardt's *Civilization of the Renaissance in Italy* (1860) entrenched the appeal of a certain sort of individualism, it shows what is clear from many of the other major thinkers around his time: they saw no tension between talking about persons and about collective spirits and minds. One just needed to consider the person and the collective as instantiations of uniqueness at different levels of analysis, almost as concentric circles of particularity, albeit that the concern with aesthetics and emotions at the level of individuals tended to morph into analysis of language and culture at the group level. Hegel discussed *Geist* and the world-historical individual. Herder, Goethe, and other German Romantics were as interested in national cultural differences as in qualitative differences between particular human beings. Hitler could talk of races and of exemplary individuals within races.

Mention of thinkers like Goethe, Burckhardt, Herder, and Hegel alongside Hitler shows the depth and breadth of the cultural-intellectual tradition under consideration. Against Hitler, the tradition was originally the offspring of the wish for peace and tolerance between collectives, just as liberalism aspired to the peaceful coexistence of literal individuals. Against the idea that the tradition was uniquely German, let us reflect on that Emerson aficionado Gandhi. Beginning at the level of the individual person, he disavowed consistency with his own prior statements in favour of 'truth as it may present itself to me at any given moment'. 'It is not necessary for me to prove the rightness of what I said then. It is essential only to know what I feel today.' He had his own 'inner voice' to guide him. As 'I am called "Great Soul"', he mused, 'I might as well endorse Emerson's saying that "foolish consistency is the hobgoblin of little minds"'. Then, moving outwards to a wider circle, with some inspiration from Emerson's meditation

---

[141] Jacob Burckhardt, *The Civilization of the Renaissance in Italy* (London: Penguin, 2004), 271.
[142] Burckhardt, *The Civilization of the Renaissance in Italy*, 271.

'Self-Reliance' Gandhi linked the inner personal concept of 'self-rule' with collect-ive Indian self-rule, *Swaraj*. The primary Indian collective he had in mind was the Hindus and, in the words of one historian, for Gandhi 'Hinduism bound all who adhered to it into a single interwoven community, in which each was allotted their appointed station.'[143]

Some of the major influences on concentric-circular thought can be located in the conflicts that reached a head in the sixteenth and seventeenth centuries, though one needs to note the deeper foundations. Rome's ascent in the central Middle Ages had been marked by great violence against 'infidels' but also against 'heretics' who as dissidents are but unsuccessful reformers—and let us not forget that the Roman Church was shaped by earlier schism with 'eastern Christianity'. Western Christendom's unity had been endangered from within by tugs of war between Papacy and Empire, which led to popes encouraging kings as opposed to successive Holy Roman Emperors. Kings could in turn present themselves as emperors within their kingdoms in order to reduce the power of feudal lords, which further strengthened monarchical power vis-à-vis the Papacy.[144] From the high Middle Ages the notion of a special *ecclesia Anglorum*, matching a supposed *gens Anglorum*, became a reference point of the later Church of England and of English distinctness, many centuries after both concepts had been invented by Pope Gregory I.[145] The consecration of the Gallican Church in 1682, which enshrined the French monarch's authority over matters temporal and civil, was the conclusion of about four centuries of drift in that direction too. The scale of destruction was extreme in the 'Wars of Religion', however, notably in the Thirty Years War. Conflict was open, very widespread, and between more evenly bal-anced though shifting parties. Instead of unconditional victory or obliteration, accommodation, as in the form of the Westphalian treaties of 1648, had to be reached between states and confessions. In the History I section we also saw that the theological and power-political developments of the time were accompanied by an efflourescence of legal and contractual theorizing, much of which enhanced the concept of subjective right as attached to individual people.

It is not paradoxical that public governance took on new dimensions as a result of this conceptualization of subjective right. One first needs to distinguish between the things to which one supposedly has rights (life, property, etc.) and the subjective right that is the power to assert the claim to those things. Both of these matters stand against the absolute ruler, but only the former limits

---

[143] 'Inner voice': from Ramin Jahanbegloo, *Gadflies in the Public Space: A Socratic Legacy of Philosophical Dissent* (Lanham, MD: Lexington, 2017), 20. All other quotes by or about Gandhi from Perry Anderson, *The Indian Ideology* (London: Verso, 2013), 30–2. On Gandhi, 'Self-Reliance', and *Swaraj*, see Alan Hodder, 'Asia in Emerson and Emerson in Asia', in Jean McClure Mudge (ed.), *Mr Emerson's Revolution* (Cambridge: Open Book Publishers, 2015), 373–405, here 394–6.

[144] Robert Fawtier, *The Capetian Kings of France* (London: Macmillan, 1960), ch. 5.

[145] Georges Tugene, *L'Image de la nation anglaise dans l'*Histoire ecclésiastique *de Bède le Vénérable* (Strasbourg: Presses universitaires de Strasbourg, 2001).

government as such. The latter, the power of assertion, which stands logically prior to the rights that the power is used to assert, may actually expand the remit of governance in the measure that its exercise expands the legitimacy of governance. 'Sovereign' individuals are drawn into the process of governance and lawmaking.[146] Governance and the State could thus acquire new moral attributes insofar as each monadic level—the individual and the State—reinforced the other. What Pufendorf called the *persona moralis composita*, ie. the sorts of social form of which the State was an especially important example, could be invoked against the monarch as the repository and executor of the will of not just an aggregation (as Hobbes had seen it) but also a more selfconscious if numerically limited and probably wealthy assembly/association of individuals. Here we see the link between Pufendorf's theory of the State and his concept of *socialitas* (p. 160).

Novel elaboration of private law was accompanied by a newly articulated public law. Describing a version of the public interest through law, as opposed to protecting the king's peace, became an important standard of legitimacy. Before being republican or liberal the concept of the public interest was above all purportedly unitary.[147] The concept of unity, with its associations of harmony, is the cue to move to the thought of Leibniz (1646–1716), which merits sustained attention given the importance of its legacy in this Part of the book.

Leibniz established a metaphysics on the basis of which individual humans, and human societies, could be envisaged in coexistence with other humans and societies. His *Monadology* was published in 1714, and his related *Theodicy* in 1710, but conceived in the 1670s–80s, when memories of the Wars of Religion were fresh and Louis XIV was breaking the peace abroad and ending religious toleration at home. Leibniz had tried to effect reconciliation between Protestants and Catholics and then between Protestants.[148] His works provided a different vision of coexistence to the contract theories with their emphases variously on self-interested toleration of others, sovereign power, or subjective rights and sovereign accountability. His account should also be set against Newton's competing view of the workings of the universe, and Pierre Bayle's denial of the compatibility of faith and reason in his *Historical and Critical Dictionary* (1695–7).

Leibniz was a rationalist of sorts but was influenced by the Neoplatonic theory of emanationism, in which all things issue and descend—with decreasing perfection and increased concreteness—from one perfect/divine source, which is

---

[146] Alvarado, *Common Law and Natural Rights*, 31–2.

[147] Zoller, *Public Law*, 70. See also on Pufendorf's conception of sovereignty as connoting the unity of the State's political will, Martin van Gelderen and Quentin Skinner (eds.) *Republicanism*, i. *Republicanism and Constitutionalism in Early Modern Europe* (Cambridge: Cambridge University Press, 2002), 232.

[148] On some of the context, Nicholas Rescher, *G.W.Leibniz's Monadology* (Pittsburgh: University of Pittsburgh Press, 1991), 5, 8, and C. A. van Peursen, *Leibniz* (London: Faber and Faber, 1969), 9. On Protestant and Catholic Relations and Theology, see Irena Backus, *Leibniz: Protestant Theologian* (New York: Oxford University Press, 2016).

sometimes called a monad to illustrate its unity. For Leibniz, the ultimate order was one of basic diversity that was only reconciled in God, there being no single correct perspective accessible to all humans. His account modifies the classical theory of monadology, as well as the Renaissance version of Giordano Bruno, who had been influenced by the Neoplatonist Nicholas Cusanus (p. 131). In fact Leibniz's work was to his time what Cusanus' had been to the crises of the fifteenth century: the latter phases of the 'Great Western Schism', the Hussite wars, and the Christian loss of Constantinople. Cusanus' thought had connotations, within limits, of unity-in-diversity, diversity as a descent from an initial unity in 'the one'.[149] His *On the Peace of Faith* (1453), written at the time of the fall of Constantinople, was an imagined dialogue between different Christian confessions, representatives of Islam, Judaism, and even of religions that would have been conceived as 'pagan'. While prejudiced in favour of Christianity, and sometimes dismissive of the beliefs of Jews, it sought to remove grounds for antagonism by casting religious disagreements as misconceived on the basis that behind their different 'rites' each religion tacitly shared the same assumptions and thus paved the way to the higher truth. Within constraints, Cusanus accepted and even welcomed 'diversity'.[150]

For Leibniz, abstract, universalizable reason alone detracted from the reality of different spiritual entities. Meanwhile a Neoplatonic blurring of the sharp Lutheran distinction between heavenly and earthly realms was necessary precisely in virtue of the fact that the earth—or in this case Europe—was divided between states, populations, and intellectuals on matters such as that distinction. Leibniz conceived of innumerable monads, of which there were different sorts and levels, as the building blocks of the world. For Leibniz, all monads were created by God, who was 'the primitive unity' (*Monadology*[151]) and all monads had the quality of a sort of soul, or 'entelechy'. Monads could enter into composites with other monads even as they retained their individuality (§51, 65, 67, 70). In recognition of change in the world, Leibniz felt that each monad was moved by an 'internal principle' (§§10–13, 22). There was some form of synchronization or harmonization of all these developing monads, pre-established by God (§§51, 78).

[149] Jasper Hopkins, *A Concise Introduction to the Philosophy of Nicholas of Cusa* (Minneapolis: University of Minnesota Press, 1978), 4, and *passim*; Marica Costigliolo, 'Organic Metaphors in "De concordantia catholica" of Nicholas of Cusa', *Viator* 44/2 (2013), 311–21, here 312, 314. See also (for some suggestive oppositions between Cusanus and the humanists on one hand and nominalism on the other) pts 10–11 of the 'Sequence on Political Ontology' of John Milbank, *Beyond Secular Order: the Representation of Being and the Representation of the People* (Hoboken, NJ: Wiley, 2013).

[150] Translated text of *De Pace Fidei*, in Jasper Hopkins, *Nicholas of Cusa's De Pace Fidei and Cribratio Alkorani: Translation and Analysis* (Minneapolis: Arthur J. Banning Press, 1994), 633–70: see esp. pt XVIII, §66 and pt XIX, §§67–8 of *De Pace Fidei* at pp. 68–70. On Cusanus' 'pluralism', see Markus Riedenauer, *Pluralität und Rationalität: Die Herausforderung der Vernunft durch religiöse und kulturelle Vielfalt nach Nikolaus Cusanus* (Stuttgart: Kohlhammer, 2007).

[151] Leibniz, 'Monadology', in Steven M. Cahn (ed.), *Classics of Western Philosophy* (Indianapolis: Hackett, 1990), 604–13 (§§47–8). Further references to section numbers will be given in the text.

This harmonization, or 'accommodation of all created things to each other, and each to all the others, brings it about that each simple substance has relations that express all the others, and consequently, that each simple substance is a perpetual, living mirror of the universe' (§56). While each monad itself comprised smaller monads, some types of monad were more fundamental in their power and significance than others (§§65, 67)—'each living body has a dominant entelechy [ie. soul]' (§70), and some elect 'souls are elevated to the rank of reason and to the prerogative of minds' (§82). There was little if any direct causal relationship between monads (they were windowless: §§7, 51), but those in closer proximity— be that within a physical body somehow subordinate to a 'mind', or embodied 'minds' within a culture—reflected more intensely on each other, and thus shared more in common, than those further removed, though all monads of whatever sort have in common that each has something of the universal in it.[152] Unlike ordinary monads with their ordinary entelechies, 'minds' are not just mirrors of the universe, but 'also images of the divinity itself, capable of knowing the system of the universe, and imitating some of it through their schematic representations'. Together they form the city of god under the divine prince (§§83–5).

When Leibniz wrote that 'Wise and virtuous persons' will 'work for all that appears to be in conformity with the presumptive or antecedent divine will' (§90), description of the universal order became prescription for those instructed in its ways. If perfections are derived from God's influence, and God's perfection is 'absolutely infinite', then minds will best emulate God if they can multiply their perspectives rather than trying to impose one. As 'the same city viewed from different directions appears entirely different' there are 'as many different universes, which are, nevertheless, only perspectives on a single one' (§§41–2, 57). Or, as he put it in 'Principles of nature and grace based on reason', 'chaque monade est un miroir vivant, . . . représentatif de l'Univers, suivant son *point de vue*'.[153] Baroque painters like Andrea Pozzo were at the time committing *points de vue* to canvas by deploying new perspectival techniques of shading-off and chiaroscuro;[154] Leibniz the ethnographer travelled and read widely to encourage a 'commerce of light' and expand his conception of reason by learning from the unique insights of different cultures.[155] Such thinking legitimated different social orders and confessions and individual minds in relation to each other, as parts and refractions of

---

[152] For an elaboration of the difficult matter of relations and reflections, and the relationship between minds and cultures, see Franklin Perkins, *Leibniz and China: A Commerce of Light* (Cambridge: Cambridge University Press, 2004), 62–5.

[153] Leibniz, 'Principes de la nature et de la grâce fondé en raison', repr. in *Gottfried Wilhelm Leibniz, Œuvres de Leibniz*, ed. M. A. Jacques (Paris: Charpentier, 1846), 479–87, here 480. Emphasis added.

[154] Egon Friedell, *A Cultural History of the Modern Age*, ii. *Baroque, Rococo and Enlightenment* (New Brunswick, NJ: Transaction, 2009), 132.

[155] Perkins, *Leibniz and China*, which is devoted in significant part to showing how Leibniz's interest in cultural exchange is consistent with his monadological thinking.

the divine. A vitiating or combustible opposition of State to divine authority was also avoided, as might be expected from a thinker who spent much of his life in the service of a middling German principality set amongst other principalities, all under an emperor.

Leibniz's linguistic theory chimed with his metaphysics. As opposed to the conception of language as a more or less reliable vessel for expressing concepts and referring to external things, for Leibniz, words and other signs played a constitutive role in thought. One of Locke's concerns about language was its potential to mislead, as with translation problems, but for Leibniz those differences reflected different ways of seeing the world. 'I really believe that languages are the best mirror of the human mind, and that a precise analysis of the significations of words would tell us more than anything else about the operations of the understanding.'[156] Understanding the essences of different languages was a key to contemplating the collective social mind of the users of that language. How precisely languages, cultures, and religions or confessions were related to each other is unclear. What matters for the following narrative is the enduring influence of monadological thought about the way that the world was divided, how it should be understood, and how it should be, *simpliciter*. As with most tales of intellectual influence, elements of Leibniz's original conception are sometimes watered down, and at other times simplified, exaggerated, and analogized.[157] The idea of cultures and then nation states as 'monads' is in any case an especially important focus of subsequent thought.

Leibniz's irenic perspectivalism is detectable in Gotthold Ephraim Lessing's play *Nathan the Wise* of 1779, with its three-sided interfaith dialogue set during the Crusades.[158] Leibniz's cosmopolitanism is manifest in Goethe's conviction that 'poetry is cosmopolitan, and the more interesting the more it shows its nationality'.[159] His metaphysics is evident in the father of 'liberal' Protestant theology, the hermeneut Friedrich Schleiermacher (1768–1834), for whom—as indeed for Clifford Geertz who in one of his voices talked of 'seeing heaven in a

---

[156] John Leavitt, *Linguistic Relativities: Language Diversity and Modern Thought* (Cambridge University Press, 2011), 51–2.

[157] I have noted elsewhere—Donald Bloxham, *Why History? A History* (Oxford: Oxford University Press, 2020), 152—the seeds of dialectical thinking in Leibniz's reflections on change within a monad stemming from an 'internal principle' of variation, such that 'the present is pregnant with the future' (*Monadology*, §§10–13, 22). This element was more conducive to Marxists than the conservatives who most wholeheartedly embraced monadic thought.

[158] Hugh Barr Nisbet, *Gotthold Ephraim Lessing: His Life, Works, and Thought* (Oxford: Oxford University Press, 2013), 512, 580, 610 on Leibniz's influence, as against others who tend to see more of Spinoza's influence on Lessing—though Nisbet recognizes Spinoza's influence too. See also Henry E. Allison, *Lessing and the Enlightenment* (New York: SUNY, 2018), ch. 4.

[159] 'Poetry' quote and further context from Longxi Zhang, *From Comparison to World Literature* (Albany, NY: SUNY, 2015), 170.

grain of sand'[160]—the infinite should be sought in the finite.[161] Such thinking gathered strength in the German reaction from the mid-eighteenth century onwards against enlightened French universalism but also against Kantian distinctions between sensibility and the understanding, the world of human affect and experience on one hand and the world of reason on the other. In that connection the thought of the deeply religious Lutheran Johann Georg Hamann (1730–88) was, despite itself, an important way station on the road to a secularized understanding of human group diversity based on language patterns and historical development.

Hamann's linguistic and aesthetic theory was suffused with his own faith, which was set against Enlightenment-compatible 'rational religion'. Applying Paul's concepts in 2 Corinthians, and consistent with Luther's view on consubstantiation, in which Christ's body and blood and bread and wine were all present in the Eucharist, Hamann disavowed any opposition between the spirit and the letter in the interpretation of language. The same went for the interpretation of the world of nature and the flesh as 'texts' more broadly defined—Hamann had something akin to a 'realist' medieval view of the world as a divine text. Language had a symbolic quality as well as referential and straightforwardly communicative capacities; it was embedded in everyday life as well as having formal properties; and the spiritual and cognitive elements were irreducibly interwined.[162] Hamann disliked the philosophical language that sought to abstract and universalize, juxtaposing it with the evocative, aesthetic qualities of poetry in which the spirit was in action to animate the meaning of words in ways that exceeded the definitions of those words. (Here there is in fact some confluence with Kant's work on aesthetics, as with Fichte's 1795 work *On the Spirit and the Letter in Philosophy*.)[163] Before the fall Adam and Eve had direct access to divine or 'angelic language'. Afterwards humans were forever engaged in a form of interpretative translation 'out of angel-speech into human language, that is, thoughts into words,—things into names,—forms into signs'. This was not, however, interpretation *ab initio*. Regarding the material world, the imagination and cognition worked on the

---

[160] Geertz sought to show that 'seeing heaven in a grain of sand is a trick that not only poets can accomplish'. 'It is in understanding [human] variousness . . . that we shall come to construct a concept of human nature that, more than a statistical shadow and less than a primitivist dream, has both substance and truth.' Geertz, *The Interpretation*, 44, 53, 52.

[161] Vladimir Latinovic, Gerrard Mannion, and Jason Welle (eds), *Catholicism Engaging Other Faiths* (Cham: Springer, 2018), 142; on Schleiermacher and the matter of each believer's experiencing religion through their individual 'Anschauung des Universums' and then each collective religion having its 'fundamental intuition'/'Grundanschauung', see John H. Smith, 'Leibniz Reception around 1800', in Elisabeth Krimmer and Patricia Anne Simpson (eds), *Religion, Reason, and Culture in the Age of Goethe* (Rochester, NY: Camden House, 2013), 209–43, here 235.

[162] Kenneth Haynes, *Hamann: Writings on Philosophy and Language* (Cambridge: Cambridge University Press, 2007), pp. xiii–xviii; Robert Alan Sparling, *Johann Georg Hamann and the Enlightenment Project* (Toronto: University of Toronto Press, 2011), 93.

[163] Clayton Koelb, *The Revivifying Word: Literature, Philosophy and the Theory of Life in Europe's Romantic Age* (Rochester: Camden House, 2008), 14–16.

experience of the senses. Authorial intent of, say, scripture, meanwhile, might be inferred and argued over, while the letter remained as a guide. When Hamann wrote that 'man' must 'take his external sense as a help, must be attentive to the given letter as the only vehicle of the Spirit which can be grasped' we can see the Neoplatonic element of his thought by which the divine and the human sphere are not entirely separate even while humans can never be certain of their inter-pretative ground. While language distances the user from original, divine mean-ing it still somehow constitutes a trace of the same, providing an oblique, mediated insight, like 'a solar eclipse which is looked at through a glass of water'.[164] Any attempt to subjugate language in the name of complete human autonomy and control was akin to the hubristic attempt to build the Tower of Babel. Reason presupposed a language in which it could be expressed, and lan-guage was inevitably interpretative, making the reader or speaker into a partici-pant in the construction of meaning as they operated from contexts that were irreducibly social and historical as well as sensuous.[165] 'In the language of every people we find the *history* of the same . . . The invisible being of our souls is revealed through words.'[166]

Events in the Garden of Eden and in 'Babel' are linked in Hamann and they are linked in the book of Genesis. In Genesis, Adam and Eve's rebellion, then the attempt to build a tower as a monument apart from god, each resulted in disper-sal and alienation, firstly of people from God, then of peoples from each other.[167] Hamann's disciple Herder (1744–1803) saw the Babel story as a cause of a linguistic-cultural diversity that was ultimately to be celebrated, with any future conceptual-ization of human unity having first to take account of diversity.[168] The religious references were, however, more by the way of adornments than architecture in the work of this erstwhile clergyman. Herder produced an almost entirely secular theory of language, replacing Hamann's historical-theological admixture with an account of historical-social evolution in which environmental factors and human reflection on sense-data also played a role, and differing religions were the prod-ucts of those different circumstances.[169] He retained Hamann's interest in para-

[164] Sparling, *Johann Georg Hamann*, 48–9, 81, 93; quotes from W. M. Alexander, *Johann Georg Hamann, Philosophy and Faith* (The Hague: Martinus Nijhoff, 1966), 84.

[165] Gwen Griffith Dickson, *Johann Georg Hamman's Relational Metacriticism* (Berlin: de Gruyter, 1995), 170. Hamann, like Herder, in the words of one scholar, asserts 'that language, not God, is the being we experience as mediating its own immediacy': Katie Terezakis, *The Immanent Word: the Turn to Language in German Philosophy, 1759–1801* (London: Routledge, 2007), 150, and see further 150–5.

[166] Quote in Alexander, *Johann Georg Hamann*, 85.

[167] James Austin, *The Tower of Babel in Genesis* (Bloomington, IN: Westbow, 2012).

[168] Michael Morton, *Herder and the Poetics of Thought* (University Park, PA: Pennsylvania State University Press, 1989), 34–6, 62, 65–6.

[169] Morton, *Herder and the Poetics of Thought*, 34–6; John R. Betz, *After Enlightenment: The Post-Secular Vision of J. G. Hamann* (Chichester: Blackwell, 2012), ch. 6; Wolfgang Proß, 'Die Begründung der Geschichte aus der Natur—Herders Konzept von "Gesetzen" in der Geschichte', in Hans Erich Bödeker, Peter Hanns Reill, and Jürgen Schlum (eds), *Wissenschaft als kulturelle Praxis, 1750–1900*

digmatic symbolic forms in language and saw poets as vital in the painting of linguistic pictures in which language-users would perceive their commonality. Historians, too, would be the handmaidens of national consciousness as they depicted the *Volk* through history. We can detect Leibniz's imprint on Herder's ethnography, not so much in the religious sense of emanation from a unity as in Herder's description of cultures as monads, each with its own 'spirit', the *Geist des Volkes*, as its developmental driving force (*Kraft*).[170] As to his own cultural group, Herder felt Protestants and Catholics would ideally be bound together by their Germanness.

Thus was entrenched a series of linked assumptions about national essences or 'spirits'—drawing on one of the related meanings of *Geist* or *pneuma*—and languages and cultures. Pushing forward into the nineteenth century, Wilhelm von Humboldt (1767–1835) wrote, in the general introduction to his study of the Kawi language of Java, that 'Language is, as it were, the outer appearance of the spirit of a people; the language is their spirit and the spirit their language . . . the structure of languages differs among mankind, because and insofar as the mental individuality of nations is itself different' and 'there resides in every language a characteristic *world-view* [*Weltansicht*]'. But Herder had also intimated that the spiritual/ideal side of a people needed an objective manifestation in the political sphere, promising gratitude to he who would 'promote the unity of the territories of Germany through writings, manufactures, and institutions'.[171] Hegel developed the concept of a fusion of the subjective and objective in his own way, but the idea is also present in the most influential strands of nineteenth-century historiography in Germany and many other places in Europe. Leopold von Ranke is an example.

Ranke's historicism aligned roughly with Leibniz's metaphysics, just as Ranke's panentheism, the belief that the universe is contained within God or is an emanation of God, derives from Neoplatonism.[172] Cultural diversity, as embodied in and safeguarded by the State, was an instantiation of the divine. In terms redolent of Leibniz's 'mirrors of the universe', Ranke wrote: 'instead of the fleeting conglomerations that the [social] contract theories invoke as if they were cloud

---

(Göttingen: Vandenhoeck und Ruprecht, 1999), 187–225; on mental reflection (*Besonnenheit*), see Helmut Gipper and Peter Schmitter, *Sprachwissenschaft und Sprachphilosophie im Zeitalter der Romantik* (Tübingen: Narr, 1979), 72–3, 151.

[170] On the links between Herder and Leibniz's monadological thought, including some peculiar appropriations thereof, see Ulrich Eisel, 'Individualität als Einheit in der konkreten Natur: Das Kulturkonzept der Geographie', in Parto Teherani-Krönner (ed.), *Humanökologie und Kulturökologie: Grundlagen · Ansätze · Praxis* (Opladen: Westdeutscher Verlag, 1992), 107–52, here 118 ff.; Hugh Barr Nisbet, *Herder and Scientific Thought* (Cambridge: Modern Humanities Research Association, 1970), *passim*; Fleischacker, *Integrity and Moral Relativism*, 217.

[171] Paul Bertagnolli, *Prometheus in Music: Representations of Myth in the Romantic Era* (London: Routledge, 2007), 146.

[172] On the relationship between panentheism and Neoplatonism, see John W. Cooper, *Panentheism—The Other God of the Philosophers* (Grand Rapids, MI: Baker, 2006), 18–19 and *passim*.

formations, I perceive spiritual essences, original creations of the human spirit—thoughts of God as one might say'. Like windowless monads, states were 'individualities, analogous to but essentially independent of each other'.[173]

How such principles of thought related to other strands of thought, how they were instrumentalized, and how they evolved in the world of peoples, states, and even economies are the central questions for the rest of this section. Accordingly, we will move away from the purely intellectual History of the last several pages to incorporate high thought into a more general historical account. The following tour is not ruthlessly governed by chronology, and no thematic survey can be. Broadly, however, it works forward from the middle of the seventeenth century to the era of the world wars, as nationalist-monadology revealed its ugliest aspect.

Like Leibniz's thought, the Westphalian treaties of 1648 bore the imprint of the Christian preoccupation with internality now applied to the level of state rather than the individual soul. The Westphalian dispensation saved the monad of Christendom by attributing something like monadic status to Christian states— and though Herderians would point out that theses states generally did not map cleanly onto cultures, they did map onto religions-of-state. The Westphalian enhancement of state sovereignty, which really meant a recognition of more and stronger poles of sovereignty as against would-be hegemonic France, the Emperor, and the Papacy, had as its corollary non-intervention by one state into the internal affairs of another. That corollary gave each state an in-principle untouchable 'internal forum' of its own as long as each respected the internal forum of other states and the further internal forum of its own religious minorities, those lower, substate monads, who in turn had to keep to their own collectively private *forum internum* of religious conscience.[174] Those states might learn from each other but under normal circumstances they must be allowed to preserve their own character and develop according to their own internal tendencies.

For its main players, the international system after the Wars of Religion rested 'on international law and the balance of power': law and power operated 'between rather than above states'.[175] The obvious contrast here is with the ecclesiological framework created within medieval western Christendom by the Papacy (how-ever limited the power of that framework often was in practice for medieval mon-archs). The explicit shift away from the medieval framework aided movement towards a proliferation of more purely secular *ecclesiae*. All the same, there remained for many centuries, and still to some degree to the present, a sense of incorporation within a higher monad, whether that be called Christendom, the West, or 'the civilized world'. Legal theorists could blend reference to national

---

[173] Ranke, 'Politisches Gespräch', *Historisch-politische Zeitschrift*, ed. Leopold Ranke, ii (1833–6), 775–807, here 794.

[174] Laurent Waelkens, *Amne adverso: Roman Legal Heritage in European Culture* (Leuven: Leuven University Press, 2015), 119 ff.

[175] Leo Gross, cited in Giovanni Arrighi, *The Long Twentieth Century* (London: Verso, 2010), 44.

customs and eternal, universal principles. Puritans in seventeenth-century New England maintained certain rights felt suitable for Old Englishmen while believing in a continuity of religious 'natural' law to positive state law, and availing themselves of the opportunity to forge this chain anew.[176]

Even as terms of collective identity changed over the following centuries, some of the principles of monadic subdivision remained the same. Thus the Augsburg and Westphalian option of emigration for those unprepared to live under the ruler's religious dispensation was replicated after the First World War when the 'option provisions' of the Paris Peace Treaties of 1919–20 provided for emigration along the lines of ethnonational division rather than confession. Likewise, the Paris peace treaties included Westphalian-analogous clauses for the protection of national and religious minorities. Overall, well into the twentieth century it remained the case that whatever the role of religious thought per se at any moment, many states and would-be states claimed something of the divine quality that Leibniz ascribed to his higher monads. The 'Enlightenment' certainly did little to militate against that conceit even when it militated against religion more generally, which was not always the case.

The German Enlightenment proved accommodating to some established Christianities,[177] but this was less true of its French equivalent. In the spirit of Bayle and under British empiricist influence too, Montesquieu's *On the Spirit of the Laws* of 1748 was a significant theoretical step in the direction of founding moral codes purely within human societies and their self-generated 'characters' rather than as an emanation of the divine, though it did not go as far as Herder towards cultural relativism. The Revolutionaries' Declaration of the Rights of Man and of the Citizen reflected secular natural-law principles more than did the Jeffersonian principles of the American Revolution, though both evinced Locke's influence.

If the agenda of the French Revolutionaries at the outset accorded with religious thought, it did so with the doctrine of the deists who emphasized the responsibility of human reason for creating the conditions for human flourishing on earth. The vessel for this flourishing was an appropriately rationalized state. The prerogatives of the Gallican Church were shattered as priests had to vow fidelity to that novel import, a constitution, and the revolutionary 'cult of reason' threatened a far more extensive de-Christianization before it was replaced by Robespierre's deistic cult of the Supreme Being. The monarchy's abolition in 1792 was also the decapitation of the Church. The easing of anticlerical repression after the Thermidorean reaction, and Napoleon's Concordat with the Papacy in 1801,

---

[176] McManus, *Law and Liberty*, 3–4.

[177] On elements of its relationship to Judaism: Michael Mack, *German Idealism and the Jew: The Inner Anti-Semitism of Philosophy and German Jewish Responses* (Chicago: University of Chicago Press, 2003).

nevertheless left the balance of Church–State relations more tilted to the secular ruler than on the eve of the Revolution.

In key respects the Revolution and its Napoleonic aftermath continued the centralizing agenda of the Bourbons, which reminds us that however much the Revolution came to be associated with the 'nation in arms', 'rationalization' and 'democratization' were not synonyms any more than the 'middle-class' lawyers over-represented in the leadership of the third estate were synonymous with the capitalists of Marx's 'bourgeoisie'. Revolutionary laws were to be the expression of the 'general will', elaborated no more unambiguously than in the work of the term's inventor. What was confirmed, though, was that the will was not ascertained by numeric calculation. This was convenient for the Revolutionary lawyers who aspired to having more in common with the nobility than with the urban and rural poor comprising the bulk of their shared 'third estate'. The monarch was as aware as these third estate leaders of the need for reform of the socio-economic order, but neither he nor they desired the end of seigneurialism. The introduction of measures to that effect in 1789–90, like the Declaration, was a concession to feared demotic forces. The same dynamics help explain the establishment of universal manhood suffrage by the Jacobins in 1792 for the election of deputies to the National Convention (that suffrage was ended by the Constitution of 1795), which only a few of them had advocated from the outset. Wariness of the masses increasingly coexisted with the desire to instrumentalize them to protect the Revolutionary state against external enemies. With the grand expansions of recruitment in 1793, an unprecedently large proportion of 'the nation' did indeed appear in arms, though not always desperately enthusiastically.

Revolutionary France expanded and then contracted, but after 1815 Napoleon's erstwhile dominions could not easily throw off all his legacies, and, like Restoration France, they did not always wish to. In many places the impact endured of attacks on clerical prerogatives, and of reforms of civil and economic institutions and even borders—consider the 'rationalization' of the principalities of the Holy Roman Empire that was inadvertently a step towards later German unification. Then there was the effect of Napoleonic constitutions. When we come to the German philosophical reaction to Revolutionary expansion, the legacy is just as ambivalent.

Like Kant, Fichte and Hegel had originally embraced the French Revolution, even if not particular deeds of the Revolutionaries. For not a few onlookers, the Revolution's attack on absolutism and tradition made it a sociopolitical embodiment of the emancipation Protestantism had supposedly brought at the spiritual level. Fichte's enthusiasm may sound odd given that his famous *Addresses to the German Nation* (1807) were shaped in reaction to the behaviour of the Napoleonic state. But his criticism of France was for its betrayal of the ideals of the Revolution as it opted for imperialism—leadership by domination rather than leadership by example. Since France was no longer the exemplar, Germany would have to be, and in order to fulfil that role (and after the defeats of 1806, to resist occupation) it would have to awaken itself as a subject of history. Or, rather, be awoken. A reader of Rousseau, Fichte would have known of his analogous efforts in trying to whip up Polish national consciousness around the time of the partition of 1772 as a way of resisting Russian, not to mention Prussian and Austrian, imperialism. Rousseau had thought it vital to shape Poles' 'minds and hearts in a national pattern that will set them apart from other peoples, that will keep them from being absorbed by other peoples and ensure that they remain patriotic'.[178] While Fichte differed from Herder given his own emphasis on 'constitutional engineering', he shared with Herder the belief that national linguistic-cultural differences amongst Europeans were 'natural' (whereas the distinction between Prussia and Germany was artificial), and that anti-imperial national-cultural self-expression would conduce to international harmony. If we can but put aside the ethnocentric leadership role in the world that Fichte arrogated to Germany, on the presumption that only Germany could act in a truly universalistic sense on behalf of all peoples, we can see the monadological logic of his pronouncement in *Patriotism and its Opposite* (1806). 'Cosmopolitanism is the dominant will that the purpose of humanity be really achieved. Patriotism is the will that that purpose be first fulfilled in that nation to which we ourselves belong', and so 'Cosmopolitanism must necessarily become patriotism'.[179]

In the 1790s, Fichte developed a view of individual identity as a product of intersubjectivity, i.e. social relations, and he fused this sound insight with his 'patriotic' agenda. The History I section mentioned a nineteenth-century reception of Fichte that focused on the egotism of the 'I' somehow 'positing' the world (p. 167). It also mentioned his point about the intentionality of consciousness, i.e. that consciousness is always consciousness of something in particular. The end of that section noted Fichte's concept of self-limiting freedom, which differed from Kant's account of self-legislating autonomy (pp. 173–4). How do we get from the first of these points to the last? Prior to there being an I at all, as in a self-conscious entity, there must be appreciation of others different to Me, but with similar capacities and rights, that have drawn my attention to my own capacities and rights. Fichte's position is anticipated by Plato's *Alcibiades*, in which the pupils of the not-I become the mirror of the I. I appreciate myself as a subject in light of the

---

[178] Cited in Mads Qvortrup, *The Political Philosophy of Jean-Jacques Rousseau* (Manchester: Manchester University Press, 2014), 78.

[179] For further elaboration of the supposed connections between individual, nations, and mankind, see Stefan-Ludwig Hoffmann, *The Politics of Sociability: Freemasonry and German Civil Society, 1840–1918* (Ann Arbor: University of Michigan Press, 2007), ch. 7, esp. 243–4. Note that *Patriotism and its Opposite* was written before the German defeat at Jena later in 1806, and thereafter Fichte's tone becomes more stridently nationalistic. On that, and on Fichte's coming vision of a German future including a 'national church' and national education in patriotism, see Helmut Walser Smith, *The Continuities of German History* (Cambridge: Cambridge University Press, 2007), 63 ff.

fact that I perceive the not-I perceiving me as an object of her similar perception. Where Descartes's appreciation of his own imperfection presupposed the idea already inserted within him of God's notion of perfection,[180] for Fichte the idea of one's freedom to posit or to affect other things presupposed the generalized idea of freedom that was accessible to others. Equally the idea of acting freely presupposed the idea of willingly limiting one's scope of action for the sake of others in the way that they must in order that I can be free. The keyword here is *Anerkennung*, i.e. recognition, which connotes a moral quality in the sense of acceptance/respect while also having the more purely cognitive sense of the word.[181] Fichte realized that relations between individuals are not unmediated but occur within contexts—and the context that he, like Herder, was most interested in was the linguistic-cultural one, which scarcely distinguishes him from some multiculturalists and conservatives today. But in address to his fellow Germans he also made a prescriptive claim based on his descriptive assumption that cultural-linguistic collectives were natural-cum-spiritual kinds.[182] It was distinctly monadological to say 'only when each people, left to itself, develops and forms itself in accordance with its own peculiar quality, and only when in each people each individual develops himself in accordance with that quality, as well as in accordance with his own peculiar quality, then, and only then, does the manifestation of divinity appear'.[183]

Karl Marx's theories were also embedded in a theory of intersubjective relations, but in their economic, political, and philosophical connotations they could scarcely have stood more at odds with Fichte's. Marx (1818–83) gave theoretical expression to the growing and very *material* discontents of the age, replacing the concept of a unifying sociocultural *Geist* with that of a dominant *ideology* spuriously legitimating the interests of one class at the expense of those of another. Urbanization, industrialization, and mass literacy started to make as much of an impact as had the Revolutionary armies produced by the *levée en masse* and the insurrections stimulated by Napoleon, and as had the 'egotistic' individualist self-assertiveness attributed to the Revolution. Accordingly the challenge for elites across the Continent, as it would be for postcolonial nationalists after the Second World War, was to keep established social orders maximally stable and unitary while harnessing, in the name of the people, the martial and productive forces unleashed by the French and English revolutions.

---

[180] Steven Crowell, 'Why Is Ethics First Philosophy? Levinas in Phenomenological Context', *European Journal of Philosophy* 23/3 (2015), 564–88, here 566.

[181] Pinkard, *German Philosophy*, 121; Eric D. Weitz, 'Self-Determination: How a German Enlightenment Idea Became the Slogan of National Liberation and a Human Right', *American Historical Review* 120/2 (2015), 462–96, here 474–6.

[182] Neither the pantheist nor the Neoplatonist—both traditions influenced Fichte—need distinguish sharply between the natural and the spiritual.

[183] Quote from Weitz, 'Self-Determination', 478–9.

The category 'English revolution' is meant to include political events between 1640 and 1688, but, in keeping with this materialist element of the discussion, my main concern is with the way in which those events channelled economic forces of revolutionary power. The absolutist agenda of Charles I that gave rise to political strife from 1640 had been born in a desire to emulate France and Spain and was given urgency by war with Scotland. The Crown's attempt to strengthen the central state and its war machine by harnessing the relatively dynamic agrarian economy through increased tax revenues was interpreted by the landed gentry as an attack on their economic prerogatives. The political 'revolution' of that moment was more an attempt to restore the status quo ante, though by 1649 it brought significant constitutional change in the identification of sovereignty in the nation, through its parliamentary representatives. Ultimately, what emerged from the early eighteenth century as the vaunted 'fiscal-military state' was the product of seventeenth-century compromises between the monarchy and the landowners in the political and economic spheres, if also of the importation of Dutch financial expertise after the Glorious Revolution of 1688. The State proved itself repeatedly in warfare against the erstwhile Continental hegemon, France, whose resulting convulsions produced the French Revolution.

England's agrarian capitalism had long since created and supplied with basic necessities a growing landless, increasingly urban population in Europe's first fully integrated internal economy. The urban population, plus the established philosophy of intensive production and enhanced labour productivity, were preconditions for the Industrial Revolution that was given a major boost by the Napoleonic Wars. Napoleon's defeat not only weakened France again, it also precipitated a globalization of British surplus capital and capital goods, hungry for new investment and sales opportunities and availing themselves of the frequently unpacific Pax Britannica. Under these specific, hegemonic conditions, Britain repudiated earlier mercantilist doctrines and followed the lead of Adam Smith.

Mercantilism had been a rather appropriate doctrine for the Westphalian era, given the synergy between state-building and national economy-building. A preoccupation with balances of trade and retention of precious metals inhibited some international commerce while binding producers and merchants alike to the state in ways that could be mutually beneficial. Merchant banks and wealthy individuals could lend to states to build the latters' capacity, while

> Partly through commands to state bureaucracies and partly through incentives to private enterprise, the rulers of France and of the United Kingdom internalized within their domains as many of the growing number of activities that, directly or indirectly, entered as inputs in war-making and state-making as was feasible. In this way, they managed to turn into tax revenues a much larger share of protection costs than [earlier economic pathbreaking polities like] the Italian city-states, or for that matter the United Provinces, ever did or could have done.

By spending these enhanced tax revenues within their domestic economies, they created new incentives and opportunities to establish ever new linkages between activities and thus make wars pay for themselves more and more.[184]

Conversely, the unimpeded commerce propounded by Britain and increasingly France from the second quarter of the nineteenth century changed the relationship between state and economy, in a way that shaped the trajectories of the disciplines of political science (and IR), sociology, and economics. By mid-Victorian times Gladstone echoed the popular aspiration 'that "government" and "economy" should be treated as separate entities in order to maintain fiscal rectitude and economic order'.[185] Such a separation—never complete—accelerated the internationalization of capital.

As 'the economy' was freed from some territorial constraints, it was attributed a transcendent quality far from unfamiliar in a Christian civilization.[186] Given the manifest power of the 'invisible hand', disbelief was scarcely an option, but its power did not always translate into legitimacy. Exegesis in the form of the theory of marginal economics was a key influence on the rational actor theory underpinning one conception of the modern human, *homo economicus*. But in the thinking of Friedrich List (1789–1846) and his successors in the German historical school of economics, there was no one economic theory, but rather a range, correlated for List with level of development and for the historical school with national history and culture and the 'universal union' that existed between each state and its people.

The argument in which different economic schools were engaged was in one way a disagreement about basic contexts of human behaviour. With the argument over primary context came the argument over primary discipline, or primary sort of discipline: deductive Ricardian economics was set against empirical economics firmly embedded in historical-cultural study of the sort that the German historicist tradition excelled in.[187] But while there was a battle for primacy between 'economic' and 'cultural' paradigms, which mapped on to the battle of a certain universalism against a certain particularism, different participants on the same 'side' by no means agreed with each other about the stakes. For some German observers, left and right, British laissez-faire economism, dubbed 'Manchesterism', indicated a despiritualized commercial civilization. For others, it indicated fragmentation, the exploitation of masses, and even of the State, by a minority class of

---

[184] Arrighi, *Long Twentieth Century*, 51.
[185] Paul Johnson, *Making the Market: Victorian Origins of Corporate Capitalism* (Cambridge: Cambridge University Press, 2010), 16.
[186] Jonathan Hearn, 'The Strength of Weak Legitimacy: A Cultural Analysis of Legitimacy in Capitalist, Liberal, Democratic Nation-States', *Journal of Political Power* 4/2 (2011), 199–216, here 205.
[187] Note that more organicist and social-collectivist accounts of the economy were never absent in the mid-Victorian period, whether among high Tories or working-class radicals and socialists. Early in the twentieth century such accounts gained greater influence.

individuals acting in its own interests.[188] Both views, as it happens, could combine in the stigmatization of Jews as parasites on 'authentic' cultures, acting above the State in mysterious ways, when the globalizing economic system experienced major shocks from 1873 to 1896 and again in the great interwar depression.

It is tribute to the remarkable adaptability of Britain's landed elite that it not only managed to maintain much of its ascendancy by the character of its relations to capitalism but also helped persuade the world that Germany constituted some special, distorted case of national development. One not-unsubstantiated allegation concerned the enduring political power of the *Junker* landowner class in Prussian-German politics, but it is the sharpness of the contrast that amuses. A more marked socio-economic contrast here is not of Germany with Britain but of Germany with an ideal(ized?) model in which 'national bourgeoisies' drove modernizing nationalist agendas against agrarian and external commercial interests.

Some of the undoubted differences between Britain and all other states may reflect nothing more than that as the first capitalist state Britain could develop at a pace and in a fashion unavailable to any other state. Every state that subsequently entered the capitalist system did so under different circumstances, and with correspondingly different pressures and imperatives. Since only one state could be first in, though, every other state shared the quality of relative 'lateness', which is why certain elements of Germany's experience were more representative of trends elsewhere on the Continent and beyond. Thus List's teaching shaped the policy of Russia under Witte, Imperial Japan, and, under the name *milli iktisat*, the late Ottoman Empire, and strongly resembled the influential doctrines of the Hamiltonian 'American school' associated with Henry Clay. For all of the other actual and would-be states seeking to develop in the interests of sovereign independence, some form of étatisme was not at all unusual. The currently dominant state, Britain, had itself explored a range of protectionisms and interventions at earlier stages of its ascent, by no means all of which had been decried by Adam Smith (who applauded the seventeenth-century Navigation Acts), and some of which survived well into the nineteenth century within Britain and in Britain's administration of its formal empire.

As the nineteenth century progressed, the link became increasingly clear between economic-industrial power and the capacity to retain sovereign independence or deny it to others—the capacity, *in extremis*, to wage war. Japan under the Meiji restoration is a prime example of a state that pursued forced-paced, *dirigiste* economic development as a route to avoid the neo-colonial fate of nearby China, which had surrendered so much to Britain in particular. In other words, while socialists and Marxists had attacked the liberal belief in an identity of interests between the individual and her society—Engels wrote of London that 'the

---

[188] Detlev Mares, 'Not Entirely a Manchester Man', in Anthony Howe and Simon Morgan (eds), *Rethinking Nineteenth Century Liberalism* (Aldershot: Ashgate, 2006), 141–60, here 154–5.

dissolution of mankind in monads, of which each has a separate principle of life and a separate goal, the world of atoms, is here carried to its utmost extremes'[189]— the Left could find some agreement with the nationalist Right on how little Adam Smith's philosophy of irenic, mutually-complementary interstate commercial relations was mirrored in reality. The expanded adoption of the gold standard from the early 1870s, while removing states' capacities to regulate the value of their currencies and aiding the acceleration of international trade, found a 'nationalist' counterpart in the coming years and decades. During the repeated depressions of the last quarter of the century, the statist element in economic and social life was enhanced in the form of customs tariffs and social legislation that sought to minimize the domestic impact of adjustments to international commerce and international economic rhythms.[190] The misadaption of Darwinism to the life of peoples contributed to the increasingly fraught competitiveness of the late nineteenth- and early twentieth-century international environment, but it also mirrored that environment. It is because of the similarity of pressures on and agendas of a range of states within that international environment that the present survey focuses more on commonalities than differences between various nationalisms.

There are other reasons for emphasizing similarity too. An influential approach in the scholarship on nationalism describes French 'Revolutionary' nationalism, like American nationalism, as a civic or constitutional nationalism, and juxtaposes this with the implicitly less healthy integral/organic/ethnic nationalisms that cropped up in Germany and in eastern and south-eastern Europe.[191] In principle the difference is clear—it is that between community defined by shared possession of a set of elective values versus a set of innate characteristics—but many qualifications are required, both of the distinction and the implied superiority of one sort of nationalism over the other.

It is more accurate to conceive of these categories of nationalism as ideal types, with reality much messier. Think of how US civic nationalism has often been flavoured by nativist racism, emphasis on America's Christian heritage, and especially more and less formal discrimination against blacks. Furthermore, granted a real or notional moment of self-constitution of the civic nation, the great majority of its citizens in subsequent generations are citizens merely in virtue of blood and soil, ie. their parentage and place of birth, while candidate citizens have, in that telling expression, to 'naturalize'. As well as changes over time and context, concepts like 'spirit' and *Kraft* blur the distinction between values (civic nationalism) and characteristics (ethnic nationalism). Spirit, *Geist*, *ésprit*, was ubiquitous. The

---

[189] Engels cited in Swaart, ' "Individualism" ', 81.
[190] Karl Polanyi, *The Great Transformation* (Boston: Beacon Press, 2001), 207–24.
[191] Liah Greenfeld, *Nationalism: Five Roads to Modernity* (Cambridge, MA: Harvard University Press, 1992); Michael Ignatieff, *Blood and Belonging* (London: Vintage, 1994), 3–6; Qvortrup, *The Political Philosophy*, 84.

Frenchman Ernst Renan called the nation 'a soul, a spiritual principle', while the Danish Bishop Grundtvig described peoples as possessing a collective 'active life-force'. Bluntschli in Switzerland and Mazzini in Italy expressed just the same sort of sentiment.[192] In some of its definitions and explanatory functions 'culture' plays much the same blurring role as 'spirit'. It is nothing if not shared, and it is the plural-but-singular element, 'the people' (consider: 'we the people'), comprising the community in whose name the State purports to act that is the source of legitimacy.[193]

Since in each 'national' case the task was of making something new from existing raw materials, it is scarcely surprising that architects seized upon those materials that seemed already hewn for the task: established ties of language or custom that lent themselves to metaphors of kinship. This approach was especially 'necessary' when the State did not already exist to provide some legal-administrative unity to the 'people' in question. Herderian thought about gathering together a politically-fragmented but (supposedly) culturally-distinct Germandom found many imitators amongst other peoples that were as yet without their own state. Rousseau's late-life work on the governance of Poland shows the increasing influence of Montesquieu on his thought in its drift away from the purest contractualism as Rousseau stressed the significance of continuity, concepts of national character, and the need for education in the Polish language rather than the language of 'foreigners'. History was important in the education process in constructing a collective memory of past greatness by way of enhancing collective Polish self-esteem.[194] We are not far from the ethos underpinning nineteenth-century German historicist thought—'informing' peoples about their collective character by revealing their past and helping individual people to orient themselves in the present in the context of larger movements that subsume them.

Let us return for a moment, then, to the influential German historical profession to assess how it reconciled its monadological-metaphysical underpinning with a political world of incipient and actual conflict. Ranke's voice comes through in an imagined dialogue of 1836—his famous *Politisches Gespräch*—when 'Friedrich' pronounces that the 'degree of independence achieved by a state dictates its standing in the world. It is accordingly obliged to marshal all its internal arrangements towards the end of asserting itself. That is its supreme law'.

---

[192] All four cited in Fleishacker, *Integrity and Moral Relativism*, 217.

[193] An example of how 'culture' can blur distinctions: Qvortrup, *The Political Philosophy*, 84, writes that 'Rousseau supported . . . a civic nationalism—not an ethnic nationalism . . . Nationalism can be an evil if it degenerates into ethnic strife—yet it can also be a force for good if it is used as a mechanism for creating cultural homogeneity'. Absent is elaboration of the relationship between this sort of homogenous order and liberalism (or multiculturalism), an account of what elements of coercion ('strife') are deemed acceptable in the creation of homogeneity, and an explanation of the relationship or apparent non-relationship of culture to ethnicity.

[194] Jean Terrier, *Visions of the Social: Society as a Political Project in France, 1750–1950* (Leiden: Brill, 2011), 54–6; Qvortrup, *The Political Philosophy*, 78–9.

This is the 'primacy of foreign policy' doctrine with which Ranke and Bismarck would become synonymous.[195] As, supposedly, in Revolutionary France, the State was the guarantor of the liberty and expression of the individuality of the nation on the stage of world history. As such, not only was it owed loyalty, it was itself a moral entity, as Pufendorf, Hegel, and later historicist historians like Gustav Droysen also maintained. Since the State was a moral entity, its prerogatives were not easily limited by recourse to the concept of external wills and moralities; its duty was at once to protect the people and express what Ranke called its 'moral energy'. Ranke evinced some awareness of the consequences of this sort of thinking, and the need for 'detachment' as prerequisite for any authentic empirically-informed intuition. Thus 'Karl' admonishes 'Friedrich': 'You look upon war's bloody handiwork as a competition of moral energies. Take care that you do not become too sublime!'[196] Clearly, then, Ranke did not feel the State could do no wrong: indeed, in keeping with Neoplatonic thought, the purest entities were the highest up the chain of being, the least coloured by the mundane and the physical, while states and their leaders had to act in an imperfect world. But by the same token it would be wrong either to expect perfection of states and statesmen or to denigrate them for their imperfection, any more than Augustine could ignore the hard choices and necessary evils of life in the earthly realm. Later in life, Ranke wrote that it would 'be infinitely wrong to seek only the effects of brutal forces in the struggles of historical powers . . . no state has ever existed without a spiritual basis and a spiritual content. A spiritual essence appears in power itself, an original genius with its own particular life.'[197]

Over time the space for reservations only dwindled. The historian Treitschke (1834–96), who we have already encountered as a theorist of political morality (p. 70) reconciled nationalistic social Darwinism with an idealist Lutheran Christianity, for if the ideal was to become real through the German state, 'good' needed to arrogate power to itself by means of which no monkish armchair moralist would approve. Arguably the last major historicist in the tradition of the Prussian school, Meinecke (1862–1954), once wrote that 'morality has not only a universal but also an individual side to it and the seeming immorality of the State's egoism for power can be morally justified from this perspective. For nothing can be immoral which comes from the innermost, individual character of a being.'[198] In other words, what Scheler and Westermarck problematized at the level of personal morality was actively supported at the level of the State.

---

[195] Ranke, 'Politisches Gespräch', 793–4.
[196] Ranke, 'Politisches Gespräch', 793–4.
[197] Leopold von Ranke, *Weltgeschichte*, ed. Alfred Dove and Georg Winter, vol. ix, pt II (Leipzig: Duncker and Humblot, 1888), p. xi.
[198] George Iggers, *The German Conception of History* (Middletown, CT: Wesleyan University Press, 2012), 9.

One of the more intringuing intellectual engagements with the interiority question is that of the Romantic pro-Revolutionary historian of France, Jules Michelet (1798–1874). He admired Leibniz and his description of France as 'a soul and as a person' has distinctly monadological overtones. This personalization of the national is the key to reconciling, on one hand, Michelet's veneration of Christian inwardness and the realm of the spirit over the world of the letter and nature and, on the other hand, his celebration of the 1789 Revolution as 'the advent of the Law, the resurrection of Right, and the reaction of Justice'. According to Michelet's own historical philosophy civilization advanced across time from east to west, and the story was of ascending liberty and consciousness as it gradually emancipated itself from an 'oriental' identification of the divine with the natural, to a focus on the realm of pure mind and spirit. Christianity was the apogee of the process. At the same time, this focus on the spiritual became distorted in the history of Christian civilization to bear overwhelmingly on the matter of grace. Michelet associated arbitrary divine favour with injustice and felt that such injustice was incarnated in the unequal society of the *ancien régime*. The Revolution marked the return of justice, which, as an essential element of love and the original Christian ideal, also restored grace by breaking its association with repression. Equally, the return of justice in a reformed national community would serve as an antidote to the individualism encouraged as Christian doctrines became more internalistic and the social structures of medieval Christian civilization collapsed. With its balance of grace and justice, revolutionary nationalism supposedly embodied the ideal attributes of religion.[199]

Beyond Michelet's personal vision, and the visions of sundry deists and panentheists who effectively contributed to the veneration of the nation(-state) as god became ever less anthropomorphic and interventionist, more orthodox-looking religious forms were adaptable too. The nineteenth century saw a proliferation of the 'national churches' that Fichte promoted in the German case and that George Bernard Shaw was to associate with 'heresy nationalism'.[200] In his *Essay On the Constitution of Church and State* (1829) the Romantic Anglican and opponent of Catholic emancipation Samuel Taylor Coleridge felt Henry VIII had not gone far enough in creating a properly national Church.[201] 'Even' in Roman Catholic countries, which one might at first blush associate with a supranational Church,

[199] Ceri Crossley, *French Historians and Romanticism: Thierry, Guizot, the Saint-Simonians, Quinet, Michelet* (London: Routledge, 1993), 193–204; Tom Conner, 'Writing History: Michelet's *History of the French Revolution*', in Gail M. Schwab and John R. Jeanneny (eds), *The French Revolution of 1789 and Its Impact* (Westport, CT: Greenwood Press, 1995), 13–22.

[200] The expression is from his *Saint Joan*. There it refers to Joan of Arc's French nationalism, and nationalism is also set alongside some version of Protestantism. Joan's heresy is to divide Christ's kingdom into nations, which is to 'dethrone Christ'. Of course the leaders and members of the national churches did not see themselves as dethroning Christ at all.

[201] Coleridge, *On the Constitution of the Church and State*, ed. John Colmer (1829; Princeton: Princeton University Press, 1976).

religion might be as important a marker of nationality as language. Consider Poland, whose epithet 'Christ among the nations' was invoked by nineteenth-century Romantics in light of the partitions of 1772–95 and then the 1830 uprising against Russia. In the 1930s Spain's Republican regime with its socialist and atheistic elements was damned by right-wing pro-clerical insurgents as the 'anti-Spain' or, like Jews, as the 'anti-nation'—either way, read: 'Antichrist'. Eastern Catholicism and various Orthodoxies were similarly adapted.

Of special relevance to the narrative of this Part of the book is how far the idea of national churches and *Volk*-spirits sustained the sort of 'heroic, folk-centred' and 'sociobiological' outlook that sundry 'Reformations' from the high Middle Ages onwards had sought to replace with a more inward spiritualism (see p. 145). Perhaps this was inevitable when the collective interior was analogized to the individual interior according to the concentric circles model of monadological thought: when talking of the interior of a nation(-state) one was perforce also talking about a worldly community of individuals within the bounds of that collective interior. Precisely this sort of logic was anathema to the existentialist Kierkegaard, who held fast to one strand of the 'Lutheran' inheritance while rejecting another. He argued that there could be no complementarity or synergy of religious and political institutions, since that would ultimately tend to the domestication of the eternal element. His abhorrence was a 'Christian state' comprising 'people's church', 'nationality', and 'popular sovereignty' in a collusive synthesis of 'official piety and socio-political convenience'.[202] Related criticisms from a slightly different perspective were expressed in Franz Overbeck's essay *Über die Christlichkeit unserer heutigen Theologie* (1873), literally 'On the Christian Character of Our Contemporary Theology', but effectively more like 'How Christian Really is Our Contemporary Theology?', and Overbeck's posthumously-published *Christentum und Kultur* (1919).

For those with an eye on politics and society, navigating the relationship between the secular and the transcendent realm might lead to one of two familiar paths being taken. One could advert to a hermetic seal between the political world and the *forum internum* of faith. This was the nature of the 'emancipation contract' offered to Jews on the terms of French 'civic nationalism' and was effectively the meaning of Jewish emancipation in Germany too: relegate your religion to the private sphere in order to participate on the same terms as everyone else in the public sphere. Or, more commonly for those in power and in majority, one could act as if the transcendent and and the political were in harmony. 'I vow to thee, my country, all earthly things above, Entire and whole and perfect, the service of my love; . . . The love that never falters, the love that pays the price, The love that makes undaunted the final sacrifice'; *dulce et decorum est pro patria mori*; and so forth. 'Gott mit uns' was etched on the belt buckles of German soldiers during the First World War, the 'war for righteousness', as well as in the 1939–45 conflict.[203] Far enough down that road, one did not need to acknowledge the divine at all, merely grateful indenture to the forces fortifying one's higher-monad: *Meine Ehre heisst Treue*, in the SS motto—my honour is loyalty.

Even internationally minded socialists remained importantly wedded to concepts of the nation. Sometimes the concept was of cultural nations enjoying autonomy within a wider, decentralized multinational state, as in the turn-of-the-century thought of some left-wing Armenians in the late Ottoman Empire or 'Austro-Marxists' like Otto Bauer. This sort of thinking would go on to shape Stalin's 1913 work *Marxism and the National Question*, and by extension Soviet nationalities policy in the 1920s and 1930s. Bauer described the nation as a *Schicksalgemeinschaft*, or community of fate/destiny with shared characteristics— a *Charaktergemeinschaft*. Stalin defined a nation as 'a historically constituted, stable community of people, formed on the basis of a common language, territory, economic life, and psychological make-up manifested in a common culture'. What ties these particular strands of socialism to more orthodox Marxist thinking about classes is the element of *collective* self-determination, the social basis of consciousness and action, as opposed to the individualism of *Manchesterthum*, and as opposed to imperial forms based on the exploitation of one people by another. Marxists were well used to thinking in terms of collective subjects like the proletariat. Like many observers of events in the age from the American revolutions to 1848, Marx was impressed by separatist and nationalist movements as agents of historical change, and the Haitian Revolution of 1791–4 had combined anti-colonialism with a successful challenge to the economic and social order of slavery. Looking forward, leftist-approved forms of national self-determination were always assumed to be intrinsically democratic, tending towards harmony between peoples and conducing to class self-expression within and across these national boundaries. The Second International stipulated 'self-determination for all peoples' in its 1896 programme, and the Russian Revolutionaries of February and October 1917 enshrined the principle of self-determination, prompting Woodrow Wilson's attempt to wrest discursive control of it.[204]

It is perhaps unnecessary to stress how little the rise of the nation state cohered with Bauer's or Herder's visions. First, whatever the 'type' of nationalism, states extant and emergent were, and remain, territorially bounded, encompassing only

---

[203] A translation of *Immanuel*, 'God is with us', *Gott mit uns* was used as a battle cry by the Christianized Roman Empire before being adopted by various Christian sects and polities. As to 'I vow to thee, my country', that was the title given to a hymn in 1921 but the words came from a poem composed before the First World War by Cecil Spring Rice. The poem was entitled *Urbs Dei/The Two Father Lands* (1908–12) and referred to the earthly and the heavenly kingdoms.

[204] Almost all of the interpretation in this paragraph, and all of the quotes, are taken from Weitz, 'Self-Determination', 480–5.

a part of the global human population, while projecting shared sentiments on that part. With the civic/ethnic nationalism distinction in mind, it is just as easy to feel superior to others who hold different values as to those with different skin colours, and both sentiments can spawn imperialism. Indeed imperial powers could alternate between the two sets of beliefs in self-justification if we but recall the importance ascribed by 'rational' *and* self-consciously white imperialists to particular, value-laden interpretations of concepts like civilization and progress.

Even if one did not feel superior to Others as such, one might nonetheless find them outside one's primary universe of obligation, which brings us back to the man with right to be considered the father of civic nationalism, Rousseau. One commentator writes that if for Rousseau all society was bad that was outside the ideal state based on the contract, then 'once the ideal state is realized, society dissolves entirely into the state'. It is not actually true that Rousseau imagined the dissolution of all bonds beneath the level of the State, because more 'natural' affections were supposedly the basis for adherence to the laws of the contractual State, that entity that embodied the 'general will' and in which a man faced no contradiction between 'his wishes and his duties'.[205] It is true, however, that 'natural' bonds were supposed to be considered less important than the bond of the general will. Rousseau allows for no limits on the sovereign power of the State vis-à-vis persons or peoples once its rule has been appropriately constituted. It is further true that interstate relations are characterized as distinctly unaffectionate in Rousseau's scheme, and he plotted no route by which the situation might be changed:

> Every patriot hates foreigners; they are only men, and nothing to him. [*Footnote in the original*: Thus the wars of republics are more cruel than those of monarchies. But if the wars of kings are less cruel, their peace is terrible; better be their foe than their subject.] This defect is inevitable, but of little importance. The great thing is to be kind to our neighbours. Among strangers the Spartan was selfish, grasping, and unjust, but unselfishness, justice, and harmony ruled his home life. Distrust those cosmopolitans who search out remote duties in their books and neglect those that lie nearest. Such philosophers will love the Tartars to avoid loving their neighbour.[206]

Self-conscious, solidaristic internal identity was necessary for state self-preservation as well as for the 'emancipation' of all contractees.

---

[205] Stanley Hoffmann, '*The Social Contract* or the Mirage of the General Will', in Christie McDonald and Stanley Hoffmann (eds), *Rousseau and Freedom* (Cambridge: Cambridge University Press, 2010), 113–41, here 134–5, cf. Roger D. Masters, *The Political Philosophy of Rousseau* (Princeton: Princeton University Press, 1968), 24–5. Quote on wishes and duties from Rousseau, *Emile* (1762; Mineola, NY: Dover, 2013), 8.
[206] Rousseau, *Emile*, 7.

To the forging of such identity, then, as in the last pages of this section we consider the means, success, limitations, and costs of the internal homogenization process. What is true of universalisms is also true of particularisms like nationalism: each begins as a concept in some specific place or mind and has to make itself be known to be true in a wider space and in other minds. The process may involve coercion as well as persuasion, and the potential for violence is not obviously less in those nationalist cases that tend to be placed more in the 'civic' than the 'ethnic' basket—which is grounds enough for bringing Michelet's vision of revolutionary 'justice' under the scrutiny of scepticism. Internal 'civilizing missions' of the 'turning peasants into Frenchmen' and 'we have made Italy, now we have to make Italians' sort were as common as external 'civilizing missions'.[207] Sometimes actions against internal opponents of the new order were as violent, as with the perhaps 200,000 killed in the Revolutionary state's campaign against the inhabitants of the Vendée from 1793 or the tens of thousands of deaths inflicted by the Italian state acting against the so-called Great Brigandage in the Mezzogiorno in the early 1860s.[208] Like Treitschke's earlier support of Prussian Germanization of Poles, in the twentieth century the new, interwar Polish state's 'Polonization' campaigns, or the massacre, dispersal, and forced assimilation of Kurds ('mountain Turks' in the Kemalist lexicon) in eastern Turkey around the same time, were all exercises in making the nation out of heterogeneous social elements while claiming that the nation provided warrant for the exercise. Hence the prominent rhetoric of '(re-)awakening' and 'renaissance' to paper over the tension.

Elsewhere, the establishment of some law-bound 'civilizations' required the eradication of potential competitors as a prerequisite of the construction project, a sort of clearing of the decks, as in the white settlement of America and Australia. In such cases civic nationalisms were constructed on the scorched earth of ethno-racial destruction, which tells us something about the limits of their inclusivity. Genocide, *strages gentium* in an earlier tongue, could be seen either as an expression of monadic unity or a way of trying to make monadology true. The latter explanation would certainly explain why some genocidaires move from target group to target group, winnowing out ever more 'enemies' (allegations of disloyalty and impurity intertwined) in some attempt to create the desired community of common purpose. It would also explain why so many *génocidaires* have perceived connections between outer enemies and inner enemies or fifth columns—there actually being no metaphysical line separating one community from another and guaranteeing the internal consistency of that which it encircles.

---

[207] Eugen Weber, *Peasants Into Frenchmen: The Modernization of Rural France, 1870–1914* (Stanford, CA: Stanford University Press, 1976). The 'Italians' quote—'Fatta l'Italia, bisogna fare gli Italiani'—has been attributed both to Massimo D'Azeglio and Ferdinando Martini.
[208] On the Italian case, including discussion of the death toll, see e.g. Roberto Martucci's pointedly titled *L'invenzione dell'Italia unita, 1855–1864* (Florence: Sansoni, 1999).

Minorities were generally imperilled and cross-border and diasporic minorities more than most. Diasporas, especially the Jewish one, presented a particular problem for Herder who liked his cultural differences to map neatly onto different territories. Since he was primarily concerned with Europe, he gave little attention to Armenians who he saw as but transient sojourners from the Orient. He reserved particular contempt for 'Indian' 'Gypsies' (*Zigeuner*) and for 'Turks' who derived from 'Turkestan' and colonized the Balkans through the Ottoman Empire.[209] Were one to map the history of ethnic cleansing and genocide in Eurasia in the century and a half after Herder's death, one would note that 'Turks' from the Balkans and elsewhere comprised one of the major victim groups up to the beginning of the First World War, as new nation states established themselves and Russia expanded itself at Ottoman expense. Then, in Anatolia in the dwindling Ottoman Empire the Armenians would be subjected to exterminatory violence during the First World War. Then Europe's Romanies were the victims of genocide in the Second World War, and not just at the hands of Nazis; like the Shoah, the Porrajmos was conducted by a genocidal alliance of several ethnonational states whose leaders enthusiastically murdered their diasporic minorities or surrendered them for murder. As to the Jews, in the longer perspective it does not look at all accidental that they should have been subjected to the most extensive and intensive of genocidal campaigns. In monadic Christian Europe, Jews comprised the ultimate ontological anomaly. Not only were they diasporans with no homeland to be pushed back to, they lacked Spirit. They lacked it by the standard Christian reading, which Hamann shared, whereby they were literalists and materialists, people of the law only.[210] By extension in this misreading, they were incapable of the internal spiritual togetherness characterizing a proper nation. They were really an anti-nation.[211]

---

[209] Karol Sauerland, ' "Die fremden Völker in Europa": Herder's unpolitische Metaphern und Bilder zu den höchst politischen Begriffen Volk und Nation', in Gesa von Essen and Horst Turk (eds), *Unerledigte Geschichten: Der literarische Umgang mit Nationalität und Internationalität* (Göttingen: Wallstein, 2000), 57–71; Sonia Sikka, *Herder on Humanity and Cultural Difference: Enlightened Relativism* (Cambridge: Cambridge University Press, 2011), 242–7.

[210] Henri Veldhuis, *Ein versiegeltes Buch: Der Naturbegriff in der Theologie J. G. Hamanns (1730–1788)* (Berlin: de Gruyter, 1994), 289 ff.

[211] As Adolf Hitler wrote in *Mein Kampf* (Manheim translation, Boston: Houghton Mifflin, 1943), 'the Jewish "State"—which should be the living organism for preserving and increasing a race—is completely unlimited as to territory. For a state formation to have a definite spatial setting always presupposes an idealistic attitude on the part of the state-race' (p. 302). Further: 'the Jew cannot possess a religious institution' because 'he lacks idealism in any form, and hence belief in a hereafter is absolutely foreign to him'. Since 'a religion in the Aryan sense cannot be imagined which lacks the conviction of survival after death in some form', it was telling that 'the Talmud is not a book to prepare a man for the hereafter, but only for a practical and profitable life in this world' (p. 306). '[The Jew's life] is only of this world and his spirit is inwardly as alien to true Christianity as his nature two thousand years previous was to the great founder of the new doctrine' (p. 307). The supposedly Jewish invention of Marxism then helps to undermine authentic civilizations by stirring up class discord and, under cover of fighting capitalism, weakening national economies (pp. 318–22). The 'power' supposedly responsible for the defeats of 1918 made preparations 'over many decades robbing our people of the political and moral instincts and forces which alone make nations capable and hence worthy of

Hamann's thought merits special attention, since it sowed the seeds of Herderian *linguistic-cultural* relativism but in *religious* terms it was not at all relativist or 'even' pluralist. He could only get to his position on the constitutive importance of language in group life given his assumptions about the spiritual element of language, and those assumptions stood in contrast to what Hamann held as simply erroneous Jewish (as well as 'Greek') ways of thinking and believing. As with all monadological thinking, thought about folk-spirits and ideal inner unity stemmed from presuppositions rooted in a particular strand of Christian thought. Any cultural doctrine that ensues from this tradition of thought, including particular sorts of cultural relativism, only works in the shadow of a certain metaphysics. The tradition is faulty.

Even when physical borders and institutions are well established, identities need not be, and for all the stress on 'positive' integration around some 'idea', it is impossible to distinguish positive from 'negative' integration against internal or external otherness. Rousseau looked this fact in the face; Herder did not, contending instead that 'Each nation has its *centre* of happiness *in itself*, like every sphere its centre of gravity.'[212] Even if one distinguishes more supposedly organic or at least 'bottom-up' nationalisms from those that are more obviously sponsored or instrumentalized from the 'top-down', it remains the fact that no peaceful coexistence between such self-constituting collectives is guaranteed because, putting things aside like battles over scarce resource, collective standards are not just matrices of things valued but things disvalued, scorned, anathematized. Unless each collective has the same values, which begs the question whether they really are different, divergent judgements of value may form the justification for conflict (even if the conflict is 'really' about resource). British national identity was forged in opposition to 'others': Spanish and French Catholic or Russian Orthodox.[213] When a British Navy League pamphlet of 1895 urged readers to submerge 'party feelings for a day; be neither Conservatives nor Liberals, but something greater and better, be ENGLISHMEN', no external party was mentioned, but it will not be ignored that the only purpose of a navy is external engagement.[214] Around the same time, the first secretary of the German Navy League said that its purpose was to 'emancipate large sections of the community

existence' (p. 327). Reversing 'racial' erosion was the purpose of the Nazi movement. Confronting the 'inner enemy' went alongside the formation of a proper 'Germanic State of a German nation', a 'national organism' (p. 329).

[212] Johann Gottfried von Herder, *Philosophical Writings*, ed. Michael N. Forster (Cambridge: Cambridge University Press, 2002), 297—emphases in original.
[213] Linda Colley, *Britons: Forging the Nation, 1707–1837* (New Haven: Yale University Press, 2005).
[214] Anne Summers, 'The Character of Edwardian Nationalism: Three Popular Leagues', in Paul Kennedy and Anthony Nicholls (eds), *Nationalist and Racialist Movements in Britain and Germany Before 1914* (Basingstoke: Macmillan, 1981), 70–87, here 77. This and the next reference I owe to an undergraduate dissertation whose author is unknown to me because of anonymity rules.

from the spell of the political parties by arousing their enthusiasm for this *one* great national issue'.[215] In the First World War the unity that had previously been sought was now proclaimed.

> Had it not been for German militarism, German civilization would have been extinguished long ago. Militarism emerged for that civilization's protection in a land that, like no other, had been afflicted for centuries by bands of raiders. The German Army and the German people are one. Today this consciousness binds in fraternity 70,000,000 Germans irrespective of education, status or party.[216]

Such was the view of the ninety-three German intellectuals who proclaimed unqualified support for the Kaiserreich in a public 'manifesto' of 4 October 1914, at much the same time as Salandra espoused Italian national *sacro egoismo*. One of the signatories was the theologian Adolf Harnack. His former student, the Swiss theologian Karl Barth, followed Kierkegaard's and Overbeck's path, rebelling against the synergy of German 'Liberal Protestantism' with German nationalism and arguing against any attempt to co-opt Christianity for any set of cultural traditions. His major First World War theological statement, published in December 1918, was *Der Römerbrief*, a commentary on St Paul's Epistle to the Romans, the book Luther had described as the most important in the New Testament. Later on, where other potential dissidents found a Protestant solution to a Protestant problem by 'internal emigration', separating their inner life from the world in which their body lived, Barth acted, becoming a founding member of the anti-Nazi German Confessing Church.[217]

It is impossible to assess the precise balance of interest and identity in explaining the rise of the nation-state system, though we may say with safety that the monadological model that would depict all as shared *Weltansicht* and the Hobbesian contractual model that would depict all as bare interest are both incorrect. 'Right or wrong, our country!' actually hints at the ambivalence, because it is not 'our country cannot be wrong'. For elements of the populace within the mainstream 'we' of 'the people' at any one moment, citizenship might be enough, as juxtaposed with previous subject-status. In principle there was more to be gained through citizenship than subjecthood, since governance was still in the name of the all even if not the each, and this might be a sufficient quid pro quo for the promotion of national loyalty above all else. Equally, and here we move more towards the preoccupations of certain established elites, and

---

[215] Holger Herwig, *The German Naval Officer Corps* (Oxford: Clarendon Press, 1973), 7.

[216] Jürgen von Ungern-Sternberg and Wolfgang von Ungern-Sternberg, *Der Aufruf 'An die Kulturwelt!'* (Stuttgart: Steiner, 1996), 158.

[217] Note, though, the limits of the Confessing Church's and Barth's position in regard of the persecution and suffering of Jews in Nazi Germany: Stephen R. Haynes, *Reluctant Witnesses: Jews and the Christian Imagination* (Louisville, KY: Westminster John Knox Press, 1995), 64–8.

particular constituencies, democracy might alter the composition of the collective's principles and threaten its security through the introduction of difference/schism by, say, the articulation of class grievances or the proportional representation of those ethnic minorities that no 'nation state' was without.[218] One more reason, then, that 'national liberation'—from, say, the apparently anachronistic and, *pace* Herder, unnatural Ottoman, Romanov, and Habsburg empires—and national self-determination might ultimately be pressed much harder than the self-determination of the individuals or subgroups within those states.

Though in nationalisms civic and ethnic the collective 'we' was clear in principle with reference to values or ethnicity, this said little to the question of who in either sort of case were the prime political constituents of the nation in practice. The French Revolution had followed Rousseau in distinguishing between active and passive citizens. Women were invariably in the latter category. When male suffrage was reduced in 1795 non-taxpaying men were returned to passive status, whence Revolutionaries of 1789 like the Abbé Sieyès had never wanted them to graduate. Fichte reproduced the active–passive distinction, with women appropriately assigned.[219] Revolutionary lexicon aside, the property and sex nexus remained important across the Continent. Locke had given theoretical imprimatur to the facts on the ground when he identified the constituents of the political nation in his England—and in eighteenth-century England the circle of the enfranchised actually fell as a proportion of the total population. Alongside the Puritan influence, Locke's conception of propertied and thus responsible man coloured the framing of the US constitution. So we already have some of the explanation in place as to why nationalism, even constitutional nationalism, even republican constitutional nationalism, had an uncertain relationship with the individual 'self-determination' implied by classical political liberalism let alone high modern democracy. Claiming to speak in the name of the people need not be justified by greatly expanded suffrage—far less by economic democracy, given the significance of landed, commercial, industrial, and military interests in the 'rationalizations' that went hand in hand with nation-state building—if the popular 'will' was purportedly monolithic or vested in a particular class of prime historical movers.

If and when the franchise was extended, that need not mean radical change in institutional arrangements in any country, given that workers could be conservative politically as well as socially. At the same time one could tinker a little with the social contract, as indeed had happened during the developments in social legislation from the late nineteenth century. Symbolic incentives (like jingoism)

---

[218] On such questions, see Michael Mann, *The Dark Side of Democracy* (Cambridge: Cambridge University Press, 2005).

[219] Christopher M. Clark, *Iron Kingdom: The Rise and Downfall of Prussia, 1600–1947* (Cambridge, MA: Harvard University Press, 2006), 377.

for the maintenance of extant hierarchies were complemented by material incentives up to rudimentary social-security arrangements. Urbanization and industrialization necessitated expanded education, sanitation works, public health measures, and, more generally, an enhanced role for the State in arbitrating the public interest. Franklin Roosevelt noted later on that it is rather a false dichotomy to think of such measures as abandoning individualism for collectivism: 'true individual freedom cannot exist without economic security and independence'.[220] It is an open question as whether granting someone a new right is acknowledging their value or appealing to their interest, or whether providing some material incentive is tantamount to bribery or a hard manifestation of moral support. Equally, it is unclear whether showing loyalty in exchange for protection (the very most basic contract) is instrumental calculation or a sign of genuine solidarity.

Obviously loyalty is not peculiar to modernity or nation states, but *pace* Weber, one characteristic of most modern states was the monopoly of organized violence, which was a powerful obstacle to the pursuit of agendas that contradicted the nationalist one—international socialism, prior to the Bolshevik Revolution, had as few divisions as famously did the pope. Again, though, the State was capable of securing not just notional rights, but also the things to which those rights pertained. Trades unions and feminists found themselves beholden to states for much these reasons, and with the advent of the First World War generally cleaved to their respective countries. Thus the State's legitimacy was expanded internally, and its power consolidated. That 'cosmopolitan' and rather pantheistic nationalist Mazzini appraised matters correctly. 'Without a country you have no name, no identity, no voice, no rights, no membership in the brotherhood of nations—you remain just the bastards of humanity. Soldiers without a flag, Jews in a world of Gentiles, you will win neither trust nor protection.'[221]

War itself can create a 'concertina effect', with social divisions reduced and conventional distinctions blurred in furtherance of a united cause, as was the case in Germany in 1914–15. But, as in Germany from 1916, and Russia in 1917, under pressure of war societies can also fragment, to be put back together, if at all, by methods that may involve extreme coercion or negative integration in the form of scapegoating. Most societies most of the time lie between the extremes of unity

---

[220] Clarke A. Chambers, *Seedtime of Reform* (Minneapolis: University of Minnesota Press, 1963), 181–2; Harold Perkin, 'Individualism versus Collectivism in Nineteenth-Century Britain: A False Antithesis', *Journal of British Studies* 17/1 (1977), 105–18.

[221] Quote and some contextualization from Donovan E. Smucker, *Origins of Walter Rauschenbuch's Social Ethics* (Montreal: McGill-Queen's University Press, 1994), 115–16. See also Stefano Recchia and Nadia Urbinati (eds), *A Cosmopolitanism of Nations: Giuseppe Mazzini's Writings on Democracy, Nation Building, and International Relations* (Princeton: Princeton University Press, 2009); a significance of the 'cosmopolitan' designation is to tie it back to Kant's universal cosmopolitanism, with the national state the intermediary in its ability to enforce the notional rights of the individual as against empires.

and disunity. Of modern state forms, paradoxically the strongest can be those held together by 'weak ties' only, admitting a plurality of individual goals, communal ends and organizations, with the ensuing gains in consent reducing the need for coercion.[222] Still, pluralism cannot shade into an infinite tolerance of practices (tolerance of beliefs is a different thing), and no liberal theorist ever suggested it could. If we take our lead from Freud and Marx as much as Leibniz or Burckhardt, we should pay as much attention to the way that some societies hang together despite not just differences but dissonances and do so not (only) because of tolerance but repression. Sometimes this repression is overt and physical, sometimes it comes in the form of carrying on as if dissonances do not exist.

The law plays an important role in carrying on despite dissonances, 'even' in liberal societies where it has the uncomfortable role of dispensing justice evenly within a social order of some degree of substantive inequality. Addressing the grey zones of informal, reproduced privilege and discrimination is not easy given the liberal conception of rights with its greater emphasis on formal legal, civil, and political equality than social and economic rights. The tension between formal equality and substantive inequality may also characterize the police's role, which contributes to the renowned difficulty in prosecuting police officers for apparent breaches of the law, and the perception by parts of the community that the police are really the servants of another part of the community. (The police clearly have a special role; the question is on whose behalf they are held to enact that role, and therefore what sorts of actions are held to contravene the underlying rules of the role.) Liberal systems can be as effective at concealing asymmetric power beneath the surface of formal equality as a vulgar Foucauldian conception of power is at removing the responsibilities of relatively powerful people.

Consistent with formal equality considerations, in criminal courts it tends to be the case that only 'physicalist' considerations like self-defence or diminished responsibility militate against prosecution or conviction. Consistent with the lesser regard for substantive equality, matters like significant material deprivation and pursuant desperation cannot have the same legal salience because they bring into question the very social system that, say, protects private property so assiduously while allowing and perhaps even promoting inequality. It was Anatole France who wrote of the 'majestueuse égalité des lois, qui interdit au riche comme au pauvre de coucher sous les ponts', the law whose sublime equality prohibits rich and poor alike from overnighting under the bridge. One outcome of formal equality before law in an unequal state: a vast disproportion in the numbers of African Americans in US prisons. Great racial disparity exists not just in prosecution but also in sentencing, though neither outcome is enshrined in statute.

---

[222] Mark S. Granovetter, 'The Strength of Weak Ties', *American Journal of Sociology* 78/6 (1973), 1360–80.

Socio-economic discrepancies might even influence unawares the interpretation given to legally salient short-range factors. 'Stand your ground' laws and other allowances for self-defence perforce bring into play subjective considerations for the defendant ('I 'felt threatened'), but they themselves may relate to objective social contexts. The perception of young black men as inherently threatening, partly because of aforementioned disparities in incarceration, which in turn reflect imbalances in social opportunity, makes it easier to get away with claiming that one felt threatened by a black teenager and 'had' to shoot him for one's own safety. An ostensibly short-range 'physicalist' factor (fear) is after all inseparable from long-range structural-cum-cultural factors, but courts have no remit to address the latter.

The legal focus is understandable for functional and psychological reasons, since a fully 'contextualized' conception of a 'criminal' mindset taken to its extreme would make a nonsense not just of any meaningful penal policy but any attribution of responsibility for humans as decision-makers. Kant's retributive principle of punishment respects this agency; punishment is a way of doing justice in both salient senses to the capacity for responsible decision-making. Once every aspect of character and thought had been attributed to some suprapersonal context, there might be nothing left of the individual on which to do justice. One would have to find some way of indicting discourses or capillaries of relational power instead of torturers, CEOs, and police chiefs. In that case justice would not be done to the 'as-if' assumption we all share about our own moral discretion, whether we are CEOs or assistant under-gardeners.

In order to obviate this particular problem, while continuing to do justice to the sense of sovereign responsibility we individually feel for our behaviour, we might, paradoxical as it might sound, do well to focus in public policy purely on sociological explanation for transgression. Sociological explanation has as its focus not moral exculpation of the actor but study of the social arrangements that mean certain sectors of society produce disproportionate numbers of transgressors, or—perhaps differently—of those convicted of transgression. A goal might be to prompt policymakers into reform of those arrangements to ensure maximally equal distribution of the moral luck that obtains before the transgressive act, in order that transgressors have nothing, morally speaking, to hide behind, and in order to ensure that the polity lives up to its rhetoric of equality in a more substantive fashion.[223] The alternative is to continue tolerating the grave social risk to, say, African Americans, which reminds us that each community is always a certain version of a community, based on exclusions as well as inclusions, and gradations of what is included. That is the perhaps obvious point with which this section reaches its terminus.

---

[223] This complements the point made about social policy and moral luck on p. 82, n. 131.

Since histories of conflict, repression, etc., have long since shown that groups are neither windowless nor internally homogeneous, which are the two criteria of a monad if the idea of a monad is to retain any distinct meaning, monadology should have been laid to rest long ago. Since monadology's description is not correct, then one might reasonably think that prescriptions for conduct based on the description cannot be correct either, however attractive the Leibnizian desire for harmony which those prescriptions might express. Perhaps my position is too absolutist, and I should think more 'realistically' on the principle that in the mundane sphere perfection is unattainable and what is to be sought instead is 'the best of all possible worlds', as Voltaire's ungenerous parody of Leibniz put it.[224] Hegel was a realist in this sense when he claimed that a certain sort of state was a condition of freedom but that there was nonetheless a price to be paid for the arrangement. If we put aside the idiosyncracies of Hegel's own vision and focus, 'realistically', on the idea of a trade-off in any social dispensation, then we might nonetheless allow that the price should not be forgotten, nor that some people and peoples have paid more of it than others.

You may think monadic thinking has shuffled off this coil. Hardly anyone uses the word 'monad' certainly. Nonetheless, as we shall see in the final historical account, History III, hand-me-down versions of monadic thought remain vital in conceptualizing—and sometimes even structuring—our world at different levels. A self-certifying 'individualism' has tightened its grip at the level of the person, whilst collective internality remains important in terms of international relations and some of the strongest traditions in the humanities and social sciences. Meanwhile—and here the thread is continued into the fourth and fifth sections of this Part of the book—even when an overarching divine unification of differing monadic perspectives is denied in the name of an ostensibly secular cultural relativism, strong traces of the religious doctrine can remain, in negative form (eg. pp. 239–40, 246–7).

Some of the developments in monadological thought addressed hereafter speak to political or economic strategies. They are prescriptions rather than descriptions. Not a few of the dispensing physicians have axes as well as medicaments to grind.

History III: To the Present

From the end of the Second World War new institutional arrangements emerged with ramifications for relations between individual people, between individuals and collectives, and between collectives. This section outlines these arrangements

---

[224] The parody is in Voltaire's *Candide, ou l'Optimisme* (1759).

and addresses influential scholarly theories that share some of their connotations. Again, the critical focus is on species of 'individualism', whether personal or collective, and on the relationship of those individuals to more than just their 'above' and 'within' (Emerson).

The post-war globalization of the nation-state system consolidated one particularly influential 'monadic' level as the imperial order in Africa and Asia broke down under the force of anti-colonial resistance and European weakness. For some anti-colonialists, control of the State and the ideology of nationalism were means of liberation and equality rather than nation-statehood being an end in itself. Equally, some perceived innate problems in the concept of the nation state. The nation-state model nonetheless entrenched itself.[225] At the same time the smallest salient monad, the individual human, was also attended to via human rights declarations. Unsurprisingly, harmonization across the monadic level of states has not been achieved any more than harmonization between the monadic level of the State and that of the individual.

The equality of states remains more formal than substantive. This is partly so despite international law: whatever the ambition towards world law as analogous to yet higher than state law, international police forces, where present at all, issue from among adversarial parties rather than a third superordinate body. (Even if today forces act under the banner of NATO, the UN, or the African Union they are still provided by particular member nation-states.) But the state of affairs also owes something to international law, which is made by treaties but also by precedents, therefore what states do, and get away with doing, is itself constitutive of international law. In other words powerful states are at an advantage not just in terms of strength but also in terms of norm arbitration. The balance of largely formal equality and substantive inequality is reflected in the mechanisms of the United Nations, where a general assembly with one vote per state was juxtaposed with a security council whose permanent membership comprised the victors of the Second World War plus France, i.e. some totalitarians and some of the most rapacious imperialists of recent centuries.

Furthermore, political independence for new states, often accompanied anyway by the enduring indirect influence of the displaced colonial power, was swiftly followed by a choice of economic alignment to the agendas of hegemonic states within either ideological bloc, or a walk along the tightrope of 'non-aligned' status. The Cold War was less a battle of freedom versus unfreedom than between economic orders and power-brokers, though it was convenient for each side to preach moral crusade, with the relationship of the 'First' and 'Second World'

---

[225] On for instance the early federalism of Léopold Sédar Senghor (president of Senegal 1960–80) and the 'departmentalization' propounded by the Martiniquean Aimé Césaire, see Gary Wilder, *Freedom Time: Negritude, Decolonization and the Future of the World* (Durham, NC: Duke University Press, 2014); cf Samuel Moyn, 'Fantasies of Federalism', *Dissent* (Winter 2015).

powers to the 'Third World' reminiscent of the relationship of the 'civilized' to the 'uncivilized world' only a generation before. The claim that capitalism and democracy (or any other form of self-determination) were twinned is a propaganda artefact of the period, one given only negative, insufficient substantiation by the obvious democratic deficit in the Eastern bloc and China. The major North-Western powers proved no friends of self-determination or the democratic process in the global South and East when that portended departure from approved developmental paths and threatened to cut off important resources from the world economic system: think of Iran in 1953 and several dozen other successful or failed attempts at 'regime change' across the world during and since the Cold War.

It is as unsatisfactory merely to attribute these interventions to US hypocrisy as it is to ignore the manifold interventions by the USSR.[226] The reason for focusing on the US is its role as lynchpin of a capitalistic economic order that was in fact *the* truly globally integrative institution during the Cold War, as beyond. However socialist some states might be internally, they still had to compete for hard currency in the international marketplace. They could not ignore the quest for surplus in their production, nor fluctuations in world markets, nor the international rules of credit.[227] 'The market' maintained some of the transcendent quality that had been established across large tracts of the globe in the nineteenth century, and the US stepped into Britain's shoes as the holder of the ring, in roughly the way described in International Relations 'hegemonic stability theory'. The rhetorical complement to this global role was that of the USA as the 'indispensible nation', the 'universal nation', i.e. at once the embodiment and protector of putatively universal values. Such a pleasing self-assessment derived from the view of the USA as having a divine mission—the 'heaven's command' once supposedly addressed to Britain.[228] An account of the thought of the eighteenth-century 'physiocrats' at the national level captures the implications of the US stance as applied to other states at many (not all) points: they 'advocate[d] both freedom from governmental influence with the market and the enforcement of this freedom by an all-powerful ruler whose self-interest is tied-up with the "right" economic system.'[229]

---

[226] Arne Westad, *The Global Cold War: Third World Interventions and the Making of Our Times* (Cambridge: Cambridge University Press, 2007) considers intervention by both sides.

[227] Ali Mazrui, 'Africa Entrapped', in Hedley Bull and Adam Watson (eds), *The Expansion of International Society* (Oxford: Clarendon Press, 1985), 289–398, here 289, 303, and more generally on the tension between the nation state and global capital.

[228] On the 'indispensible nation' and its religious hinterland, Christopher J. Fettweis, *The Pathologies of Power* (Cambridge: Cambridge University Press, 2013), 21. 'Heaven's command' is from James Thompson's early eighteenth-century 'Rule, Britannia'.

[229] Albert O. Hirschman, *The Passions and the Interests: Political Arguments for Capitalism Before Its Triumph* (Princeton: Princeton University Press, 1997), 98.

To see the way in which certain economic arrangements can infringe sovereignty in the absence of any formal political intervention we need look no further in recent decades than the conditions attached to loans to states from international financial institutions operating according to 'Washington consensus' economics. The Nobel Laureate in economics Joseph Stiglitz puts it thus:

> We tell developing countries about the importance of democracy, but then, when it comes to the issues they are most concerned with, those that affect their livelihoods, the economy, they are told: the iron law of economics gives you little or no choice [so . . .] you must cede key economic decisions, say, concerning macroeconomic policy, to an independent central bank, almost always dominated by representatives of the financial community; and to ensure that you act in the interests of the financial community, you are told to focus exclusively on inflation—never mind jobs or growth; and to make sure you do just that, you are told to impose on the central bank rules, such as expanding the money supply at a constant rate; and when one rule fails to work as has been hoped, another rule is brought out, such as inflation targeting. In short, as we seemingly empower individuals in the former colonies through democracy with one hand, we take it away with the other.[230]

Decades before the International Monetary Fund started dispensing these prescriptions, it was fundamental to US economic policy that other states should open their markets for international commerce and their natural resources for exploitation. Woodrow Wilson's limited support for national self-determination sat easily with the existence of some European empires elsewhere as long as the latter did not place obstacles in front of the 'open door'. Thus, for instance, US oil companies entered 'mandatory' Iraq under conditions provided by British interwar rule there.[231] The Atlantic Charter of 1941 proposed a world of states with equal access to 'trade and to the raw materials of the world which are needed for their economic prosperity', as if all states were capable of taking equal advantage of this arrangement. Despite professed Anglo-American 'respect' for 'the right of all peoples to choose the form of government under which they will live', the corollary of the economic aspiration was that those who did not wish to open themselves risked being forced open. Precise American policies varied due to Cold War exigencies. But in principle the economic openness of others was tied in with US narrower self-interest and a harmonious world order, which is why it could be a condition of America's respecting the sovereignty of other states.

As far as the Charter of the United Nations was concerned, the only condition for respecting a state's internal sovereignty was that the State respected the

---

[230] Foreword to Polanyi, *The Great Transformation*, p. xvi.
[231] Donald Bloxham, *The Great Game of Genocide* (Oxford: Oxford University Press, 2005), 190–1.

sovereignty of other states by not invading them. For all of the human rights talk from 1945, older and newer states were *the* building blocks of international order. They, rather than anything above them, were seen as the primary guarantors of the supposedly universal human rights of their citizens. Ultimately they had great de facto discretion in the *means* by which they imposed internal order on their people, even if the ideological *ends* of that internal policy might attract the interest of a superpower. The Universal Declaration of Human Rights was hortatory, as was the UN Convention on the Prevention and Punishment of Genocide, and while one should not underestimate the power of aspirations to articulate norms that may come to influence behaviour, it is telling that there was even less capacity for enforcement of either proclamation than had been the case in the interwar years with the League of Nations' remit for protection of minorities in certain states.[232] The victorious Allies effectively decreed the undesirability of the *forum internum–forum externum* principle of State–minority relations that was pioneered in the peace treaties of the sixteenth and seventeeth centuries and redeployed via the minorities protection clauses of the post-1918 peace treaties. Thus was removed a 'monadic' layer between the State and individual people.

From a rights perspective it is incongruous that minority protection was downgraded after all the violence perpetrated in the name of nationalism and ethnic and homogeneity in the era of the Second World War. The strategic perspective makes sense of things given the association of the minorities question with instability and interstate war. The interwar minorities clauses had been intended as a measure to smooth the way towards minorities' assimilation into titular majorities. 'Munich', in 1938, dealt the death blow to that arrangement: Hitler's claim to speak on behalf of suffering Czech Germans had provided the justification for imperialist expansion and the cannibalization of a neighbouring state, and it was external war, rather than the character of Nazi rule internally, that ultimately concerned the architects of the world order. In his closing speech at the Nuremberg trial of the major German war criminals US chief prosecutor Robert Jackson reflected that the 'intellectual bankruptcy and moral perversion of the Nazi regime might have been *no concern to international law* had it not been utilized to goosestep the Herrenvolk across international frontiers'.[233]

At war's end, the policy in Europe was no longer that of trying to draw borders around national groups while providing protection in principle for minorities within those borders, nor of relying on the mere possibility of emigration for minorities in one country to join the titular minority in another country as in the 'option' provisions of the 1919–20 peace treaties. The model was that of the 1923

---

[232] Mark Mazower, *No Enchanted Palace* (Princeton: Princeton University Press, 2009), 130–3, 141–3.
[233] Kirsten Sellars, *'Crimes Against Peace' and International Law* (Cambridge: Cambridge University Press, 2013), 119, emphasis Sellars's.

Lausanne Treaty which had given international legitimation to the ethnic cleansing of Muslims from Greece and Greek Orthodox subjects from Anatolia. People were moved to fit new boundaries in the interests of creating more supposedly homogeneous populations and reducing the prospects for future irredentist disturbances of the international peace. In quantitative terms, the main European victims of this ethnic unmixing were ethnic Germans from beyond the German state now driven into Germany, though many other eastern Europeans were also moved around like chattels on a board. When these Europeans are added to the even greater numbers of Muslims and Hindus fleeing in either direction on Indian partition around the same time we are talking about the fates of around 27 million people.

Such realignment of people to borders was not practicable everywhere. Of the Middle East early in the interwar period one US diplomat scorned: 'if every group in the world which desires independence were satisfied there would be thousands of peanut states and the map would look more like chickenpox than Wilson ever believed when he created [*sic*] the slogan of "self-determination"'.[234] After 1945 in the world as after 1918 in Europe, the process of post-imperial territorial subdivision had to stop somewhere, even if that meant the reproduction of some imperial dynamics on a smaller scale. Ask the animists and Buddhists of the Chittagong Hill Tracts as they tried to fight off internal colonization by the nation state of Bangladesh which had itself emerged in blood from quasi-colonial subservience in the state of Pakistan, which had in turn emerged in the violence of Indian 'partition'. As this example suggests, sometimes, though rarely, new national borders have been established to modify the territorial order established at decolonization; more often it has been a matter of internal repression, up to and including genocide, or, where forces are more evenly matched, struggle for control of the State within its 'given' borders.

Given previous experience of imperial rule and the live possibility of neo-imperial intervention, including at the economic level, postcolonial states were as loud as any in defending the principle of state sovereignty and an internal free hand. Depending on circumstances, the attitude to sovereignty could either be universalist or particularist-relativist. Before and during decolonization aspirations for independence from colonial rule had often been phrased in the universalistic idiom with appeals for human rights universality at the level of the individual person accompanying calls for collective self-determination, in a way that harked back to nationalism's association-by-analogy with liberalism. More relativistic stances arose later, and had direct counterparts in academic debate. This shift occurred as a number of postcolonial states fell prey to authoritarian regimes from the later 1960s, and also because of the suspicion that human rights discourse was a Trojan horse for neo-imperial agendas. Intonations of the

---

[234] Bloxham, *The Great Game of Genocide*, 192.

inviolability of local knowledge and values were a way of rejecting external rights-based criticism and demanding respect for cultural difference.[235] Neither tendency could be said to be anathema to the stipulated principles of world order; the UN Charter did not specify anything about the internal structure of states, their governing philosophies, or the type of nationalism guiding national self-determination.

Some of the arrangements outlined hitherto met with criticism in influential trends in the Western social sciences and humanities, but those intellectual trends are relevant here because they also replicate some of the conceptual and norma-tive problems of elements of the set-up. We will begin with the anthropologist Marshal Sahlins, as he focused on the relationship between global (economic) system and culture, without considering the intercultural level. Then we will examine other famous anthropologists whose relativistic theories imply too much within-group homogeneity and so obscure much about intracultural relations. Then we will move to the almost 'anti-cultural' prescriptions of Michel Foucault, and the problems of that and other individualisms for the conceptualization of interpersonal relations. In closing the section, we will try to establish some overall impression of the relationship between individuals, states, and the global system at the time of writing.

Looking back from 1995 on his work since the 1970s, Sahlins invoked the Herderian origins of the concept 'of cultures as distinct forms of life' in oppos-ition 'to bourgeois-utilitarian reason'. This is a bit of a caricature of the thought against which Herder set himself but that can pass. Sahlins reflected on a recent history of many peoples' 'announcing the existence of their culture', of a 'marked self-consciousness of "culture"', and saw this as reproducing Herder's moment, with particularistic culture standing against pseudo-universalistic market forces. 'The anthropological concept of culture as a specific form of life thus emerged in a relatively backward region [i.e. Germany], and as an expression of that com-parative backwardness, or of its nationalist demands, as against the hegemonic ambitions of Western Europe.' Sahlins interpreted the burgeoning cultural self-consciousness of recent decades likewise as a response by the 'victims and erst-while victims of Western domination', a response more specifically to 'the planetary juggernaut of Western capitalism'. 'Ojibway Indians in Wisconsin, Kayapo in Brazil, Tibetans, New Zealand Maori, Kashmiris, New Guinea Highland peoples, Zulus, Eskimo, Mongols, Australian Aboriginals, and . . . Hawaiians: all speak of their "culture," using that word or some close local

---

[235] On the rights debates, Raymond Burke, *Decolonization and the Evolution of International Human Rights* (Philadelphia: University of Pennsylvania Press, 2010). In the shifts Burke details there are echoes of the interwar world in which some nationalists, disappointed at the limited realization of 'Wilsonian' self-determination, turned sharply away from liberal internationalism even as they main-tained their anti-imperialism. See David Motadel, 'The Global Authoritarian Movement and the Revolt against Empire', *American Historical Review* 124/3 (2019), 843–77.

equivalent, as a value worthy of respect, commitment and defense.'[236] The Vietnam War, with its connotations of imperialism and capitalist aggression, was influential in Sahlin's conception of non-Western resistance to Western domination.[237] Yet cultural destruction was not the solve preserve of Westerners, and, there being no pure, determinant economic sphere, it was not just capitalism doing the work of intrusion and destruction of indigenous peoples. In places like Bangladeshi Chittagong destruction was wrought on animists and others in the name of titular majorities with *their* particular cultures and desire to survive in a competitive world, just as had been the case in the extreme example of Europe earlier in the century. Recall, too, Herder's decided ambivalence towards diasporic minorities: how do they feature in a vision like that of Sahlins?

Sahlins's work had been shaped by the theory of structuralism, whose anthropological variant attained its greatest influence in the third quarter of the twentieth century, at precisely the time of the global consolidation of the nation-state system. The father of anthropological structuralism was the avowed anti-imperialist Claude Lévi-Strauss (1908–2009). While structuralism differed from historicist monadology, leaning ultimately more to the tradition of *Erklären—* generalizing model-building—than *Verstehen*—hermeneutic understanding—there are key similarities. As German defeat in 1945 discredited a great deal of obviously German-derived thought, structuralism, with its apparent francophone pedigree, stepped into the shoes of monadic doctrines. Idealist conceits about nations as expressions of divine 'mind' or Geist were replaced by more secular ideas of collective representations, or Bloch's mentalités, (pp. 21–22) which left unaddressed the questions of how to conceptualize culture-internal disagree-ments, present-changing agency, and, ultimately, within-group politics. Again, the problem of this sort of thinking is that it implies too great a homogeneity within the culture in question.

Strictly, structuralism is a purely formal doctrine. Structuralist linguistics posits that meanings are constructed not by reference to a world outside language but by differences internal to language—be the differences phonetic (matters of sound) or semantic (matters of meaning as in left–right, night–day)—and by syn-tax, ie. the placing of words in relation to other words. Anthropological structur-alism expanded this conception of meaning-construction to non-linguistic realms like mores, morality, and aesthetics. Thinking to the deeper German heri-tage, Lévi-Strauss accepted the description of his structuralism as 'Kantianism without the transcendental subject'.[238] There are indeed parallels at the formal level between Kant's 'categories' of the understanding and Lévi-Strauss's idea of

---

[236] All quotes from Marshall Sahlins, *How 'Natives' Think: About Captain Cook, for Example* (Chicago: University of Chicago Press, 1995), 12–14.
[237] See 'In the Absence of the Metaphysical Field: an Interview with Marhsall Sahlins', *Exchange* (2006) online at http://ucexchange.uchicago.edu/interviews/sahlins.html.
[238] Claude Lévi-Strauss, *The Raw and the Cooked* (New York: Harper and Row, 1969), 11.

the basic structures shared by minds 'civilized' and 'savage' alike, as they mediated nature to create culture. Where Kant speculated to gain insight into the categories, Lévi-Strauss inferred them from formal similarities amongst otherwise very different cultures. For Kant there was ultimately one true reason available to any and all rational individuals. For Lévi-Strauss rationalities vary with communities. His formalism related to the universal, which permits the creation of a value-neutral scientific metalanguage of study, and implies equality at the formal level, but on the *content* and evaluation of different meaning and value systems the structural anthropologist is entirely relativist. Indeed, when we compare structuralism's relativizing logic to the logic of monadology, we see that structuralism completes the step begun by Herder as he moved away from Hamann's religious concepts. Travelling further backwards along the same intellectual chain, Marcel Hénaff is surely correct to characterize Lévi-Strauss's structuralism as 'Leibnizianism without divine understanding'.[239] Where in Leibniz's thought lower monads provided differing perspectives on something above, in structuralism there was no substantive, higher reconciliation, only formal similarities. As in Herderian monadic thinking, anthropological structuralism concerns wholes; both doctrines are internalist in their consideration of order, and structuralism's internal oppositions, relativized to a coherent system, are the architecture of the whole, not evidence against it. Or, to flip things round, monadic culturalism easily accommodates structuralist propositions. 'Shortcoming and virtue always dwell together in one human hut', Herder wrote, and 'good and evil are only relational terms'.[240]

Geertz's later symbolic anthropology has much the same holistic connotations, which often equates to anthropology with the politics removed and an implied within-group homogeneity at many levels. Consider his famous essay on the symbolism of the Balinese cockfight. He claimed extravagantly that the event embodied 'almost every level of Balinese experience . . . animal savagery, male narcissism, opponent gambling, status rivalry, mass excitement, blood sacrifice . . . [and binds] them into a set of rules, . . . a symbolic structure in which . . . the reality of their inner affiliation can be intelligibly felt'. The assertion captures elements of anthropologist Christopher Herbert's thinking on 'wholeness', Ruth Benedict's conception on 'cultural wholeness', and E. E. Evans-Pritchard's view of the Azande people's 'web of belief in which every strand depends upon every other strand'.[241] While structuralist anthropology has syntactics (word relation-

---

[239] Marcel Hénaff, *Claude Lévi-Strauss and the Making of Structural Anthropology* (Minneapolis: University of Minnesota Press, 1998), 109.

[240] Herder, *Philosophical Writings*, 295, and also 294; Michael Mack, *Spinoza and the Specters of Modernity* (New York: Continuum, 2010), 59. On Burke and Montesquieu, Charles Edwyn Vaughan, *Studies in the History of Political Philosophy Before and After Rousseau* (1925; New York: Russell & Russell, 1960), 299 ff.

[241] All cited in Li, 'Marshal Sahlins and the Apotheosis of Culture', 217–19.

ship) as its paradigm, the paradigm of Geertzian symbolic anthropology is semantics, or semiology (the meaning of signs). Nonetheless what Jacques Derrida said of Lévi-Strauss—that his social systems appear as if all having fallen into place simultaneously, without regard to past and ongoing processes—might be said of Geertz as he described 'man [as] an animal suspended in webs of significance'.[242] Programmatic Geertzian statements included comprehending 'what the devil they [ie. inhabitants of other societies] think they are up to', and describing data as 'really our own constructions of other people's constructions of what they and their compatriots are up to'. Yet since he observed that 'culture is public because meaning is', and so meaning could be divined by 'reading' public practices as one would a text, one could cut out the middleman, which is the route to portraying people as but pedantic followers of a given cultural script, with 'culture' the only actual agent. Geertz owed an interpretative debt to Dilthey, who in turn felt that hermeneutic techniques could lead to understanding people of the past better, in some ways, than they understood themselves, but like many historians Dilthey had no other way of approaching (dead) people than through their meaning-laden objectifications. Not so fieldwork anthropology which, in the words of the anthropologist Handelman, 'is unlike any of the humanities and other social sciences in that it is not a text-mediated discipline in the first place. Consequently, it is the sole discipline that struggles with the turning of subjects into objects.'[243]

The difficulty of reconciling holistic cultural interpretation with the realities of social schism and the present-changing capacity of political agency is illustrated in Geertz's engagement with the massacre of around half a million Indonesians in 1965. They were killed by fellow Indonesians on the basis of their actual or supposed association with far-left politics. The shortcoming in Geertz's approach is accentuated here because the massive, ethno-religiously diverse archipelago comprising Indonesia would seem not to admit of any monadic characterization. Geertz himself repeatedly emphasizes diversity, claiming that 'it has been the refusal, at all levels of the society, to come to terms with [diversity] that has

---

[242] Geertz, *The Interpretation of Cultures*, 5; Aletta Biersack, 'Local Knowledge, Local History', in Lynn Hunt (ed.), *The New Cultural History* (Berkeley and Los Angeles: University of California Press, 1989), 72–96, here 80, which also problematizes Geertz's claim. Derrida passage from Jacques Derrida, *Writing and Difference*, ed. Alan Bass (London: Routledge, 2005), 367–9. Further on the problems of this ahistorical approach, see Mark Hobart, 'As They Like It: Overinterpretation and Hyporeality in Bali', in Dilley (ed.), *The Problem of Context*, 105–44, esp. 112–13.

[243] Geertz's 'what the devil' cited and scrutinized in Vincent P. Pecora, 'The Limits of Local Knowledge', in H. Aram Veeser (ed.), *The New Historicism* (London: Routledge, 1989), 243–76. Handelman quote and Geertz quotes on constructions on culture/meaning as public cited in Katherine E. Hoffman, 'Cultures as Texts: Hazards and Possibilities of Geertz's Literary/Literacy Metaphor', in Susan Slymovics (ed.), *Clifford Geertz in Morocco* (London: Routledge, 2013), 97–110, here 97–100. Further on interpretative problems in Geertz, especially concerning the viewpoints of those studied, Biersack, 'Local Knowledge', 79 and Hobart, 'As They Like It'. On the general problems of Geertian understandings of the relations of 'texts' to 'contexts', Levi, 'I pericoli del Geertzismo'.

impeded Indonesia's search for effective political form', and in many ways this case does shed important light on the discontents of the globalization of the nation-state system with its drive for homogeneity. Nonetheless both of the key elements of crude monadology are present in Geertz's essay: windowlessness and the presumption of internal congruity of perspective in relevant respects. One of the striking things is how little attention Geertz pays to outside *forces*, as if adhering to Leibniz on the lack of direct causal impact of one monad on another. One would not guess from his account the role of international Cold War politics: the USA supported the military and political ringleaders of much of the violence, and had previously supported an attempted coup against the 'guided democracy regime' of President Sukarno, whose experiment in holding the ring between Westernizer 'developmentalists', Islamic political forces, and communists was brought to such a bloody end in 1965. Geertz is certainly interested in 'outside' ideologies, and insofar as he provides an explanation for the massacres (obvious causes are absent, with major agents like the military unnamed) it is in the form of Indonesian rejection of such ideologies—or at least rejection of one of them, namely Marxism, since capitalism subsequently flourished. Interestingly, the primary sociocultural tendencies that Geertz sees as doing the rejecting are themselves testament to internal heterogeneity. These forces are named as 'disbelief and disorder', 'dissensus, ambivalence, and dis-orientation'. Nonetheless for Geertz this is still 'indigenous', 'Indonesian' dissensus (etc.), which still admits of discussion under the rubric 'Indonesian culture'. That the fundaments of monadology remain in place is highlighted by Geertz's concluding lines—the aforementioned quote from Burckhardt on the impossibility of evaluating the 'character', the 'conscience' of a people, whose 'defects have another side, where they reappear as peculiarities or even virtues'.[244] Yet we are not dealing with a singular 'people' here but rather a large number of individual people murdered by a large number of other people in an attempt to entrench a particular ideology of social cohesion and development, and ultimately, in the long run, to create a particular 'Indonesian culture'. (As to Burckhardt, for all the relativistic overtones of his cultural holism, he had views developing from the same basis as Herder's attitude towards Jews. Indeed Burckhardt's opposition to Jewish emancipation in Switzerland would prevent Jews being considered a proper part of the relevant 'people' to begin with.[245])

The difference was noted earlier between today's neo-historicism and classical nineteenth-century historicism: many historians today have a more absolute sense of difference across time culture as well as across place culture. A sense of

---

[244] See 'The Politics of Meaning', in Geertz, *The Interpretation of Cultures*, 311–26, quotes from 315, 318, 325, 326. My interpretation of Geertz on the massacres has been shaped by Pecora, 'The Limits of Local Knowledge'.

[245] Richard Franklin Sigurdson, *Jacob Burckhardt's Social and Political Thought* (Toronto: University of Toronto Press, 2004), 147–9.

temporal difference was not at all absent from Ranke or Droysen, but they had a sense of cultural unity-amidst-flux. Not so that large number of intellectuals under the influence of anyone from Marx and the classical economists (who despite their different inflections emphasized economic epochs related to changing modes of production) to classical sociology ('traditional' community versus 'modern' society) to postmodernism (which is parasitic upon certain assumptions of classical sociology) to theorists of the State (the nation state versus absolutism or feudalism). Thomas Kuhn's blockbuster *The Structure of Scientific Revolutions* (1961) achieved much the same thing for the History of science with his consideration of scientific paradigms that dominated for long periods before being overthrown by others. At around the same time Kuhn shot to fame, one of the best known and most rigid historical periodizations emerged from Michel Foucault's early work on 'epistemes'. In one definition, an episteme is 'the system of concepts that defines knowledge for a given intellectual era'.[246] The similarity is clear with the underlying generative grammar of structural linguistics and the formal subterranean structures of structural anthropology. Periodically, in an 'epistemological rupture'—the concept is that of Foucault's influence Gaston Bachelard—the system is replaced wholesale by another system, meaning that we move from a Renaissance to a Classical then Modern episteme. Foucault's 'archaeological' approach to the History of knowledge indicates the layering process here, as the shared basic assumptions of an 'era', within a particular civilization, shape a host of knowledge-claiming activities much more than the diachronic internal development of any one such activity over longer periods of time. All of this Foucauldian theorizing gave a harder, scientistic edge to the sorts of things that Romantic scholars of art had been intimating for over a century as they mused to the effect that

> Each epoch of history . . . had its distinctive institutions. Men were molded and remolded by these changing social forms. Thus men could not be regarded as the same throughout history. The peculiar institutions and the corresponding psychology of each period gave rise to different styles and standards of art. The merits of each artistic style were relative to the prevailing social institutions.[247]

As it happens, Foucault's epistemes have some of the same problems as the monadic cultural thought examined above: specialist scrutiny has revealed heterogeneity within the supposed boundaries of Foucault's epistemic epochs, and some continuity of thought across those boundaries.[248] Nonetheless, the hard

---

[246] Gary Gutting (ed.), *The Cambridge Companion to Foucault* (Cambridge: Cambridge University Press, 2005), 9.

[247] Wolfenstein, 'The Social Background of Taine's Philosophy of Art', 337.

[248] Critics including Ian Maclean, 'Foucault's Renaissance Episteme Reassessed: An Aristotelian Counterblast', *Journal of the History of Ideas* 59/1 (1998), 149–66, and those cited in José Guilherme

temporally-contextualizing, often relativizing neo-historicist spirit from which Foucault fed and to which he contributed is alive and well in the human sciences.

The question remains as to how far to drive neo-historicist division and sub-division beyond the level of 'culture' or 'episteme', because logically the process could go on ad infinitum, well beyond how someone's precise circumstances shaped their identity or perspective on Thursday morning as opposed to Wednesday night. Foucault himself contributed to this process of subdivision with his later concept of power whereby the 'subject' is produced at the contingent meeting point of a particular combination of discourses. And given Foucault's academic influence as the latest in a long line of hard contextualizers, it is more than noteworthy that when he moved to prescriptive mode, away from his critical descriptions of the conditions of thought and the workings of power, he reinforced individualistic tendencies that already had a strong hold in the culture from which he sprung.

Foucault's individualism is anything but 'Protestant' in the sense that it does not stem from an intellectual rejection of structuralist-type thinking—even as he attempted to surpass structuralism he was clearly influenced by it—but it coheres with a dislike of the implications of structuralist-type insights. Let us hypothesize that the moral and political attractions of structuralism were strongest for those who defined themselves against colonialism and externally intrusive behaviour, while opposition to its connotations was more attractive for those defining themselves against totalitarianism and the internally intrusive state. The distinction is purely heuristic, thus not watertight in practice. In elementary terms, anti-colonial critiques attacked civilizational hierarchies, their supporting thought-systems, and the drive to control 'others' beyond the metropole. The main beneficiaries of anti-colonial critiques were non-Westerners who could then determine their own futures according to their own lights. They, and some anti-imperial Westerners too, applauded the 'equalizing' or in fact relativizing implications of structuralism. Anti-totalitarian critiques, conversely, sought to interrogate the pathology of specific institutional and philosophical tendencies that had manifested themselves most extremely within the West, prior to the horrors of Maoist China from the later 1950s and Cambodia from 1975 to 1978: tendencies that sought to control the minds of those already under the rule of the totalitarian regime. The main beneficiaries of these critiques in the first instance would be Westerners who were enjoined to reject external conditioning in the name of liberation. Foucault falls more into the category of thought shaped by anti-totalitarianism than anti-colonialism, even though his analyses rarely focus on totalitarian regimes and are concerned with what had been considered mainstream modern European social development, especially in 'rationalist' France but also under strands of social

Merquior, *Michel Foucault* (Berkeley and Los Angeles: University of California Press, 1985), 27, 29. For analogous criticisms, see Derrida, *Writing and Difference*, 368.

and economic liberalism. Yet whatever the critiques he seemed to have applied to neo-liberalism, some of his leanings, especially in his later career, are neo-liberal as well as being libertarian and in some modified sense liberal.[249]

Foucault's particular brand of individualism brings him closer to the existentialist Jean-Paul Sartre than is generally thought, whatever their different relations to Marxism. True, Foucault replaced Sartre's call for 'authenticity' with one for 'self-creation', but it is not clear that these cash out differently in practice, especially since one of Sartre's most famous formulations was to reverse the Platonic hierarchy of essence and 'mere' existence. Existence, Sartre claimed, comes before essence, which meant a prioritization of ongoing choice and responsibility. Nor is it clear how different late Foucault's 'self-creation' is than the 'experiments in living' that John Stuart Mill advocated.[250] Elements of all three of these men's thought are foreshadowed by Aristotle's injunction to shape one's *hexis* by *praxis*, which coheres with a more general intellectual turn to virtue ethics in post-war occidental moral philosophy. And at a less rarefied level, we ought not ignore the cross-over of Foucault's performative agenda with the general antinomianism of 1960s youth counterculture, enshrined in a poster of Paris's 1968 May days: 'it is forbidden to forbid'.[251] Overall, in elements of his lifestyle and his prescriptions Foucault exemplifies what the historian of morality Rubin calls a 'morality of self-fulfilment'.[252] Yet according to the distinction between morality and ethics stipulated earlier (p. 141) in Foucault's case at least what we are actually talking about is an *ethics* of self-fulfilment rather than a morality of same. After all, the self rather than the 'other' is still the point of departure and reference, as in Foucault's 'technologies of the self' and his *rapport à soi*, or relationship to oneself.[253]

Like philosopher Alan Gewirth,[254] Rubin argues that 'moralities' of self-fulfilment, as they reject higher causes like *raison d'état*, also rethink relations to 'others' who would before have been seen as supporters of opposing causes. They create the potential for imagining a broader community of obligation of the sort recently expressed in heightened internationalism or, better, post-nationalism. In principle this philosophy is unlike classical liberalism with its conception of the other as a

---

[249] On neo-liberalism, and this despite Foucault's renowned work on governmentality and micropolitics, see Daniel Zamora (ed.), *Foucault and Neoliberalism* (Cambridge: Polity Press, 2016); Michael C. Behrent, 'Liberalism without Humanism: Michel Foucault and the Free-Market Creed, 1976–1979', *Modern Intellectual History* 6/3 (2009), 539–68. When invoking Foucault's liberalism I am thinking of classically liberal causes like prison-reform, as well, of course, as his obvious interest in self-determination, however characterized.

[250] Anthony Kwame Appiah, *The Ethics of Identity* (Princeton: Princeton University Press, 2007), 18–19 on Sartre and Foucault, 142 and 147 on Mill. On similarities between Sartre and Foucault, Ian Hacking, 'Between Michel Foucault and Erving Goffman', *Economy and Society* 33/3 (2004), 277–302, here 288.

[251] On the poster and cultural antinomianism, Eric Hobsbawm, *Age of Extremes* (London: Joseph, 1994), 332.

[252] Edward L. Rubin, *Soul, Self, and Society* (Oxford: Oxford University Press, 2015), ch. 3.

[253] Foucault, *Ethics: Subjectivity and Truth*, 223 ff., 263, 269 ff.

[254] Alan Gewirth, *Self-Fulfillment* (Princeton: Princeton University Press, 1998).

limiting influence on my liberties, and it might even lead to the realization that self-fulfilment can only really be attained in mutually fulfilling relationships. Yet questions must still remain about the thickness of the sense of obligation that can be elicited. As for the specific dimensions of Foucault's thought, whatever his claims that he was not just validating individualism in his emphasis on self-styling, he provided little substantiation for his claim that care for others would follow from the practice of 'care of the self'.[255] It is by no means obvious that it should. When praising justice as perfect virtue 'because its possessor can practice his virtue towards others and not merely by himself', Aristotle noted that 'there are plenty of people who can behave uprightly in their own affairs, but not when they come to deal with others'.[256] Nevertheless, Foucault wrote: 'Care for others should not be put before the care of oneself. The care of the self is ethically prior in that the relationship with oneself is ontologically prior.'[257] It is no doubt damnably unfair to pair this claim with one of Margaret Thatcher's around the same time that 'No one would remember the Good Samaritan if he'd only had good intentions; he had money as well.'[258] The serious point is that, as had been true earlier (pp. 168–9), the romantic individualism of which Foucault and significant elements of later twentieth-century counterculture were offshoots did not provide much of a bulwark against economic individualism, now turbocharged by neo-liberalism, and in some ways dovetailed with it, as the 'cultural Left' enjoyed significant success in the same societies in which the economic Right prospered.[259]

Whatever the laudable concerns about power and domination that led Foucault to his conclusion about self and others,[260] the reasoning is debatable. There is at least one important sense in which it is not at all obvious that the relationship one has to oneself is prior to the relationship one has with others. This is the sense touched on in Plato's *Alcibiades* in discussion of the reflective pupil, and analysed by Fichte's consideration of *Anerkennung*, 'recognition', in which one only apprehends oneself in relationships (pp. 188–9). The concept of recognition was developed from phenomenological principles in accordance with a recognizably Jewish ethics of obligation to 'the other', and in rejection of Fichtean nationalism, by Foucault's older contemporary the French-Jewish philosopher Emmanuel Levinas

---

[255] 'Care of the Self' being the subtitle of the third volume of Foucault's *History of Sexuality*. On care for others, see Foucault, *Ethics: Subjectivity and Truth*, 287 ff. and 271 on his claim that this is not just what his interviewer called a 'version of our self-absorption'.

[256] Aristotle, *Ethics*, 142 (bk V, ch. 1).   [257] Foucault, *Ethics: Subjectivity and Truth*, 287.

[258] Margaret Thatcher, interview for London Weekend Television *Weekend World*, 6 January 1980.

[259] e.g. Samuel H. Beer, *Britain Against Itself: The Political Contradictions of Collectivism* (New York: Norton, 1982); Prince and Riches, 'The Holistic Individual'. On Foucault as a new sort of Romantic, see Quentin Skinner (ed.), *The Return of Grand Theory in the Human Sciences* (Cambridge: Cambridge University Press, 1990), 10.

[260] On those concerns, see Paul S. Chung, *The Hermeneutical Self and an Ethical Difference: Intercivilizational Engagement* (Cambridge: James Clarke and Co., 2012), 172–3.

(1906–95).[261] Furthermore, while some have attributed significant political connotations to this element of Foucault's thought, Foucault himself was more hesitant.[262] Indeed this titan of the postmodern 'Left' has no social or political theory to propound, and most of what he implies about the State is negative, which is a pity since as well as witnessing the most destructive state behaviour to date, the twentieth century also provided the best-developed intimations of a state that was more than just the enforcement arm of some particular class interest.

Where it existed, the more representative state came under increasing pressure in the final quarter of the twentieth century with the rise of 'neo-liberal' economics. Especially but not only in the Anglo-Saxon states the 'third way' accepted much of the new economic orthodoxy. New conservatives—different to their patrician predecessors—and third-wayers were primarily separated by the latter's *social* liberalism, which met with significant success in the removal of formal barriers to emancipation on a number of fronts. Nonetheless, as with burgeoning rights discourse that tended to favour civic and political over social and economic rights, such emancipation only had a limited impact on informal structural obstacles to substantive, especially economic equality, and did little to counteract the atomizing logic of the prevailing economic doctrine with its own vast hinterland. Some distilled spirit of *The Wealth of Nations* was hived off from the concepts of obligation and government-enforced justice embodied in Smith's earlier *Theory of Moral Sentiment*. The 'invisible hand' remained but not Smith's 'impartial spectator' who might restrain the exercise of naked greed. Neo-liberal economics produced a 'social' theory that society really was nothing more than acquisitive individual behaviour multiplied. In 1997 the economist and Republican US House Majority Leader Dick Armey pronounced that 'markets punish immorality', which works if one equates that which is immoral with that which is antithetical to market norms and confirms that anyone who fails by the rules of the market is morally deficient. This indicates the colonization of the social by the economic, rather than the utilization of the economic by the social for the social once the social had been freed from the State.[263]

So what is the relation now between the global market system, the national state, and the individual person? We ought not conclude that the rise of multinational corporations and borderless finance renders the State marginal, any more than the rise of mercenaries makes armies redundant. Even if we only say

---

[261] Emmanuel Levinas, *Totality and Infinity* (Pittsburgh: Duquesne University Press, 1969).

[262] Chung makes the positive claim in *The Hermeneutical Self*, 172–3. On the underdeveloped political element of his salient thought, see Foucault, *Ethics: Subjectivity and Truth*, 294. For an analysis of the political and moral shortcomings of his theory of care in light of such political and moral claims as Foucault does make for it, see Ella Myers, *Worldly Ethics: Democratic Politics and Care for the World* (Durham, NC: Duke University Press, 2013), 34–9. See also Behrent, 'Liberalism without Humanism'.

[263] On Smith and Armey, Don Erler, *Lone Star State of Mind* (Lanham, MD: Lexington, 2002), 75–6.

that the State is instrumentalized by greater powers for the coercion of labour and protection of property, the fact that it is a useful instrument is itself telling, as is the fear of the vacuum created by 'failed states'. But there is more to be said. Genuinely global, fully State-transcending economic integration, while in the interests of a genuinely free market logic, would actually not be in the interest of tax-haven users or multinationals who benefit from the race to the bottom in terms of competing State tax rates and labour costs. In any case we know that states remain vital to the making of markets, by investing in infrastructure and 'human capital' and by appropriate legislation regarding property rights, and to compensate for market failures. And their very existence as vertical subdivisions of humanity hinders horizontal solidarity with/of the exploited. It is also in the interests of richer states and economic alliances of states to maintain some of the circumstances that conduce to very different national GDP rates, as they maximise prosperity for at least some domestic constituencies while explaining any reduction in material fortune by reference to the nature of interstate economic competition at which one must simply become better.

If statespeople can often appear to be little more than conduits of corporate power, they can also portray themselves as defenders of the people against said power—or at least against migrants who might compete with the people for jobs and threaten the culture, or against assorted 'enemies within' as well as without. The ploy of negative integration by scapegoating confirms that patriotism can be the last resort of the scoundrel (in more conceptual terms, the *identity* card is played against select 'others' to enhance *solidarity* among the 'we-group') but its success is not thereby explained. Some of the reasons for its success were outlined in the History II section, but even if, given the spread of 'individualist' consumerism, states cannot get away as frequently as before with claims to embody values, they can still claim to be the guarantor of certain things that are valued. Above all today in the West that seems to mean a technocratic commitment to economic growth and, beyond dwindling social security, security of property and actual physical security.

The currently hegemonic 'securitization' agenda, in Barry Buzan's term, was partly anticipated by Jacob Burckhardt.[264] As well as sounding post-ideological, which all the most successful ideologies do, it is wonderfully subjective, because who can gainsay someone else's feeling insecure? And this is before we get to iterations of the security agenda like 'resource security', which forestall equitable distribution of finite, diminishing resources between states and peoples, and in a neat circularity turn the desperate into potential security threats. As we continue to turn the planet into a second Mars through climate change and environmental

---

[264] Barry Buzan, Oly Wæver, and Jaap de Wilde, *Security: A New Framework for Analysis* (Boulder, CO: Lynne Rienner, 1998), 23ff; Jacob Burckhardt, 'On Fortune and Misfortune in History', in Meyerhoff (ed.), *The Philosophy of History in Our Time*, 273–90, here 279.

spoliation we are likely to see the production of many more refugees and of the accompanying 'fortress' plans to keep them away from 'our' doors. This is no approximation to the monadological ideal that Leibniz entertained.

The logic of arrangements is that states compete with states and individuals with individuals even while the image is that individuals and states enjoy the negative liberty that permits 'self-determination' according to one's own lights. The arrangement is given a gloss of harmonizing transcendence at national and global levels via claims of trickle-down economics, comparative advantage, and even wealth convergence. Of course the economic 'game' is not a zero-sum undertaking and it would be absurd to ignore the material benefits that it has brought about. Nonetheless, benefits are spread in vastly unequal measures, and this within states as well as between them.[265] A lesson of political economy as of psychology is that collectives and individuals are as concerned about relative standing as absolute gain—none of these entities actually being windowless monads whose opinion of themselves is entirely centred in themselves.

Moving Beyond 'Their Own Terms'

This section contrasts internalist conceptions of morality with relational conceptions, arguing for the superior empirical foundation of the assumptions upon which the relational conception rests. To make the contrast clear it helps to summarize the problems of that internalist model which we have called 'monadic', remembering of course that Leibniz should not be held responsible for all of the iterations of the model.

As its name indicates, monadic thinking is concerned with oneness, whether of the individual human, the linguistic-cultural community, or the entirety of spiritual existence. From the perspective of the smallest significant monad, let us say the person looking outward/upward, different monadic levels appear as widening concentric circles of identity. From the perspective of larger monads looking inward, the 'relationship' of the smaller monads is something akin to cells in a honeycomb, each harmoniously coexisting with adjacent cells, at most being influenced by its neighbours in some unspecified but basically non-intrusive sense. Insofar as this model addresses change, it is change roughly analogous to the way that genes shape attributes, i.e. from within. If the monadological model is to work, descriptively and normatively, it can only do so if it works evenly, all

---

[265] It will also be noted that the states that achieved the most formidable economic growth in the later twentieth century, primarily in eastern Asia, have worked on neo-mercantilist principles rather than accepting Washington consensus doctrine. Economically illiberal China's growth in the late twentieth and early twenty-first century has been responsible for the bulk of global success in recent decades in bringing people out of poverty.

the way up, from the lowest monad to the highest and most completely inclusive, such that particular differences at one level are resolved at the next level above.

Looking 'downwards', it is no good if smaller monads have to be coerced into accepting the broader arrangements within which they are situated. The same is the case, now looking 'upwards' from the people/State, if monadology stops at some supranational universal like the Umma or the 'civilized world', because then there are still elements whose difference cannot be reconciled in a higher unity. In that event we are in the realms of exclusionary inclusion. 'Free trade' blocs only promote free trade from within; externally, they are protectionist. Alliances of countries presuppose countries not in the club. Leibniz fell into this pattern, at once criticizing Louis XIV's disruptions in Europe and his failure to direct his martial energies outside Christendom, 'against the barbarians', i.e. the Ottomans.[266] The Westphalian 'principle' of non-intervention and the just war innovations of the period did not apply outside Europe; norms of war-conduct were likewise restricted. Apart from the extension of European exceptionalism to lands of white settlement in the wider world, the situation largely endured into the twentieth century. Indeed, it is unclear that 'we' have yet escaped from these prejudicial presumptions. A variation on exclusionary inclusion is the tradition of acknowledging a higher unity, such as 'humanity', and purporting to act in its name whilst crushing parts of it.

The precepts of liberal economics and liberal political theory have the individual person as the basic actor, while international relations and culturalist thought focus upon the State and the nation respectively, and culture and nation are supposedly brought together in the nation state. The most influential forms of moral relativism prioritize cultural 'contexts' over others. The pre-eminent and mostly German founders of the modern study of culture can also lay claim to being the founders of cultural relativism. It is no paradox that German intellectual traditions were later implicated in the destruction of cultures and their peoples, because while relativism is often invoked in an irenic sense, it can also have aggressive-defensive expression. It is a matter of historical contingency which element is emphasized.

To illustrate one extreme potentiality of relativist thinking, let us turn to the sense of ineradicable difference that Nazis perceived in the Jews. Put aside some of Hitler's more overtly religious or mystical utterances and contemplate the likes of the senior civil servant in the Nazi interior ministry, Wilhelm Stuckart, who claimed in the late 1930s that Jews were different but not inferior, whilst of course vigorously persecuting them.[267] Stuckart's position is not incompatible with

[266] Simon Kow, *China in Early Enlightenment Political Thought* (Abingdon: Routledge, 2017), 87.
[267] Mark Roseman, 'Beyond Conviction?', in Frank Biess, Mark Roseman, and Hanna Schissler (eds), *Conflict, Catastrophe, and Continuity* (New York: Berghahn, 2007), 83–103, here 95.

relativism, to which the next section devotes sustained attention. Not a huge distance ideologically from Nazism was Benito Mussolini, who averred that

> If relativism signifies contempt for fixed categories and men who claim to be the bearers of an objective, immortal truth . . . then there is nothing more relativistic than Fascist attitudes and activity . . . From the fact that all ideologies are of equal value, that all ideologies are mere fiction, the modern relativist infers that everybody has the right to create for himself his own ideology and to attempt to enforce it with all the energy of which he is capable.[268]

Thus does the monad become the antinomian, with relativism its sword against others and its shield against judgement. Whatever the difference in temper, Mussolini's logic is not so very different to Jacob Burckhardt's reasoning that 'the people of Europe can maltreat, but happily not judge one another'.[269] It is an open question as to whether that 'heroic realist', the SS's Werner Best, was closer to Mussolini or Burckhardt when claiming that 'in times of conflict we will of course pursue the vital interests of our people even to the extent of annihilating the opponent—but without the hatred and contempt of any value judgement'.[270] It is not reassuring that maltreatment through annihilation need not be accompanied by value judgement, but the case shows shows that relativism can be co-opted for 'heroic realism' as much as for more peaceable agendas. Best also felt, by the way, that 'We can respect even those whom we fight and whom we may have to exterminate'.[271]

We need little more than Mussolini's words to conclude that groups cannot—whether directly or through the agendas of their internally legitimate leaders—be the only arbiters of the rectitude of their actions any more than can individuals, because they do not exist in a state of isolation any more than in a state of absolute unity. The idea of a 'we' or 'our values' presupposes an idea of a 'them' and 'their values', quite as much as, in Fichte's account, the idea of an I presupposes the idea of a not-I. We cannot effectively say that a belief in one's own, or one's religious community's or State's illumination/predestination/righteousness plus the power to realize one's agendas renders the agendas beyond criticism, lest we arrive at a modified version of the obviously faulty doctrine 'might makes right'. The modification is that 'might is right if it believes itself so'. Assuming that the we-group will always be happy with its own arrangements if it is tightly enough defined (by whom—its most powerful 'representatives', its 'active citizens', its sympathetic historians?), then adopting this position has the peculiar corollary

---

[268] Quoted in Maria Baghramian, *Relativism* (London: Routledge, 2005), 117.
[269] Burckhardt, *Civilization*, 271.
[270] Herbert, 'Ideological Legitimation', 105; Roseman, 'Beyond Conviction?, 92.
[271] Roseman, 'Beyond Conviction?', 93.

that the only people who are qualified meaningfully to criticize those arrangements are the ones who already support them. As with matters of the individual interior, the only way that the collective interior can be left to legislate for itself is in matters that are solely interior. In the unlikely event that *Volk*-spirits exist, they, like human souls, cannot be meaningfully evaluated in this world, but any action that is mandated by the bearer of the collective *Geist*/soul is a candidate for external evaluation.

It is eminently understandable why, when confronted with imperialists' assertions of their own moral superiority, the victims of imperialism, or those Westerners who purport to speak for the victims, might propound relativism in moral self-validation (though we have seen that just as frequently anti-imperialists have used the language of universalism in their resistance). Equally, however, it is often convenient for elements on both 'sides' to inflate criticism across cultures to a zero-sum game, because that is a good way of rallying everyone to the flag, silencing internal criticism. Thereby a particular interpretation of a culture is promoted to a position of internal pre-eminence and its proponents promoted as the only face of the culture presented to the external antagonist. Every sphere of life within the society is tightly interrelated, it is claimed: one understands nothing unless one understands the whole, so considering the parts without ability to consider the whole issues in error; and when the whole is viewed as self-sufficient and independent, then there is after all no means of judging the whole. If for Burckhardt and Geertz judgement was beyond human ken, for that bestselling interwar philosopher of History Oswald Spengler it was a highly subjective matter that properly belonged to the aesthetic not the moral realm. A society may sanction practices like chattel slavery, which look wrong to Us, but one may not pronounce on that because the same seed that produced the institution may also have produced other institutions eminently conducive to human wellbeing. Herder coined a 'principle of displaced alternatives' to explain the inevitable losses as well as benefits entailed in *any* 'decision'. While this sounds like the economist's concept of 'opportunity cost', Herder could in fact use the language of evaluation to argue the impossibility of evaluation. At the individual as at the societal level, the different gestalt configurations of human life that existed before and after the decision were matters for empathetic understanding only.[272] That elucidator of the 'spirit of the laws', Montesquieu, warned against measures that might lead to changing 'the general spirit of a nation'. 'If the character is good, what difference do a few faults make? One could constrain its women, make laws to correct their mores and limit their luxury, but who knows whether one would not lose a certain taste that would be the source of the nation's wealth and a politeness that

---

[272] F. M. Barnard, 'Self-Direction: Thomasius, Kant, and Herder', *Political Theory*, 11/3 (1983), 343–68, here 348–9.

attracts foreigners to it.'[273] Under Montesquieu's influence, Edmund Burke made the same point. Laws and norms could not be transferred from one society to another (save in Montesquieu's limited endorsement of imperialism!), nor elaborated from abstract principle as the contractualists tried to. Changes even in small areas of what Burke called this 'mysterious incorporation' might upset the delicate balance of the whole, which is why Montesquieu's thought was so attractive to anti-revolutionaries like Burke—and why it remains attractive to conservatives.

Rather than leaping to monadological internalism, the way to obviate blanket judgements about 'ways of life' is to depart from the view, common to Burkeans, Burckhardtians, and Bolsheviks, that societies are coherent wholes to be accepted or rejected en bloc.[274] If one criticizes the practice of female genital mutilation, one is not criticizing the entirety of the cultures from which that practice contingently springs. If one spends one's life lobbying against Western intervention in the Middle East, one may well be commenting on some of the pathologies of great power politics and the domestic arrogance that encourages them, but one is not necessarily opposing 'the Western way of life', whatever that might be. A New York socialite and a farmer from the Franche-Comté both partake of that 'way' but would seem to have as little in common as a Mumbai millionaire and a Deccan peasant, even if the first two each know a smidgeon of Voltaire and the latter pair can quote bits of the Bhagavadgita. The untenable monadic view is as injurious to certain forms of *internal* criticism as anything else, since it removes the huge menu of political options between absolute continuity and fullscale social revolution.

That the monadic philosophy and its kin like structuralism do not 'work' in the relevant sense is why a critique of certain species of relativism—such as the critique provided below—that appeals to relational criteria cannot be exploited in the name of some total critique of any given society. One of the many problems with imperial agendas is that they tend towards that sort of total critique. They often involve changing other ways of life, either to conform to that of the imperialists, or to facilitate the serving of the imperialists. They operate, that is, at a wide range of levels and in a large number of spheres in the recipient society. The act of intervening in another society with a view to directing its affairs may presuppose

---

[273] Cited in Appiah, *Ethics of Identity*, 150.

[274] I relate certain conservatives and revolutionaries for these reasons: 'If the present has its roots deep down in the past, by the same principle the future must draw its life from the present. And when one generation allows abuses to go unchecked and uncorrected, the next generation, or those that come after, must look to pay the penalty. That penalty may take one of two forms. It may either lie in the increased difficulty of rooting out an abuse which has been suffered to grow and spread beyond all knowledge, or it may lie in the blind fury of a revolution which will sweep away the good with the bad, the wheat with the tares, in a whirlwind of indiscriminating vengeance' (Vaughan, *Studies in the History of Political Philosophy Before and After Rousseau*, 300). There is a counter-argument about conservatives as apostles of incremental change, but the concept is rather slippery since there is no agreed definition of an increment's authorship, size, frequency, direction—i.e. whether the increment ameliorates or exacerbates, conceals, distracts from, etc., the abuses in question.

or at least encourage among the interveners an attitude of general society-to-society superiority rather than a focus on the specific contrast that has been made in one area of social practice. But it is precisely at the level of 'ways of life' that we cannot make evaluations because they are multifaceted, incorporating a whole range of more-and-less discordant and malleable aesthetic and moral tenets.

Unlike an internalist paradigm, a relational paradigm is concerned with interactions within and between different 'ones'. Whether the focus is on interactions between different influences within the organic individual, or among individuals within groups, groups within societies, or societies amongst other societies, the concern is with the element of relation and interaction between non-identical entities, rather than with unity or identity. This interaction is a key driver not just of change but of self-definition, self-development, differentiation from others, and finally alliances and antagonisms with others. A relational model contrasts with the monadic model where the person or the culture just has a character that wells up from some internal or ideal source. In the camp of those finding monadic claims to cohesion inaccurate would come Freud at the level of the 'individual' or the subject (ego, id, superego, or drives, socialization, etc.), Marx at the level of society (conflicting classes), 'realist' IR theorists at the supranational level, and postmoderns concerned with the 'difference' that goes all the way down, as opposed to the monadology that supposedly goes all the way up. To the list we might add Machiavelli, at least according to one interpretation. Contrary to the view of Machiavelli as envisaging the neutralization of internal social conflict through citizenship in the republic, Étienne Balibar depicts Machiavelli's political science as being concerned with negotiating ongoing conflict.[275] This disagreement about the man so often called the father of modern political thought points to the very heart of the distinction between monist and relational models. Where monadic models are apolitical in either their starting assumptions (about unified entities) or their vision of the final state (when unity has been achieved), relational models assume the endless existence of some level of friction between entities in relations of interactive definition and development.

Balibar is a Marxist and well before postmodern anthropologists and post-Parsonian sociologists developed theories of 'difference' and conflict, Marxists had provided a counterpoint to much classical sociology and historicist monadology by focusing on social faultlines, competition, and unevenness. While (as pp. 21–2) ideal type theories or accounts of *répresentations collectives* that draw on societal cross-sections are apt to miss the element of conflict that can emerge from factoring in temporal processes, some Marxist theorists have used the idiom of different temporalities to discuss dissonance in the frozen moment of the cross

---

[275] Etienne Balibar, '*Essere Principe, Essere Populare*: The Principle of Antagonism in Machiavelli's Epistemology', in Fillipo Del Lucchese et al. (eds) *The Radical Machiavelli: Politics, Philosophy, and Language* (Leiden: Brill, 2015), 349–67, here 355–6.

section too. It is one of those confusions caused by little more than nominal similarity that the Marxist Louis Althusser (1918–90), who drew on Freud, was frequently known as a structuralist, when amongst other things he tried to come up with a non-determinist theory of change that involved reference to social structures-plural. He was concerned with the interaction of heterogeneous structural elements within the same society—say religious, educational, economic, and political institutions all with their own internal cultures and subsystemic logics. Social change might come as structures of different ages/states of development, embodying different social principles, clashed with one another. Althusser himself owed a debt to Gramsci's thought: Gramsci illustrated how the 'present' of any given state is fractured, say between metropoles and rural peripheries, and between different classes.[276] And in his 1935 work *The Heritage* [or *Inheritance*] *of Our Times*, Ernst Bloch deployed the idea of the 'non-contemporaneity of the contemporaneous' (*ungleichzeitigkeit des Gleichzeitigen*) to indicate the way in which some social and cultural structures of the past continued to exist alongside capitalist ones, and not necessarily just as dwindling, irrelevant anachronisms.[277] Each of these theories militated against the viability of what Althusser called 'expressive' social models whereby economic, political, or moral arrangements somehow emanate as harmonious phenomena from a shared essence, as in Montesquieu's 'spirit of the laws'. They also stood opposed to the structuralist model with its centred balance and even gravity.[278]

Bringing together Marxism and anthropology, Eric Wolf saw

civilizations as social sets, in which the elements are linked to each other in a large variety of ways and with very different degrees of cohesion. Methodologically, this means that we do not have to account for all the elements contained in the array or in the set—only for those we hold to be significant. Our account need in no case assume that civilizations are special wholes; they are only temporarily occurring arrays or sets . . . There does not seem any need

---

[276] Althusser, 'Contradiction and Overdetermination', in Althusser, *For Marx* (Harmondsworth: Penguin, 1969), 89–116, with reference to Gramsci at 114 and more traces of Gramsci's influence on the matter of cultural 'survivals' at 114–16. Further to Althusser's theory of 'aleatory materialism', with its emphasis on chance, Louis Althusser, *Écrits philosophiques et politiques*, i (Paris: Éditions Stock, 1994), 21 and *passim*. As to Gramsci's relevant thought: Morera, *Gramsci's Historicism*, 34–5; Peter D. Thomas, 'Althusser's Last Encounter: Gramsci', in Katja Diefenbach et al. (eds), *Encountering Althusser* (London: Bloomsbury, 2013), 137–52, here 141–3; Peter D. Thomas, *The Gramscian Moment: Philosophy, Hegemony and Marxism* (Leiden: Brill, 2009), 327; Sue Golding, *Gramsci's Democratic Theory: Contributions to a Post-Liberal Democracy* (Toronto: University of Toronto Press, 1982),148 n. 25.

[277] Bloch, *Erbschaft dieser Zeit* (Zurich: Oprecht and Helbling, 1935).

[278] Althusser 'Contradiction and Overdetermination', 103; Althusser, 'The Object of Capital' in Louis Althusser and Étienne Balibar, *Reading Capital*, pt 2 (London: New Left Books, 1970), 71–98, here esp. 94–6, 186–7.

to deal with civilizations as wholes characterized, in [the sociologist Pitirim] Sorokin's phrase, by 'immanent self-determination'.[279]

One reason to reject Sorokin's rather Leibnizian 'immanent self-determination' is a cause of change that is underemphasized in Gramsci and Althusser. That cause is cross-cultural contact. The world historian William H. McNeill is only one of the most prominent scholars to observe that cultural contact has been the key historical driver of social change—precursors include Jean Bodin in the sixteenth century and the Cambro-Norman cleric Gerald of Wales in the twelfth century.[280] In the 1950s the anthropologist George Peter Murdock described 'cultural borrowing' as 'by far the most common and important' of 'all forms of innovation'. Murdock's American culture took language from England, alphabet from the Phoenicians, numerical system from India, family and property structure from medieval Europe. Ancient Babylon provided the fundaments of its systems of banking, credits, loans, and so forth, after refinements from Italy, the Netherlands, and England. Its favourite ice cream flavours—chocolate and vanilla—were taken from the Aztecs. The USA's major religion was and remains an assemblage of inputs from the ancient Hebrews, Egyptians, Babylonians, and Persians, and, one might add, its systems of morality are just as heterogeneous.[281]

Not absolutely always but very, very often, societies have rubbed along in inter-relationships of coexistence as well as conflict. Trade, slavery, interbreeding, warfare, colonization, migration, and investment have left their marks. All societies with access to other societies engage in appropriation to some degree and some, like Indonesia, are renowned for their syncretic openness,[282] which makes Geertz's Burckhardtian talk of 'Indonesian culture' all the odder (pp. 217–18). China has been famously less forthcoming about its borrowings, and on the whole that is true of Western civilization too, but that does not mean there have been none.[283] Given all such intercourse, Wolf wrote:

> The habit of treating named entities such as Iroquois, Greece, Persia, or the United Slates as fixed entities opposed to one another by stable internal architecture and external boundaries interferes with our ability to understand their mutual

[279] Eric R. Wolf, 'Understanding Civilizations: A Review Article', *Comparative Studies in Society and History* 9/4 (1967), 446–65, here 448–9.

[280] McNeill, 'The Changing Shape of World History', *History and Theory* 34/2 (1995), 21. Cf. Jean Bodin, *Method for the Easy Comprehension of History* (New York: Octagon, 1945), ch. 9; Gerald of Wales, *Giraldus Cambrensis: The Topography of Ireland* (Cambridge, ON: In Parentheses, 2000), distinction III, ch. 10.

[281] Murdock, 'How Culture Changes', in Harry L. Shapiro (ed.), *Man, Culture, and Society* (1956; New York: Oxford University Press, 1960), 247–60, here 253–4.

[282] J. D. Legge, *Indonesia* (Sydney: Prentice Hall, 1977).

[283] Consider some of the West's claims to unique ownership or origination critically examined in Jack Goody, *The Theft of History* (Cambridge: Cambridge University Press, 2012), and also Goody's comments at pp. 120–1 on cultural exchange.

encounter and confrontation. One need have no quarrel with a denotative use of the term *society* to designate an empirically verifiable cluster of interconnections among people, as long as no evaluative prejudgments are added about its state of internal cohesion or boundedness in relation to the external world.[284]

The anthropologist Alexander Lesser likewise suggested 'adopt[ing] as a working hypothesis the universality of human contact and influence', and thinking 'of human societies—prehistoric, primitive, or modern—not as closed systems, but as open systems' which are 'inextricably involved with other aggregates, near and far, in weblike, netlike connections'.[285]

Whatever hypothesis we favour, the evidentiary record of cross-cultural exchange also shows how overblown are some of the concerns, developed under the shadow of structuralism, about conceptualizing change purely from within a closed system of culture, power, or whatever, by deconstruction or by a Foucaultian self-reinvention whose conditions of possibility are, given his account of power-knowledge and discourse, obscure. These empirics suggest, whatever the claims about the impossibility of an 'outside' in the thought of, say, Foucault, or Jean-Luc Nancy, that there is indeed always some 'outside' that may intrude on the 'inside', even though it is not a transcendent outside, just a foreign country making contact.[286] True, there will be a perimeter—that surrounding the shifting totality of human ways of being and acting under the sun—which one cannot outside, but the humanist would well ask: what *on earth* would it mean to get outside it? Once one adopts a relational paradigm as descriptively better than an internalist paradigm, one can not only secularize and demystify the question of exteriority (i.e. the exterior entity need not be a lawgiving deity), one is always guaranteed another exteriority. That is the condition of politics, not of politics' end in some monadic ideal condition.

In one sense it is of the utmost importance to remind ourselves that we are always within some context, but in another sense it is banal because there are so many sorts of context and our power to modify them is so variable. The interaction of two elements can produce a third, 'emergent' structure just as the encounter of two people can produce a unique structure of understanding which only exists between them rather than within either on their own. This also means

---

[284] Wolf, *Europe and The People without History*, 18.

[285] Cited in Wolf, *Europe and The People without History*, 19.

[286] Jean-Luc Nancy and Richard Livingston, 'The Unsacrificeable', *Yale French Studies* 79 (1991), 20–38, here 37; on Foucault's pronouncements on outsides, Michel Foucault, *Michel Foucault: Power/Knowledge: Selected Interviews and Other Writings 1972–1977*, ed. Colin Gordon (London: Harvester Press, 1980), 141, 142, and Robert M. Strozier, *Foucault, Subjectivity and Identity* (Detroit: Wayne State University Press, 2002), 57. Derrida's claims that 'there is no outside-text [*hors-texte*]', sometimes translated as 'there is nothing outside the text', and his similar claim about outside-context, are slightly different to these other cases in Derrida's meaning (though not always in Derrida-exegesis), while arising from a related tradition of thought: Derrida, *Limited Inc.*, 9, 136, 148, 152.

that to talk about contexts in the sense of structures, and to talk about human relations across the boundaries of those contexts, is not to talk about things that need be conceptually opposed.

Tolerance, Respect, Relativism

This section brings out the implications of relational thought for moral evaluation across all cleavages, and does so by engaging in philosophical debates. The focal point is cultural contextualizations. To refresh the memory, 'cultural' contextualizations are contextualizations to different value systems, as opposed to 'functional' contextualizations that imply a common value system applied to special situations (see p. 39).

Reflection on cultural differences has prompted at least three sorts of arguments against evaluation, and all three will be shown to be wanting. One set of arguments is relativist. The varieties and complexity of relativist positions mean that they are accorded most attention hereafter. A second argument abjures evaluation in the name of tolerance but falls down because it fails to consider the conditions of tolerance. The third argument is more patronizing and therefore implicitly judgemental anyway. The three positions are now considered in reverse order.

The third argument is that there is no point criticizing people who could not have known *better*. This is already a thorny area given that it raises questions about who and on what bases the better is judged, but the automatic assumption that 'we' know morally better than predecessors can give a distinct slant to the whole discussion. It is the sort of assumption decried by Nietzsche and Ranke, as they criticized that form of History that depicted the latest arrival in the development of manners as *ipso facto* the greatest form of humanity to date, as if moral advancement marched forward as surely as technological sophistication.[287] The key issue is that disapprobation is implicit in all such assumptions. It is only the forbearance towards the ignorant bearers of the relevantly inferior culture that varies, as if in accordance with Thomas Aquinas's claim that an errant conscience still binds provided that its bearer was not ignorant of a law that she *should* have known. In the Catholic tradition such a state of innocent ignorance is known as *invincible ignorance*, as contrasted with vincible ignorance.

---

[287] Joseph McBride, 'Tragic Philosophy and History in the Thought of Friedrich Nietzsche', *Maynooth Review* 5/2 (1979), 25–33, here 30; Leopold von Ranke, *The Secret of World History: Selected Writings on the Art and Science of History*, ed. Roger Wines (New York: Fordham University Press, 1981), 160–1, including: 'We can assume in the areas of material interest an absolute progress, a highly decisive ascent which would require an enormous upset to bring about a decline. But we cannot find a similar progress in moral affairs.'

Let us contemplate such thinking as applied to the present, before turning to its application to the past. Consider the Rwandan genocide of 1994, in which up to 800,000 people, mostly Tutsis, were murdered by the 'Hutu Power' regime. If we suggest that Africans, or perhaps inhabitants of the Balkans, are more likely to murder each other than Western Europeans, owing perhaps to some primitive atavism, or some childlike state then we would rightly be accused of racism as applied to the groups in question even as we seem to be absolving the relevant members of those groups from blame for their actions. We are saying that the collective 'they' did not know better, that their cultures lacked the resources for the sort of moral discernment that 'we' have. The remotest acquaintance with the cultures in question shows that their bearers had the resources to make the relevant moral distinctions. Mass murder was the outcome of specific, conscious political projects, not of some general cultural disposition. In both cases mass murder was a concerted attempt to change the world not a reproduction of entrenched ways of being in the world. The perpetrators of genocide need to be judged morally as relevantly discerning beings.

In popular culture there is often no equivalent stigma attached to saying the same sorts of patronizing things about cultures of the past. Some of the first responses to ethnic cleansing in Yugoslavia invoked its 'medieval' quality, as did much of the rhetoric around the murderous Islamic State movement in Syria and Iraq from 2014. On a personal note, I am struck by the number of university students who, when they encounter them, wrongly regard medieval peasants collectively as dimwits lacking any discernment except that forced upon them by Church and State. Not blaming these students for what are inculcated views, I blame tendencies in a society (ours) that has, since the Renaissance and with additional force since Voltaire and Condorcet, developed a knee-jerk assumption of its superiority over some of its own historical antecedents, associating the Middle Ages with barbarity and so forth. This sort of attitude, which can produce the conviction that moral advance has occurred in much the same way as technological advance, was what Ranke had wished to counter. The reaction to the *Lumières* judgementalism also helped to shape the profession's opposition to evaluation more generally.[288] Clearly this book does not argue against evaluation as such. What it does reject—and this without prejudice to the obvious fact that certain moral concepts were unavailable to certain inhabitants of the past owing to the concepts' being developed later on—is the default assumption of the present's full spectrum, society-to-society level superiority over the past. Under that wrong-headed assumption, any given problematic practice in the past appears as a predictable manifestation of a general moral deficiency back then. Equivalent terms for racism or ethnocentrism that encapsulate such retrospective stereotyp-

---

[288] On the—to him misplaced—fear of yielding a 'gratuitous victory to Voltaire', Lord Acton, *Lectures on Modern History* (London: Fontana, 1960), 38–9.

ing of whole societies might be *epochalism* or *chronocentrism*. In sum: even when epochalism or chronocentrism is deployed 'positively', in the sense of absolving past people for their not being as morally advanced as 'us', it is still implicitly deprecating of their world.

When History is written under the assumption of general contemporary moral superiority there is either a pseudo-evaluation where the conclusion is known before the process begins, or a putatively anti-evaluative stance that is actually premised upon evaluation. Any proper process of evaluation cannot start from such positions. The same sort of reasoning stands in rebuttal of that smaller but not insignificant band of proper reactionaries who assume that our forebears were *better* than us. Since this book argues for a non-relativist position *in practice* (see below for possible distinctions in *theory*) it is important to distinguish non-relativism from ethnocentrism/chronocentrism. For the sake of ease let us just focus on ethnocentrism, though the same considerations apply to chronocentrism. Ethnocentrism it is not the same as anti-relativism despite the effective titular equation of the two in the exchange between the anthropologist Clifford Geertz and the philosopher Richard Rorty, when the former's 'anti-anti-relativism' was met with the latter's 'anti-anti-ethnocentrism'.[289] To be sure, anti-relativism and ethnocentrism can contingently accompany each other and often have done. The assumption of their logical linkage has been reinforced by strands of postmodern and anti- and postcolonial scholarship that tie anti-relativism to universalism and at the same time depict universalism as nothing but ethnocentrism spuriously generalized.[290] Nevertheless, there is no logical linkage. Practical non-relativism implies that it is meaningful, intellectually defensible and sometimes necessary to make judgements across, say, cultural boundaries. Ethnocentrism is the belief that one's own culture's arrangements are always the better, and it is closely related to the imperialist's prejudicial society-to-society comparison debunked above (pp. 228–30). The inquirer who rejects ethnocentrism along, for practical purposes, with relativism, as this inquirer does, must be open to the prospect that some of the principles and practices of other societies in the past (as in the present) are *preferable* to certain principles and practices in his or her own society. That is what it means not to prejudice the inquiry.

The second argument against judgement tries to excise evaluation because judgement is deemed to be incompatible with tolerance. Traces of the argument that historical study is conducive to tolerance are there in Descartes, and it is

---

[289] Clifford Geertz, 'Distinguished Lecture: Anti Anti-Relativism', *American Anthropologist*, NS 86/2 (1984), 263–78; Richard Rorty, *Objectivity, Relativism, and Truth* (Cambridge: Cambridge University Press, 1991), 203 ff.

[290] Overall it is important to establish whether the objection is to universalism per se (in the name of something like relativism) or to pseudo-universalism (in the name of genuine universalism) or whether one is saying (in the name of scepticism) that it is impossible to distinguish universalism from pseudo-universalism.

explicit in the writing of Henry St John, Viscount Bolingbroke (1678–1751), Collingwood, Butterfield, and Richard Evans. What are the prospects for this History as tolerance? When Evans, for instance, claims that History will encourage democratic pluralism by encouraging the historian to tolerate human variety, he is prejudicing the issue.[291] The attitude that is supposed to be inculcated by studying the past is imposed, or already possessed, prior to any encounter with the past, otherwise there is no guarantee of the right outcome.

'Tolerance' is not even the correct category if one wishes to avoid judgement, as most of its proponents do. It has been said that for Spinoza, one of the most influential early modern thinkers on toleration, that 'Toleration is not a maxim of mutual indifference laid down by raison d'état (Hobbes and Locke), a negative limit to a rational requirement of conformity: it is mutual understanding based on recognition of the variety of the human imagination; that is, charity made scientific by the new science of hermeneutics.' The first definition resembles tolerance as practical necessity: the second tolerance as principle.[292] Clearly tolerance based on mutual understanding sounds more attractive than that based on mutual indifference, but either way there must be limits. Mutual indifference can no longer suffice when interaction becomes necessary, and here some attempt at mutual understanding provides the alternative to obliteration or enslavement. Mutual understanding may pave the way for provisional harmony but understanding is inter alia a precondition for disagreement, and one can only 'agree to disagree' up to the point that resolving disagreement is the only alternative to physical conflict—a conflict the end point of which will in any case be the resolution of disagreement in favour of one party. Tolerance of either sort is a principle which will have at points to compete with other principles.[293] One cannot say in advance of encountering a specific practice that one will be tolerant of it. That would be to forswear the possession of any other principle than tolerance, indeed to render oneself so completely mutable as to have no identity as a value-bearing individual qualified to be tolerant.[294]

---

[291] Examples of conceiving History as a tutor of tolerance range from Lord Bolingbroke, *Letters on the Study and Use of History* (London: T. Cadell, 1779), 25–7, to Evans, 'What Is History', 5, 7. For other examples see the works cited in the Introduction, p. 8 n. 22.

[292] Norman O. Brown, *Apocalypse and/or Metamorphosis* (Berkeley and Los Angeles: University of California Press, 1991), 107; Adam Sutcliffe, *Judaism and Enlightenment* (Cambridge: Cambridge University Press, 2003), 213–14.

[293] I stress 'at points', not 'all the time'. My target is the argument that it is both possible and desirable to be tolerant of *all* other practices, indiscriminately. Manifestly there are matters of, for instance, manners and etiquette that vary from setting to setting and about which tolerance is eminently possible if it is actually deemed relevant (the very idea of tolerating something can imply distaste for it and differing manners need not prompt distaste). The problem comes with extending tolerance beyond some borderline between matters like dining etiquette and matters like sending children down coal mines. To be sure, the borderline itself may be blurred but that only means that certain cases are marginal—many others are not.

[294] Arthur O. Lovejoy, *The Great Chain of Being* (Cambridge, MA: Harvard University Press, 1964), 312: 'To say "Yes" to everything and everybody is manifestly to have no character at all.'

It might be objected that 'tolerance' retrojected is different to tolerance practised in the here and now. The encounter with denizens of the past is notional, and as such does not *really* bring the potential conflict of tolerance with other principles, does not really engage the pragmatic judgement that guides action. If that is so, then the point undermines the proposition that studying History can/will make one tolerant. After all, it is only if tolerance costs something that it is true tolerance. If the previous paragraph pointed to the limits of tolerance, here we have the condition for tolerance. Via both we corroborate the semiological claim that tolerance only acquires its meaning in differential relation to the concept intolerance.

One can take one of two directions. One can take talk of tolerance seriously. This would mean that at times, after every effort of understanding and perspective-taking, one would also have not to be tolerant towards some bits of the past; this disposition is that of the author, but it is not what advocates of tolerance generally mean. Alternatively, one discards the notion of tolerance along with intolerance. If carried through, this would issue in a sort of natural-scientific positivism resembling the utterly disinterested observation of, say, termite cultures. Even if operable, which is unclear, that attitude does not seem desirable when discussing other humans. We will return to the question of tolerance and intolerance during discussion of relativism.

Let us open the discussion of relativism with a stance sometimes called *descriptive moral relativism*. At its most elementary this position simply recognizes diversity in norms across cultures, perhaps observing how culture A has a sharply different view to culture B of a particular practice or set of practices. As such it does not really qualify as relativism, because it is more a report about different standards than any attempt to establish or reject criteria for evaluating such standards from a position outside any given culture. At best it is a description from which one makes an inference about relativism, perhaps on the basis that different moral systems appear to be so different for that difference to be categorical.[295] But the relativist needs to take at least one more step if she is to give that inference more than purely suggestive force. The step may be onto the terrain sometimes marked *meta-ethical moral relativism*, or *meta-ethical relativism*, though each is a potentially confusing moniker not adopted by everyone who discusses the position it denotes.

One definition of meta-ethical moral relativism is this: 'The truth or falsity of moral judgments, or their justification, is not absolute or universal, but is relative to the traditions, convictions, or practices of a group of persons.'[296] Meta-ethics is

---

[295] On descriptive relativism, Baghramanian, *Relativism*, 270–1; Claudio Corradetti, *Relativism and Human Rights: A Theory of Pluralistic Universalism* (Dordrecht: Springer, 2009), 37–8.

[296] Chris Gowans, 'Moral Relativism', in Edward N. Zalta (ed.), *The Stanford Encyclopedia of Philosophy* [online] (Summer 2019 edn), quote from section 2 of 'Moral Relativism'. Also on

not a study of what is good or bad per se, but rather of what moral theories are about and how they function. The usual starting point is that the world does not seem to contain any mind-independent property of goodness/rightness, so we need an explanation of what claims like 'justice is good' or 'greed is good' mean that does not interpret them as made true by mind-independent properties.[297] The only sort of explanation that works, so the argument goes, is that groups produce their own moral conventions embedded in particular historico-cultural circumstances and for particular purposes. Philosopher Gilbert Harman wrote: 'What is morally right in relation to one moral framework can be morally wrong in relation to a different moral framework. And no moral framework is object-ively privileged as the one true morality.'[298]

Let us be clear about what meta-ethical relativists reject (though I do not imply that only meta-ethical relativists reject the following positions). They reject *tran-scendent* sources of morality, the most obvious examples of which are divinely-inscribed stone tablets. They also rule out *moral objectivism*. Under some definitions moral objectivism, like the concept of *moral realism*, incorporates transcendent concepts of morality of the sort just mentioned—think back to the medieval 'realists', as opposed to the nominalists, discussed in the History I sec-tion. Moral objectivism/realism can also incorporate the idea that moral codes are somehow woven into the material stuff of the world, testable against the evi-dence in much the way one could establish the law of gravity. Relativists cannot accept either of those positions because relativists see moral codes as being gener-ated within minds and cultures, not by things external to them. Indeed post-religious 'naturalistic' or scientific understandings of the world have given great impetus to relativism precisely on the grounds that nature does not seem to have an inherent moral quality. (Again, compare this view with that of medieval theo-logical 'realists' who associated transcendent morality with the material world as the 'book of God'.) Now many non-relativists would also reject the idea of moral transcendence and objectivism or realism under any of the foregoing definitions. Things get more interesting when non-relativists come up with arguments that are compatible with naturalistic precepts because they do not appeal to moral properties of the natural or supernatural world. An obvious example of such non-relativistic thought is the Kantian suggestion that human rationality (as opposed to anything that can be tested against evidence in the material world) working on its own (absent divine decree) is capable of justifying moral rules that are in principle binding on all rational beings. Meta-ethical relativists reject Kant-like

meta-ethical moral relativism, Baghramanian, *Relativism*, 281 ff.; and for different versions of what he calls meta-ethical relativism, Corradetti, *Relativism and Human Rights*, 40.

[297] See e.g. the clarifications in Alex Miller, *Contemporary Metaethics: An Introduction* (Cambridge: Polity, 2013), ch. 1.
[298] Cited in Baghramanian, *Relativism*, 285.

positions as well, arguing that there are no conceptual foundations or yardsticks for values and evaluation outside any and all societies against which the values or the value-generating mechanisms of any given society can be measured.

Philosophical debate endures between non-relativistic moral rationalists and meta-ethical relativists, and your author is not competent to arbitrate between the positions. Fortunately he does not need that competence, since the intention here is the more modest one of showing only that the most powerful moral relativisms do not produce logical or moral objections to relevant forms of moral *judgement*. Pursuant to substantiating these more modest claims, the present argument warns relativists away from any negative argument about the morally transcendent/objective that implicitly depends on the idea of the transcendent/objective for its efficacy. As suggested earlier, the doctrine of moral relativism developed at the point of the secularization of religious metaphysics, with the disappearance of the divine-universal force in whom all differing earthly perspectives were supposedly reconciled. Yet the scenarios are not symmetrical. An absence does not work in the same way, or rather it does not work in the equal-but-opposite way, as a presence. To build a positive theory on the basis of the absence of an external moral authority or source is to make the absence into an 'absolute ground' or 'foundation'—and it is precisely the absence of such 'foundations' that relativists appeal to in the first place.

An example of a species of moral relativism that falls into just this trap is the popular theory that has variously been called *vulgar (moral) relativism* and *naïve relativism* and is sometimes included under the rubric of *normative relativism*. The claim of this theory is something like: 'the only standard by which to judge the practices or concepts of a culture is the standard provided by that culture and it would be wrong to use other standards' or, slightly differently, 'it is wrong for members of one group to judge the values of another group'. This species of relativism is self-undermining because it makes a non-relativized judgement about what is right and wrong while trying to argue for relativism in judgements about what is right and wrong. It proposes a group-transcending, universal moral standard for the principles of judging across group boundaries whilst denying the existence of such group-transcending moral standards.'[299]

Emphasizing the flaw in this species of relativism strikes at the heart of the idea that relativism can provide us with any instruction about how to think beyond the level of abstract thought about the constitution of values. Assuming that some relativisms are coherent, they only have implications at the level of the meta-ethical rather than the ethical (or moral, in the terms of this book)—they cannot provide practical guidance on adjudging this or that practice/value good or bad. It is the

---

[299] For the labels 'vulgar' and 'naïve', see Baghramian, *Relativism*, 274 (and also for hints of self-refutation in what she calls normative ethical relativism, 279); on identical self-refutation problems in what he calls normative relativism, Corradetti, *Relativism and Human Rights*, 37.

mistake of equating moral relativism with any particular practical position that led the intellectual historian Hayden White to proclaim 'relativism to be the basis of social tolerance'.[300] White's position is adopted by the historiographer and postmodernist Keith Jenkins, who bases tolerance on 'moral relativism'.[301] The claim is most famously associated with the anthropologist M. J. Herskovits.[302] 'Has any group been *less* culturally relative than the Nazis?' asks literary theorist Robert Eaglestone in what he wrongly takes to be a rhetorical question.[303] Obviously many Nazis and Fascists were not remotely relativist, but we have already encountered Mussolini and the Nazi Werner Best in relativist mode (pp. 70–71, 226–7).

Putting aside the aforementioned fact that tolerance cannot be infinite and indiscriminate, one may be tolerant in addition to being a relativist, or, equally, intolerant. The strongest anti-relativism is no more incompatible than relativism with tolerance or respect. A belief that one's beliefs are right in an absolute sense can sit easily, all else equal, with tolerance or respect for the differing beliefs and belief-related practices of others. It is unsurprising that tolerance and relativism are often confused, because they seem to have the same function of avoiding conflict, but there is no conceptual relationship between them. No more than universalists or sceptics do relativists comprise a particular character-type with a common civic or affective disposition.

If someone claims to be a relativist that tells us nothing about their specific, effective conceptions of what is right and wrong, good and bad, nor about how they will judge or act upon those conceptions in any concrete situation. In actual interactions, i.e. beyond abstract discussions about the nature of value justification, it makes no difference if one identifies as a constructivist, relativist, universalist, particularist, etc. This is a reason that we need not associate relativism with the absence of any criteria of judgement, even nihilism. The relativist will still have local standards of judgement to adhere to and will adhere to these just as strongly as someone who believes in absolute standards—indeed the relativists' philosophy must lead them to the conclusion that local standards are all that there are, such that whatever their local standards are at any given moment, those standards are, for them, effectively absolute in their force. That also applies to the relativist's encounters with someone else who holds different local standards when they differ on some substantive moral matter.

At the same time, relativism in the abstract, ie. without thinking about specific judgements, will not be welcomed by all the peoples of the world, however much it has been associated with anti-imperialism and tolerance. Say that the relativist

[300] White, *Content*, 227.
[301] Keith Jenkins, *Re-Thinking History* (London: Routledge, 2003), 68.
[302] Melville J. Herskovits, *Cultural Relativism* (New York: Random House, 1972), 31.
[303] Robert Eaglestone, *Postmodernism and Holocaust Denial* (London: Icon, 2001), 6.

contemplates another culture whose inhabitants conceive of some value as objectively given, perhaps because it was articulated by a deity. (Of course many such people exist in 'our' culture too.) While the relativist accepts 'their' belief as valid, in the sense of being regulative 'for them', he does not accept as correct their *estimation* of their belief—as in correct in virtue of the particular justification they claim for the belief. In denying that their values really are objectively given, the relativist claims a higher insight than the relevant members of that culture into the *nature* of their values. In the event that inhabitants of this culture get to hear of the relativist's thoughts, they will reasonably infer that the relativist believes their belief system to be conceptually wrong—and since their morality is justified on the particular conceptual basis that the relativist finds to be conceptually wrong they will after all see relativism as an attack on their moral system. If relativism is irrelevant where it might be thought to matter in *practice*, i.e. in 'real-life' interactions, there is no guarantee that people will welcome relativism in *principle*, as a concept.

The last few paragraphs help remove some of the moral baggage that has become attached to arguments for and against relativism. Neither relativism in its most persuasive iterations nor non-relativism should be conceived as being good or bad in the moral sense, even while each of them obviously pertains to how good and the right and bad and the wrong are conceived. They are rarefied conceptual arguments 'only', not moral arguments. Having already contended that the more sophisticated relativisms do not rule out cross-cultural judgements on moral and otherwise practical grounds, let us now work our way through the issues in order to substantiate the claim that they do not rule out relevant judgements on conceptual grounds either.

If, for argument's sake, we granted that moral relativists are correct to deny the existence of Kant-like as well as objective/transcendent grounds of moral arbitration,[304] it would remain a matter of debate as to what relevantly follows. One could still adopt non-relativistic positions including scepticism about the possibility of knowing moral truths of any sort, or reject any system of validating moral claims, including relativistic systems.[305] More importantly for the present argument, even if one accepted that it makes no sense to talk about matters bearing on all societies from a point conceptually outside them all, one could still talk about matters between societies, and matters common among societies. In pursuing those thoughts it helps to address the matter of conceptual *incommensurability*.

---

[304] One need not grant this position, though, again, your author is not qualified to argue either way. See e.g. the groundwork towards the argument in support of some measure of normative absolutism in Paul Boghossian, 'Relativism about Morality' at: http://as.nyu.edu/content/dam/nyu-as/asSilverDialogues/documents/PBoghossian-RelAboutNorm-final-SilverDialogues%20v3.pdf and Boghossian, 'Should We Be Relativists about Morality?', at https://cpb-us-e1.wpmucdn.com/sites.northwestern.edu/dist/1/1221/files/2016/09/BoghossianPublicHandout-1kxhlx0.pdf.

[305] Gowans, 'Moral Relativism', section 6.

Incommensurability means the absence of any standard by which two or more things can be considered comparatively. Ruth Benedict harnessed the term to her own relativistic wagon in discussion of three particular cultures: 'They differ . . . because they are oriented as wholes in different directions. They are travelling along different roads in pursuit of different ends, and these ends and these means in one society cannot be judged in terms of those of another society, because essentially they are incommensurable.'[306] We do have good reasons to believe that some values are indeed incommensurable: how, for instance, does one adjudge—instead of just asserting—that social equality is a higher or lower value than personal liberty? But disagreement over those two values can exist within the confines of a single culture as well as across cultures.[307] The same goes for different systems of moral thought: deontology and consequentialism, for instance, can clearly exist in the same society, but are incommensurable as frameworks for moral decision because of the concept of the individual within their schemes.[308] Identifying such cases of incommensurability substantiates an argument for value pluralism, which is itself important, but it does not itself justify a more broad-ranging relativism and obviously it does not justify the equation that is sometimes made of incommensurability with incomprehensibility or 'talking past' one another: consequentialists and deontologists understand and argue with each other about the superiority of their positions all the time, as do the sides in the liberty–equality battle. Incommensurability in certain areas of value does not imply incommensurability in all and there is no reason to think such incommensurability as exists must be specially and extensively tied to intercultural differences unless one has already adopted a sort of whole-culture, monadic view of things, as in Benedict's quote above. Such whole-culture views are consistent with the particular secularized-religious view of the nature of cultures as they developed from Leibniz to Herder, which should sound alarm bells for aforementioned reasons. We need again to be sure that when rejecting the religious-metaphysical assumptions on which monadological thinking was based (*Geist*, God, and so forth) we do not keep the rest of the monadological structure, either at the level of the individual or the collective.

One flaw in whole-culture views, as if any given culture were the product of logical extension from a differing founding axiom, with each part of that culture infused with the unique character of its parent axiom, is that just as any given culture can be riven over some value dispute, some commonality in value exists across many cultures. Something can be universalized, in the sense of gaining general assent as a good idea or practice, or the best of the menu of options that

---

[306] Benedict, *The Chrysanthemum and the Sword*, 223.
[307] See e.g. the discussion of Isaiah Berlin in Baghramian, *Relativism*, 294–8, which also distinguishes between pluralism and relativism.
[308] Larry Alexander, 'Deontology at the Threshold', *San Diego Law Review* 37 (2000), 893–912, here 911–12.

appear to be available given what outcomes it produces in the world, without being found as an injunction carved on tablets of stone or stemming from a set of rational principles whose force is universally evident. Differently, some arrangements might turn out to be necessary in the ordinary, non-philosophical sense of the word. They might for instance just turn out to be functionally necessary for humans living in at least some non-conflictual relations to other humans.[309] The relativist might wish to call these arrangements 'ubiquitous' as opposed to 'universal',[310] but there is no harm in calling them contingent, effective universals. Contingent universals are already observed in cultures, in shared bans on arbitrary killing and arbitrary violence more generally, or shared promotion of truthfulness, which are presumably pretheoretical and functional in origin, requiring retrospective anthropological genealogies to explain their evolution, but not to commend them, for their justification has already been provided by the human coexistence to which they conduce. In summary, to deny transcendent morality and moral objectivism in the foregoing sense of moral realism is to make a claim about what is (and is not) and can (and cannot) be the case, whereas to deny universals in principle (as opposed to being sceptical about any particular universalist claim) is to forestall a possibility that might come to pass—or to refuse to recognize one that actually, if contingently, exists. This point will be elaborated no further here, given that the historian is concerned with the past, rather than possibilities for the future, and given, too, that historians, like anyone else, are entitled to concern themselves with the areas in which groups differ morally, rather than in the areas of effectively universal common ground.

Another challenge to cultural hermeticism (Benedict's claim that the incommensurability of entire culture A and cultures B, C, D, etc. automatically implies that any given practice or concept in culture A cannot meaningfully be judged from within cultures B, C, D) is the empirical one, elucidated in the section Moving Beyond 'Their Own Terms' that cultures just do change as a result of intercultural contact as well as internal conflict. This historical and sociological fact bespeaks general cultural syncretism rather than substantiating a view of any given culture as tantamount to the genetically determined product of a unique

---

[309] Combining this sort of sociological perspective with the insights of theories about evolutionary theory and developmental psychology, David B. Wong, *Natural Moralities* (Oxford: Oxford University Press, 2009) produces a pluralistic account of morality based on the naturalistic criteria that the relativist Gilbert Harman sees as tending to conduce to relativistic conclusions. See p. xv for the contrast with Harman, and Wong's claim that his own theory is pluralistic 'because it recognizes limits on what can count as a true morality'. Note, though, in connection with the discussion in n. 307 about Baghramian's distinction between relativism and pluralism that Wong's book is subtitled *A Defense of Pluralistic Relativism*, and before his account of his theory's pluralism he notes that 'theory is relativistic because it holds there is no single true morality'. However Wong conceptualizes the relationship between pluralism and relativism, he clearly holds the adjective 'pluralistic' to qualify the reach of the noun 'relativism'.

[310] For reasons highlighted in J. David Velleman, *Foundations for Moral Relativism* (Cambridge: Open Book, 2015), 93–4.

seed. Cultures comprise a variably related set of structures among other sets of structures in which people can express themselves and which mutate in virtue of internal action and external engagement.[311]

Recognition of the way cultures change by a combination of internal argument and external contact brings us to the point that, depending upon the species of relativism, relativists cannot rely for support on the doctrine of social construct-ivism. Constructivism is not identical to relativism, though it has enough family resemblances to appear the same to the casual observer. Here the sole focus is social construction of the cultural world, because the issues around the social construction of the natural world are sufficiently different as to cause confusion when discussed under the same rubric.[312] Indeed, it is tautological to talk of the social construction of the cultural world, but not of the natural world—which is not to say that there will not be debate about the interpenetration of the two worlds and the location of the border between them.

Constructivism implies variety (as relativism does) but also potentially endless mutability so can, as one possibility, envisage fusion and even convergence between different cultures' norms and practices across time. It is perfectly pos-sible to be a constructivist who also believes in contingent universals even if con-structivists, like relativists, tend to reject moral objectivism and the idea of transcendent morality. The constructivist may be contrasted with the cultural essentialist, whereas it is perfectly possible to be a relativist and a cultural essen-tialist. Some postmodernists fail to see this distinction, emphasizing their com-mitment to contingency and difference/particularity as against necessity (in its philosophical rather than everyday sense) and universality respectively, while overlooking the fact that one could appeal to contingent universals (the con-structivist possibility) or necessary particulars (the essentialist-relativist proposition).[313] Herder's thought was essentialist-relativist, whilst globalizing consumer-capitalism, with its homogenizing potential, represents a strand con-sonant with constructivism-universalism. Stalinism evinced both tendencies at different points as the regime variously embraced the annihilation or forced reconstruction of 'enemies', as well as sometimes encouraging the expression of cultural difference amongst the USSR's constituent peoples in what one scholar has called 'affirmative action'.[314] Imperialism also expressed different modes of

---

[311] This is shown by those instances when certain harmful social practices have been jettisoned as a result of the development of an attitude of shame towards them and is also shown by, say, the case of the end of foot-binding in early twentieth-century China, when shame was stimulated by outside scorn (but note also that shame about that practice did not equate to a wish to abandon all traditions). See Appiah, *The Honor Code*, on that case of 'moral revolution' plus the cases of the end of duelling in nineteenth-century Britain and the suppression of the Atlantic slave trade.

[312] On the differences, see Hacking, *The Social Construction of What?*.

[313] For key distinctions made here, see Steve Fuller, *The Philosophy of Science and Technology Studies* (New York: Routledge, 2006), 35–7.

[314] Terry Martin, *The Affirmative Action Empire: Nations and Nationalism in the Soviet Union, 1923–1939* (Ithaca, NY: Cornell University Press, 2001).

thought across time and place. In one example, in India the British sometimes gave great interpretative authority to conservative Brahmins whose advice about the way things were turned out to be a scheme of how they wanted things to be.[315] In that instance, as at points in the colonial rule of Ireland, gaining some version of 'local knowledge' of 'difference' was important to the imperial power, as opposed to imposing metropolitan views of difference.[316] In further British examples, the more 'optimistic' 'civilizing mission' of the earlier nineteenth century, with its intimations of convergence in accordance with the tenets of British 'universalism', gave way later on to the more 'pessimistic' attitude of problem-management as concepts of irreconcilable/essentialist difference and enmity gained credence in the era of social Darwinism and 'scientific racism'. It is probably the impact of imperialism, with its shifting combination of universalism (which points towards convergence) and racism (which is a species of essentialism) that led to the alliance of resistance between relativists and constructivists, but the alliance is politically contingent and conceptually problematic.

The fact that constructing oneself, i.e. changing oneself, can involve cross-cultural judgements about desirability, in the sense of what to assimilate, and undesirability, in the sense of what to define oneself against, is evidence that cross-cultural judgement is not a *meaningless* activity in political or existential terms. Moral relativism need not imply the conceptual meaninglessness or non-sensicality of such judgements either—and as previously noted, relativists who contend that such judgements are *morally* right or wrong undermine their own relativism. All that the moral relativist necessarily contends, and here we are really discussing the meta-ethical moral relativist, is that there is no ground, rational or otherwise, on which to prioritize any value judgement as having some kind of universal, transcultural authority. The thrust is that one cannot force by reason relevantly different others into accepting one's standards of judgement. If correct, that position is only a problem in theory for those who seek to create or believe themselves already to be in possession of a moral theory to which everyone *should* subscribe in virtue of its persuasive force. The relativist could not gainsay the empirical point that moral argument across (say) cultural borders *can* change views. Nor need the relativist consider it pointless or irrational to make cross-cultural judgements if they fail to persuade members of the group whose practice is under criticism. This is an important point because to take a contrary view would be another instance of labouring under the influence of a religiously inflected monadic paradigm of conscience, where the individual interior is the ultimate locus of interpretation and the decisive factor is whether or not the

---

[315] O'Hanlon and Washbrook, 'After Orientalism', 210–11; see also Nicolas Argenti and Deborah Durham, 'Youth', in John Parker and Richard Reid (eds), *The Oxford Handbook of Modern African History* (Oxford: Oxford University Press, 2013), 396–413, here 398–9, 401–2.

[316] Niall Ó'Ciosáin, 'The Poor Inquiry and Irish Society—A Consensus Theory of Truth', *Transactions of the Royal Historical Society* 20 (2010), 127–39, here 132–3.

individual offers up a 'free confession'. At the level of the cultural interior the mind goes back to Burckhardt's conviction that however poorly the peoples of Europe treated each other, they could 'happily not judge one another';[317] of course they could judge each other, and frequently did, but Burckhardt's mistaken belief was that this judgement had no meaning given that cultures were answerable only to what Emerson called the within and the above.

Beyond conceptually legitimating moral judgement in the relevant cases one needs to establish the particular character or focus of that judgement. Moral theory revolves around two fundamental questions. The questions are: 'what is good/ right?', which is a matter of *value*, and 'what ought one do?', which is a matter of *obligation*.[318] In the terms of moral judgement we say of the convicted criminal that what he did was bad/wrong, which we can call the *evaluative* element, and that he ought not have done it, which we can call the *normative* element. (Different scholars would give different names to these two elements in judgement, and of course different accounts exist of the relation between value and obligation in moral theory.)[319] Whatever additional purposes the distinction between the evaluative and normative elements has served in moral inquiry, it merits a particular emphasis when we are thinking about judgment across the boundaries of different value systems. As opposed to the case of the convicted criminal in 'our' society, it would be odd to tell actors in another society that they should have acted differently when they behaved in ways that were morally justified by their lights. The normative element, in the sense defined above, does not then apply. But the evaluative element may still apply as regards the lights according to which those actors acted given, say, the implications of the mandated practice for other people within or beyond that society.[320] If this distinction holds for the person looking at the diverse world around herself, it has at least as much weight for the

---

[317] Burckhardt, *Civilization*, 271.

[318] Bayles (ed.), *Contemporary Utilitarianism*, 2.

[319] Ralph Wedgwood provides the evaluative-normative duo used above, while Christine Tappolet refers to evaluative and deontic elements respectively. See Wedgwood, 'The "Good" and the "Right" Revisited', *Philosophical Perspectives* 23 (2009), 499–519, here 499; Tappolet, 'La Normativité des concepts évaluatifs', *Philosophiques* 38/1 (2011), 157–76.

[320] This position seems consistent with Gilbert Harman's distinction between 'using the word "wrong" to say that a particular situation or action is wrong from using the word to say that it is wrong of someone to do something. In the former case, the word "wrong" is used to assess an act or situation. In the latter case it is used to describe a relation between an agent and an act.' That distinction is an expression of Harman's distinction between 'inner judgements' and other judgements. He wrote: 'My relativism is a thesis only about what I will call "inner judgments," such as the judgment that someone ought or ought not to have acted in a certain way or the judgment that it was right or wrong of him to have done so. My relativism is not meant to apply, for example, to the judgment that . . . a given institution is unjust.' Harman's conception of 'inner judgement' here, which could actually be accommodated within what this book earlier called moral contextualism, is related to the 'motivational internalism' and 'judgement internalism' strands of ethical theory mentioned in this Part's Introduction (p. 127, n. 1). As noted, these sorts of internalism are related to the monadic internalism with which the main text has been so preoccupied. For the relevant quotes, see Harman, 'Moral Relativism Defended', in Russ Shafer-Landau, *Ethical Theory: An Anthology* (Chichester: Wiley-Blackweel, 2013), 35–43, here 37, 36.

historian who is sensitive to the moral content of the past but appreciates the fatuity of issuing oughts and ought-nots to the dead. In other respects, distinctions are more apparent than real between judgements on things past and things present.

The philosopher Bernard Williams, influential at many points in this book, would not agree with the latter claim, and this section closes by countering his argument as to the *relativism of distance*. The first step in Williams's argument is consistent with arguments above about the practical irrelevance of relativism in real-life, say cross-cultural, encounters. Williams observes that at the moment of contact it is already 'too late' for relativism to be relevant, because on contact there is no separate 'us' and 'them', but rather 'a new "we" to be negotiated'.[321] Precisely because of the encounter it is impossible to sit back and think abstractly about cultural difference, because the relationship has to be continually negotiated, whether to find some common ground or to fight it out in some more or less literal fashion. The present work concurs with this argument, though it departs from Williams's further argument as it contrasted the interactive attitudes that we must adopt towards 'others' who we encounter in the present with the attitude which we can adopt towards past times or far-off others with whom we have nothing more than notional contact. The contrast does not relevantly work, even if one cannot engage in an argument with people in the past.

As against Williams's 'relativism of difference' argument, even in the event of clear water between 'them' and 'us', what seems from a distance like a homogeneous 'them' might fragment under the sort of scrutiny that the historian brings to their affairs. Depending on their social set-up and our knowledge of its ramifications, we may not be able to talk of 'their values' in the collective singular, and the character of social relations might stimulate the evaluative faculties. A hypothetical example illustrates.

Say that in reading some historical evidence I discover a practice that seems to bring happiness or suffering to some member(s) of the past foreign society in question. My immediate reaction on encountering the practice is to think how favourably or unfavourably that compares with some approximately equivalent practice to which I am accustomed, or just to think how pleasant or unpleasant the practice seems, period. Does the relevant relativist (or for that matter the nonrelativist advocate of blanket tolerance) tell me that I cannot have that initial, let us call it 'gut', reaction? If so, then he is whistling in the wind. As well as the matter of the impossibility of my controlling my gut reaction, the question of desirability comes in to play here. First and foremost, in encountering this practice I am recognizing that something is being brought to bear on one or more entities who are humans as well as being members of such-and-such a group. With that

---

[321] Bernard Williams, *In the Beginning Was the Deed*, 68–9. For an extension of the argument, see his *Ethics and the Limits of Philosophy* (London: Routledge, 2006), ch. 9.

recognition come a host of assumptions about significantly shared cognitive capacity, shared capacity to experience pain, humiliation, joy, pride, love, shared capacity to act and to perceive others to have acted well, poorly, justly, unjustly, whatever the local standards of good and bad may be. The baseline parameter whereby one assumes some shared humanness, in which 'the human' is not just an empty, formal category, is presumably also subscribed to by most relativists. This is what was meant at the outset of this book by the claim that relativism is, generally speaking, an anthropocentric conception. If any given relativist does not subscribe to that parameter, they need to clarify what their parameter is, because relativism without a parameter to which things are relative does not make sense.

Perhaps, instead of protesting against the 'gut' reaction, the relativist tells me that I cannot progress from that reaction to any further cognitive processing that might result in a reasoned value judgement, whether less or more favourable? If so, then even if such a dictum can really be followed in practice, it cannot remove my initial reaction, so my visceral impression will remain the same, and will merely be unadulterated by any reflection. This is a shame: the relativist will actually hinder any understanding of the other society, as that understanding might be furthered by contextualized comprehension of the practice—comprehension of its social function, of the theories underlying it, of the attitudes to it of various practitioners, including the issue of how far those attitudes vary along power cleavages, and so forth. Any prospect of sympathetic or admiring understanding is thereby excluded alongside condign judgmentalism.

Perhaps the relativist permits the cognitive process up to but excluding any evaluation that I might make about the practice. Can such a dictum really be followed? Possibly, insofar as it is true that, while understanding and evaluation are not opposed—the former should aid the latter—they are not the same thing. Yet actually no, insofar as the drive to understand in this scenario was provided precisely by the desire to progress beyond the initial judgemental reaction. Even without some formal conclusion to top off the whole business of reflection, it will be impossible to ignore the way in which the greater understanding negated, reinforced, or diluted my initial reflex-appraisal. Evaluation is already upon me whether its result is positive, negative, or neutral. The only question at this stage is whether the evaluation will be informed or uninformed, reflective or unreflective. Then the question comes as to how I should present the matter to my audience, which returns us to the considerations raised in Part 2 of this book.

Past and Present in Conversation

Relational thought does not just lift conceptual silos surrounding discrete individuals or groups in the past; it also removes some of the sharper divisions between past and present. In closing this Part of the book, with a mind to Part 4, let us return to Williams's concept of the relativism of distance. Another problem with that argument is that it can elide different meanings of 'distance' between past and present. To be sure, there will be temporal distance, but that is not the only sort of distance in question. Williams's formula does not make sufficient allowance for the proximity or even contiguity of past and present in at least a significant subset of historical inquiries.

Williams understandably seems to consider causality or its absence only in so far as it flows from 'us', here and now, to 'them', whether past or elsewhere in the present. The causal relationship of us to them has indeed been the main issue at stake in the debates over Western foreign policy, where relativism relates to questions of intervention, i.e. what it is legitimate for 'us' to do to 'them'. Such dilemmas of *self*-justification include when and whom it is legitimate for us to arm/bomb/sanction/economically-penetrate/rule. The question of reciprocity is rarely raised, namely when it is legitimate for 'them' to tell 'us' that our behaviour is unacceptable, and to take remedial action. This is generally not a practical concern these days, given extant power relations; one reason terrorism has become a preoccupation of the world's most powerful states is that it is one of the few effective weapons that otherwise weak people can use. However, there can be influence from 'them' in the past to 'us' in the present, in the form of all sorts of material bequests and identity legacies mediated inter alia by historians. The next part of the book addresses these past–present relationships.

PART 4

HISTORY, IDENTITY, AND THE PRESENT

Introduction

This, the final Part of the book, considers the role of historical consciousness in the shaping of social and political identity. It is critical of prejudicial, upper-case 'Identity History', while calling upon historians to embrace their roles in historical arguments that pertain to identity. The balancing act is difficult. One needs to distinguish between ways of participating in these identity arguments. It helps the process of elucidation to address inconsistencies in the way some historians navigate connections and disconnections with the past.

Distinguishing between the practices of different scholars within the discipline of History also means refuting some of the general characterizations of historians and their craft that are in circulation. These critical depictions may apply to certain works of History but not all. Consequently, as shown in the first section, such 'solutions' as are prescribed for the discipline by critical theorists are often remedies for problems that do not exist at the relevant level. That first section clarifies what falls outside the definition of pejorative Identity History, noting that a great deal of excellent historical scholarship pertains to identity and even serves identity goals without being prejudicial in the way Identity History is.

The second section highlights where historians working on identity matters are likely to fall into conceptual difficulty. The relationship between past and present is complex indeed and raises the question of how distant our ancestors are from us when we depart from purely temporal senses of 'distance'. Is the relationship between 'them' and 'us' a matter of identity or difference or a bit of both? The answer has significant ramifications for how 'we' relate to 'their' behaviour. Identity History is inconsistent in this area, with different attitudes taken depending on whether that past behaviour was good or bad by present lights. In the confrontation with what can be argued to be historical injustices, when the knee-jerk response is not that 'our' past should be left to 'us' to investigate, which is a species of ethnocentrism, it tends to be that the past should be left in the past, which is only ever a selectively implemented doctrine that finds its greatest employment among those whose constituencies have most benefited from the past in question.

There are consequences for the historian's engagement with past rights and wrongs, harms and benefits, because claims on these matters constitute stakes in the identity game whose winner gets to decide what is desirable in the here and now. The third section develops such themes and distinguishes between more and less appropriate idioms for characterizing the relationship between contemporary polities and social groups on one hand and the deeds of relevant 'forebears' on the other hand. It is a mistake to talk of contemporary guilt, or for that matter virtue, in light of what one's predecessors did, but the language of shame or pride may be perfectly appropriate, and both pride and shame can influence one's orientation in the present, as Part 3 of this book was at pains to illustrate.

The fourth section addresses the material legacies of past action. It considers compensation, repatriation, and redistribution as significant political and moral issues in their own right. That discussion also gives an obviously practical focus to what can be abstract discussions about the legacy of the past as a bone of contention in the present. To the broader matter the concluding section returns.

Influential Misunderstandings

For most of its history, albeit with many exceptions, the occidental discipline of History focused upon elites, the big battalions, wars and other matters of State and Church, and national development. One reason is that History was often written by members of elites for other members of elites.

An extensive and concerted challenge to these tendencies was the twentieth-century proliferation of social History, broadly defined, as it grew from seeds planted in earlier centuries. The rise of social History can be attributed to the rise of new social movements from the nineteenth century, the general spread of literacy, then the broadening of participation in higher education. In its own way the new cultural History of the final decades of the century further diversified historical focus, while the recent trend towards global and world History has expanded it yet further. The common factor in all of these 'turns' is a shift away from elite actors to broader forces and to the conditions, movements, and experience of life of the many within and then beyond the global North-West.

Changes in historical focus have often been justified in ways in which the political and the moral elements are intertwined. The Australian historian Greg Dening talked of studying those 'on whom the forces of the world press most hardly'.[1] Dening's principle inheres in the very name of the intellectual project

---

[1] Denning, cited in Klaus Neumann, 'History, Memory, Justice', in Prasenjit Duara, Viren Murthy, and Andrew Sartori (eds), *A Companion to Global Historical Thought* (Oxford: Blackwell, 2014), 466–81, here 470.

and publication series *Subaltern Studies*, while the popularity of 'History from Below' showed the appetite for such a refocusing. Rendering 'ordinary' people into more than abstractions also dignifies them with the recognition that they were not just grist to the mills of greater forces. History is in principle the record of all human experiences and experiments, however much erasure of the traces of the marginalized limits History's practice, and however much some historians of power equate invisible with irrelevant. The importance of such projects as women's History is intrinsic but also instrumental, in the sense of being counter-pre-emptive. Women's History, or the History of African Americans that buttressed the civil rights movement, or the History of the working classes, and, more recently, of people with different sexual orientations, and so much more besides, seeks to disturb established presuppositions about what merits study, drawing attention to what have too often been caricatures, or silences. Social Histories bore implicit or explicit critiques of the prevailing dispensations at the time of their writing, since even if important social conditions had changed over the centuries, patriarchal, racist, and economic inequality had proved capable of reproducing itself by adaptation. Such History not infrequently implied a critique of the social arrangements of past worlds too, as most obviously when E. P. Thompson invoked an imperative to 'take sides' with one or other historical party.[2]

If some of these Histories were politically forthright, or romanticizing, this was not without reason.[3] Sometimes their authors felt more obligation to those groups than to the national professions—not to mention states—that had marginalized them. While establishments might charge these new Histories with politicization, we need to consider what this 'politicized History' was implicitly being contrasted with, and to disavow any presupposition that more established sorts of History were somehow more objective or apolitical, or unromanticized, or that their sole concern was 'the past for its own sake'. Social History was given impetus by the desire to challenge the way in which many earlier high political and constitutional historians forged coherent national stories out of the record of heterogeneous and sometimes antagonistic social forces or just ignored such forces and focused on national figureheads, and durable institutions. Indeed we can chart a moderately strong correlation between the disavowal of overt moral judgement in a profes-sionalizing nineteenth-century historiography and the desire for domestic unity in the face of other states, as well, sometimes, as the desire for interstate harmony in the face of international tensions: moral judgement, like focus on social disunity, might be politically divisive.[4]

Any charge of politicization can elide distinctions between History written for political reasons, History with political ramifications, History in which

---

[2] Thompson, *The Making*, 226.
[3] See Barbara Ehrenreich and Deirdre English's reflective introduction to the 2nd edn of their *Witches, Midwives and Nurses* (New York: Feminist Press, 2010).
[4] Bloxham, *Why History? A History*, ch. 6.

uncomfortable or thesis-challenging evidence is omitted for political ends, and History whose content is manipulated by parts of its audience for political reasons. There is no necessary contradiction between faithfulness to procedure and political engagement. It is a fallacy to think that the commitment to truthfulness and rigour in the drawing of inferences from evidence must be undermined if the historian writes with additional motives. One cannot judge the validity of people's intellectual claims by their motives for making them. A criticism of some narrative of the 'rise of X' or 'the benevolence of Y' could at once be politically motivated and more plausible—better substantiated—than the narrative under criticism. Now consider the historian who wishes to write the History of group X 'back into the historical record' out of some sense of injustice, or fidelity to group X in the present. Obviously the writing 'back' can be done in better and worse ways in the procedural sense but if one has evidentiary warrant to infer that group X has been the subject of an enduring cultural stereotype, or suffered historically, or made some contribution hitherto ignored in the historiography, then undermining the stereotype or recording the suffering or contribution can serve such political motives as the historian may have while honouring the precepts of robust investigative procedure.

Whatever your author's sympathies with so many of these Histories, whatever his gratitude that they exist and belief that we need many more of them, there nonetheless should not be a rule about what or who any given historian chooses to study. A general principle of historianship such as the one this book explores cannot be tied to specific objects of historical inquiry—high politics versus everyday affairs, men versus women, dominators versus subalterns. Besides, if the emphasis is on relative power rather than elites per se, a change of focus to 'newer' objects of historical inquiry does not automatically solve the problems perceived as inherent in elite History. However widely 'great man' History has been lampooned, the concept of a 'great man', or great woman, is always relative to the scale of the historical drama under scrutiny.[5]

Historians of causation have good reason to focus on the powerful irrespective of sympathies, antipathies, or moral indifference towards them, because the powerful are disproportionately influential in bringing about change or, what is just as significant and contrived, ensuring reproduction in conditions. For the same reason of causal efficacy, it is a mistake to equate all work on the powerful with elitism in the pejorative sense meant by references to the 'great man school of History'. After all, part of women's History has been to show the causal role of women too—the chief consideration for the causal historian is causal significance, thus relative power, and as soon as, say, the relevant women are shown to be causally effective they must become part of the causal account too, or it is deficient

---

[5] Plekhanov, *The Role of the Individual*, 62.

causal History. Elitism in the pejorative sense only comes into the picture if the historian of the texture of life focuses on the relatively powerful as somehow especially important as manifestations of that texture—as if what the king felt about his realm, separately to anything he did about that perception, was more important in telling us about life in that country than what any given peasant thought.

In order to clear the ground to focus on the implications of the position about *how* historians discuss bits of the past rather than *what* bits they discuss, it is necessary to address five clusters of well-meaning but flawed arguments to the contrary. We may approach the first cluster of arguments by way of psychoanalyst Shoshana Felman's claim that 'history by definition silences the victim, the reality of degradation and of suffering—the very facts of victimhood and abuse—are intrinsically inaccessible to history'.[6] She does not tell us who penned this peculiar definition, but it is probably drawn from the philosopher Emmanuel Levinas or the cultural critic Walter Benjamin.[7] The literary theorist Robert Eaglestone draws on Levinas to make a similar point.[8] Amongst other things, Levinas wrote that

The judgment of history is set forth in the visible. Historical events are the visible par excellence; their truth is produced in evidence. The visible forms, or tends to form, a totality...The invisible must manifest itself if history is to lose its right to the last word, necessarily unjust for the subjectivity, inevitably cruel....The invisible is the offense that inevitably results from the judgment of visible history, even if history unfolds rationally. The virile judgment of history, the virile judgment of 'pure reason', is cruel. The universal norms of this judgment silence the unicity in which the apology is contained and from which it draws its arguments.

But however Levinas has been interpreted, his main target was Hegelian speculative philosophy of history, with its *Aufhebung*, its onward march of spirit, its supra-historical progress, and so forth. Whatever else Levinas was doing, he was scarcely engaging with the artisanal practice of all the historians in universities of his time or subsequently.[9] Benjamin's thought too was oriented to 'progressive' philosophies of the 'historical process'.

---

[6] Shoshana Felman, 'Theaters of Justice: Arendt in Jerusalem, the Eichmann Trial, and the Redefinition of Legal Meaning in the Wake of the Holocaust', *Critical Inquiry* 27/2 (2001), 201–38, here 229.

[7] Walther Benjamin, *Illuminations*, ed. Hannah Arendt (New York: Shocken, 1968), 253–64, esp. 256. Levinas, *Totality and Infinity*, 241–3.

[8] Robert Eaglestone, *The Holocaust and the Postmodern* (Oxford: Oxford University Press, 2004), 157.

[9] Quote from Levinas, *Totality and Infinity*, 243. Dennis Beach writes that 'For Levinas, "history" is almost always Hegelian history': Beach, 'History and the Other: Dussel's Challenge to Levinas', *Philosophy and Social Criticism*, 30/3 (2004), 315–30, here 318. Indeed in reference precisely to the reproduced passage that Eaglestone also cites from Levinas about the 'judgment of history', Leslie MacAvoy notes: 'In *Totality and Infinity* Levinas writes disparagingly of history, particularly what he calls the judgment of history, which he consistently associates with totality. It is clear that he has

The second flawed strand of argument can be a secularized derivative of the first, or a homespun wisdom. It is that History is always written by the victors, the powerful, the winners, and therefore amongst others the killers. The problem with the victors' claim is that even in the unlikely event no one in the victors' camp is capable of self-criticism, victors themselves get defeated over time and new ones arrive. The arrivistes need not have the same reservations as their predecessors about criticizing those predecessors' activities. Germany illustrates the point as well as any state, as it has developed a culture of contrition, memorialization, and historical scholarship about the once-dominant 'Third Reich'.

The third strand of argumentation can draw on either of the first two. The claim here is that 'to focus on a dominant process is *necessarily* to celebrate its outcome'.[10] On some accounts, such celebration may have implications of backing the winner in some meta-historical development, or it may just be a way of focusing on historically dominant elements in order to entrench a certain idea of History and vindicate the position of such dominant elements in the process. A variation on the claim that writing about a historical force somehow celebrates that force is the claim that writing about the force actually reinforces it. This is the fourth strand of arguments, and the sort of thing to which the historian of Africa and imperialism Frederick Cooper alluded when talking about the difficulty of studying imperial rule during his graduate years (1969–74): 'studying precolonial history or resistance constituted genuine African history, but bringing a similar specificity of inquiry to that which was being resisted risked having one's project labeled as a throwback to imperial history'.[11]

The postcolonial theorist Gyan Prakash threw out an accusation analogous to the one Cooper feared when he wrote that historical research necessarily 'functions to universalize capitalism and the nation-state', without ever illustrating why this was so.[12] Prakash raised 'the narrativization of Indian history in terms of the development of capitalism' and asked: 'How is it possible to write such a narrative, but also contest, at the same time, the homogenization of the contemporary world

Hegel's teleological conception of history in mind' Leslie MacAvoy, 'Levinas and the Possibility of History', *Philosophy Today* 49/5 (2005) (suppl.), 68–73, here 68. See also on mistaken identity Levinas, *Totality and Infinity*, 247: 'What is above all invisible is the offense *universal* history inflicts on particulars'; 'the visible judgment of history which seduces the *philosopher*'. Emphases added.

[10] David D. Roberts, *Nothing But History: Reconstruction and Extremity After Metaphysics* (Berkeley and Los Angeles: University of California Press, 1995), 287, emphasis in Roberts. Roberts criticizes the sort of claim in question, and he has in mind Joan Scott's position in her dispute with the conservative historian Gertrude Himmelfarb that culminated in the article Joan Scott, 'History in Crisis? The Others' Side of the Story', *American Historical Review* 94/3 (1989), 680–92. See more generally Roberts's discussion at pp. 262–5, 280–90.

[11] Frederick Cooper, 'Conflict and Connection: Rethinking Colonial African History', *American Historical Review* 99/5 (1994), 1516–45, here 1522.

[12] Gyan Prakesh, 'Subaltern Studies as Postcolonial Criticism', *American Historical Review* 99/5 (1994), 1475–90, here 1489.

by capitalism?'[13] Unless this question is set up to be construed in a circular fashion, the answer is: easily enough, if one writes critically about capitalism.

There is only a problem here if one is labouring under a sort of discursive idealism whereby even criticism of something buttresses its reality by dint of invoking it. To be sure, that is a real concern in issues of, say, ascribed gender roles, where the repeated use of 'man' or 'woman' in certain connections reinforces a perception about 'naturalness' or propriety in relation to such-and-such a capacity and activity. But that case is not analogous to the one in hand, because Prakash claims to identify something true about capitalism (its homogenizing tendency) while seeking to combat that thing. Contesting something presupposes some knowledge of it, and knowledge of the sort in question can only be acquired and transmitted discursively, so Prakash is in a dilemma.[14]

Prakash's confusion is of the same sort as when terms like 'Eurocentrism' or 'Western-centrism' are bandied about without due regard for what the work in question is actually saying about Europe or the West, and what the author's stated or inferable attitudes are to non-Europeans or non-Westerners. The broad selection of people to whom Eurocentrism might be and indeed has been applied

> includes racists who insist on the natural superiority of Europeans over Asians, Africans, and indigenous Americans; cultural chauvinists who think that, for whatever reason, 'the West' has achieved a higher level of cultural development and 'rationality' that has given it an advantage in every other respect; environmental determinists who believe that Europe has some distinct ecological advantages; non-racist historians who neglect or underestimate the role of Western imperialism in European history; and [those], who are neither racists, nor cultural chauvinists, nor ecological determinists, nor inclined to underestimate the evils of imperialism, but who believe that certain specific historical conditions in Europe, which have nothing to do with European superiority, produced certain specific historical consequences—such as the rise of capitalism.[15]

The quoted words are Ellen Meiksins Wood's and it is to be hoped that the foregoing historical critiques, and indeed this whole book, fall into her final category:

---

[13] Gyan Prakash, 'Writing Post-Orientalist Histories of the Third World', in Vinayak Chaturvedi (ed.), *Mapping Subaltern Studies and the Postcolonial* (London: Verso, 2012), 163–90, here 177.

[14] As Rosalind O'Hanlon and David Washbrook point out in their 'After Orientalism: Culture, Criticism and Politics in the Third World', in Chaturvedi (ed.), *Mapping Subaltern Studies*, 191–219.

[15] Ellen Meiksins Wood, *The Origin of Capitalism: A Longer View* (London: Verso, 2002), 27–8; Wood, 'Eurocentric Anti-Eurocentrism', *Against the Current* 92 (May/June 2001), 29–35. Note that in Wood's original text the word 'Marxists' appears where I have used the parenthesized 'those'. This is not because I wish to hide the role of Marxists in the sort of project with which Wood is sympathetic—quite the opposite. It is just that excerpted from the context of the book and article cited above, with its specific focus on Marxism and theories of capitalism, the quote might give the impression that only Marxists opposed Eurocentrism in this way, or that no Marxist had ever been Eurocentric, both of which are wrong.

this study is Occident-focused through and through because it is concerned with some influential, and in important ways faulty, occidental ways of seeing things. The basic point as applied to historiography is that there is no such thing as a conservative, or authoritarian, or radical (or whatever) choice of historical topic, only a conservative, or authoritarian, or radical (or whatever) way of dealing with that topic.

The fifth relevant strand of arguments contested here derives from the idea that 'the archive' binds the historian to the perspective of those who produced the records in it. Unlike the first three strands, the historian is not a dictator to the historical record and her contemporary world, nor an executor of some grand philosophy of History. Rather, she is helpless in the face of what 'the documents' tell her to think and who to sympathize with. It is true, for instance, that in the historiography of the Highland Clearances of the nineteenth century, those who have used the estate records of the evictor-landlords have sometimes clashed with those working from the testimonies of the evictees. The mind also goes back to Ulrich Bonnell Phillips 1918 account *American Negro Slavery* which infamously replicated American slave-owners' view of themselves as paternalistic, the slaves as content—a view that survived in some form through some major academic works of the 1950s.[16] But the implicit equation must be resisted that the use of a certain set of sources *necessarily* makes the historian identify with the people whose sources they were, since that would lead us to the curious conclusion that Roberts Conquest and Service are morally sympathetic to Stalin or Ian Kershaw taken in by his biographical subject Hitler.

Many of these stances and others like them have been adopted in recent years in the historiography of the Holocaust, especially as regards which elements of the genocide different historians focus on. Historian Omer Bartov asserts, without substantiation, that 'Writing the history of genocide only from the perspective of the killers, whatever one's intentions, leads to writing a history of atrocity lacking a human face, thereby becoming complicit in the depersonalization, not to say dehumanization of the victims sought by the perpetrators'.[17] Note that writing *about* the killers becomes in this understanding writing '*from the perspective* of the killers'. Historian Alexandra Garbarini writes, with another historian's remarks about the importance of studying perpetrators in mind, that

> Perhaps genocide prevention and activism could be equally well served by people considering deeply, and empathizing with, the historical experiences of genocide victims *as well as* perpetrators. Activism does not necessarily follow

---

[16] Ulrich Bonnell Phillips, *American Negro Slavery* (New York: Appleton and Company, 1918); Davis, 'Reflections', 157.

[17] Bartov in 'Review Forum: Donald Bloxham, *The Final Solution: A Genocide*', *Journal of Genocide Research* 13/1–2 (2011), 107–52, here 128.

from people getting in touch with their own ability to violate others' human rights. It may just as much follow from people understanding those whose rights have been violated.[18]

Consider the phraseology. In one case it is a matter of scholars *understanding those who have been violated*. In the other it is scholars *accessing their own ability to violate*. This is much the same as implying that an interest in the causes of crime makes the criminologist herself an aspiring criminal. Historian Doris Bergen pronounces that the 'biggest challenge'—not one of many big challenges but the biggest challenge—'facing scholars of the Holocaust and of every case of extreme violence is how to develop methods to talk about the people on the receiving end of persecution and abuse'. She also implies that only the historian who examines victim experiences can be said to evince 'understanding'.[19] Like Bartov, Bergen provides no philosophical justification of her position, and she does not tell her readers what she understands by 'understanding'. Nonetheless she has assigned herself the role of awarding praise or criticism to works of Holocaust History depending on the extent to which they address victim experiences.[20]

A peculiar logic is in play when historians are told what to study by Bergen as she adopts a quantitative approach, as if dedicating x number of pages to matter a incurs a moral responsibility to devote x number of pages to matter b, which would mean only giving half of the attention one felt merited to matter a or writing a book twice as long.[21] Ultimately the quantitative attitude gives the game away in its implication that there is a sort of accounting balance to be struck—as if the moral negative of focusing on perpetration had to be countered by the moral positive of focusing on victims. Certainly Bergen's school of thought would see that it might be *intellectually* complementary to focus on both perpetration and victims, and depending on precise line of inquiry that is surely right. But in *moral* terms the assumption is of antagonism between the two lines of inquiry, which is incorrect. There is no reason why focusing on perpetration cannot be complementary in moral terms to the important task of examining victims'

---

[18] Alexandra Garbarini, 'Reflections on the Holocaust and Jewish History', *Jewish Quarterly Review* 102/1 (2012), 81–90, here 90.

[19] Bergen, in 'Review Forum: Donald Bloxham, *The Final Solution: A Genocide*', 134.

[20] As opposed to her criticisms locatable via n. 19, see Bergen's positive review of Garbarini's *Numbered Days: Diaries and the Holocaust* (New Haven: Yale University Press, 2006) in *Central European History* 42/2 (2009), 364–6. Note that Bergen is also inconsistent in her reasoning. In reviewing Garbarini's *Numbered Days* she linked it explicitly to Saul Friedlander's 'integrated history' which weaves together accounts of perpetration and victims' experiences, even though, as Garbarini's title suggests, her book is about victims and their accounts, not perpetrators or perpetration. In this review the relevant connotations of 'integrated' are not about incorporating different angles of inquiry at all; they amount to the study and use of personal victim accounts and what Bergen asserts, without defining, as 'profound and critical empathy'. 'Empathy' and its connotations will be considered below.

[21] For Bergen's remarks on book size and representative proportions, 'Review Forum: Donald Bloxham, *The Final Solution: A Genocide*', 134.

experiences, just as there is no reason focusing on the mechanisms of empire cannot be morally complementary to studying the victims of exploitation.

The matter hinges on the quality of evidence to some degree, a little more on skill in interrogating evidence, and most of all on purposes in so doing. The only point at which the operations of the historian of Hitler, Himmler, or the lowliest Ukrainian auxiliary policeman become problematic in moral terms is when these historians move from explanation/understanding to justification or obfuscation of what they brought about. Justification, or at least a tortuous mitigation, was the problem with Ernst Nolte's *The European Civil War* (see p. 108). The historian Michael M. Gunther opened his *Armenian History and the Question of Genocide* claiming to provide 'an objective analysis of the Turkish point of view', which is at once disarmingly frank and raises the question of what it is that he meant to be objective towards—the official Turkish view is the one he broadly adopts over the coming pages, so he could be said to have reproduced that 'objectively'. (One suspects that this is not what he meant.)[22] Clearly not all historical accounts legitimate in this way, though, because explanation and justification are not necessarily the same things, though Holocaust historian Saul Friedlander, who is probably the inspiration behind Bergen's and Bartov's assertions, does sometimes conflate them. He wrote that 'no one of sound mind would wish to interpret the events from Hitler's viewpoint'.[23] Here Friedlander depicts 'interpretation' in just the problematic way that Gustave le Bon defined proper understanding (p. 105). However 'interpretation' could alternatively pertain to an explanation in which the historian recognizes that Hitler was a virulent anti-Semite and shows how that world-view affected Hitler's actions, but in which the historian does not take on that world-view. The evidence for the viability of the latter interpretation of 'interpretation' is widespread in the historiography of the Holocaust.

If one wishes to clear up these conceptual misunderstandings then conceptual precision is all important, especially as regards that protean term 'empathy', which has been hovering around this whole conversation and is weaponized by Bergen alongside 'understanding'.[24] Conceptual precision is not aided by the fact that salient definitions have differed across time and between contemporaries. Kant, for instance, distinguished between *Mitleidenschaft* and *Teilnehmung*.[25] The former, meaning compassion or commiseration, was passive. The latter connoted a more active participation in others' feelings and experiences. The former coincides with at least one important definition of sympathy, while the latter coincides with at least one important conception of empathy, which is the focus here.

---

[22] Michael M. Gunther, *Armenian History and the Question of Genocide* (New York: Palgrave Macmillan, 2011), p. ix.

[23] Friedlander, 'The "Final Solution"', 32.   [24] See nn. 19 and 20.

[25] Anna Wehofsits, *Anthropologie und Moral: Affekte, Leidenschaften und Mitgefühl in Kants Ethik* (Berlin: De Gruyter, 2016), *passim*, esp. 140.

In much nineteenth-century thought, through R. G. Collingwood's version of it, empathy was considered a cognitive, not affective, matter. It was a way of thinking, a form of temporary perspective-understanding, not a way of feeling in the emotional sense. This changed, at least in common usage, at some point in the twentieth century, and empathy gained stronger affective connotations in much usage. But even working with the more recent popular affective conception of empathy, there is no need to read into empathy any of the warmth or solicitousness that we might imply by use of the word sympathy (in one of its common usages). The understanding-of-the-other that is the only necessary component of empathy—the only component without which the concept is incapable of performing the work of any definition of it—will be shown by the competent torturer or boxer just as much as the friend or therapist. In other words, if empathy does have an affective component, it has no inherent normatively 'positive' calibration.[26]

Once we have accepted that study of the powerful can be complementary rather than antipathetic to the concerns of those examining the experience of power's victims, we are actually back to a fairly standard ethics of historical practice, subject to the arguments of this book hitherto about factoring in 'external' moral evaluation in the characterization of acts. Precisely because historians need not identify with particular past actors when engaged in transmitting to their readers what they infer about those actors, the politics of the past need not be reproduced with the historian as witting or unwitting advocate for one side. Indeed we may need to take issue with those historians who do identify in this way in the event that their identification affects the moral contextualization of relevant historical actors and the characterization of their acts. So we come to examine how History that is relevant to identity, i.e. lower-case identity History, might metamorphose into a more problematic upper-case Identity History.

Relating to the Past

The influence of past on present comes in many forms, through many channels. There just are some ways in which the past shapes us that exist independently of what we say about it—say economic, legal, or environmental structures into which individuals or polities are born. This does not mean what we say about those structures cannot contribute to their alteration, which is important in subsequent sections. The present section focuses not on enduring material structures but on the sort of 'inheritance' that is more completely shaped by how it is

---

[26] I thank David Deutsch, whose speciality this is, for insights on empathy, including, if my memory is correct, the example of the torturer.

discussed, which is where historians—professional, amateur, official—and the heritage industry are key players.

The issues are especially challenging in identity History because of the tension between *historicity*, meaning the embeddedness of oneself in historically shaped contexts and by extension the relevance and conceptual proximity of the past, and *modern historical consciousness*, with its connotations of the past's separateness from the present. Some wordplay helps elucidate. 'Relative' roots two different things. 'Relativism' points to moral-cultural difference and accords with the neo-historicist orthodoxy of treating the historical actor as a distant 'other'. 'Relatives', or 'relations', points to proximity or similarity in some respects. The perception of some proximity or similarity, embedded in the sense of historicity, explains why so many Americans are interested in American History, so many French people in French History, etcetera. Herein lies the difference between many sorts of History and anthropology.

Despite the formal and logical similarities between understanding people in the context of their times and of their culture, History in the global North-West has had more difficulty with negotiating the ramifications of relativism/relationality than has anthropology in most of its historical variants. This is because with anthropologists (generally speaking), the consideration of temporal change comes 'after' the apprehension of cultural difference. Anthropologists generally locate physically and culturally distant 'others' in the present and may study 'their' past to shed further light on them, but the historical element of the examination has few ramifications for reflection on their 'otherness' from the perspective of any present-day interface between 'us' and 'them'. In other words, study of the pasts of 'others' does not close such anthropological gaps as have already been opened by distinguishing between their ways and our ways in the present. Conversely, the societies that have produced most paid historians have produced, in numbers disproportionate to the total, historians who study the History of their own society. For the French historian of France, the route may begin by charting 'otherness' in the past, but in the knowledge that at some point there may be a convergence between Their ways and Our ways, between Them and Us. In the title *A History of the English-Speaking Peoples* the temporal differentiation indicated by *History* is tempered by the identity of cultural-linguistic commonality. In *The Rise of the West*, historical movement ('rise') exists alongside referential stability ('West').

Histories with a major identity component tend to rely especially on *genealogy*, *analogy*, or *metonym*, though these are not always distinct and the genealogical element tends to run through each. Identity by genealogy is a question of connecting oneself to those whom one chooses as relevant forebears. An especially influential genealogical type is the 'national story', which is concerned with epochs, episodes, and people from a given nation's past.

National genealogy can help to establish that *Wir-Gefühl*, that sense of 'We-hood' or 'Us-ness' that was promoted by historians in early medieval Saxony, as by the monk Bede (*c*.673–735) in England or the Royal Frankish Annals whose production coincided with Charlemagne's founding of a grand public court.[27] Coleridge's *The Constitution of Church and State* invoked a national clerisy of schoolteachers tasked 'to preserve the stores, to guard the treasures, of past civilization, and thus to bind the present with the past; to perfect and add to the same, and thus to connect the present with the future.'[28] Coleridge bears out the conviction of one scholar of nationalism that if 'there is no memory, there is no identity; no identity, no nation.'[29] An issue for the nation-builder is that 'On the one hand, the nation is always coming into being but not yet fully itself, *hence the need for it to be educated about itself.* On the other, it has always already existed, is eternal, and its people are linked with one another in a linear fashion through history, hence the need for the nation's past to be vindicated.'[30]

Confronting the education issue was the historian and journalist Max Hastings (b. 1945), one of the most prominent pundits on historical issues in Britain's national press. He mused as follows on school curricula.

[The Labour Government's Qualifications and Curriculum Authority report of 2005] argues that schools 'undervalue the overall contribution of black and other minority ethnic peoples to Britain's past, and...ignore their cultural, scientific and many other achievements'... Yet how is it possible to do much of this in a British school without distorting the western experience, which anyone living here is signed up to? Pupils in modern African or Indian schools obviously focus their historical studies on the experience of subject races under foreign rule. But, as a profound sceptic about multiculturalism, I can't see the case for such an agenda, unless the vast majority of British people are to pretend to be something they are not....History is the story of the dominance, however unjust, of societies that display superior energy, ability, technology and might. If one's own people were victims of western imperialism, it is entirely understandable that one should wish to study history from their viewpoint. But, whatever the crimes of our forefathers, this is the country of Drake, Clive and Kitchener, not of Tipu Sultan, Shaka Zulu or the Mahdi....At the weekend, I glanced at some of my old school essays.... They were no more 'relevant' to middle-class white teenagers then than to schoolchildren of West Indian or Muslim origins

---

[27] Wolfgang Eggert and Barbara Pätzold, *Wir-Gefühl und Regnum Saxonum bei frühmittelalterlichen Geschichtsschreibern* (Cologne: Böhlau, 1984); Rosalind McKitterick, 'Constructing the Past in the Early Middle Ages', *Transactions of the Royal Historical Society*, 6th ser., 7 (1997), 101–29, here 115.

[28] Coleridge, *On the Constitution*, 43–4.

[29] Anthony D. Smith, 'Memory and Modernity: Reflections on Ernest Gellner's Theory of Nationalism', *Nations and Nationalism* 2/3 (1996), 371–88, here 383.

[30] Richard Seymour, 'The British Have Invaded 90% of the World's Countries: Ha ha?', *The Guardian*, 6 November 2012. Emphases added.

now. We addressed them, first, because education is properly about learning to think, and objectively to assess evidence; second, so that we knew something about a broad sweep of the history of the society to which, whether by birth or migration, we belonged. We were developing a sense of British cultural identity, which no amount of social engineering can honestly relocate far from Crecy and Waterloo, Pepys and Newton[31]

Oddly, Hastings distinguishes his recommendations from 'social engineering', which he associates with 'multiculturalism'. He dislikes multiculturalism, but since a certain level of multiculturalism is the current state of affairs, he must mean to endorse altering the fact of diversity by policy. It is hard to see this as anything other than social engineering. His agenda is forging a We in the present by 'appropriate' historical instruction, which is a common form of History as national genealogy.

Identity by *analogy* operates along some of the same lines as the classical and medieval idea of History as moral instruction by examples. We might alternatively call it the 'contemporary relevance' strand. It primarily concerns identification with or against bygone *doing* in the form of discrete events or the actions of personages. For the significance of political analogies long after most academic historians decided that exemplarity was an outdated conceit, one need only consult Yuen Foong Khong's *Analogies at War: Korea, Munich, Dien Bien Phu, and the Vietnam Decisions of 1965.*[32] The most attractive analogies are substantive as well as logical. In a substantive analogy the comparison is not only effective in its reasoning across the case in question and the analogized case (which suffices to make a logical analogy), there is some plausible identity between the objects comprising the analogy and the situation to which the analogy is made. What constitutes a substantive analogy is in the eye of the beholder, as when the failure of appeasement in the 1930s was invoked to justify—amongst many actions at other times—the 2003 invasion of Iraq.[33] An alternative substantive analogy to the invasion was the story of earlier counter-productive and self-interested Western meddling in the Middle East.

Metonymy means using one thing to refer to something else associated with it or of which it is part. 'The guillotine' is a metonym for the French Revolution, not an analogy to or metaphor for it, because it is part of what we understand by the Revolution and represents the whole. Since the conceptualization of the whole varies among historians, it is not always easy to distinguish metonymical references from genealogical or analogical ones in Identity Histories. Episodes in the

---

[31] Hastings, 'This Is the Country of Drake and Pepys, Not Shaka Zulu', *The Guardian*, 27 December 2005.

[32] (Princeton: Princeton University Press, 1992).

[33] For many such examples of appeasement as a 'lesson of history', Sidney Aster, 'Appeasement: Before and After Revisionism', *Diplomacy and Statecraft* 19/3 (2008), 443–80.

past of 'Great Britain' can be used genealogically in the sense of that past being related developmentally to the British present, as one would think of a grandparent; they can be used analogically or metaphorically as points of alleged similarity that just happen to be from the history of Great Britain but could be part of any polity's history; or they can be used metonymically in the sense of establishing identity between past and present Great Britains, such that past episodes of British history stand for Britain today.

Adapting the terms of historian Charles Maier, we may dub as matters of 'hot memory' those specific bits of the past on which identity Historians are especially apt to alight, whether they deploy genealogy, analogy, or metonym.[34] Golden ages, bygone empires, and famous victories vie with defeats, servitude, and dark ages. Images or triumph and success need not win out—one may relate positively to failures. Vainglory is a resource, as shown by the use of Serbian memories of defeat by the Ottomans in 1389, or my adopted country's unofficial national anthem, 'Flower of Scotland'. Lachrymose uses of identity can be just as useful as positive images, as the competitive identity politics of victimhood in the contemporary USA shows. It might seem, intuitively, that the hottest memories are apt to concern the more recent past, as with, say, the idea of the Italians as the *brava gente* of the Second World War Axis alliance, France with its Vichy syndrome and *résistancialisme*, the Soviet Great Fatherland War, and so on. But not only are heat and proximity relative concepts, in some cases the very distance of the salient past is itself the point. To those Lebanese who still proudly call themselves Phoenicians, or those early medieval Franks or Anglo-Normans like Henry of Huntingdon who claimed lineage from the Trojans, the antiquity of the reference point is an important indicator of civilizational pedigree. In such cases, as with aristocrats tracing family trees, the more distant the relevant past, the better. In order to substantiate its self-congratulatory claims about the progressive evolution of English liberties, 'Whig' History required an assimilation of the ostensible disruption of the Norman Conquest into a yet longer island story. Judging by references to such things as the 'classical heritage', or Judaeo-Christian civilization, occidental identity goes deep and, with it comes a very long History of 'othering', selective borrowing, and selective acknowledgement of debt. Those Serbian nationalists who hark back to the 1389 defeat at Ottoman hands on the 'field of blackbirds' in Kosovo in substantiation of their claim to the province do not perceive the intervening years to have diminished the relevance of the historical episode. Such demands, and the counter-demands that may ensue, illustrate the general selectivity of the politics of History, but they also show why one does not need to be an historian of the modern to get an animated audience that extends well beyond the academy of vocational scholars.

---

[34] Charles Maier, 'Mémoire chaude, mémoire froide: Mémoire du fascisme, mémoire du communisme', *Le Débat* 122/5 (2002), 109–17.

When historians write on matters of hot memory, they are doing their most sensitive work. Different historians not only write for different audiences—the popular market, the profession in general, the *Annales* editorial board, the currently fashionable crowd in the American Historical Association—but they cater to differing degrees to what they might perceive those audiences want from them. The catering might take the form of style or jargon, and is often just a harmless form of window dressing, but we would scarcely have to tax ourselves to find examples where History is tailored altogether more in terms of content than which theorist or potential referee one finds it professionally expedient to cite. Whence and whither the identity thrust cannot be codified, but the inclinations, expectations, foreknowledge and forejudgement of present audience and social order can be powerful influences on the historian who is a member of one or more identity groups prior to and after becoming a historian of one of those identity groups. The result is not necessarily circular reinforcement of a given world-view: many 'self'-critical Histories exist even if they are not abundantly represented in cases like some of those recently mentioned.

Inconsistencies, moral and otherwise, can ensue as scholars advertently or inadvertently cross the line between identity-relevant History and prejudicial Identity History. Three examples from my island context illustrate. The historians in question have been chosen not because they are intellectually unusual but because they evince common contradictions and have a voice beyond the academy.

The first case is the aforementioned Geoffrey Alderman. He was the historian who argued in 2008 against posthumous pardons for 'witches' and 'deserters' (p. 116). What was 'then' considered ' "right" may now be considered very wrong', he found. Understanding of the past was to be separated from present concerns by the application of neo-historicist principles. Alderman's opinion was different when in 2010 he commented on the new Conservative government's proposal to rewrite the national school History curriculum in a spirit contradictory to that of the report of the Qualifications and Curriculum Authority under the previous Labour government—the report of which Max Hastings disapproved (p. 263). 'History', Alderman wrote, 'is the collective memory of society. It is that memory which informs society's attitude to itself and to the world around it.' That is why he disapproved of the teaching in schools of what he understood to be an 'essentially negative impression of British political and social development over the past 500 or so years'. Let us underline that Alderman was no longer objecting to the idea of positive or negative impressions of the past as anachronistic failures to observe the historicist principles that he urged in the contemplation of deserters and witch-trials. He merely wished for a more positive view of the past, as in his enthusiasm for the sort of History he had learned at school: 'Above all, perhaps, I was taught that imperialism had its virtues as well as its vices.'[35]

Other historians only need the space between one sentence and the next to shift from 'neutral' to partisan status. Our second case is the military historian Antony Beevor, who wrote:

> I would never argue that historians or history teachers have a moral role. Their main obligation is to understand the mentality of the time and to pass on that understanding: it is not to apply 21st-century values in retrospect. Nor should they simplify for moral effect. It is absolutely right to convey the horrors of the Atlantic slave trade, but the role of African leaders themselves in promoting slavery must also be explained. So must the fact that the eastern slave trade, mainly to the Arabian peninsula, was older and more lethal. Certainly it led to the death of more victims in peculiarly horrible circumstances.[36]

The only consistency of this passage lies in its defensiveness. In the first three sentences Beevor plays the neo-historicist, seeking only to comprehend the difference of foreign countries past. In the next three he is advocate for the defence, using evocative and evaluative language to stigmatize others more than the Atlantic slave-traders. Historians and history teachers should not have a moral role—except where they *must* remind their audience that others have done worse things than the British, and so should have more of any blame that is to be spread around.

We return to Max Hastings for the third case. We will bear in mind his recommendations for the teaching of History at school (pp. 263–4), which is a topic that binds together all three of these historians. In that manifesto he acknowledged in passing 'the crimes of our forefathers',[37] but it is unclear what he was prepared to do with such recognition. In one of his review essays, entitled 'High-handed moral condemnation' (somehow 'vindication' is never conceived as high-handed), he noted:

> All participants in all wars are in some degree morally compromised by the experience. [The philosopher Anthony] Grayling seems to have nothing more useful to tell us about the [Allied Second World War] bomber offensive than writers who inveigh against, say, the conduct of the British empire in the 18th century. We know that today we would do it all differently, but that is not the point.[38]

---

[35] Geoffrey Alderman, 'Bring on the History Revolution in Schools', *The Guardian*, 3 June 2010.
[36] Antony Beevor, 'Antony Beevor in Defence of History', *The Guardian*, 12 November 2010.
[37] Hastings, 'This Is the Country of Drake and Pepys'.
[38] Hastings, 'High-Handed Moral Condemnation', *Daily Telegraph*, 19 February 2006.

What of the conduct of the British Empire not in the eighteenth century, but the 1950s, then? When Hastings was brought by a pair of accounts of the British counter-insurgency war in Kenya (the 'Mau-Mau' conflict) to acknowledge the 'painful' truth of what had been done there—painful, that is, to those who still sympathize with some of the British Empire's projects, not to the erstwhile victims and their families—he objected forthrightly to any compensation for survivors of torture by the British army, and advocated leaving the matter to historians alone.[39]

Hastings was keener that non-historians take a definite stand when it came to British preparations for centenary commemorations of the outbreak of the First World War. He chastised politicians for their reticence on 'the virtue of Britain's cause, or the blame that chiefly attaches to Germany for the catastrophe that over-took Europe': the government, he mocked, 'calls this a "non-judgmental" approach. The rest of us might call it a cop-out.'[40] This judgement was in the same spirit of his claim that 'Winston Churchill was the greatest Englishman and one of the greatest human beings of the 20th century, indeed of all time.'[41] But it was also made shortly after he reviewed another book on the Allied bombardment of Germany in which he concluded that a 'sensible judgment about wartime bomb-ing, as about almost everything in life, must lie somewhere in the middle ground.'[42]

Opaque in all this is just where Hastings stands on evaluation and the relation-ship between historicism and historicity. He has some concept of anachronism, albeit not one that hinders the occasional transhistorical judgement about 'great-ness'. In his curricular recommendations he professed authority on what History's remit is, though his prescriptions alternated between the story of dominant 'soci-eties' and the story of one's own society. Even then 'society' was not the correct word for what he was really getting at: dominant states, classes, or sexes would have been more appropriate given that he selected Newton, Pepys, Clive, Kitchener, Drake, and some wars as his emblems of Britishness/Englishness, rather than, say, Victorian child labourers, deported convicts, executed 'deserters', persecuted homosexuals, or African slaves in Britain's transatlantic dominions. In sum, it was not just a matter of trying to homogenize the present We by appropri-ate historical education; it was a matter of selectively constructing an 'ideal' past We to which the present We was supposed to relate. Hastings's principles of anachronism do not sit easily with these identity interests. On one hand Britons born and naturalized are supposed to immerse themselves in British History for

---

[39] Hastings, 'The Dark Side of the Empire', *Daily Telegraph*, 11 January 2005; Hastings, 'The Folly of Judges, Vulture Lawyers and a Nation Addicted to Masochism', *Daily Mail*, 16 July 2012; and in the same vein, 'Yes, Slavery Was Evil: But It Would Be Insane to Force Us to Pay Damages for Age-Old Wrongs', *Daily Mail*, 11 March 2014.

[40] Hastings, 'Sucking Up to the Germans Is No Way to Remember Our Great War Heroes, Mr Cameron', *Daily Mail*, 11 June 2013.

[41] Hastings, *Finest Years: Churchill as Warlord 1940–1945* (London: Harper Collins, 2010), p. xv.

[42] Hastings's review of Richard Overy, *The Bombing War: Europe 1939–1945* (London: Allen Lane, 2013), *Sunday Times, Culture* magazine, 29 March 2013, 38.

the present (anachronism ignored), while on the other hand matters like carpet bombing of cities or the conduct of the British Empire are dismissed as having nothing to do with identity (anachronism invoked).

If Hastings sees himself as tolerant towards the inhabitants of the past then he only achieves this selectively. Since the actions of eighteenth-century imperialists and twentieth-century bombers had huge, deleterious repercussions for the people on the receiving end, tolerance of the perpetrators in this sense is tantamount to taking sides. If he does have some properly relativistic account of difference, rather than the sort of absolutism that he attributes to Grayling, some further explanation is needed as to why he only applies that relativism inconsistently. Given his 'We know that today we would do it all differently' he will also need to clarify why his conception of different standards is *not* also a claim of the superiority of today's moral sensibility. If he forbears from explicit judgement on grounds of sufferance, then he has already made up his mind that past or otherwise different worlds are morally inferior to Ours such that we can adopt a paternalistic attitude to them. If chronocentrism/ethnocentrism is indeed his position he needs to be open about it—though that will show him to be thoroughly embroiled in judgementalism.

Hastings's sometime pose as detached neo-historicist notwithstanding, he fully understands History's power to shape identity (a sense of historicity) in the present, as his intervention on curricula matters shows, and this explains his attempt to have his cake and eat it. For Hastings, British History is for actual and would-be Britons, against the backdrop of an empire that sought to make the world England. The past means everything and nothing. We have triumphs without real slaughter, enrichment without real exploitation, expansion without real dispossession, historically informed identity without historically derived identity challenges. 'Our historical identity' turns out to be highly selective between the good and the bad, even before we get to the crass politicians who wax populist about Our Island Story, or whatever the equivalent narrative elsewhere is.

These tendencies and variants on them are anything but unusual. Judgement is made where it suits identity purposes, and the relativism of distance invoked where it does not. Inhabitants of the past are of 'us' in certain ways but not in others, and their allocation to either side of the divide conveniently maintains the integrity of our usable past. The enduring greatness of Greek civilization is neatly separated from Greek slavery, which of course has nothing to say to Us, Now. Compare and contrast this treatment with the long-standing focus on the violence of the Mongols as somehow definitive of their record, as opposed, say, to the provision for cultural exchange and mutually enriching commerce of the Pax Mongolica. Victorians are men of Their times when massacring Africans or deploying child labour (of course we'd do things differently now), but Our forebears when it comes to their achievements in industry, engineering, and civics. The latter achievements become common cultural property, as Englanders with no technical training whatsoever bask in the reflected glory of 'Western medicine' or 'technology' or the parliamentary tradition as if this were a mark of personal achievement. But then we change our minds when it comes to things like colonialism: nothing to do with me, m'lud—unless we are among that not insignificant band still prepared to argue that colonialism was a Good Thing.

The former Australian premier John Howard exemplified the tensions and resolved them, to his own satisfaction at least. On historical violence and discrimination towards the indigenous peoples of Australia, Howard stated repeatedly to the effect that we should 'understand the past in its own terms', not in accordance with 'our own contemporary standards',[43] yet as with Alderman and Hastings the moral separation of past from present militated against his desire to celebrate, as he once put it, what 'many generations of Australians have worked hard to secure'.[44] Sensitive to the contradiction, it seems, Howard resorted to that treacherous rhetorical device, the language of balance: 'I believe that the balance sheet of our history is one of heroic achievement and that we have achieved much more as a nation of which we can be proud than of which we should be ashamed.'[45] Given the much greater weight of good in the scales, a weight established 'by assertion rather than audit',[46] it hardly made sense to dwell too long on any marginal flaws.

The selectivity deployed in Identity History is a world away from the sort entailed in cross-cultural borrowing (pp. 232–3). Each sort of selectivity involves value judgements in the comparison/contrast between some of 'their' practices and 'ours'. The difference between the sorts of selectivity is the difference between the effort of reflection and the complacency of self-satisfaction. The nineteenth-century historian and political philosopher Ernest Renan identified the selective memory required for the construction of nationalism's 'imagined communities', and the basic point has been handsomely extended by studies such as Marc Ferro's *Comment on raconte l'histoire aux enfants*.[47] For Identity historians, whether in the university or beyond, it is not a matter of casting a genuinely critical eye over aspects of the past and employing consistent evaluative thought. It is a matter of surreptitious, partial evaluation that ends in excusing, justifying, spuriously mitigating, or minimizing or otherwise obfuscating those aspects.

---

[43] Bain Attwood and S. G. Foster (eds), *Frontier Conflict: The Australian Experience* (Canberra: National Museum of Australia, 2003), 13–14. For further evidence of his abhorrence of anachronism, see John Howard, 'Practical Reconciliation', in Michelle Grattan (ed.), *Reconciliation: Essays on Australian Reconciliation* (Melbourne: Black Inc., 2000), 95.

[44] John Howard, 'The Liberal Tradition: The Beliefs and Values Which Guide the Federal Government' (18 November 1996), 10. Online at: https://pmtranscripts.pmc.gov.au/release/transcript-10171

[45] Howard, 'The Liberal Tradition', 9.

[46] Quote from Stuart Macintyre and Anna Clark, *The History Wars* (Melbourne: Melbourne University Press, 2004), 139.

[47] (Paris: Payot, 1981).

Some things are just convenient to avoid: 'Forgetting is the shears with which you cut away what you cannot use, doing it under the supreme direction of memory. Forgetting and remembering are thus identical arts', as Kierkegaard put it.[48] On the other side of Kierkegaard's coin, accentuation can take the form of preferential treatment for chosen historical agents. So Identity historians become judges in their own case, albeit judges who, like Michael Howard, rule in preliminary hearings that their case should never reach court.

Pride and Shame about the Past

Moral evaluation seems apt to lose its compass in the choppy waters of identity-relevant History, where judgements have most contemporary relevance because they relate directly to people's sense of historicity. The philosopher Frank Ankersmit pinpoints why fear of the intrusion of the historian's moral and political commitments might exceed fears of other sorts of intrusion, such as writing-style, adherence to an interpretative tradition, and so forth:

> style, affinity with a certain kind of topic, scholarly affiliation, etc. are clearly all attributes of the historian that do not have their counterpart in the 'objective' past itself. So we shall immediately recognize them for what they are—namely, immixtures of the subject—and we shall never be tempted to project them onto the past itself... [Conversely, m]oral and political values have their existence in both the subject and the object... [and are] feared so much by historians because the spheres of the object (the past) and of the subject come infinitesimally close to each other... Not only may historians be tempted to project their own moral and political values on the past, but it may also happen that the moral and political values active in the past invade the world of historians and of their contemporaries.[49]

Those historiographical areas in which moral judgement might seem most applicable and straightforward, i.e. in the treating of cultures that seem closest to 'ours', or the encounter with events most salient by analogy, are precisely the areas in which we might be lured into disregarding important contextual differences. Thus confused, one might act against Collingwood's warning, falling 'into the fallacy of imagining that somewhere, behind a veil, the past is still happening'.[50] All that can be done is to acknowledge this very real danger and to try to avoid it.

---

[48] Cited in Donald W. Shriver, *Honest Patriots* (Oxford: Oxford University Press, 2005), 15.

[49] F.R. Ankersmit, 'The Ethics of History: From the Double Binds of (Moral) Meaning to Experience', *History and Theory* 43/4 (2004), 84–102, here 86–7.

[50] Collingwood, *The Idea of History*, 404.

In the terms of Part 1, engaging in such projection is to fall at the first hurdle of moral contextualism.

There are at least two ways of falling at this hurdle, and one tends to be less well advertised than the other. Butterfield's warning that the 'whig' historian might exercise her moral opinions on things 'anathema only to the whigs' can be read as a warning against the historian's bringing historical Others towards her, enlisting Them in her own political battles. But we must guard equally against the historian's aligning herself with historical actors without moving them. This tendency does not always appear to be anachronism, because it is ostensibly the reverse of the most obvious anachronism.

'Reverse' anachronism just means that the historian's viewpoint and that of her chosen historical objects coincides, and each is used to legitimate the other. Consider the scholarship of pro-imperial British scholars like Niall Ferguson and Andrew Roberts, whose own world-views resemble in some respects the world-views of their historical objects. Instead of appearing to apply present values to the past, they use the past to validate some present attitudes towards (neo-) imperialism, a certain Anglo-Saxon political culture, and so forth.

Consider in particular Ferguson's pro-imperial blockbuster *Empire: How Britain Made the Modern World*. Rather than its overtly political stance, let us focus on an issue that sheds light on the relationship between its politics and Identity History: its relationship to counterfactuals. This issue merits attention since Ferguson's career was partly built on the use of the counterfactual as a device for contemplating historical contingency,[51] yet in *Empire* he vacillates on the utility of the tool. He begins by claiming that 'while it is just about possible to imagine what the world would have been like without the French Revolution or the First World War, the imagination reels from the counter-factual of modern history without the British empire'. Then he dictates that whatever that unknowable counterfactual world would have been like, it would not have been as good.[52] Ferguson's inconsistency should not obscure the importance of contingency: quite the opposite. His agonizing over his primary counterfactual would be irrelevant to the historian who really understood contingency, one of whose implications is not oracular insight into alternative universes but intellectual humility. One of the things Ferguson could safely say about an alternative history without the British Empire is that in that scenario there would be no one socialized like him into pronouncing on why he could not conceive of modern history without the British Empire. The words of the German Jewish philosopher Theodor Lessing (1872–1933) are appropriate for *Empire*. Lessing wrote that our relationship

---

[51] Niall Ferguson (ed.), *Virtual History: Alternatives and Counterfactuals* (London: Picador, 1997).
[52] Ferguson, *Empire* (London: Penguin, 2004), p. xxii; cf. p. xxviii with its rhetorical question of 'whether there could have been a less bloody path to modernity', to which the rest of the book supposedly provides the implicit answer.

towards the past often seems to resemble 'a fabric in which, like the spider in its web, we always constitute the centre and the origin of all the threads'.[53] The subtext of Ferguson's teleological bias is: without that past you wouldn't have this present—and his book hinges on the idea that a particular sort of economic globalization is a Good Thing for which we can thank the 'Anglobalization' of the British Empire. By such reasoning the past can be viewed positively or negatively in correspondence to one's perception of the present, but what E. P. Thompson called the deafening propaganda of the status quo stacks the deck in favour of particular contemporary arrangements.

The commonplace that we can only know who we are by knowing where we come from can rather lead from open inquiry to a protectiveness towards one's identity group's path through History. Again in Lessing's words:

> We adjudge, for example, the old Roman Empire's hideous orgies of blood as historically reasonable and necessary because we see ourselves as the ultimate outcome of the empire, though we would probably have considered no curse too harsh for it had we remained slaves under its yoke. We judge even the most senseless historical reality of Tamerlane's bloodshed and horrors to be historic- ally inevitable and necessary, because without Tamerlane's historical appearance the Turks would be ruling in Europe today and our own treasured world history would not have transpired at all.[54]

Burckhardt had made much the same point in 1871: our 'self-seeking first regards those times as happy which are in some way akin to our nature. Further, it con- siders as praiseworthy such past forces and individuals on whose work our pre- sent existence and relative welfare are based', 'as if the world and its history had existed merely for our own sakes!' It would be worth conducting an opinion sur- vey to test the endurance into the present of those reflex historical convictions that Burckhardt observed in his time, such that 'It was fortunate that the Greeks conquered Persia, and Rome Carthage; unfortunate that Athens was defeated by Sparta in the Peloponnesian war; ... fortunate that Europe, in the eighth century, on the whole held Islam at bay; ... fortunate that first Spain, then Louis XIV were eventually defeated in their plans for world domination.' With such deep civilization- grounding consensus established, he went on, there might be scope for a little disagreement on more local matters.[55]

Scholars with the established fact of various forms of hegemony—patriarchal, capitalist, Marxist-Leninist, statist, imperial, or whatever—behind them can pose as neutral in their views towards past as well as present. It is rare these days to

---

[53] Lessing, *Geschichte als Sinngebung des Sinnlosen* (Munich: Beck, 1921), 14–15.
[54] Lessing, *Geschichte als Sinngebung des Sinnlosen*, 14–15.
[55] Burckhardt, 'On Fortune and Misfortune in History', 274, 281.

find someone sympathetic to the Soviet experiment, though it may be that, had the Eastern bloc prevailed in the Cold War, more historians would be found speaking in the idiom of eggs and omelettes while identifying with the chefs in the Kremlin. Being 'neutral' here *may* be to prejudice one's History in favour of forces that are influential in the present as well as the past, and this is no more evident than in 'national story' genealogical historiography. The practice of understanding the past then equates to reiterating the ascent of history's victors by colourfully recounting the stories of national figureheads, decisive military campaigns, forms of governance, and the contributions thereto of 'universal' qualities such as sacrifice, heroism, far-sightedness, and strong leadership.

Having discarded the detritus of failed alternatives, competent national Identity historians will be able to assimilate more successful opposition movements in the form, say, of organized labour, or drives for female emancipation or religious reform. The success of those erstwhile 'others' is assimilated into the narrative as further proof of the inherent, inclusive reasonableness of the tradition. Consider the extent to which the historiography of slavery in Britain was for so long really the historiography of slavery's abolition, as if that negated all that went before, as if abolition were just a natural part of the maturation process, rather than something a dedicated minority had to fight for, alongside resistant slaves themselves, in the face of greed and racist violence. A compelling circularity is created. Those who remain 'othered' by being defeated, dominated, or dismissed, be they internal or external to the culture, must simply have been irreconcilable or not have had anything to offer in the first place. What 'we' did to 'them' becomes understandable in the overall scheme of things. Those who are to some extent incorporated by making themselves sufficiently amenable or by mobilizing effectively, are told that the advances they have secured are precisely in the right measure. Any more would be unreasonable—until, that is, the reflective equilibrium shifts again and a new base standard of reasonableness is established, from which, for the time being, it would be unreasonable to diverge, as if W. G. Sumner were correct that it is 'the times' that change and people that follow, rather than people changing 'the times' by refusing to put up with existing arrangements (p. 123). The concept of 'reasonableness' is then projected backwards via the Identity historians and a parameter of reasonable disagreement and tone is created, transgression of which renders one anachronistic, ahistorical, presentist, and so on. One of Britain's finest journalists, Gary Younge, encapsulated the tendency in 2018 in a discussion of the American commemoration of the murder of Martin Luther King:

> the US will indulge in an orgy of self-congratulation, selectively misrepresenting King's life and work, as if rebelling against the American establishment was, in fact, what the establishment has always encouraged...the struggle is to ensure that King's legacy isn't eviscerated of all militancy so that it can be repurposed as

one more illustration of the American establishment's God-given ability to produce the antidote to its own poison.[56]

Dissident scholarship—marked purely negatively, in terms of opposition to whatever the prevailing order may be—can look anachronistically 'presentist' simply by looking unreasonable in the present (see pp. 100–101). That need only tell us about the present. There may come a point in which it seems more significant to dwell on the monumental atrocity that followed Columbus' arrival in the Americas than the manly spirit of 'discovery' occasioning his advent. The Columbian events themselves will not have changed in the interim, but one can infer something about the sort of society that prioritizes the record of the one over the other.[57] And it is contemporary societies doing their memory work that we are now concerned with, which is why, given the inherently ethical nature of relationality to one's forebears, and the moral quality of their relationship to others, this book can only commend more systematic and consistent moral reflection on the past as an element of present-day political practice.

Elaborated counterfactuals can be just as much of a problem here (see also pp. 78–80), as selectively disavowed counterfactuals à la *Empire*. When they are not just a waste of time, elaborated counterfactuals can well turn into validations of what transpired by invocation of worse alternatives or—the reverse—validations of imagined ideal alternatives by contrast with the real course of events. In either case the exercise is prejudiced in some direction by the choice of counterfactual and when to graft that diverging counterfactual branch onto the trunk of the empirically inferable. Moral evaluation provides a course different both to the contemplation of frictionless alternative worlds—utopia meaning famously 'no-place'—and to the worship of 'the god of things as they' that mascarades as open-minded interest in contingency.

Just because the past turned out as it did, we owe some normative account of what was done to make it so. We must provide that account precisely because there is no overarching course of history whose advancement automatically legitimates the costs incurred, because, against some of the scholarship examined earlier (pp. 114–15), history cannot be reduced to a sort of niche-adaptivity (the triumph of the morally 'best-fitted') and because the analogy between the maturing individual and the nation is a misleading artefact of that thinking-in-concentric-circles that is characteristic of certain monadic doctrines. Since the undertaking of History is not the same as ideal theorizing, the question is never about what they in the past should have done by some ideal-universal standard, but about the character of what 'they' did, just as in the world today the question is not of

---

[56] Gary Younge, 'Martin Luther King: How a Rebel Leader Was Lost to History', *The Guardian*, 4 April 2018.

[57] Howard Zinn, *A People's History of the United States, 1492–Present* (London: Routledge, 2003), 9.

imposing a utopian blueprint on a *tabula rasa*, it concerns what we do in the circumstances prevailing now.

Just as no book can cover everything and no reader can read everything, and no community can practise an undifferentiated cult of remembrance,[58] so it is vital to interrogate what we do choose to remember, to contemplate chosen actors and acts not just in their 'own terms' but also as regards their effects in the world. Apropos the discussion of historiographical misunderstandings in the first section of this Part, it is not necessarily a question of which actors one focuses upon but rather how one handles that which is in focus. Think back to the sort of allegations levelled at historians of the perpetrators and perpetration of the Holocaust (pp. 258–60), as if their concentration on such matters alone in any given work must somehow connote lack of sympathy or concern for victims. Sometimes these allegations have gone further. Saul Friedlander associated a perpetration-centred approach with 'the (mostly involuntary) smugness of scholarly detachment', and he once wrote of the historian's placing the reader 'in a situation not unrelated to the detached position of an administrator of extermination. Interest is fixed on an administrative process, an activity of building and transportation, words used for record-keeping. And that's all.'[59] The impression is that historians of the Nazi machinery are in the business of contemplating trains to Auschwitz but without giving any thought to what Auschwitz was. Perhaps some are, but it is deeply hazardous to generalize from any individual case. One retort would be that the very name 'perpetrator research' or *Täterforschung* in German, connotes awareness of the significance of things done: the root of the German word for perpetrator is *Tat*, act or deed, i.e. something done in the world, in this case something done to someone else—the victims. It is eminently possible for a historian to devote a book to the study of Holocaust perpetrators without concealing from herself or the reader the moral gravity of the perpetrated deeds.[60]

One can, conversely, think of regions of historical discourse in which what was brought about is minimized, marginalized, or substantially ignored. In American-led wars over the last few generations, six to seven million Koreans, Vietnamese, and Iraqis died, mostly civilians, compared to the combined American death toll of *c*.96,000, the vast majority servicepeople. The millions barely register in American national consciousness.[61] The American historiography of, say, the Vietnam War has been complicit in this. Accompanying the prevailing fascination with the military and political history of the conflict is a preoccupation with

---

[58] That is Tzvetan Todorov's phrase.
[59] Saul Friedlander, *The Years of Extermination: Nazi Germany and the Jews, 1939–1945* (London, Harper Collins, 2007), p. xxvi; Friedlander, *Reflections of Nazism: An Essay on Kitsch and death* (New York: Harper and Row, 1984), 90–1.
[60] e.g. Browning, *Ordinary Men*.
[61] John Tirman, *The Deaths of Others: The Fate of Civilians in America's Wars* (New York: Oxford University Press, 2011).

its impact on American society, which looks like an extension of the partisan concern displayed during the war itself.

Tendencies towards narcissism may be found in the imperial endeavours of many states, where signifiers like 'Suez' or 'Dien Ben Phu' indicate how much more We tend to be concerned with the moments at which imperial matters disagreeably affect Us rather than anyone else. While the actual empire clearly forms part of British History, it is absent from many Britons' sense of historicity. To be sure, that sense may be informed by the notion of having had an empire, especially what Joseph Conrad called 'the idea', meaning the 'good faith' justifications for empire. But it is generally much less well informed by an awareness of actual policies and deeds. To the extent that this is different in France, Algeria is the major variable, being that territory that was not only geographically close to home but actually claimed as part of Metropolitan France. Only in recent years has Belgium's 'great forgetting' of mass slaughter and hyper-exploitation in the Congo been somewhat rectified by the memory guardians who previously espoused the self-comforting 'civilizing process' line.[62] The conventional focus on self-justifications explains why it is not necessarily effective for critics of, say, that 'Victorian Titan' Salisbury, to describe his views as imperialist. It is not just a historicization of Salisbury that works in his defence, but an enduring view amongst a sizeable part of the British public today that imperialism was merited *simpliciter*, not just 'legitimate' according to the standards of its times. Such views have their own moral or quasi-moral facets, so their proponents are in no position to delegitimate additional moral argument. A proper moral accounting would take cognizance of the baser motives of many imperialists and, irrespective of motives, empire's deleterious effects.

One possible inference from so much talk of evaluation is that this book is suggesting that bearers of a historically informed identity (everyone) might bear the same virtue or guilt as certain historical forebears. That is not the implication. One cannot talk of individual or collective credit or guilt for acts preceding the given individual or generation of the collective. Mention of guilt, and its counterpart innocence, is a red herring anyway; it is the wrong idiom, carrying the wrong connotations. A better idiom is that of pride and shame,[63] on which Michael Howard alighted and which we have already encountered in some of its social valences.

---

[62] Adam Hochschild, *King Leopold's Ghost* (London: Pan Macmillan, 1999), ch. 19 'The Great Forgetting'; on civilizing mission rhetoric and limited attempts to change the picture, Alex Marshall, 'Belgium's Africa Museum Attempts to Lose "Pro-Colonialism" Image with Redesign', *The Independent*, 10 December 2018.

[63] On the idiom of pride and shame, W. H. Walsh, 'Pride, Shame and Responsibility', *Philosophical Quarterly* 20/78 (1970), 1–13; Farid Abdel-Nour, 'National Responsibility', *Political Theory* 31/5 (2003), 693–719.

Unlike in the discussion of the Homeric Greek case (pp. 139–42), this section is concerned with feelings of pride or shame around things that one has not oneself done. Manifestly many people feel pride in what they see as the achievements of their identity group(s)—and this was also true of the Homeric Greeks. One may be proud of oneself but also proud of some person or persons X with whom one perceives some form of connection. To be proud of X in that way is in an important sense not (or not just) to be vicariously proud of them, as in the way that one might empathize with the doings of another person of whatever background as revealed in her autobiography, or the way that one might act vicariously for another in some professional capacity (eg as an estate agent). It is to be proud because in some respect X is held to exhibit some identity with oneself. This shared element might be 'blood' in the familial or nationalistic sense, or a shared experience of suffering and resistance, and so on for as many iterations as there are types of identity collective. All the same considerations apply to being 'ashamed of…'. One may be ashamed of oneself or of X.[64]

Now shame is not a popular feeling for much the same reasons that costs are less popular than benefits and the memory of suffering endured is more powerful than that of suffering inflicted. Yet historically oriented pride is alive and well 'even' in those cultures that supposedly have a 'modern' or neo-historicist historical consciousness. And pride is sensitive. Those who criticize, say, the record of imperialism or slavery quickly discover this when they are labelled self-haters and suchlike. The aggressive-defensive response is self-evidently not a consequence of the responders' having a relativistic or neo-historicist historical consciousness that sees judgement on the foreign country of the past as a category error. Thus a July 2014 poll of more than 1,700 British adults recorded 59 per cent as 'proud' of the British Empire and 19 per cent as 'ashamed'. Perhaps all of the 23 per cent responding 'don't know' rejected historical evaluation in principle. It is more probable that that attitude was significantly less well represented, vying with ignorance and equivocation on empire's merits and demerits.[65] Clearly enough, given pride, shame is not some anachronistic residue that can be discarded out of hand. If shame is to be jettisoned as a possible response to the past, then so must be pride, at which moment we can say that the historical part of identity has lost its purchase. Opinions divide on whether an all-embracing capacity to disregard the past would be a good or a bad thing, but for the while it is most unlikely.[66]

---

[64] Abdel-Nour, 'National Responsibility', 693–719; Appiah, *The Honor Code*, 63–4.

[65] YouGov survey results, fieldwork 24–5 July 2014, sample size 1,741 British adults, survey question 'Thinking about the British Empire, would you say it is more something to be proud or
    more something to be ashamed of?' Survey results available online at: http://cdn.yougov.com/cumulus_uploads/document/6quatmbimd/Internal_Results_140725_Commonwealth_Empire-W.pdf.

[66] See David Rieff's stimulating *In Praise of Forgetting: Historical Memory and Its Ironies* (New Haven: Yale University Press, 2016).

Since people are apt to disagree over what in the past merits pride or shame, arguments ensue about what is, good, bad, right, and wrong. When these arguments are about the past they are nonetheless arguments for the present. In them, moral judgement about the past is unavoidable and ramifies on political orientation in the present: a moral reckoning with the British Empire cannot but affect visions of what Britishness should be today.

With the empire example in mind, we hear quite a lot about the need for postcolonial states and others affected by North-Western foreign policy not to live in the past, take responsibility for their own ills, and so forth. Sometimes these sorts of remarks are made in good faith, after extensive, sensitive inquiry. They may find support among members of postcolonial communities themselves, as in the work of the novelist V.S. Naipaul, or the Cameroonian philosopher Achille Mbembe. Sometimes the sentiments express the aggressive-defensiveness that stems from cognitive dissonance, as when the then British chancellor of the Exchequer, later prime minister, Gordon Brown, decreed that 'the days of Britain having to apologize for its colonial history are over. We should move forward.' By 'moving forward', he did not mean putting the past entirely in the past, such that any evaluative attitude towards it, positive or negative, was inappropriate. With the self-serving inconsistency familiar from recent pages he claimed: 'We should celebrate much of our past rather than apologise for it.'[67] (Some observers reasonably queried when Britain had started apologizing.[68]) Sometimes the issue is simple bad faith, as those who stress the historical identity of their own seem unprepared to contemplate how deeply others might be shaped by intrusive historical processes. One way of knowing whether the stance is the product of sympathetic reflection is to see whether it is arrived at by weighing the arguments of the Mbembes against the opposing arguments of the likes of Edward Said and the Australian academic and Australian indigenous rights activist Aileen Moreton-Robinson. But ultimately, however well informed the ensuing conclusion of the argumentative process, it is beside the point when contemplating 'our' identity-relevant History. It was Butterfield who wrote that the acme of effrontery is telling someone else to turn the other cheek.[69] In the identity vein, the we-group's responsibility is to reflect on what its salient 'members' have done through time, not to pronounce on how anyone else should respond to those deeds.

The vocational historian can have an important role to play in all this. In clarification of some of the parameters of that role it is important to address the point made by the historian Mark Edele that bad History may make good politics, in the sense that some tales about the past are politically useful for various purposes

---

[67] Benedict Brogan, 'It's Time to Celebrate the Empire, says Brown', *Daily Mail*, 15 January 2005; editorial, 'An Imperial History Lesson for Mr Brown', *The Independent*, 16 March 2005.

[68] Owen Jones, 'William Hague Is Wrong…We Must Own Up to Our Brutal Colonial Past', *The Independent*, 3 September 2012.

[69] Butterfield, *Christianity and History*, 63.

whatever their evidentiary warrant.[70] We need not contest this point. Nothing follows from it for the vocational historian. If 'bad' History here does not mean deliberately misleading History it must mean demonstrably weak History, in the sense of poorly substantiated or feebly argued; it cannot reasonably mean History that has been empirically or conceptually superseded, because that happens to some degree to all historianship, however well regarded. Politicians can always find something in historiography to use to their advantage, and they may be as adept at exploiting bad History as good. Edele is only necessarily at loggerheads with the present argument if he is proposing, as he does not seem to be, that vocational historians deliberately write poor or misleading History in the hope that it will be used for some good purpose. That prescription would assume a level of control over how a work of history is read that is disconfirmed by the record of politicians and activists exploiting such works. It is as likely as not to result in discrediting the historian, removing her from the ranks of those who warrant particular trust as interpreters of the past.

Saying historians cannot control how they are used by those who do not share their procedural ethos is not, however, the same as saying that historians cannot establish criteria by which certain readings may be adjudged *illegitimate*. They can, within limits. Attention to especially sensitive contexts of dissemination is important, which means embracing one's responsibilities to speak without fear or favour, and can sometimes imply saying what one believes a particular audience should hear, irrespective of what it may want to hear. (This is not the same as the undesirable practice of saying one thing to one group and a contradictory thing to another group.) Yet one will never be able to anticipate all potential audiences. No: since this is a matter of procedural ethos, the key level of arbitration is that of process and methodology, of what one might call 'working' in very loose analogy to mathematical working.

This working, i.e. the moral reasoning that the first three Parts of this book have tried to provide some grounds and guidelines for, is simultaneously functional and performative. In making clear the relationships between historical empirics, moral concepts, and evaluative conclusion it lays down a challenge for competing accounts to do the same. Now of course one cannot stop historians who are intent on pursuing another course under any circumstances, or readers who want some Identity matter validated at all costs—such people certainly exist alongside others who study the past with open identity questions in mind rather than prefabricated Identity answers. Yet commending more consistency and transparency in evaluative thought means not only that those who have fallen unawares into the ways of Identity History may have the tendency raised to

---

[70] Mark Edele, 'The Ethics and the Politics of History: Beyond the "Moral Turn"', Monash University Symposium 'The Ethics *of* History, Morality *in* History', 21–2 July 2016.

consciousness, but also that those who deliberately persevere as Identity historians will be more easily exposed in light of it.

How far can or should the process of historical self-interrogation proceed? Since societies need narratives about themselves, too much historical criticism might contribute to social dissensus, demoralization and the collapse of shared projects.[71] So goes the argument and it merits serious attention given that the historian who heeds the moral weight of the past seems unlikely to disregard questions of human coexistence in the present. A response would be that historically oriented shame, like shame of any provenance, can be just as 'positively' reconstructive as pride is constructive. That is the function of shame, full stop, which is why it is not some remnant of the collectivist past that the good modern individualist needs to shake off. The fear of social fragmentation, if we assume it to be sincere rather than just a spectre raised to sustain any given social arrangement, is in danger of assuming an initially monadic condition from which self-criticism portends a radical departure. But contrary to what Hastings desires for the present and wishes to impose in the study of the past, the present is no more monadic than the past. The 'we' is always already just one coalition of individuals and factions, and the point of politics is to articulate disagreements between such factions and find ways to accommodate them while moving into a future that is always somehow different from the present. Discussions about the past are reference points for contestation about choice in the present. In the here and now the state of Guatemala, for instance, has a reality that cannot be ignored, a reality comprising the legacies of its past as well as other matters like its topography. Whatever might happen in future, the present question is of the stewardship and direction of the good ship Guatemala.

Some of the most striking instances of historical reckoning have occurred in the context of regime transition, as in the Nuremberg Trials or the truth commissions established in South Africa and South America, yet consolidated social orders, including consolidated democracies, may obviously also feature historically inherited social injustices.[72] Consequently, certain pasts that are not presently matters of hot memory for the majority may need to be made into such in the interests of driving social justice in the present, on the principle that marginalization or denial of past oppression may lead to relevant constituencies distrusting broader society and its governing institutions.[73] Furthermore, even absolute consensus within a polity may not be enough in the event that members of an external entity have some historical grievance. All shareholders are stakeholders but not all stakeholders are shareholders, as is clear to anyone outside the USA who is

---

[71] As discussed in Abdel-Nour, 'National Responsibility'.
[72] On the latter cases, Bashir Bashir, 'Reconciling Historical Injustices: Deliberative Democracy and the Politics of Reconciliation', *Res Publica* 18/2 (2012), 127–43.
[73] Bashir, 'Reconciling Historical Injustices', 133.

affected by decisions of internally elected US politicians and internally account-able US security services.

Material Legacies

While it would be wrong to hold individuals or groups responsible for things done by salient predecessors, they can be held responsible for the way in which they act in relation to those things. In material terms just as much as in other terms, the past saw the creation of losers and beneficiaries. The inheritance of ill-gotten gains presents a moral problem for beneficiaries. Owing to the individual-ism that permeates social and economic thought today, popular discussion of inheritance is apt to be shot through with inconsistencies, but it is inheritance at the collective level with which this section is principally concerned.

The first question to address is that of statutes of limitations, whether in the literal, legal sense or the sense of 'mere' matters of principle. Such statutes need not correspond to the lifetime of individual humans or generations of humans. Where the matter is of state policy, for instance, international law provides for inherited obligations in virtue of the quasi-permanence of state structures. Individual generations and regimes pass but the State remains, which is essential for issues like the honouring of loan repayments over the long term, or the adher-ence to treaties signed decades before by state governments of different outlooks to the present one.

States are not the only sort of *universitas* with lifespans of a different scale to that of humans; all *corporate* entities potentially have this quality. A corporation denotes people united in a collective for some common purpose. It derives from the Latin *corpus*, body. The modern corporation has more than just nominal similarity. It is a legal person under law, with accompanying rights and liabilities, and exists from the moment of legal incorporation to that of liquidation, whether that be days or centuries.[74] During its lifespan any number of people may pass through it as successive officeholders and partake of it as shareholders. As long as the corporation 'lives', however, it bears some of the same responsibilities as the organic individual.

Whether at the level of the individual or the *universitas*, a culpable relationship of actor to earlier misdeed by another is captured by the legal concept of the accessory after the fact. The analogy of the accessory after the fact may sometimes be replaced by the analogy of the recipient of stolen goods—as legal concepts the

---

[74] Susan Mary Watson, 'The Corporate Legal Person', *Journal of Corporate Law Studies* 19/1 (2019), 137–66.

latter developed out of the former anyway.[75] The actions of the Turkish state in the years and generations after the Armenian genocide illustrate both relationships. In most instances of genocide or genocide-like massacre perpetrators have got away not just with the murder or expulsion of the victim group, but its dispossession. The Armenian genocide involved a huge capital transfer, partly to the State, partly to regional bigwigs best positioned to get in on the pilfering of land, buildings, and businesses, and partly to more and less organized groups which predated upon the deported Armenians who carried what they could into the deserts of Syria and Mesopotamia. Many orchestrators of genocide went on to form the administrative elite of the Republic of Turkey that emerged from the Ottoman carcass, and many descendants of the private profiteers still head businesses stolen in 1915.

The way in which wealth is distributed can at once expand the circle of beneficiaries and complicate the issue of liability. (Note that 'liability' is not used in a narrowly legal sense.) Wealth taken, then invested, may now constitute the fabric of the social infrastructure of many more people than the initial appropriators and their immediate, greatest beneficiaries. Ditto the fruits of labour extracted by slavery. The appropriation of common land that has characterized modern state-development projects—accompanied by destructive contempt for subsisting peasants and hunter gatherers across the globe—is now thoroughly 'normalized' and very often its economic consequences have been diffused, unevenly, via the market mechanism. With relevant considerations in mind John Stuart Mill opined:

> It may seem hard that a claim originally just, should be defeated by mere lapse of time; but there is a time after which...the balance of hardship turns the other way. With the injustices of men as with the convulsions and disasters of nature, the longer they remain unrepaired, the greater become the obstacles to repairing them, arising from the after-growths which would have to be torn up or broken through.[76]

What should we make of this?

One response to Mill would be to distinguish between what we can expect from individual beneficiaries and from the polities within which those beneficiaries live—polities that may themselves have benefited, of course. If under certain circumstances it may be very difficult, perhaps illusory, or by Mill's account even

---

[75] 'Receiving the Proceeds of Stolen Goods as a Criminal Offense', *Columbia Law Review* 19/3 (1919), 229–33.

[76] John Stuart Mill, *Principles of Political Economy*, i (London: Parker, 1848), 257 (bk II, ch. 2 §2).

wrong to seek redress from individuals, that says nothing to the possibility and desirability of restitution by relevant polities.[77]

Secondly, Mill's point, at once of practicality and principle, is not an argument to neutrality or any sort of historically oriented relativism, but groundwork towards the consideration of recompense. It is curious how many parties to such debates fail to realize that they are already engaged in the evaluative exercise even when arguing against restitution. Take the matter of repatriation of culturally valuable property from foreign private or public collections. The argument against repatriation that is based on the claim that the initial acquisition of the property was consensual not only opens the door to argument about what consent means in the context of historically inequitable power relations, it also tacitly affirms that repatriation is appropriate in cases of non-consensual acquisition. It is sometimes said that the Parthenon frieze, aka the 'Elgin Marbles', was legitimately taken from Athens since *in situ* it would, neglected, have fallen into disrepair. This argument is roughly one of holding in trust. If it is accepted, then once arrangements have been made in Greece for appropriate care of the antiquities, they should be returned.

Thirdly, Mill does not specify the 'time' after which 'the balance of hardship turns the other way', because the principle and the pragmatics will vary with each other. That is, one may not stipulate that in principle all claims stemming from before a certain time should automatically be rejected. Nor should complex practicalities automatically rule out the pursuit of an earlier claim. It may be that there is no way to be found, but a will is needed to look for the way in the first place, even if only to establish its impossibility. Sometimes the will is palpably lacking, as in the thirty years, at the time of writing, from 1989, during which the US Congress annually rejected HR 40, the Commission to Study Reparation Proposals for African Americans Act.[78]

When the dispossessed or their disadvantaged descendants are around to make a legal or moral case for a reckoning, it is only half the battle to raise awareness among beneficiaries, whether they be individuals or polities. It is one thing for recipients to abhor the ill-getting of gains, another for them to reconcile themselves to surrendering gains that have landed in their lap. Moral pressure might be needed.

It was contended earlier on that justice is the highest virtue because it can be demanded in the way that its traditional competitor for the title, love, cannot be (p. 139). Demanding something does not mean one will receive it, but that one

---

[77] Of course a beneficiary society contains its own winners and losers, and the poorest in a population may be affected most by measures taken on behalf of the whole, as noted by Neil MacCormick, *Practical Reason in Law and Morality* (Oxford: Oxford University Press, 2008), 140. Some principles of compensation that may militate against this tendency in an analogous case are outlined towards the conclusion of Christian Baatz, 'Responsibility for the Past? Some Thoughts on Compensating Those Vulnerable to Climate Change in Developing Countries', *Ethics, Policy and Environment* 16/1 (2013), 94–110.

[78] Ta-Nehisi Coates, 'The Case for Reparations', *The Atlantic* (June 2014).

asserts a claim as of legal and/or moral right. Demanding reparations or restitution is a way of self-assertion and a way of *shaming*. Reparations have more than
material connotations—or, rather, material connotations are rarely 'just' material,
as the German etymological equation of debt and guilt makes clear (p. 147). The
German for reparation is *Wiedergutmachung*, literally 'making good again'. It
compounds the noun *Gut*, which like its English equivalent 'good' at once connotes property and the opposite of evil.

Returning to Mill, we need to note a major qualification. 'It is scarcely needful
to remark', he wrote, 'that these reasons for not disturbing acts of injustice of old
date, cannot apply to unjust systems or institutions; since a bad law or usage is not
one bad act, in the remote past, but a perpetual repetition of bad acts, as long as
the law or usage lasts.'[79] Some continuities are less obvious than others, but no less
important for that. When one talks of the reproduction of power across time,
cleavages may remain similar while social forms change—discrimination over
centuries on grounds of sex and 'race' being emblematic. Legal scholar and civil
rights lawyer Michelle Alexander's coruscating *The New Jim Crow: Mass
Incarceration in the Age of Colorblindness* concludes that 'we have not ended racial
caste in America; we have merely redesigned it' for a post-civil-rights era in which
laws are supposedly colour-neutral.[80] Social prejudices and unequal social structures continue to perform the work to which legalized segregation had previously
contributed. As in accessory-after-the-fact scenarios, the relationship of beneficiaries to legacies may buttress the reproduction of elements of the power relations that conduced to the historical act in the first place, even if other parts of the
overall context-nexus have shifted. Armenian claims for genocide recognition
and compensation are met with implicit threats against the small Armenian
minority still in Turkey, threats justified with the same rhetoric of alien disloyalty
that spawned the genocide in the first place. The much greater openness among
former perpetrators of mass violence in Indonesia can serve the same function, as
celebration of the political slaughter of 1965 serves as an ongoing warning to any
contemporary dissidents.

In the case of laws that remain in force in their original form, it is easier to
ascertain continuities or Mill's 'repetitions', though that is a far cry from saying it is
easier to change the situation. Consider the matter of land right disputes. Are states
whose topography is still shaped by historical sequestration simply able to dismiss
arguments for redress on the grounds of anachronism, in the sense that when the
land was taken the expropriators believed themselves to be in the right and had the
power to assert that right by law as well as force? This is not quite the same issue as
the one in cases where law 'preserves its force long after the reasons, occasions, and

---

[79] Mill, *Principles*, i. 258 (bk II, ch. 2 §2).   [80] (2010; New York: New Press, 2012), 2.

time itself from whence it was created, is erased from memory',[81] because the original reasons may still be present to mind. The question of when earlier authority is to be deemed invalid is nonetheless common to both situations.

The issue around anachronism in landownership cases is less, *pace* Alderman on 'witches' (pp. 116–17), about whether one is doing justice to the values and intentions of earlier lawgivers and more about whether the sway those earlier lawgivers hold is unreasonable in the present. For defenders of the status quo in Australia, however, the very fear that the past is not so 'past' after all issues in a firm determination to enshrine it as such, while at the same time trying to preserve its legacy in the present. In protest against the very modest 'native title' measures that were given force of new law under the *Wik* judgment of December 1996, Queensland premier Rob Borbidge impugned the relevant High Court judges as 'dills about history'. Note, though, that even the dissenting judges who argued against native title's coexistence with established settler pastoral leases recognized that the 'principles of the law' that they had applied 'reveal "a significant moral shortcoming" which can be rectified only by legislation or by the acquisition of an estate which would allow the traditions and customs of the Wik and Thayorre Peoples to be preserved and observed'.[82]

Legal and constitutional History get their general relevance from the fact that laws, along with other sorts of rules, traditions, and precepts provide some of the sinews that hold corporations and polities together over time, while zeitgeists and 'great men' wheel and pass. The neo-historicist view can tend to obscure this truth. The same sort of emphasis of 'horizontal', synchronic contextualization that has shaped recent intellectual History against an older tradition more preoccupied with 'vertical', diachronic connections[83] characterizes the work of the 'law and society' school as it reacted against the older 'black letter' tradition of legal scholarship. The 'law and society' approach seems much more professionally 'historical' insofar as the black letter tradition has overtones of whiggishness and even teleology. But in bringing the law overly into social and economic History, the law and society approach might in fact impose what one scholar calls 'epistemological closure'.[84] By this expression he means giving effective capacity to entities like society and the economy as they operate at any one point, let us say synchronically, whilst removing such a capacity from 'the law'—i.e. its canon and specific institutional history—as might radiate outwards to affect the other entities. Much the same goes for separating what historians used to call the (say)

---

[81]   This analysis of the endurance of antiquated authority comes from Lord Mansfield's 1772 judgment of the English Court of King's Bench in the *Somerset* v *Stewart* case, 98 ER 499, available online at: http://www.commonlii.org/int/cases/EngR/1772/57.pdf.

[82]   Bryan Horrigan, *Adventures in Law and Justice* (Sydney: University of New South Wales Press, 2011), 207–8.

[83]   Stephan Collini, 'Intellectual History', at: http://www.history.ac.uk/makinghistory/resources/articles/.

[84]   Johnson, *Making the Market*, 20.

Western artistic canon, or the history of treatment of mental illness, into discrete time periods as if some temporal 'context' cut one epoch off entirely from its predecessor. For historians who like to talk of the context of the times, the 'temptation', to quote the scholar of the Enlightenment Norman Hampson, 'is always to look away from the work of art itself and the technical evolution of a particular genre, 'to "influences" which, whatever their social importance in general, may have had little significance for the artist himself'. Such examples could be multiplied in other areas or art and science but also in everyday discourses such as that of sexism.[85]

In sum, we need to take care that recourse to the particular *neo-historicist* use of the language of context does not hinder *historical* understanding of balances of continuity and change—or, better put, we must insist that historical understanding is not automatically equated with neo-historicist precepts. In the legal connection we need not reproduce all of the blind spots of the black letter tradition to note that the law has some institutional autonomy and self-generated influence; of course it changes across time but that does not mean its rhythms are all dictated from outside its own variable precincts. Here is a prime example of the point that societies comprise tendencies and institutions of different historical 'age', of different temporality, in the terms of Ernst Bloch or Gramsci (p. 231).

By the same token, one cannot use the historical givenness of certain legal dispensations as a way of rendering something sacrosanct and unarguable in the present. In land-right disputes, the law is central to debates over what sort of state one wants to live in. Many opponents of indigenous land rights are really seeking to indenture any such vision of the future to the fait accompli created by earlier invasion. So it is not always enough to defer to the meanings and intentions of the original lawgivers, because it may be necessary to take issue with the system of precedent and statute by which their interest-value amalgam entrenched itself through the present at the expense of Others' ways of life. In plain language, that means saying that you dissent from the justice of those lawgivers—saying you think them wrong.

It is in the areas of law, economics, philosophy, and political science that principles of restitution and restitution's relative, affirmative action, will be worked out, if at all; it is in the political domain that the principles will be acted upon, if they are. The central concerns of this book are less with the nature, range, and sum of apologies, pardons, and awards, and more with the process of self-reflection that is not subject to any statute of limitations.

---

[85] For the quote, Hampson, *The Enlightenment*, 108. On treatment of the mentally ill, Merquior, *Michel Foucault*, 27; for important social discourses in which continuity across large tracts of time is just as marked as change, see Wahrman, 'Change and the Corporeal'.

Closing Thoughts

A final note on self-reflection concerns that part of the material inheritance from the past which is the focus of cultural geographers, students of the politics of space and of material culture. Civic buildings; monumental architecture; public space; sacred space: each of these categories brings together material and ideal/mental components of identity. Think of those grand municipal structures, town houses and country dwellings built on the proceeds of slave labour, or the Turkish roads and landmarks named after the perpetrators of the Armenian genocide. Think too of those kitsch appropriations of extinguished cultures like 'Cherokee' jeeps or 'Apache' helicopters—there is nothing like celebrating the noble savage once 'he' has been eradicated. And think of monuments like the one erected in 1907 in Berlin to the colonial Schutztruppe which had recently conducted the campaign of extermination against the Herero people in the Imperial German colony that later became Namibia. In Namibia itself, a statue of the leading perpetrator, General Lothar von Trotha, marks the site of a former German concentration camp from the genocide, and his name was given to a street in the capital Windhoek.[86]

During a visit to Namibia in 1998, the President of Germany, Roman Herzog, declared that 'too much time has passed for a formal apology to the Hereros to make sense'. He also tried to argue that German actions had not contravened international law at the time—a legalistic argument (itself of dubious strength) that was somewhat undermined by the fact that avoiding an apology was patently a matter of avoiding an admission that might facilitate compensation claims.[87] Clearly there are all sorts of practical and political reasons for a head of state to try to limit his country's liability for past crimes, or, in the German case, to try to restrict critical reflection to the Nazi period alone in order that other periods might be salvaged. The problem with the historicizing argument to the passage of time and the changing legitimacy of colonialism across time is that Germany's civic landscape still featured the 1907 monument to the perpetrators—the monument, and that for which it stood, was a part of Germany's present. Only in the twenty-first century, some thirteen years after Herzog's statement, and after extensive pressure from activists, was another monument erected next to that one. The

---

[86]   Chris Johns and Rob Russell, 'Germany's Forgotten Genocide: The Lasting Effects of the German Colonial project in Namibia', *New Histories* (online), 4/5 (10 May 2013); Jasmin Rietdorf, 'Tracing Marks of German Colonialism in the Cities of Berlin and Windhoek' (Berlin: Entwicklungspolitisches Bildungs-und Informationszentrum, 2010), available at http://www.epiz-berlin.de.

[87]   Quote and contextualization in Tom Bentley, *Empires of Remorse: Narrative, Postcolonialism and Apologies for Colonial Atrocity* (London: Routledge, 2015), ch. 3, which also examines the self-serving, circumscribed nature of the apology that did materialize. On some of the associated legal arguments, see also Catherine Lu, *Justice and Reconciliation in World Politics* (Cambridge: Cambridge University Press, 2017), 122.

new monument was dedicated to the victims of German rule in Namibia—though the appropriate noun 'genocide' was not employed, merely 'colonial war'.[88]

With statues like that of Robert Clive, 'Clive of India', adorning Whitehall and that of Cecil Rhodes, Oxford University, a good question would be: why does our civic landscape give the impression that 'we' are the opposite of ashamed of what the likes of Clive did? Destroying these statues is not the only alternative. Like Confederate flags and busts of Stalin they are a species of sociohistorical evidence, so destroying them would be like burning records in an archive. (Admittedly one only needs so many duplicates of a record…) They need not even be removed from public space, merely relocated within it—away from parks and pantheons and universities and city halls and into museums, though this does not mean museums dedicated to the lifetimes of those whom the statues honoured. These statues belong in an exhibit of cultural anthropology reflecting on the most recent time in the relevant culture at which it was deemed acceptable to have them standing proudly outside museums.

History, as a form of 'openness to other human beings',[89] must have as its accompaniment more than just the capacity to discover, in the words of the German historian of classical antiquity Barthold Georg Niebuhr (1776–1831), what 'even the greatest and highest spirits of our human race' do not understand, namely 'how their eyes only acquired by chance the way in which they see'.[90] Genuine openness must imply the preparedness, the imperative under some circumstances, to try to change one's own way of seeing. That claim does not contradict this book's argument about the irrelevance of relativism and the limits of tolerance when contemplating the foreign country of the past; it is a corollary of the argument. One cannot disengage the moral faculties in the study of history, and one should not aspire to.

[88] Rietdorf, 'Tracing Marks', 3.
[89] François Bédarida, 'The Modern Historian's Dilemma: Conflicting Pressures from Science and Society', *Economic History Review*, NS 40 (1987), 335–48, here 343.
[90] Niebuhr, *Lebensnachrichten über Barthold Georg Niebuhr*, ii (Hamburg: Perthes, 1838), 480.

Bibliography

Newspapers, Journals, and Official Records

Acta Classica
Against the Current
Ajatus
American Anthropologist
American Foreign Policy Interests
American Historical Review
American Journal of Sociology
American Quarterly
American Scholar
American Sociological Review
Ancient Society
Armenian Review
Asian Journal of Social Science
The Atlantic
British Journal of Educational Studies
Central European History
Christian Century
Columbia Law Review
Common Knowledge
Comparative Studies in Society and History
Critical Inquiry
Critical Quarterly
Daily Mail
Daily Telegraph
Diplomacy and Statecraft
Dissent
Economic History Review
Economy and Society
Emotion Review
Ethics
Ethics, Policy and Environment
Exchange
Gender and History
Georgetown Law Journal
The Guardian
Hansard
Harvard Law Review
Historical Journal
Historisch-politische Zeitschrift
History

History and Theory
History of European Ideas
History of Philosophy Quarterly
History Workshop Journal
Human Studies
Humanity
Independent
International Politics
Jewish Quarterly Review
Journal of Advanced Nursing
Journal of Applied Philosophy
Journal of British Studies
Journal of Corporate Law Studies
Journal of Criminal Law and Criminology
Journal of Genocide Research
Journal of the History of Ideas
Journal of Literary Theory Online
Journal of Peace Research
Journal of Philosophy
Journal of Political Power
Le Débat
London Review of Books
Maynooth Review
Michigan Law Review
Midland History
Modern Intellectual History
Modern Law Review
The Nation
Nations and Nationalism
New Centennial Review
New German Critique
New Histories
New York Times Magazine
Philosophical Review
Philosophical Perspectives
Philosophical Quarterly
Philosophical Studies
Philosophiques
Philosophy and Public Affairs
Philosophy and Social Criticism
Philosophy Today
Political Theory
Praxis International
Quaderni storici
Religion and Human Rights
Res Publica
Reviews in American History
Revue de métaphysique et de morale
San Diego Law Review

Science
Security Studies
Slavic Review
Sunday Times
Theory and Society
The Times
Toronto Globe and Mail
Traditio
Transactions of the Royal Historical Society
University of Chicago Record
Viator
Washington Post
William and Mary Quarterly
Yale French Studies
Zeitschrift der Savigny-Stiftung

Online Sources

Boghossian, Paul, 'Relativism about Morality', online at http://as.nyu.edu/content/dam/nyu-as/asSilverDialogues/documents/PBoghossian-RelAboutNorm-final-Silver Dialogues%20v3.pdf.

Boghossian, Paul, 'Should We Be Relativists about Morality?', online at https://cpb-us-e1.wpmucdn.com/sites.northwestern.edu/dist/1/1221/files/2016/09/BoghossianPublicHandout-1kxhlx0.pdf.

Howard, John, 'The Liberal Tradition: The Beliefs and Values which Guide the Federal Government': https://pmtranscripts.pmc.gov.au/release/transcript-10171.

http://www.history.ac.uk/reviews/.

http://www.history.ac.uk/makinghistory/resources/articles/.

Mansfield, Lord, 1772 judgment, *Somerset* v *Stewart* case, 98 ER 499: http://www.commonlii.org/int/cases/EngR/1772/57.pdf.

Stanford Encyclopedia of Philosophy: https://plato.stanford.edu/.

YouGov poll on British attitudes towards empire: http://cdn.yougov.com/cumulus_uploads/document/6quatmbimd/Internal_Results_140725_Commonwealth_Empire-W.pdf.

Zunjic, Bob, 'The Sermon on the Mount: an outline': http://jakavonyte-philosophy.yolasite.com/resources/Zujnic%20on%20Sermon%20on%20the%20Mount.pdf.

Books

Acton, Lord John, *Historical Essays & Studies* (London: Macmillan, 1908).

Acton, Lord John, *Lectures on Modern History* (London: Fontana, 1960).

Alexander, W. M., *Johann Georg Hamann, Philosophy and Faith* (The Hague: Martinus Nijhoff, 1966).

Allison, Henry E., *Lessing and the Enlightenment* (New York: SUNY, 2018).

Althusser, Louis, *For Marx* (Harmondsworth: Penguin, 1969).

Althusser, Louis, *Écrits philosophiques et politiques*, vol. i (Paris: Éditions Stock, 1994).

Althusser, Louis, and Balibar, Étienne, *Reading Capital*, pt 2 (London: New Left Books, 1970).

Alvarado, Ruben, *Common Law and Natural Rights* (Aalten: Wordbridge, 2009).

Anderson, Perry, *The Indian Ideology* (London: Verso, 2013).

Appiah, Kwame Anthony, *The Ethics of Identity* (Princeton: Princeton University Press, 2007).

Appiah, Kwame Anthony, *The Honor Code: How Moral Revolutions Happen* (New York: Norton, 2010).

Applebaum, Arthur Isak, *Ethics for Adversaries: The Morality of Roles in Public and Professional Life* (Princeton: Princeton University Press, 1999).

Aquinas, Thomas, *Summa Theologica*, trans. The Fathers of the English Dominican Province (Raleigh, NC: Hayes Barton Press, 2006).

Arendt, Hannah, *Between Past and Future* (Harmondsworth: Penguin, 1985).

Arendt, Hannah, *Eichmann in Jerusalem* (Harmondsworth: Penguin, 1994).

Aristotle, *Ethics*, trans. J. A. K. Thompson (Harmondsworth: Penguin, 1966).

Arrighi, Giovanni, *The Long Twentieth Century* (London: Verso, 2010).

Attwood, Bain, and Foster, S. G. (eds), *Frontier Conflict: The Australian Experience*, (Canberra: National Museum of Australia, 2003).

Augustine of Hippo, *The Works of Aurelius Augustine: A New Translation*, ed. Marcus Dods, vol. v (Edinburgh: Clark, 1872).

Augustine of Hippo, *City of God*, ed. David Knowles (Harmondsworth: Penguin, 1972).

Augustine of Hippo, *St. Augustine's Anti-Pelagian Works*, ed. Philip Schaff (Woodstock, ON: Devoted, 2017).

Austin, James, *The Tower of Babel in Genesis* (Bloomington, IN: Westbow, 2012).

Backus, Irena, *Leibniz: Protestant Theologian* (New York: Oxford University Press, 2016).

Bayles, Michael D. (ed.), *Contemporary Utilitarianism* (New York: Anchor, 1968).

Beiser, Frederick C., *The German Historicist Tradition* (Oxford: Oxford University Press, 2011).

Benedict, Ruth, *The Chrysanthemum and the Sword: Patterns of Japanese Culture* (Boston: Mariner, 2005).

Benedict, Ruth, and Weltfish, Gene, *The Races of Mankind* (New York: Public Affairs Committee, 1943).

Benjamin, Walter, *Illuminations*, ed. Hannah Arendt (New York: Shocken, 1968).

Bentley, Michael, *Lord Salisbury's World: Conservative Environments in Late-Victorian Britain* (Cambridge: Cambridge University Press, 2004).

Bentley, Tom, *Empires of Remorse: Narrative, Postcolonialism and Apologies for Colonial Atrocity* (London: Routledge, 2015).

Berger, Adolf (ed.) *Encyclopedic Dictionary of Roman Law* (Clark, NJ: The Lawbook Exchange, 2004).

Berlin, Isaiah, *Historical Inevitability* (New York: Oxford University Press, 1954).

Berlin, Isaiah, *Four Essays on Liberty* (Oxford: Oxford University Press, 1969).

Berman, Harold J., *Law and Revolution: The Formation of the Western Legal Tradition* (Cambridge, MA: Harvard University Press, 1983).

Berman, Harold J., *Law and Revolution II: The Impact of the Protestant Reformations on the Western Legal Tradition* (Cambridge, MA: Belknap Press, 2003).

Bertagnolli, Paul, *Prometheus in Music: Representations of Myth in the Romantic Era* (London: Routledge, 2007).

Betteridge, Tom, *Literature and Politics in the Tudor Reformation* (Manchester: Manchester University Press, 2004).

Betz, John R., *After Enlightenment: The Post-Secular Vision of J. G. Hamann* (Chichester: Blackwell, 2012).

Biess, Frank, Roseman, Mark, and Schissler, Hanna (eds), *Conflict, Catastrophe, and Continuity* (New York: Berghahn, 2007).

Bishop, Robert C., *Philosophy of the Social Sciences* (London: Bloomsbury, 2007).

Blight, David W., *Race and Reunion* (Cambridge, MA: Belknap Press, 2001).

Bloch, Ernst, *Erbschaft dieser Zeit* (Zurich: Oprecht and Helbling, 1935).

Bloch, Ernst, *Natural Law and Human Dignity* (Cambridge, MA: MIT Press, 1996).

Bloch, Marc, *The Historian's Craft* (New York: Vintage Books, 1953).

Bloch, Marc, *Feudal Society* (London: Routledge, 1989).

Bloxham, Donald, *The Great Game of Genocide* (Oxford: Oxford University Press, 2005).

Bloxham, Donald, *Why History? A History* (Oxford: Oxford University Press, 2020).

Bödeker, Hans Erich, Reill, Peter Hanns, and Schlumbohm, Jürgen (eds), *Wissenschaft als kulturelle Praxis, 1750–1900* (Göttingen: Vandenhoeck und Ruprecht, 1999).

Bodin, Jean, *Method for the Easy Comprehension of History* (New York: Octagon, 1945).

Bolingbroke, Lord Henry St John, *Letters on the Study and Use of History* (London: T. Cadell, 1779).

Bourdieu, Pierre, *Practical Reason* (Cambridge: Polity Press, 2001).

Bourdieu, Pierre, and Wacquant, Loïc J. D., *An Invitation to Reflexive Sociology* (Cambridge: Polity, 1992).

Bowie, Norman E., and Simon, Robert L., *The Individual and the Political Order* (Lanham, MD: Rowman and Littlefield, 2008).

Briggs, Charles F., *The Body Broken: Medieval Europe, 1300–1520* (London: Routledge 2011).

Brooker, Peter, Gąsiorek, Andrzej, Longworth, Deborah, and Thacker, Andrew (eds), *The Oxford Handbook of Modernisms* (Oxford: Oxford University Press, 2010).

Brown, Norman O., *Apocalypse and/or Metamorphosis* (Berkeley and Los Angeles: University of California Press, 1991).

Browning, Christopher, *Ordinary Men: Reserve Police Battalion 101 and the Final Solution in Poland* (New York: Harper Collins, 1993).

Browning, Christopher, with Matthäus, Jürgen, *The Origins of the Final Solution* (Lincoln, NE: University of Nebraska Press, 2005).

Bryant, Michael, *A World History of War Crimes* (London: Bloomsbury, 2016).

Buber, Martin, *I and Thou* (Mansfield, CT: Martino, 2010).

Bull, Hedley, and Watson, Adam (eds), *The Expansion of International Society* (Oxford: Clarendon Press, 1985).

Burckhardt, Jacob, *The Civilization of the Renaissance in Italy* (London: Penguin, 2004).

Burke, Edmund, *Reflections on the French Revolution*, ed. W. Alison Phillips and Catherine Beatrice Phillips (Cambridge: Cambridge University Press, 1912).

Burke, Raymond, *Decolonization and the Evolution of International Human Rights* (Philadelphia: University of Pennsylvania Press, 2010).

Butterfield, Herbert, *Christianity and History* (London: G. Bell and Sons, 1949).

Butterfield, Herbert, *The Whig Interpretation of History* (New York: Norton, 1965).

Buzan, Barry, Wæver, Oly, and Wilde, Jaap de, *Security: A New Framework for Analysis* (Boulder, CO: Lynne Rienner, 1998).

Cahill, Edward, *Liberty of the Imagination* (Philadelphia: University of Pennsylvania Press, 2012).

Cahn, Steven M. (ed.), *Classics of Western Philosophy* (Indianapolis: Hackett, 1990).

Calvin, Jean, *Institutes of the Christian Religion* (Woodstock, ON: Devoted, 2016).

Card, Claudia, *Confronting Evils: Terrorism, Torture, Genocide* (Cambridge: Cambridge University Press, 2010).

Carlyle, Thomas, *Heroes and Hero-Worship, Past and Present* (London: Ward, Lock and co., 1892).

Cassirer, Ernst, *The Philosophy of the Enlightenment* (Princeton: Princeton University Press, 2009).

Cavell, Stanley, *The Claim of Reason* (New York: Oxford University Press, 1999).

Certeau, Michel de, *The Practice of Everyday Life* (Berkeley and Los Angeles: University of California Press, 1988).

Chambers, Clarke A., *Seedtime of Reform* (Minneapolis: University of Minnesota Press, 1963).

Chaturvedi, Vinayak (ed.), *Mapping Subaltern Studies and the Postcolonial* (London: Verso, 2012).

Chibber, Vivek, *Postcolonial Theory and the Specter of Capital* (London: Verso, 2013).

Chung, Paul S., *The Hermeneutical Self and an Ethical Difference: Intercivilizational Engagement* (Cambridge: James Clarke and Co., 2012).

Cicero, Marcus Tullius, *Cato: or, An Essay on Old-Age* (London: J. Dodsley, 1773).

Cioffi-Revilla, Claudio, *Politics and Uncertainty* (New York: Cambridge University Press, 1998).

Clark, Linda (ed.), *The Fifteenth Century*, v. *Of Mice and Men: Image, Belief and Regulation in Late Medieval England* (Woodbridge: The Boydell Press, 2005).

Coady, C. A. J., *Messy Morality: The Challenge of Politics* (Oxford: Oxford University Press, 2010).

Coleman, Janet, *Ancient and Medieval Memories: Studies in the Reconstruction of the Past* (Cambridge: Cambridge University Press, 2005).

Coleridge, Samuel Taylor, *On the Constitution of the Church and State*, ed. John Colmer (Princeton: Princeton University Press, 1976).

Colley, Linda, *Britons: Forging the Nation, 1707–1837* (New Haven: Yale University Press, 2005).

Collingwood, R. G., *An Essay on Metaphysics* (Oxford: Clarendon Press, 1969).

Collingwood, R. G., *The Idea of History* (rev. edn, Oxford: Oxford University Press, 2005).

Commager, H. S., *The Search for a Usable Past* (New York: Knopf, 1967).

Confino, Alon, *Foundational Pasts: The Holocaust as Historical Understanding* (Cambridge: Cambridge University Press, 2012), 83–96.

Connelly, Mark, *Reaching for the Stars: A New History of Bomber Command in World War II* (London: Tauris, 2001).

Connor, Robert, *Thucydides* (Princeton: Princeton University Press, 1987).

Cooper, John W., *Panentheism—The Other God of the Philosophers* (Grand Rapids, MI: Baker, 2006).

Corradetti, Claudio, *Relativism and Human Rights: A Theory of Pluralistic Universalism* (Dordrecht: Springer, 2009).

Crick, Bernard, *In Defence of Politics* (London: Penguin, 1964).

Croce, Benedetto, *History as the Story of Liberty* (Chicago: Regnery, 1970).

Crofts, Penny, *Wickedness and Crime: Laws of Homicide and Malice* (London: Routledge, 2013).

Crossley, Ceri, *French Historians and Romanticism: Thierry, Guizot, the Saint-Simonians, Quinet, Michelet* (London: Routledge, 1993).

Crowe, Michael Bertram, *The Changing Profile of The Natural Law* (The Hague: Nijhoff, 1977).

Davies, Brian, and Stump, Eleonore (eds), *The Oxford Handbook of Aquinas* (Oxford: Oxford University Press, 2012).

De Mauro, Tullio, and Formigari, Lia (eds), *Leibniz, Humboldt and the Origins of Comparativism* (Amsterdam: Benjamins, 1990).

Del Lucchese, Fillipo, Frosini, Fabio, and Morfino, Vittorio. (eds) *The Radical Machiavelli: Politics, Philosophy, and Language* (Leiden: Brill, 2015).

Derrida, Jacques, *Limited Inc* (Evanston, IL: Northwestern University Press, 1988).

Derrida, Jacques, *Writing and Difference*, ed. Alan Bass (London: Routledge, 2005).

Descheemaeker, Eric, and Scott, Helen (eds) *Iniuria and the Common Law* (Oxford: Hart, 2014).

Dickson, Gwen Griffith, *Johann Georg Hamman's Relational Metacriticism* (Berlin: de Gruyter, 1995).

Diefenbach, Katja, Ferris, Sara R., Kirn, Gal, and Thomas, Peter D. (eds), *Encountering Althusser* (London: Bloomsbury, 2013).

Dierken, Jörg, *Selbstbewusstsein individueller Freiheit: Religionstheoretische Erkundungen in protestantischer Perspektive* (Tübingen: Mohr Siebeck, 2005).

Di Leo, Jeffrey R. (ed.), *Federman's Fictions* (Albany, NY: SUNY, 2011).

Dilley, Roy (ed.), *Context and Social Anthropology* (New York: Berghahn, 1999).

Dilthey, Wilhelm, *The Formation of the Historical World in the Human Sciences*, ed. Rudolf A. Makreel and Frithjof Rodi (Princeton: Princeton University Press, 2002).

Dobson, R. B. (ed.) *The Peasants' Revolt of 1381* (London: Macmillan, 1970).

Donagan, Alan, *The Later Philosophy of R. G. Collingwood* (Oxford: Clarendon Press, 1962).

Donnelly, Jack, *Realism and International Relations* (Cambridge: Cambridge University Press, 2002).

Dower, John, *War Without Mercy: Race and Power in the Pacific War* (New York: Pantheon, 1986).

Drapkin, Israel, *Crime and Punishment in the Ancient World* (Lexington, KY: Lexington Books, 1989).

Duara, Prasenjit, Murthy, Viren, and Sartori, Andrew (eds), *A Companion to Global Historical Thought* (Oxford: Blackwell, 2014).

Durkheim, Émile, *Sociology and Philosophy* (New York: The Free Press, 1953).

Eaglestone, Robert, *Postmodernism and Holocaust Denial* (London: Icon, 2001).

Eaglestone, Robert, *The Holocaust and the Postmodern* (Oxford: Oxford University Press, 2004).

Edwards, Mark U., *Luther's Last Battles: Politics and Polemics 1531–1546* (Minneapolis: Fortress, 2004).

Eggert, Wolfgang, and Pätzold, Barbara, *Wir-Gefühl und Regnum Saxonum bei frühmittelalterlichen Geschichtsschreibern* (Cologne: Böhlau, 1984).

Ehrenreich, Barbara, and English, Deirdre, *Witches, Midwives and Nurses* (New York: Feminist Press, 2010).

Ellingson, Mark, *The Richness of Augustine* (Louisville, KY: Westminster John Knox Press, 2005).

Elton, G. R., *The Practice of History* (Sydney: Sydney University Press, 1967).

Emerson, Ralph Waldo, *The Essays of Ralph Waldo Emerson* (Cambridge, MA: Belknap Press, 1987).

Erler, Don, *Lone Star State of Mind* (Lanham, MD: Lexington, 2002).

Essen, Gesa von, and Turk, Horst (eds), *Unerledigte Geschichten: Der literarische Umgang mit Nationalität und Internationalität* (Göttingen: Wallstein, 2000).

Evans, Richard J., *In Defense of History* (New York: Norton, 1999).

Farmer, Sharon, and Rosenwein, Barbara H. (eds), *Monks and Nuns, Saints and Outcasts: Religion in Medieval Society* (Ithaca, NY: Cornell University Press, 2000).

Fasolt, Constantin, *The Limits of History* (Chicago: University of Chicago Press, 2004).

Fawtier, Robert, *The Capetian Kings of France* (London: Macmillan, 1960).

Ferguson, Niall (ed.), *Virtual History: Alternatives and Counterfactuals* (London: Picador, 1997).

Ferguson, Niall, *Empire* (London: Penguin, 2004).

Ferguson, Niall, *The War of the World: History's Age of Hatred* (London: Penguin, 2009).

Fettweis, Christopher J., *The Pathologies of Power* (Cambridge: Cambridge University Press, 2013).

Firth, Raymond, *Elements of Social Organisation* (London: Watts, 1963).

Fleischacker, Samuel, *Integrity and Moral Relativism* (Leiden: Brill, 1992).

Foucault, Michel, *Michel Foucault: Power/Knowledge: Selected Interviews and Other Writings 1972–1977*, ed. Colin Gordon (London: Harvester Press, 1980).

Foucault, Michel, *Ethics: Subjectivity and Truth*, ed. Paul Rabinow (New York: New Press, 1997).

Fowler, Loretta, *Shared Symbols, Contested Meanings: Gros Ventre Culture and History, 1778–1984* (Ithaca, NY: Cornell University Press, 1987).

Freire, Paolo, *Pedagogy of Hope* (London: Continuum, 1998).

Frey, R. G., and Morris, C. W. (eds), *Violence, Terrorism and Justice* (Cambridge: Cambridge University Press, 1991).

Friedell, Egon, *A Cultural History of the Modern Age*, ii. *Baroque, Rococo and Enlightenment* (New Brunswick, NJ: Transaction, 2009).

Friedlander, Saul, *Reflections of Nazism: An Essay on Kitsch and Death* (New York: Harper and Row, 1984).

Friedlander, Saul, *The Years of Extermination: Nazi Germany and the Jews, 1939–1945* (London: Harper Collins, 2007).

Fulda, Daniel, *Wissenschaft aus Kunst: Die Entstehung der modernen deutschen Geschichtsschreibung, 1760–1860* (Berlin: de Gruyter, 1996).

Fuller, Steve, *The Philosophy of Science and Technology Studies* (New York: Routledge, 2006).

Gaddis, John Lewis, *The Landscape of History* (Oxford: Oxford University Press, 2004).

Geertz, Clifford, *The Interpretation of Cultures* (New York: Basic Books, 1973).

Geertz, Clifford, *Works and Lives: The Anthropologist as Author* (Stanford, CA: Stanford University Press, 1988).

Gerald of Wales, *Giraldus Cambrensis: The Topography of Ireland* (Cambridge, Ontario: In Parentheses, 2000).

Gewirth, Alan, *Self-Fulfillment* (Princeton: Princeton University Press, 1998).

Giddens, Anthony, *The Constitution of Society: Outline of the Theory of Structuration* (Cambridge: Polity Press, 1984).

Ginzburg, Carlo, *The Judge and the Historian* (London: Verso, 2002).

Gipper, Helmut, and Schmitter, Peter, *Sprachwissenschaft und Sprachphilosophie im Zeitalter der Romantik* (Tübingen: Narr, 1979).

Golding, Sue, *Gramsci's Democratic Theory: Contributions to a Post-Liberal Democracy* (Toronto: University of Toronto Press, 1982).

Goody, Jack, *The Theft of History* (Cambridge: Cambridge University Press, 2012).

Gordley, James, *The Jurists: A Critical History* (Oxford: Oxford University Press, 2013).

Gottlieb, Erika, *The Orwell Conundrum: A Cry of Despair or Faith in the Spirit of Man?* (Ottawa: Carleton University Press, 1992).

Grattan, Michelle (ed.), *Reconciliation: Essays on Australian Reconciliation* (Melbourne: Black Inc., 2000).

Greenfeld, Liah, *Nationalism: Five Roads to Modernity* (Cambridge, MA: Harvard University Press, 1992).

Guevara Jnr, Nick J., *West Point, Bataan, and Beyond: Santiago Guevara and the War in the Philippines* (Silver Spring, MD: Garfield Street Publishing, 2016).

Gunther, Michael M., *Armenian History and the Question of Genocide* (New York: Palgrave Macmillan, 2011).

Gutting, Gary (ed.), *The Cambridge Companion to Foucault* (Cambridge: Cambridge University Press, 2005).

Habermas, Jürgen, *The Philosophical Discourse of Modernity* (Cambridge, MA: MIT Press, 1990).

Haberski Jr, Raymond, and Hartman, Andrew (eds), *American Labyrinth: Intellectual History for Complicated Times* (Ithaca, NY: Cornell University Press, 2018).

Hacker, Paul, *The Ego in Faith: Martin Luther and the Origin of Anthropocentric Religion* (Chicago: Franciscan Herald Press, 1970).

Hacking, Ian, *The Social Construction of What?* (Cambridge, MA: Harvard University Press, 1999).

Hague, William, *William Wilberforce, The Life of the Great Anti-Slave Trade Campaigner* (London: Harper Perennial, 2008).

Haikola, Lauri, *Gesetz und Evangelium bei Matthias Flacius Illyricus: Eine Untersuchung zur Lutherischen Theologie vor der Konkordienformel* (Lund: Gleerup, 1952).

Hampson, Norman, *The Enlightenment* (London: Penguin, 1990).

Haslam, Jonathan, *The Vices of Integrity: E. H. Carr, 1892–1982* (London: Verso, 1999).

Hastings, Max, *Nemesis: The Battle for Japan, 1944–1945* (London: Harper Perennial, 2008).

Hayek, F. A., *The Constitution of Liberty* (London: Routledge and Kegan Paul, 1960).

Hayes, Peter (ed.) *Lessons and Legacies: The Meaning of the Holocaust in a Changing World* (Evanston, IL: Northwestern University Press, 1991).

Haynes, Kenneth, *Hamann: Writings on Philosophy and Language* (Cambridge: Cambridge University Press, 2007).

Haynes, Stephen R., *Reluctant Witnesses: Jews and the Christian Imagination* (Louisville, KY: Westminster John Knox Press, 1995).

Hearn, Jonathan, *Theorizing Power* (Houndmills: Palgrave, 2012).

Hegel, G. W. F., *The Philosophy of Right* (Oxford: Clarendon Press, 1952).

Heidegger, Martin, *Sein und Zeit* (Tübingen: Niemeyer, 1967).

Herder, Johann Gottfried von, *Philosophical Writings*, ed. Michael N. Forster (Cambridge: Cambridge University Press, 2002).

Herskovits, Melville J., *Cultural Relativism* (New York: Random House, 1972).

Herwig, Holger, *The German Naval Officer Corps* (Oxford: Clarendon Press, 1973).

Hill, Christopher, *Reformation to Industrial Revolution* (London: Penguin, 1969).

Hill, Christopher, *The World Turned Upside Down* (London: Penguin, 1991).

Himmelfarb, Gertrude, *The Moral Imagination: From Adam Smith to Lionel Trilling* (Lanham, MD: Rowman and Littlefield, 2012).

Hirschman, Albert O., *The Passions and the Interests: Political Arguments for Capitalism Before Its Triumph* (Princeton: Princeton University Press, 1997).

Hitler, Adolf, *Mein Kampf* (Boston: Houghton Mifflin, 1943).

Hobart, Mark, and Taylor, Robert H. (eds) *Context, Meaning and Power in Southeast Asia* (Ithaca, NY: Cornell University Press, 1986).

Hobsbawm, Eric, *Age of Extremes* (London: Joseph, 1994).

Hochschild, Adam, *King Leopold's Ghost* (London: Pan Macmillan, 1999).

Hoffmann, Stefan-Ludwig, *The Politics of Sociability: Freemasonry and German Civil Society, 1840–1918* (Ann Arbor: University of Michigan Press, 2007).

Hopkins, Jasper, *A Concise Introduction to the Philosophy of Nicholas of Cusa* (Minneapolis: University of Minnesota Press, 1978).

Hopkins, Jasper, *Nicholas of Cusa's* De Pace Fidei *and* Cribratio Alkorani: *Translation and Analysis* (Minneapolis: The Arthur J. Banning Press, 1994).

Horsman, Reginald, *The Origins of Indian Removal, 1815–1824* (East Lansing, MI: Michigan State University Press, 1969).

Houlgate, Stephen, and Baur, Michael (eds) *A Companion to Hegel* (Oxford: Wiley-Blackwell, 2016).

Howe, Anthony, and Morgan, Simon (eds) *Rethinking Nineteenth Century Liberalism* (Aldershot: Ashgate, 2006).

Hruschka, Joachim, *Kant und der Rechtsstaat: Und andere Essays zu Kants Rechtslehre und Ethik* (Freiburg: Karl Alber, 2015).

Hughes, Philip, *History of the Church*, vol. iii (London: Sheed and Ward, 1947).

Hughes, Richard A., *Pro-Justice Ethics* (New York: Lang, 2009).

Hull, David L., and Ruse, Michael (eds), *Cambridge Companion to the Philosophy of Biology* (Cambridge: Cambridge University Press, 2007).

Hunt, Lynn (ed.), *The New Cultural History* (Berkeley and Los Angeles: University of California Press, 1989).

Iggers, George, *The German Conception of History* (Middletown, CT: Wesleyan University Press, 2012).

Ignatieff, Michael, *Blood and Belonging* (London: Vintage, 1994).

Ignatieff, Michael, *The Lesser Evil: Political Ethics in an Age of Terror* (Princeton: Princeton University Press, 2005).

Jahanbegloo, Ramin, *Gadflies in the Public Space: A Socratic Legacy of Philosophical Dissent* (Lanham, MD: Lexington, 2017).

Jameson, Fredric, *The Political Unconscious* (London: Routledge, 1983).

Jenkins, Keith, *Re-Thinking History* (London: Routledge, 2003).

Johnson, Chalmers, *Blowback: The Costs and Consequences of American Empire* (New York: Henry Holt, 2001).

Johnson, Paul, *Making the Market: Victorian Origins of Corporate Capitalism* (Cambridge: Cambridge University Press, 2010).

Johnston, William M., *The Formative Years of R. G. Collingwood* (Leiden: Martinus Nijhoff, 1968).

Jones, Dan, *The Plantagenets* (London: Harper, 2013).

Kant, Immanuel, *Religion Within the Boundaries of Mere Reason and Other Writings* (Cambridge: Cambridge University Press, 1998).

Kant, Immanuel, *Lectures on Ethics*, ed. Peter Heath and J. B. Schneewind (Cambridge: Cambridge University Press, 2001).

Kantorowicz, Ernst H., *The King's Two Bodies: A Study in Medieval Political Theology* (Princeton: Princeton University Press, 2016).

Kapuściński, Ryszard, *The Other* (London: Verso, 2008).

Kennedy, Paul, and Nicholls, Anthony (eds), *Nationalist and Racialist Movements in Britain and Germany Before 1914* (Basingstoke: Macmillan, 1981).

Kenny, Anthony, *A New History of Western Philosophy* (Oxford: Clarendon Press, 2010).

Kenny, Anthony, and Kenny, Charles, *Life, Liberty and the Pursuit of Utility* (Exeter: Imprint Academic, 2006).

Khong, Yuen Foong, *Analogies at War: Korea, Munich, Dien Bien Phu, and the Vietnam Decisions of 1965* (Princeton: Princeton University Press, 1992).

Kierkegaard, Søren, *Kierkegaard's Concluding Unscientific Postscript* (Princeton: Princeton University Press, 1961).

Kitson Clark, George, *The Critical Historian* (London: The History Book Club, 1968).

Klein, Laurence E. (ed.), *Shaftesbury: Characteristics of Men, Manners, Opinions, Times* (Cambridge: Cambridge University Press, 1990).

Kleist, E. E., *Judging Appearances: A Phenomenological Study of the Kantian* sensus communis (Dordrecht: Springer, 2012).

Knowles, David, *The Evolution of Medieval Thought* (Baltimore: Helican, 1962).

Koelb, Clayton, *The Revivifying Word: Literature, Philosophy and the Theory of Life in Europe's Romantic Age* (Rochester, NY: Camden House, 2008).

Kow, Simon, *China in Early Enlightenment Political Thought* (Abingdon: Routledge, 2017).

Kozicki, Henry (ed.), *Developments in Modern Historiography* (Basingstoke: Palgrave, 1998).

Krimmer, Elisabeth, and Simpson, Patricia Anne (eds), *Religion, Reason, and Culture in the Age of Goethe* (Rochester, NY: Camden House, 2013).

Lang, Berel, *Act and Idea in the Nazi Genocide* (Syracuse, NY: Syracuse University Press, 2003).

Latinovic, Vladimir, Mannion, Gerrard, and Welle, Jason (eds), *Catholicism Engaging Other Faiths* (Cham: Springer, 2018).

Lawson, Tom, *The Church of England and the Holocaust: Christianity, Memory and Nazism* (Martlesham: Boydell, 2006).

le Bon, Gustave, *The Psychology of Revolution* (Sioux Falls, SD: NuVision Publications, 2010).

Leavitt, John, *Linguistic Relativities: Language Diversity and Modern Thought* (Cambridge University Press, 2011).

Lee, Steven Hugh, *Outposts of Empire: Korea, Vietnam and the Origins of the Cold War in Asia, 1949–1954* (Liverpool: Liverpool University Press, 1995).

Leerssen, Joep, and Rigney, Ann, *Historians and Social Values* (Amsterdam: Amsterdam University Press, 2000).

Lefever, Ernest, *Ethics and United States Foreign Policy* (New York: Living Age Books, 1959).

Leff, Gordon, *William of Ockham: The Metamorphosis of Scholastic Discourse* (Manchester: Manchester University Press, 1975).

Leibniz, Gottfried Wilhelm, *Œuvres de Leibniz*, ed. M. A. Jacques (Paris: Charpentier, 1846).

Leibniz, Gottfried Wilhelm, *Discourse on Metaphysics and The Monadology*, trans. George R. Montgomery (Mineola, NY: Dover, 2005).

Leiter, Brian, and Rosen, Michael (eds), *The Oxford Handbook of Continental Philosophy* (Oxford: Oxford University Press, 2007).

Lenin, V. I., *Selected Works*, 2 vols. (Moscow: Foreign Languages Publishing House, 1947).

Lessing, Theodor, *Geschichte als Sinngebung des Sinnlosen* (Munich: Beck, 1921).

Lévi-Strauss, Claude, *The Raw and the Cooked* (Harmondsworth: Penguin, 1969).

Levin, David, *History as Romantic Art* (Stanford, CA: Stanford University Press, 1959).

Levinas, Emmanuel, *Totality and Infinity* (Pittsburgh: Duquesne University Press, 1969).

Levy, Ariel, *Female Chauvinist Pigs* (New York: Free Press, 2006).

Loewen, Harry, *Luther and the Radicals* (Waterloo, ON: Wilfrid Laurier University Press, 2010).

London, Louise, *Whitehall and the Jews* (Cambridge: Cambridge University Press, 2001).

Loughlin, Martin, *Foundations of Public Law* (Oxford: Oxford University Press, 2010).

Lovejoy, Arthur O., *The Great Chain of Being* (Cambridge, MA: Harvard University Press, 1964).

Lu, Catherine, *Justice and Reconciliation in World Politics* (Cambridge: Cambridge University Press, 2017).

Lukes, Steven, *Moral Relativism* (New York: Picador, 2008).

Luther, Martin, *Commentary on Paul's Epistle to the Galatians* (Lafayette, IN: Sovereign Grace, 2001).

Luxemburg, Rosa, *Prison Letters to Sophie Liebknecht* (London: Independent Labour Party, 1972).

Lynch, Joseph H., and Adamo, Phillip C., *The Medieval Church* (London: Routledge, 2014).

MacCormick, Neil, *Practical Reason in Law and Morality* (Oxford: Oxford University Press, 2008).

McDonald, Christie, and Hoffmann, Stanley (eds), *Rousseau and Freedom* (Cambridge: Cambridge University Press, 2010).

McInerny, Ralph, *A History of Western Philosophy from St. Augustine to Ockham* (Notre Dame, IN: University of Notre Dame Press, 1963).

McIntire, C. T., *Herbert Butterfield: Historian as Dissenter* (New Haven: Yale University Press, 2004).

Macintyre, Stuart, and Clark, Anna, *The History Wars* (Melbourne: Melbourne University Press, 2004).

Mack, Michael, *German Idealism and the Jew: The Inner Anti-Semitism of Philosophy and German Jewish Responses* (Chicago: University of Chicago Press, 2003).

Mack, Michael, *Spinoza and the Specters of Modernity* (New York: Continuum, 2010).

McMahon, Robert J., *The Cold War* (Oxford: Oxford University Press, 2003).

McManus, Edgar J., *Law and Liberty in Early New England* (Amherst, MA: University of Massachusetts Press, 1993).

Macmurray, John, *Persons in Relation* (London: Faber and Faber, 1995).

Mahmood, Saba, *Politics of Piety: The Islamic Revival and the Feminist Subject* (Princeton: Princeton University Press, 2005).

Mäkinen, Virpi (ed.), *Lutheran Reformation and the Law* (Leiden: Brill, 2006).

Makkreel, Rudolf A., *Dilthey: Philosopher of the Human Sciences* (Princeton: Princeton University Press, 1992).

Malinowski, Bronisław, *Argonauts of the West Pacific* (London: Routledge and Kegan Paul, 1922).

Mann, Michael, *The Dark Side of Democracy* (Cambridge: Cambridge University Press, 2005).

Marenbon, John, *The Philosophy of Peter Abelard* (Cambridge: Cambridge University Press, 1999).

Marincola, John, Llewellyn-Jones, Lloyd, and Maciver, Calum Alasdair (eds), *Greek Notions of the Past in the Archaic and Classical Eras: History without Historians* (Edinburgh: Edinburgh University Press, 2012).

Martin, Terry, *The Affirmative Action Empire: Nations and Nationalism in the Soviet Union, 1923–1939* (Ithaca, NY: Cornell University Press, 2001).

Martucci, Roberto, *L'invenzione dell'Italia unita, 1855–1864* (Florence: Sansoni, 1999).

Marx, Karl, and Engels, Friedrich, *Karl Marx and Friedrich Engels—Selected Works in Three Volumes*, vol. i (Moscow: Progress, 1966).

Masters, Roger D., *The Political Philosophy of Rousseau* (Princeton: Princeton University Press, 1968).

Mastnak, Tomaž, *Crusading Peace: Christendom, the Muslim World, and Western Political Order* (Berkeley and Los Angeles: University of California Press, 2002).

Mays, Michael, *The Cultures of Irish Nationalism* (Lanham, MD: Lexington Books, 2007).

Mazower, Mark, *No Enchanted Palace* (Princeton: Princeton University Press, 2009).

Mearsheimer, John J., *The Tragedy of Great Power Politics* (New York: W. W. Norton, 2001).

Melvin, Mungo, *Manstein: Hitler's Greatest General* (London: Weidenfeld and Nicolson, 2010).

Menzler-Trott, Eckart, *Gentzens Problem: Mathematische Logik im nationalsozialistischen Deutschland* (Basel: Springer, 2001).

Merquior, José Guilherme, *Michel Foucault* (Berkeley and Los Angeles: University of California Press, 1985).

Meyerhoff, Hans (ed.), *The Philosophy of History in Our Time* (New York: Anchor, 1959).

Milbank, John, *Beyond Secular Order: The Representation of Being and the Representation of the People* (Hoboken, NJ: Wiley, 2013).

Mill, John Stuart, *Principles of Political Economy*, vol. i (London: Parker, 1848).

Miller, Alexander, *Contemporary Metaethics: An Introduction* (Cambridge: Polity, 2013).

Mitchell, Timothy, *Rule of Experts: Egypt, Techno-Politics, Modernity* (Berkeley and Los Angeles: University of California Press, 2002).

Mommsen, Hans (ed.), *The Third Reich Between Vision and Reality* (Oxford: Berg, 2002).

Montmarquet, James A., *Epistemic Virtue and Doxastic Responsibility* (Lanham, MD: Rowman and Littlefield, 1993).

Moore, R. I., *The Formation of a Persecuting Society* (2nd edn, Oxford: Blackwell, 2007).

Morera, Esteve, *Gramsci's Historicism: A Realist Interpretation* (Abingdon: Routledge, 1990).

Morton, Michael, *Herder and the Poetics of Thought* (University Park, PA: Pennsylvania State University Press, 1989).

Mudge, Jean McClure (ed.), *Mr Emerson's Revolution* (Cambridge: Open Book Publishers, 2015).

Mulligan, William, *The Great War for Peace* (New Haven: Yale University Press, 2014).

Murray, Alexander, *Conscience and Authority in the Medieval Church* (Oxford: Oxford University Press, 2015).

Myers, Ella, *Worldly Ethics: Democratic Politics and Care for the World* (Durham, NC: Duke University Press, 2013).

Nagel, Thomas, *Mortal Questions* (Cambridge: Cambridge University Press, 1979).

Neuhouser, Frederick, *Rousseau's Critique of Inequality* (Cambridge: Cambridge University Press, 2015).

Niebuhr, B. G., *Lebensnachrichten über Barthold Georg Niebuhr*, vol. ii (Hamburg: Perthes, 1838).

Nietzsche, Friedrich, *On the Advantage and Disadvantage of History for Life* (Indianapolis: Hackett, 1980).

Nietzsche, Friedrich, *On the Genealogy of Morality*, ed. Keith Ansell-Pearson (Cambridge: Cambridge University Press, 2006).

Nisbet, Hugh Barr, *Herder and Scientific Thought* (Cambridge: The Modern Humanities Research Association, 1970).

Nisbet, Hugh Barr, *Gotthold Ephraim Lessing: His Life, Works, and Thought* (Oxford: Oxford University Press, 2013).

Nolte, Ernst, *Der europäische Bürgerkrieg 1917–1945* (Berlin: Propyläen, 1987).

Norrie, Alan, *Crime, Reason and History: A Critical Introduction to Criminal Law* (Cambridge: Cambridge University Press, 2014).

Oakeshott, Michael, *Rationalism in Politics and Other Essays* (London: Methuen, 1962).

Olzak, Susan, *The Dynamics of Ethnic Competition and Conflict* (Stanford, CA: Stanford. University Press, 1992).

Orwell, George, *Critical Essays* (London: Secker and Warburg, 1946).

Orwell, George, *Facing Unpleasant Facts: Narrative Essays*, ed. George Packer (Boston: Mariner, 2009).

Parker, John, and Reid, Richard (eds), *The Oxford Handbook of Modern African History* (Oxford: Oxford University Press, 2013).

Parker, Robert, *Miasma: Pollution and Purification in Early Greek Religion* (Oxford: Clarendon Press, 1991).

Patterson, David, *Genocide in Jewish Thought* (Cambridge: Cambridge University Press, 2012).

Perkins, Franklin, *Leibniz and China: A Commerce of Light* (Cambridge: Cambridge University Press, 2004).

Phillips, Ulrich Bonnell, *American Negro Slavery* (New York: Appleton and Company, 1918).

Pinkard, Terry, *German Philosophy 1760–1860: The Legacy of Idealism* (Cambridge: Cambridge University Press, 2002).

Pippin, Robert B., *Modernism as a Philosophical Problem* (Oxford: Blackwell, 1999).

Plamenatz, John, *Man and Society*, vol. i (London: Longmans, 1969).

Plekhanov, Georgi, *The Role of the Individual in History* (London: Camelot Press, 1950).

Polanyi, Karl, *The Great Transformation* (Boston: Beacon Press, 2001).

Polybius, *The Rise of the Roman Empire*, trans. Ian Scott-Kilvert (London: Penguin, 1979).

Popper, Karl Raimund, *The Open Society and Its Enemies*, vol. ii (London: Routledge, 2003).

Powell, Thomas, *The Persistence of Racism in America* (Lanham, MD: Littlefield Adams, 1993).

Praeg, Leonhard, *The Geometry of Violence: Africa, Girard, Modernity* (Stellenbosch: SUN, 2007).

Pyrhönen, Heta, *Mayhem and Murder: Narrative and Moral Issues in the Detective Story* (Toronto: University of Toronto Press, 1999).

Qvortrup, Mads, *The Political Philosophy of Jean-Jacques Rousseau* (Manchester: Manchester University Press, 2014).

Rand, Ayn, *The Virtue of Selfishness: A New Concept of Egoism* (New York: Signet, 1964).

Rand, Ayn, *The Journals of Ayn Rand*, ed. Leonard Peikoff (Harmondsworth: Penguin, 1999).

Ranke, Leopold von, *Weltgeschichte*, ed. Alfred Dove and Georg Winter, vol. ix, pt II (Leipzig: Duncker and Humblot, 1888).

Ranke, Leopold von, *Aus Werke und Nachlass*, vol. ii, ed. Theodor Schieder and Helmut Berding (Munich: Oldenbourg 1971).

Ranke, Leopold von, *Aus Werke und Nachlass*, vol. iv, ed. V. Dotterweich and W. P. Fuchs (Munich: Oldenbourg 1975).

Ranke, Leopold von, *The Secret of World History: Selected Writings on the Art and Science of History*, ed. Roger Wines (New York: Fordham University Press, 1981).

Reardon, Bernard M. G., *Religion in the Age of Romanticism* (Cambridge: Cambridge University Press, 1985).

Recchia, Stefano, and Urbinati, Nadia (eds), *A Cosmopolitanism of Nations: Giuseppe Mazzini's Writings on Democracy, Nation Building, and International Relations* (Princeton: Princeton University Press, 2009).

Reichertz, Jo, and Schneider, Manfred (eds) *Sozialgeschichte des Geständnisses: Zum Wandel der Geständniskultur* (Wiesbaden: VS, 2007).

Rescher, Nicholas, *G. W. Leibniz's Monadology* (Pittsburgh: University of Pittsburgh Press, 1991).

Riedenauer, Markus, *Pluralität und Rationalität: Die Herausforderung der Vernunft durch religiöse und kulturelle Vielfalt nach Nikolaus Cusanus* (Stuttgart: Kohlhammer, 2007).

Rieff, David, *In Praise of Forgetting: Historical Memory and its Ironies* (New Haven: Yale University Press, 2016).

Rigby, S. H., *English Society in the Later Middle Ages: Class, Status and Gender* (Manchester: Manchester University Press, 1995).

Rist, John M., *Augustine Deformed: Love, Sin and Freedom in the Western Moral Tradition* (Cambridge: Cambridge University Press, 2014).

Roberts, Charlotte, *Edward Gibbon and the Shape of History* (Oxford: Oxford University Press, 2014).

Roberts, David D., *Nothing But History: Reconstruction and Extremity After Metaphysics* (Berkeley and Los Angeles: University of California Press, 1995).

Robinson, Ronald, and Gallagher, John, with Denny, Alice, *Africa and the Victorians: The Official Mind of Imperialism* (London: Macmillan, 1961).

Roller, Matthew B., *Constructing Autocracy: Aristocrats and Emperors in Julio-Claudian Rome* (Princeton: Princeton University Press, 2001).

Roper, Lyndal, *Martin Luther: Renegade and Prophet* (London: Bodley Head, 2016).

Rorty, Richard, *Objectivity, Relativism, and Truth* (Cambridge: Cambridge University Press, 1991).

Rousseau, Jean-Jacques, *The Social Contract and the Discourses* (London: Dent and Sons, 1973).

Rousseau, Jean-Jacques, *Emile* (Mineola, NY: Dover, 2013).

Rubin, Edward L., *Soul, Self, and Society* (Oxford: Oxford University Press, 2015).

Rubinoff, Lionel, *Collingwood and the Reform of Metaphysics: A Study in the Philosophy of Mind* (Toronto: University of Toronto Press, 1970).

Rubinstein, William D., *The Myth of Rescue: Why the Democracies Could Not Have Saved More Jews from the Nazis* (London: Routledge, 2000).

Rublack, Ulinka (ed.), *A Concise Companion to History* (Oxford: Oxford University Press, 2011).

Runciman, W. G., *A Treatise on Social Theory*, vol. i (Cambridge: Cambridge University Press, 1993).

Rüsen, Jörn, *Rekonstruktion der Vergangenheit. Grundzüge einer Historik II: Die Prinzipien der historischen Forschung* (Göttingen: Vandenhoeck und Ruprecht, 1986).

Russell, James C., *The Germanization of Early Medieval Christianity: A Sociohistorical Approach to Religious Transformation* (Oxford: Oxford University Press, 1996).

Sahlins, Marshall, *How 'Natives' Think: About Captain Cook, for Example* (Chicago: University of Chicago Press, 1995).

Sartre, Jean-Paul, *Anti-Semite and Jew* (New York: Schocken, 1948).

Sartre, Jean-Paul, *Being and Nothingness* (London: Methuen, 1957).

Sartre, Jean-Paul, *Existentialism Is a Humanism*, trans. John Kulka (New Haven: Yake University Press, 2007).

Schaff, Philip, *History of the Christian Church*, vol. viii (Grand Rapids, MI: Eerdmans, 1969).

Schwab, Gail M., and Jeanneny, John R. (eds), *The French Revolution of 1789 and Its Impact* (Westport, CT: Greenwood Press, 1995).

Scott, James Brown, *Law, the State, and the International Community* (Clark, NJ: Lawbook Exchange, 2003).

Scott, James C., *Weapons of the Weak: Everyday Forms of Peasant Resistance* (New Haven: Yale University Press, 1985).

Scott, James C., *Seeing Like a State: How Certain Schemes to Improve the Human Condition Have Failed* (New Haven: Yale University Press, 1998).

Sellars, Kirsten, *'Crimes Against Peace' and International Law* (Cambridge: Cambridge University Press, 2013).

Sewell, William G., *Logics of History: Social History and Social Transformation* (Chicago: University of Chicago Press, 2005).

Shafer-Landau, Russ, *Ethical Theory: An Anthology* (Chichester: Wiley-Blackwell, 2013).

Shapiro, Harry L. (ed.), *Man, Culture, and Society* (New York: Oxford University Press, 1960).

Shell, Susan Meld, *Kant and the Limits of Autonomy* (Cambridge, MA: Harvard University Press, 2009).

Shoemaker, Karl, *Sanctuary and Crime in the Middle Ages, 450–1500* (New York: Fordham University Press, 2011).

Shriver, Donald W., *Honest Patriots* (Oxford: Oxford University Press, 2005).

Sigurdson, Richard Franklin, *Jacob Burckhardt's Social and Political Thought* (Toronto: University of Toronto Press, 2004).

Sikka, Sonia, *Herder on Humanity and Cultural Difference: Enlightened Relativism* (Cambridge: Cambridge University Press, 2011).

Slymovics, Susan (ed.), *Clifford Geertz in Morocco* (London: Routledge, 2013).

Smith, Adam, *The Theory of Moral Sentiments* (6th edn, London: Cadell, 1790).

Smith, D. Livingstone, *The Most Dangerous Animal* (New York: St Martin's Press, 2007).

Smith, Helmut Walser, *The Continuities of German History* (Cambridge: Cambridge University Press, 2007).

Smucker, Donovan E., *Origins of Walter Rauschenbuch's Social Ethics* (Montreal: McGill-Queen's University Press, 1994).

Snyder, Timothy, *Bloodlands: Eastern Europe between Hitler and Stalin* (London: The Bodley Head, 2010).

Southern, R. W., *History and Historians: Selected Papers of R. W. Southern*, ed. R. J. Bartlett (Oxford: Blackwell, 2004).

Sparling, Robert Alan, *Johann Georg Hamann and the Enlightenment Project* (Toronto: University of Toronto Press, 2011).

Stern, Fritz (ed.), *The Varieties of History* (New York: Meridian, 1956).

Stocking, George W. Jnr. (ed.), *Volksgeist as Method and Ethic: Essays on Boasian Ethnography and the German Anthropological Tradition* (Madison: University of Wisconsin Press, 1996).

Strohm, Paul, *Conscience: A Very Short Introduction* (Oxford: Oxford University Press, 2011).

Strozier, Robert M., *Foucault, Subjectivity and Identity* (Detroit: Wayne State University Press, 2002).

Stuart, Matthew (ed.), *A Companion to Locke* (Oxford: Blackwell, 2016).

Stubbs, William, *The Constitutional History of England in Its Origin and Development*, vol. iii (Oxford: Clarendon Press, 1890).

Sullivan, Shannon, and Tuana, Nancy (eds) *Race and Epistemologies of Ignorance* (Albany, NY: SUNY, 2007).

Sumner, W. G., *Folkways* (New York: Dover Publications, 1959).

Sutcliffe, Adam, *Judaism and Enlightenment* (Cambridge: Cambridge University Press, 2003).

Swain, Harriet (ed.), *Big Questions in History* (London: Jonathan Cape, 2005).

Teherani-Krönner, Parto (ed.), *Humanökologie und Kulturökologie: Grundlagen · Ansätze · Praxis* (Opladen: Westdeutscher Verlag, 1992).

Tentler, Thomas N., *Sin and Confession on the Eve of the Reformation* (Princeton: Princeton University Press, 2015).

Terezakis, Katie, *The Immanent Word: the Turn to Language in German Philosophy, 1759–1801* (London: Routledge, 2007).

Terrier, Jean, *Visions of the Social: Society as a Political Project in France, 1750–1950* (Leiden: Brill, 2011).

Thibodeaux, Jennifer D. (ed.), *Negotiating Clerical Identities* (Basingstoke: Palgrave, 2010).

Thomas, Peter D., *The Gramscian Moment: Philosophy, Hegemony and Marxism* (Leiden: Brill, 2009).

Thompson, E. P., *The Making of the English Working Class* (Harmondsworth: Pelican, 1968).

Tillich, Paul, *The Protestant Era* (London: Nisbet, 1955).

Tillich, Paul, *A History of Christian Thought* (New York: Touchstone, 1968).

Tillinghast, Pardon E., *The Specious Past* (Reading, MA: Addison-Wesley, 1972).

Tirman, John, *The Deaths of Others: the Fate of Civilians in America's Wars* (New York: Oxford University Press, 2011).

Tong, Yanqi, and Lei, Shaohua, *Social Protest in Contemporary China, 2003–2010: Transitional Pains and Regime Legitimacy* (Abingdon: Routledge, 2014).

Tooke, Joan D., *The Just War in Aquinas and Grotius* (London: SPCK, 1965).

Topping, Richard R., and Vissers, John A. (eds), *Calvin@500: Theology, History and Practice* (Eugene, OR: Wipf and Stock, 2011).

Toulmin, Stephen, *The Place of Reason in Ethics* (Cambridge: Cambridge University Press, 1950).

Toynbee, Arnold, *Greek Historical Thought* (New York: Mentor Books, 1952).

Treitschke, Heinrich von, *Politics*, vol. i (New York: MacMillan, 1916).

Tucker, Aviezer (ed.), *A Companion to the Philosophy of History and Historiography* (Chichester: Wiley-Blackwell, 2011).

Tugene, Georges, *L'Image de la nation anglaise dans l'*Histoire ecclésiastique *de Bède le Vénérable* (Strasbourg: Presses universitaires de Strasbourg, 2001).

Tuninga, Matthew J., *Calvin's Political Theology and the Public Engagement of the Church: Christ's Two Kingdoms* (Cambridge: Cambridge University Press, 2017).

Tutino, Stefania, *Shadows of Doubt: Language and Truth in Post-Reformation Catholic Culture* (Oxford: Oxford University Press, 2014).

Ungern-Sternberg, Jürgen von, and Ungern-Sternberg, Wolfgang von, *Der Aufruf 'An die Kulturwelt!'* (Stuttgart: Steiner, 1996).

Vaihinger, Hans, *Die Philosophie des Als Ob* (Lepizig: Feliz Meiner, 1922).

van Gelderen, Martin, and Skinner, Quentin (eds) *Republicanism*, i. *Republicanism and Constitutionalism in Early Modern Europe* (Cambridge: Cambridge University Press, 2002).

van Liere, Frans, *An Introduction to the Medieval Bible* (Cambridge: Cambridge University Press, 2014).

van Peursen, C. A., *Leibniz* (London: Faber and Faber, 1969).

Vaughan, Charles Edwyn, *Studies in the History of Political Philosophy Before and After Rousseau* (1925; New York: Russell & Russell, 1960).

Veeser, H. Aram (ed.), *The New Historicism* (London: Routledge, 1989).

Veldhuis, Henri, *Ein versiegeltes Buch: Der Naturbegriff in der Theologie J. G. Hamanns (1730–1788)* (Berlin: de Gruyter, 1994).

Velleman, J. David, *Foundations for Moral Relativism* (Cambridge: Open Book, 2015).

Vermeulen, Hans F., *Before Boas: The Genesis of Ethnography and Ethnology in the German Enlightenment* (Lincoln, NE: University of Nebraska Press, 2015).

Waelkens, Laurent, *Amne adverso: Roman Legal Heritage in European Culture* (Leuven: Leuven University Press, 2015).

Walter, Natasha, *Living Dolls* (London: Virago, 2010).

Waltz, Kenneth N., *Theory of International Politics* (New York: McGraw Hill, 1979).

Weber, Eugen, *Peasants Into Frenchmen: The Modernization of Rural France, 1870–1914* (Stanford, CA: Stanford University Press, 1976).

Weber, Max, *Max Weber: Essays in Sociology*, ed. and trans. H. H. Gerth and C. Wright Mills (New York: Oxford University Press, 1946).

Weber, Max, *Gesammelte Aufsätze zur Wissenschaftslehre* ed. Johannes Winckelmann (Tübingen: Mohr, 1985).

Weber, Max, *Max Weber: Schriften 1894–1922*, ed. Dirk Kaesler (Stuttgart: Alfred Kröner, 2002).

Wehofsits, Anna, *Anthropologie und Moral: Affekte, Leidenschaften und Mitgefühl in Kants Ethik* (Berlin: De Gruyter, 2016).

Weitz, Eric, *A Century of Genocide: Utopias of Race and Nation* (Princeton: Princeton University Press, 2009),

Westad, Arne, *The Global Cold War: Third World Interventions and the Making of Our Times* (Cambridge: Cambridge University Press, 2007).

Wilder, Gary, *Freedom Time: Negritude, Decolonization and the Future of the World* (Durham, NC: Duke University Press, 2014).

Williams, Bernard, *Shame and Necessity* (Berkeley and Los Angeles: University of California Press, 1993).

Williams, Bernard, *Truth and Truthfulness: An Essay in Genealogy* (Princeton: Princeton University Press, 2002).

Williams, Bernard, *In the Beginning Was the Deed* (Princeton: Princeton University Press, 2005).

Williams, Bernard, *Ethics and the Limits of Philosophy* (London: Routledge, 2006).

Williams, Bernard, *Moral Luck* (Cambridge: Cambridge University Press, 2012).

Wong, David B., *Natural Moralities* (Oxford: Oxford University Press, 2009).

Wood, Andy, *The Politics of Social Conflict: The Peak Country, 1520–1770* (Cambridge: Cambridge University Press, 1999).

Wood, Andy, *The 1549 Rebellions and the Making of Early Modern England* (Cambridge: Cambridge University Press, 2007).

Wood, Ellen Meiksins, *The Origin of Capitalism: A Longer View* (London: Verso, 2002).

Wormald, Patrick, *Legal Culture in the Early Medieval West* (London: Hambledon, 1999).

Zagorin, Perez, *How the Idea of Religious Toleration Came to the West* (Princeton: Princeton University Press, 2005).

Zamora, Daniel (ed.), *Foucault and Neoliberalism* (Cambridge: Polity Press, 2016).

Zecha, Gerhard, and Weingartner, Paul (eds), *Conscience: An Interdisciplinary View* (Dordrecht: Reidel, 1987).

Zhang, Longxi, *From Comparison to World Literature* (Albany, NY: SUNY, 2015).

Zinn, Howard, *A People's History of the United States, 1492–Present* (London: Routledge, 2003).

Zoller, Elizabeth, *Introduction to Public Law: A Comparative Perspective* (Leiden: Martinus Nijhoff, 2008).

Index

For the benefit of digital users, indexed terms that span two pages (e.g., 52–53) may, on occasion, appear on only one of those pages.

Abelard, Peter 150–2, 174–5
absolutism 62–4, 68, 160, 187–8, 218–19, 269
Acton, Lord John 116
Agathias of Myrina 109–10
Alderman, Geoffrey 116–17, 120, 133–4, 266, 270, 286
Alexander, Michelle 285
Althusser, Louis 230–2
anachronism 3–4, 7–8, 77–8, 93, 116–17, 268–9, 272, 285–6
Anerkennung 188–9, 222–3
Ankersmit, Frank 271
Annales 21–2, 266
Aquinas, Thomas 83–4, 152–4, 234
Arendt, Hannah 119
Aristotle 139, 150–1, 173–4, 221–2
Augustine of Hippo 33–4, 138, 142–4, 149–51, 153–4, 156–9, 166, 194–5
autarkeia 175

Bachelard, Gaston 218–19
Balibar, Étienne 230–1
Balzac, Honoré 169
Barth, Karl 203
Bartov, Omer 258–9
Bauer, Otto 198–9
Bayle, Pierre 178, 186
Bede 263
Benedict, Ruth 131–3, 136–7, 145, 216–17, 243–5
Benjamin, Walter 255
Bergen, Doris 259–60
Best, Werner 70–1
Beevor, Anthony 267
Biggar, Nigel 4–5
Bloch, Ernst 165–6, 215, 230–1, 287
Bloch, Marc 2–3, 10, 18–22, 27, 36, 39, 50, 71–2, 78–9, 81, 89, 146
  and mentalité 21, 27, 215
Boas, Franz 131–2
Bodin, Jean 160, 232
Bolingbroke, Viscount Henry St John 236–7
Bourdieu, Pierre 123, 136–7

Bruno, Giordano 178–9
Buber, Martin 167–8
Burckhardt, Jacob 175–7, 205–6, 217–18, 224–5, 227–9, 232, 246–7, 273
Burke, Edmund 57–9, 72, 228–9
Butterfield, Herbert 3, 8, 11, 71–2, 83–4, 134–5, 175, 236–7, 272, 279
Buzan, Barry 224–5

Calvin, Jean 155–60, 162–3
Card, Claudia 134–5
Carlyle, Thomas 116
Carr, E. H. 66, 116
Castellio, Sebastian 159
cause (*causa*) 2, 30–9 passim, 41–2, 47, 58, 80–1, 84, 104, 109, 112–13, 125, 179–80, 217–18, 254–5
  causation 10, 23, 30–9 passim, 80–1, 90, 250, 254–5
Chakrabarty, Dipesh 43–4
Chatterjee, Partha 43–4
Chibber, Vivek 43–4
chronocentrism 235–6, 269
Cicero 33, 137
Clay, Henry 192
Coleridge, Samuel Taylor 196–7, 263
collectivism 204–5, 281
Collingwood, R. G. 8, 110–11, 236–7, 261, 271–2
Commager, H. S. 2–3, 10
Condorcet, Nicolas de 8, 235–6
Confino, Alon 41–2
Connor, Walter Robert 97–8
Conrad, Joseph 277
Conscience 133, 137, 152, 156–8, 173–4
  conscientia 137, 152, 159, 164–5
  synderesis 152, 164–5
  syneidêsis 137, 152
  see also *forum internum/conscientiae*
conscientia, see conscience
consequentialism 63–4, 68, 243
constructivism, International Relations theory of 69, 72–3
constructivism, social/cultural 245–6

context 3–4, 11–14, 16–18, 30–52 passim, 58
contextualization 3–4, 8–14, 17, 18–30 passim,
    39–52 passim, 55–60, 72, 87, 93–4, 102,
    112–13, 128–30, 207, 219–20, 234, 249,
    261, 271–2, 286–7
    see also decontextualization
Cooper, Frederick 256
counterfactual History 78–80, 85–6, 272–3, 275
Crofts, Penny 148–9
Crowley, Robert 49–50
crypto-normativity 117–20, 128–9
cultural turn 16–17, 40–1
Cusanus, Nicholas 131, 178–9

Darwinism 69–70, 108, 117, 192–3, 195, 245–6
decontextualization 74–6, 140–1
de Valera, Éamon 175
deontology 63–4, 243
Derrida, Jacques 216–17
Descartes, René 154, 188–9, 236–7
determinism 11, 17–18, 32–8, 161–2, 230–1
    teleological determinism 33–5, 37–8
    mechanistic determinism 35, 37–8
Dilthey, Wilhelm 110–11, 135–6, 216–17
discourse, Foucault's concept of, see Foucault,
    Michel
Droysen, Gustav 130, 194–5, 218–19
Duns Scotus 150, 153–4, 158
Durkheim, Émile 21–2, 90, 114–15

Eaglestone, Robert 240–1, 255
Edele, Mark 279–80
Elton, Geoffrey 86
Emerson, Ralph Waldo 165, 167–8, 175–7,
    208–9
Engels, Friedrich 192–3
epochalism 235–6
Erklären 215
ethnocentrism 16–17, 235–6, 251–2, 269
Evans, Richard 2–3, 10–12, 76, 80, 82, 89, 94–6,
    100, 236–7
Evans-Pritchard, E. E. 216–17

Fasolt, Constantin 3–4
Febvre, Lucien 36
Felman, Shoshana 255
Ferguson, Niall 272–3
Ferro, Marc 270
Fichte, Johann Gottlieb 164–7, 173–4, 182–3,
    187–9, 196–7, 204, 222–3, 227–8
formalism, ethical 164–5
formalism of structuralist theory 215–16
forum externum 151–2, 165–6, 211–12

forum internum/conscientiae 151–2, 165–6, 185,
    197–8, 211–12
Foucault, Michel 47, 117–21, 123, 206, 214,
    218–23, 233
Freud, Sigmund 40, 165, 205–6, 230–1
Friedlander, Saul 51–2, 260, 276

Gaddis, John Lewis 79
Gallagher, John 22–7, 50, 105
Galtung, Johan 58–9
Garbarini, Alexandra 258–9
Geertz, Clifford 41–2, 45, 131–2, 181–2, 216–18,
    228–9, 232, 236
Geist 133–4, 176, 183–4, 189, 193–4, 215,
    227–8, 243
Gerald of Wales 232
Gesinnungsethik 165–6
Gewirth, Alan 221–2
Gibbon, Edward 96–7, 134–5
Giddens, Anthony 36
Ginzburg, Carlo 18–19, 89
Gobineau, Joseph Arthur de 69–70
Goethe 176–7, 181–2
Gramsci, Antonio 120–1, 124–5, 230–2, 287
Gratian 143–4, 147, 150–1, 157–8, 166
Grayling, Anthony 267, 269
Grotius, Hugo 160–1
Grundtvig, Bishop N.F.S. 193–4
Gunther, Michael M. 260

Hamann, Johann Georg 181–4, 201–2, 215–16
Hamilton, Bernard 21–2
Hampson, Norman 286–7
Harman, Gilbert 238–9
Harnack, Adolf 203
Hastings, Max 263–4, 266–70, 281
Hayek, Friedrich 122
Hegel, Georg Wilhelm Friedrich 164–7, 176–7,
    184, 187–8, 194–5, 208
    Hegelian speculative philosophy of
    history 255
hegemony 120–1, 124–5, 273–4
Heidegger, Martin 110–11
Hénaff, Marcel 215–16
Herbert, Christopher 216–17
Herder, Johann Gottfried 131–2, 164, 176–7,
    183–5, 187–9, 194, 198–9, 201–4,
    214–18, 228–9, 243, 245–6
hermeneutics 107–11, 156, 215–17, 237
heroic realism 61, 69–72, 85, 227
    see also realism, International Relations
    theory of
Herskovits, M. J. 240–1

Hill, Christopher 122
historicism (*Historismus*) 8–9, 16–17, 40–3, 128,
    131–2, 184–5, 191–2, 218–19, 268–9
   German historicism 16–17, 194–5
   see also neo-historicism
historicity 262, 268–9, 271, 277
historicization 8–9, 21–2, 128–9, 277
Historische Zeitschrift 57
Hobart, Mark 106
Hobbes, Thomas 159–63, 166, 170–1, 177–8, 237
Homer 139–41
Horseman, Reginald 50–1
Howard, Michael 277
Humboldt, Wilhelm von 184
Hume, David 164
Hutcheson, Francis 160–1

idealism 40–1, 65–6, 215
Identity History 14–15
   and genealogy 262–5, 273–4
   and analogy 262, 264–5
   and metonymy 262, 264–5
incommensurability 242–5
individualism 130, 132–3, 140, 148–9, 163,
    168–74, 175–208 passim, 209, 214,
    218–22, 282
internalism 109–11, 127–34 passim, 138, 140–1,
    148–9, 158–9, 163–4, 185, 208, 215–16,
    225, 230
   see also Monadological thought
internalization 140–1, 154
International Relations (IR) theory 64–9,
    210, 226
   see also constructivism, International
    Relations theory of
   see also liberalism, International relations
    theory of
   see also realism, International Relations
    theory of

Jameson, Fredric 128
Jenkins, Keith 240–1
Joachim of Fiore 155
John of Salisbury 129–31

Kant, Immanuel 32, 61–2, 106–7, 138, 150,
    163–7, 182–3, 187–9, 207, 215–16,
    242, 260
Kantianism 61–4, 129, 170, 181–2, 215–16,
    239–40
Kertész, Imre 45, 47
Khong, Yuen Foong 264
Kierkegaard, Søren 158–9, 197, 203, 271

Kitson Clark, George 89, 91–2, 94–5, 104–5,
    134–5
Kraft 183–4, 193–4
Kuhn, Thomas 218–19

Lang, Berel 51–2
Le Bon, Gustav 104–5, 260
Lee, Stephen Hugh 109
legitimacy 64, 113–26 passim, 128–9, 178, 191,
    193–4, 205, 288–9
Leibniz, Gottfried Wilhelm 131–3, 160–1, 178–86,
    196, 205–6, 208, 215–18, 224–6, 232, 243
   Monadology 178–80
Lenin, V. I. 32–3, 116
Lesser, Alexander 233
Lessing, Theodor 272–3
Levin, David 168–9
Levinas, Emmanuel 139, 222–3, 255
Lévi-Strauss, Claude 132–3, 215–16
Levy, Ariel 171
liberalism, International Relations theory
    of 65–6, 68–9,
liberalism, philosophical and political 129–30,
    168, 173–4, 176–7, 204, 213–14, 221–2
liberalism, social 223
List, Friedrich 191–2
Locke, John 160–1, 173–4, 181, 186, 204, 237
Lombard, Peter 152
Luther, Martin 131–2, 145, 154–60, 164, 166–7,
    173–4, 179–83, 195, 197, 203

Machiavelli, Niccolò 62–4
Malinowski, Bronislaw 104–5
Marx, Karl 32–3, 59–60, 117–18, 168–9, 187,
    189, 198, 205–6, 218–19, 230
Marxism 33–4, 40–1, 117, 120–1, 165–6, 192–3,
    198, 217–18, 221, 230–1, 273–4
   vulgar Marxism 117–18
Matt, Susan J. 110–11
Mazzini, Giuseppe 193–4, 205
Mbembe, Achille 279
McMahon, Robert J. 108–9, 113
Mead, Margaret 131–2
Meinecke, Friedrich 9–10, 69–70, 95–6, 98, 195
Melvin, Mungo 77–8
Michelet, Jules 196–7, 200
Mill, John Stuart 173–4, 221, 283–6
Mommsen, Theodor 88–9
monadological thought 131–3, 175–234 passim,
    243, 246–7, 275–6, 281
   see also Leibniz, Gottfried Wilhelm,
Montaigne, Michel de 47
Montesquieu 46, 113, 186, 194, 228–31

Montmarquet, James A. 52
moral contextualization 8, 11–13, 51–2, 72, 87,
    93–4, 112–13, 261
moral luck 81–2, 207
moral objectivism 239–40, 243–6
    see also realism, moral
moral positivism 116–17
moral 'relational' thought, see relational moral
    thought
moral relativism, see relativism
moral responsibility 31, 109
moralism 10, 15, 61, 65–6, 69, 74–6, 85, 171
Moreton-Robinson, Aileen 279
Morgenthau, Hans 61–2, 64–6
Murdock, George Peter 232
Musson, Anthony 114–15

Naipaul, V. S. 279
Nancy, Jean-Luc 233
nationalism 129–30, 169, 193–4, 196–204,
    208–25 passim
    civic nationalism 193–4, 197–200, 204
    ethnic nationalism 193–4, 198–9, 204
    constitutional nationalism 193, 204
    Imagined Communities and 270
neo-historicism 40–1, 45, 55–6, 128, 218–20,
    266–7, 269, 278, 286–7
    see also historicism
neo-liberalism 220–3
neoplatonism 160–1, 167–8, 178–80, 182–5,
    194–5
Newton, Isaac 178
Niebuhr, Barthold Georg 289
Nietzsche, Friedrich 40, 123, 135–6, 165–6,
    169–70, 234
Nolte, Ernst 108, 260
nominalism 153–4, 156, 159, 161–2, 165–7,
    239–40

Oakeshott, Michael 2–3, 89
Ormrod, W. M. 114–15
Orwell, George 52–4, 58–9, 102–3
Overbeck, Franz 197, 203

Parsons, Talcott 47
particularism 191–2, 200, 213–15, 241
Phillips, Ulrich Bonnell 258
Phylarcus 102–3
physis 143–4, 154
Plato 129–30, 137, 141–2, 153–4, 188–9, 222–3
Platonism 221
    see also neoplatonism
Plekhanov, Georgi 33–4
pneuma 133–4, 143–4, 154, 165–6, 184

Polybius 102–4
Popper, Karl 116
Porter, Bernard 5–8
postcolonialism 43–4, 236, 256–7, 279
postmodernism 218–19, 222–3, 230–1, 240–1,
    245–6
post-nationalism 221–2
Prakash, Gyan 256–7
Protestantism 161–2, 167–9
Proudhon, Pierre-Joseph 106
prudence 83–4
Pufendorf. Samuel 160–2, 177–8, 194–5

Rand, Ayn 169–70
Ranke, Leopold von 8–9, 40–1, 115, 128, 184–5,
    194–5, 218–19, 234–6
realism, International Relations theory of 65–9,
    72–3
    see also heroic realism
realism, literary 97–8
realism, metaphysical/theological 153–4, 159,
    165, 182–3
realism, moral 65–6, 239–40, 243–4
relational moral thought 134, 225, 230, 233–4,
    249–50, 262
relativism, cultural and moral 13–15, 128,
    213–16, 226–7, 234–49 passim, 262,
    269, 289
    cultural relativism 13, 133, 186, 202, 208,
        214–16, 226–30
        see also monadological thought
    moral and cultural relativism distinguished 8,
        243–5
    moral relativism 8–14, 54–5, 128, 133–4,
        238–50, 289
        descriptive moral relativism 238
        meta-ethical (moral) relativism 238–40,
            246–7
        naïve (moral) relativism 240
        normative relativism 240
        relativism of distance 248–50, 269–70
        vulgar moral relativism 240
Renan, Ernest 193–4, 270
reparations 284–5
Richards, Robert A. 96–7
Rickert, Heinrich 88
Rigby, Steve 92–4
Roberts, Andrew 272
Robespierre 19, 140, 186–7
Robinson, Ronald 22–7, 50, 105
Romanticism 40–1, 58, 166–9
Rorty, Richard 236
Rousseau, Jean-Jacques 136–7, 161–4, 187–8,
    194, 199, 202–4

Rubin, Edward L. 221–2
Rubinstein, William D. 85–6
Runciman, W. G. 101–2

sacro egoismo 175, 203
Sahlins, Marshal 40–1, 131–2, 214–15
Said, Edward 43–4, 279
Salisbury, Lord Robert Cecil 73, 277
Sartre, Jean-Paul 51–4, 221
Scheler, Max 170–1, 195
Schell, Jonathan 97–8, 102–4
Schleiermacher, Friedrich 181–2
Schopenhauer, Arthur 165–6
Scott, James C. 119–20
Seneca 137, 174–5
Sewell, William H. Jr. 16
Shaftesbury, Third Earl of 160–2, 164, 168–9
Shaw, George Bernard 196–7
Shorter, Edward 121
Smiles, Samuel 168
Smith, Adam 48, 140–1, 190, 192–3, 223
Snyder, Timothy 27–31, 39, 54–5
socialitas 160–1, 177–8
Socrates 137
Sorokin, Pitrim 232
Southern, R. J. W. 110–11
Spengler, Oswald 228–9
Spinoza, Baruch 37, 237
Stiglitz, Joseph 211
stoic tradition 33, 137, 141–2, 145, 165–6,
        174–5
Stone, Dan 128
Strohm, Paul 170–1
structuralism 16–17, 90, 123, 215–17, 220–1,
        229–31, 233
    anthropological structuralism 215–17
Stubbs, William 156
Subaltern Studies 252–3
subjectivism 150–1, 154, 171, 173–4
Suetonius 134–5

Sumner, W. G. 114–15, 120, 123
Sybel, Heinrich von 57
synderesis, *see* conscience
syneidêsis, *see* conscience

Taine, Hippolyte 114–15
Tardío, Manuel Alvarez 56–7
Thompson, E. P. 170, 252–3, 272–3
Thucydides 66, 97–8
tolerance 15, 234–49 passim, 289
Tolstoy, Leo 35–6, 104–5
Tolstoy, Nikolai 53–4
Toulmin, Stephen 123–4
Treitschke, Heinrich von 69–70, 88–9, 195, 200
Trevelyan, G. M. 88–9
Tyndale, William 173–4

universalism 16–17, 181–2, 187–8, 191–2, 200,
        213–15, 236, 241, 245–6
universitas 131, 156, 282–3

Verstehen 215
Volksgeist 133–4, 176
Voltaire 8, 168–9, 208, 235–6

Walter, Natasha 171
Weber, Max 74, 88–90, 165–6, 205
Westermarck, Edvard 129, 195
Wheatcroft, Geoffrey 99
White, Hayden 240–1
William of Ockham 153–4, 156, 163–4
Williams, Bernard 248–50
Wolf, Eric 231–3
Wood, Andy 122
Wood, Ellen Meiksins 257–8

Younge, Gary 274

Zeitgeist 176
Zetkin, Klara 34